GROWING WITH MY CHILDREN

A Jewish Mother's Diary

GROWING WITH MY CHILDREN

A Jewish Mother's Diary

Sarah Shapiro

CIS PUBLISHERS

New York · London · Jerusalem

First published 1990

ISBN 0-944070-21-3

Phototypeset at Targum Press

Published by:
Targum Press Inc.
22700 W. Eleven Mile Rd.
Southfield, Mich. 48034

Distributed in U.S., Canada and Overseas by:
C.I.S. Publishers and Distributors
180 Park Ave. Lakewood, N.J. 08701
Tel: (201) 905-3000 / 367-7858 / 364-1629 Fax: (201) 367-6666

Distributed in U.K. and Europe by:
C.I.S. International
1 Palm Court, Queen Elizabeth Walk
London, England, N16
Tel: 01-809-3732

Distributed in Israel by:
Nof Books Ltd.
POB 23646
Jerusalem 91235

Printed in Israel

For My Mother and My Father

That which a person gives to another is never lost. It is an extension of his own being. He can see a part of himself in the fellow-man to whom he has given. This is the attachment between one man and his fellow to which we give the name 'love.'

Rabbi Eliyahu Dessler
Michtav MiEliyahu

Rabbi CHAIM P. SCHEINBERG
KIRYAT MATTERSDORF
PANIM MEIROT 2
JERUSALEM, ISRAEL

הרב חיים פנחס שיינברג
ראש ישיבת "תורה אור"
ומורה הוראה דקרית מטרסדורף
ירושלים טל.ל.ל.ל.ל

Mothers of large families know that the blessing of children brings with it a host of challenges. Mrs. Sarah Shapiro has written a realistic work that deals honestly with some of these challenges. The Jewish mother's struggle to raise many young children and at the same time develop her own *middos* and *yiras shomayim* is an issue that should be aired, so that women will realize that they are not alone in their battle against fear and doubt. An honest look at motherhood, written by a woman who has tried to follow *daas Torah* in her role as mother, can give immense *chizuk* to the women who are the mothers of this and the next generation. I am pleased to hear of the publication of such a work, and wish Mrs. Shapiro *hatzlachah* and much *nachas* from her family.

Rabbi Chaim P. Scheinberg

RABBI ZELIG PLISKIN
Director
Aish HaTorah Counseling Center

The Vilna Gaon wrote that our prime purpose in life is to strive constantly to break our negative traits. Every life situation is an opportunity to help us grow spiritually.

One of life's biggest challenges and opportunities is child raising. There is a strong bond of love between a parent and child. Children can be the source of a parent's greatest joy. But raising children can also generate much frustration, anger and resentment. These negative feelings can lead to many counterproductive statements.

A child's self-image is greatly dependent on the respect or lack of it that he or she experiences from parents. A parent who is calm can focus on the best possible approach for each individual child. On the other hand, when a parent is angry, harmful words are spoken. Besides one's own obligation to work on character traits, one owes it to one's children to be in control of what one says.

Growing With My Children is an inspiring journal that will give insight and encouragement to many parents. While each individual is unique, and the particular struggles and difficulties of one person are different from those of another, every parent can gain awareness and sensitivity from the author's personal experiences. It takes courage to admit that one has made mistakes. Reading this journal will make it easier for other parents to become aware of their own tendencies towards anger and feelings of unresourcefulness.

The growth expressed in this work will serve as a positive model for the reader. By becoming aware of your own counterproductive attitudes and behavior, you will be able to find approaches, concepts and techniques that will make you both a better person and a better parent.

Rabbi Zelig Pliskin
Author of *Gateway to Happiness*

When in 1986 I suggested to the participants of a summer parenting workshop that they keep diaries, I had no idea where this would lead.

I am so pleased to see in this book the principles which I teach, brought to life so meaningfully. Sarah Shapiro models for us the difficult process of change. Possessed of high ideals, she endeavors to achieve a balance between a relentless striving for perfection and a realistic appreciation of human nature.

The parent-child encounters to be found here will be familiar to many of us. We laugh through whimsical, touching, and sometimes hilarious episodes, funny because they are universal.

Sarah Shapiro's diary provides us with a rare opportunity to get a glimpse into a private struggle, replete with great insights into the issues of life that concern us all.

Miriam Levi
Author of *Effective Jewish Parenting*

Sarah Shapiro's book is both a beautifully written and tremendously honest account of the day-to-day struggles of a conscientious mother who wants to bring up her children with the proper blend of loving-kindness and protective discipline. She has an amazing ability to accurately convey the reality of motherhood—the tensions, conflicts, fears, joys and triumphs involved in child rearing. Sarah is fiercely determined to succeed and become the best mother possible. Her book will give *chizuk* to all mothers who want to bring up their children in the true spirit of Torah.

Miriam Adahan
Author of *Raising Children to Care*

Acknowledgments

I am indebted to Miriam Levi and Miriam Adahan for the effect they have had on the course of my life.

My gratitude to Rabbi Zelig Pliskin, who gave many hours to review the manuscript.

It was a joy and a privilege to work together with the staff of Targum Press. A special thank you to my editor Ita Olesker for her encouragement, personal insight and keen literary sensitivity.

I am grateful to live in Jerusalem, where there are so many women who try to live according to their ideals. May we continue to share with one another what we learn day by day.

Above all, I thank my husband, Yaacov Zvi Shapiro. Many an author cites one person without whom his book could not have been written, but I can only wonder if it's always as true as it is in this case. It was my husband who instilled in me the self-confidence to continue the diary when in 1986 I was going to put it aside. It was he who gave support and advice along the way, and he who on countless occasions took care of the children and helped me with housework so that I could write down that day's entry. He repeatedly fixed my typewriter, did the initial proofreading of the manuscript, and provided me with a title.

May his dedication to Torah study be rewarded.

Sarah Shapiro
Cheshvan 5750

The names of most of the people who appear in this book have been changed. Relatives and well-known personalities appear under their real names, as do the following individuals:

Mrs. Benjamin	Esther Linder
Diane	Esther Lomnitz
Bracha Goetz	Nina
Honey	Beyla Potash
Mr. and Mrs. Israel	Rivka Rappaport
Happy Klein	Mrs. Schlesinger
Dori Lewis	Channy Stark
Linda	Sarah and Sender Tannenbaum

The author apologizes if she has misrepresented the ideas of any of the teachers who are quoted herein.

A Note to My Children and to the Reader

Thank you, children, for trustfully letting me share you with an unknown public.

The reader is asked to bear in mind that generally speaking, the purpose of this journal has been to focus on problems and challenges of child raising. A second volume would be needed to adequately describe my children's virtues: their zeal to do *chessed*, their finely tuned sensitivity to the feelings and needs of others, their uncanny grasp of the concept of working on one's *middos*, and the enormous pleasure they take in Torah and in life itself.

This diary does not purport to be a child raising manual. Nor is its purpose to condone behavior on the part of adults which is contrary to Torah, such as anger, intolerance, judgmentalness or lack of *emunah*. Its intention is to reveal a *baalat teshuvah*'s growth process, the striving towards Torah values and self-mastery.

Sarah Shapiro

Contents

Prologue

On the cover was a fair-haired, smiling, ethereal-looking lady, enclosed delicately in some sort of mist. The book appeared on the coffee table one Friday when my sister came home from college for the weekend. It surprises me now to realize that I was only nine. I would never dream that a nine-year-old understands so much of what's talked about among adults: I knew my sister had learned from this book, in one of her classes at Sarah Lawrence, that my mother had wasted her life. My mother had been fooled and misused, tricked into sacrificing her potential as a person for the sake of her husband and children. How lucky that at least now, we, the younger generation, could wake up and avoid making the same horrible mistake.

I don't recall whether any of the conversations turned into arguments, but an explosion occurred, even if a silent one.

It was entitled *The Second Sex*. Did that mean that women really were second, or that they really weren't second? I looked at the pretty lady on the cover and wished I looked like her. She was fair and blonde. I was dark. Her gentle, knowing, far-away smile hinted that whatever "second" was, she wasn't. Or was she? Maybe she was second *because* she was pretty. I couldn't be sure.

When my sister went back to college on Sunday, the peace to

which she abandoned us was a vague indictment of our plight: stuck at home, safely away from the storms of truth going on among the searching, intellectually alive college students and their brilliant professors. The world was out there, and I was only nine. I had a long way to go. At home.

If I remember being surprised that on Monday morning my mother got up as usual and rushed to cook us all breakfast, and rushed, as usual, to get my father to his train on time, and was doing the ironing when I got home from school, then my memory is imprecise. How could this routine ever have surprised me?

What had changed, to be more exact, was that her selflessness had all of a sudden become dishonorable in my eyes. And I thought I could discern in *her* eyes a new, frightened defensiveness: "So maybe I *have* been misused, maybe I *have* given up too much," my mother's expression seemed to say. "But this is my job and I'm going to do it right!"

Nineteen years later I was in Jerusalem, an observant Jew, married and pregnant (though I didn't know it yet) with twins. I looked forward to a wonderful life, of which I was at once the star and the coming attractions. I was to be surrounded, in their supporting roles, by a devoted husband and an intelligent, special baby who would love me and justify my existence.

Before my marriage, an Israeli friend had told me gravely that marriage meant a lot of hard work, and she wondered if I'd be able to handle it, given the fact that I was not yet familiar with brooms and pans and sponges and other things of that nature. This was insulting. I was sure I would do just fine. Within me surged the tremendous power of my own goodwill and the determination to make my dreams come true. Side issues faded.

As far as becoming a mother was concerned, however, I did have some worries: all those baby undershirts and nighties, for one thing. The books said you needed a lot of them. Would I be able to keep the baby's clothes clean and organized, when I had never been able to do as much with mine? I was also concerned about bathing the baby: a wet infant must be so slippery! Another thing that kind of bothered me was the idea of having to be mother to this as yet unknown person for the rest of my life. The rest of my life!

In my seventh month, my husband and I took a trip back home. I felt like a queen in front of my parents and sisters. And all the relatives, whom we'd seen through the years at Thanksgiving and the Passover seder, before whom I had always cowered shyly, little Sarah, were shaking their heads and murmuring, "Well, well, well, maybe her becoming religious wasn't such a bad thing after all. Nice-looking husband, she's smiling a lot..." I felt fulfilled, successful, a walking *Kiddush HaShem*. I asked my mother for advice about taking care of a baby. "Well, I think the most important thing is to be gentle." This was most encouraging, for I was nothing if not gentle. Kind, dreamy and gentle Sarah, that's how I'd always been known.

When I gave birth to twins, a boy and a girl, my husband and I cried together in our joy. I thought to myself fervently, "G-d has been so kind. I'll never experience jealousy again." The next morning, there was a call for me at the nurses' station. "It's from America!" said the nurse. I tore out of bed.

"Yes, Daddy! Yes! I know!" I sang into the telephone. "Isn't it amazing?"

My mother got on the phone. "Sarah...Sarah..." I heard her give something like a laugh and a cry. "How did you do it?" (She'd never had twins, nor boys.) My father got back on. "I got the news when I was on the golf course, and the rest of the day I was two feet off the ground!"

I've made them so happy, I said to myself. *I've made them proud.*

"You have a whole family now, Sarah," my mother was saying with quiet wonder. "A boy and a girl! It's...it's unbelievable. You don't even need to have more."

In 1986, a sign turned up on our building's bulletin board. Someone named Miriam Levi was going to be giving a free talk to the neighborhood women on the subject of "Discipline With Love." My heart stirred with guilt and hope. I knew intuitively that somehow I should be disciplining my children more, but was secretly proud that the authoritarian image had never suited me. Who, me, discipline? I'm too compassionate. And even if I wanted to, I had no idea how: I just screamed. Besides, I'd come of age as a member of the generation that scorned absolutes. Who was I to be absolutely sure of anything? What was to be forbidden? What permitted? It was with free choice that as a young adult I had taken on the do's and don'ts of Judaism, and I wanted my children to experience the religion with equal eagerness and joy. Wouldn't forcing it upon them poison their observance? More than anything else as a parent, I feared hindering the free expression of their feelings. I feared doing anything that might stunt their emotional and psychological growth, make them neurotic—all of which results from too much discipline, not too little. Right? But discipline with love, that sounded perfect. Pushing the baby carriage, I rushed, as usual, to the supermarket, and rushed, as usual, through the shopping, to get back home in time for the four kids' return from school.

A few weeks later, there I was in my second-row seat, hoping to learn the secret, and two months later, I organized an intensive, twice-weekly Miriam Levi summer workshop in my home. A crash course. This was something I wanted to learn quickly.

Mrs. Levi told the women who signed up that anyone so inclined might find it useful to keep a journal for the three-week duration of the workshop.

1

Elephants in Quicksand

June 22, 1986

Tonight at eight is the first workshop, and it's going to be at our house. It's only three in the afternoon, but I'm already plotting how to get the children into bed on time. I pray they fall asleep quickly, before the class starts.

I've never offered our home for an evening activity before. If my children were the kind who would stay in bed as instructed, in spite of a noisy gathering of adults in the living room, and were I the kind of mother who wouldn't get embarrassed by their disobedience, then I wouldn't need this thing in the first place. Mrs. Levi, however, told me last week that they once had problems with someone's rebellious child during a workshop, and he ended up serving quite nicely as a demonstration model. So I feel secure that in case of trouble, there will be something to fall back upon. Besides, I wouldn't mind the children getting some unsolicited discipline at the hands of a pro.

I took no chances. It's ten to eight and all of them are asleep. An incredible achievement, yet I can't overlook the irony: I nearly killed my children so they wouldn't get in the way of my learning about discipline with love.

It's twenty to twelve. I went in to talk to Yaacov after the women left, and was disappointed to see he'd already fallen asleep. I've been bumbling around the apartment, trying to relax myself with a cup of hot milk and an old *Jewish Woman's Outlook* magazine from Purim 1983. But I can't sleep.

Throughout the workshop, scenes of my day with the children kept rising up to mind, like undeveloped, shadowy negatives coming into bright focus before my eyes.

It's so sad.

I just made myself another cup of warm milk. I wish there were something good to eat in the refrigerator.

Miriam Levi warned tonight that an excessive sense of guilt is usually not constructive, and wrong from a Torah point of view. (I really can't go along with that. Doesn't a sense of guilt inspire one to change? How else can one be motivated?) But I am choked with guilt now, and rightly so. If in the course of one unexceptional day I managed to make so many harmful mistakes, I wonder what in the world I'm doing to my children. These are incidents which normally I'd regret but then forget, or simply not recognize as incidents in the first place. They're the sort of things that happen while I'm putting out a tremendous amount of energy and effort, trying to get everything accomplished, and all I know afterwards is that I feel vaguely rotten and disappointed. I usually chalk it all up, as I exult over the fact that they're finally in bed, to plain tiredness. Isn't tiredness, after all, an inevitable consequence of motherhood? Doesn't every mother of young children feel at the end of the day as if she's been run over by a truck?

I now suspect, however, that tiredness is the name I give to my discouragement.

Mrs. Levi started out tonight by presenting us with an imaginary situation, one which by no means, however, was unfamiliar to anyone: You're on the way out the back door of an Egged bus, let's say with two baskets of fruit and vegetables from the *shuk*, when the driver lurches forward and slams the door shut on you. You barely make it out in one piece, and forget about the peaches. What would your reaction be?

"I'd be furious," said one of the women.

"I'd get his registration number and report him," said another. "If I did something about it, I'd feel better."

"Most of us would be angry?" Mrs. Levi asked. We nodded. "Now, let's say, though, that one woman out of a hundred comes along, and when this happens to her, she doesn't feel any anger. What would you say about that?"

"Well, it could be that she has strong *bitachon*," one woman volunteered, "and she recognizes immediately that it's a small *kapparah* and it's good nothing worse happened."

"I'd say a person like that is out of touch with her feelings," said someone else. "Anyone in his right mind would feel angry at something like that."

"Yes, that's what I think, too," I said. "Maybe she can calm herself down, but the initial reaction has to be something like indignation. Unless she's a doormat."

"Anything else?" Mrs. Levi inquired.

"It could be that that's her nature, not to get angry."

Another woman objected. "Oh, no, I don't buy that. She's human, isn't she? She's probably trying to prove to herself what a *tzadekkes* she is and thinks that means she has to be beyond normal human reactions."

"So would all of you say that anger is the most appropriate response to this situation?" Mrs. Levi asked.

"Well..." People mumbled a moment and started to debate. "It's not the most appropriate, but it's inevitable." "No, it's wrong to get angry about it. We have to have self-control." "But it's just a natural human reaction, and it's not healthy to repress it."

"All right, now," Mrs. Levi interjected. "If we really want to get a better understanding of the difference between the woman who gets angry at this mishap and the one who doesn't, we have to take a look at something else. We have to look at what they're thinking. Right at that moment the door closes on you, what kind of thoughts are going through your mind?"

Two women raised their hands. "I'd think, 'What a terrible thing! He could have really hurt me!'"

"I'd think, 'What an irresponsible bus driver. He has no right being so careless.' "

"O.K.," said Mrs. Levi. "Let's put all this into one central idea. The person..."

I interrupted. "Wait a minute. Excuse me. You said that in order to determine the difference between the two women, you have to look at what they're thinking. But thoughts are just the superficial expression of what a person is feeling. I'd say that to find out why one woman gets angry and the other doesn't, you'd have to look much more deeply than their thoughts."

"It's a commonly held erroneous notion," replied Mrs. Levi, "that if we want to understand some problem we're having, we have to delve deeply into our psyches. Yet all we really need to do is to modify our present way of thinking about events. That will automatically cause us to feel differently about them."

I sat back in my chair, wary. Maybe I was in the wrong class. It sounded like one of these radical behaviorist theories that reduce human beings to mechanical entities without deep feelings. It wasn't for me.

"You know what," Mrs. Levi declared, "I'd rather come back to this a little later. What concerns us right now is examining the thoughts. What does the person who gets angry think?"

The woman sitting next to me raised her hand. "Things like this shouldn't happen! Drivers shouldn't go around slamming doors on human beings!"

Mrs. Levi nodded. "What's the main word there?"

A few of us chimed in, "Shouldn't."

"Yes. *Shouldn't*. That is the main idea behind anger. 'This shouldn't be! It shouldn't happen!' But if even only one person out of a thousand doesn't get angry in a particular situation, it proves the possibility that it may not be the outer event which causes the anger. The door slamming shut was not in itself what made all those other women mad." Silence. Some doubtful stares. "Oh, by the way, I prepared some nametags for all of you." Mrs. Levi leaned down and took from her big bag a plastic container of straight pins and a little pile of white cards. Some of us smiled at this flashback to grade school. As she passed them around, Sharon raised her hand.

"What you were saying about anger, Mrs. Levi, on one hand you're saying you don't have to delve deeply into the psyche, and on the other hand that the real reason someone gets angry is on the inside, not in the outer event. So which is it?"

"What I'm trying to get across here," said Mrs. Levi, "is that the cause of the anger is within the person. It's internal, not external. And when we recognize this fully, we are less prone to become puppets of external events. That's not to say you have to be above reacting to things. Sometimes an extreme emotional reaction is desirable and even necessary. Nonetheless, at least on a theoretical level, a person *could* eliminate emotional pain from his life merely by changing the way he views so-called painful events. Since for most of us this is an unrealistic goal, it behooves us simply to recognize that a good portion of the pain we experience is brought on by our habitual ways of thinking and perceiving. People tend to view events in the same characteristic way they did as children, and this is a perspective which often brings us pain. That pain can be diminished by training ourselves to change our perspectives. But it's not an easy process. It will not happen overnight, just because one wills it."

Miriam Levi smiled. "I didn't really expect to get into this so much tonight. We'll come back to this a little farther down the road, all right? Now we're going to shift the focus. Now that we're out of the bus, let's go back home. Imagine that one of your children is hitting the other. Gripping his arm, you shout loudly: 'How would you like someone to do that to you!' " She paused. Yes, it sounded familiar.

"Now visualize the scene again. You don't yell. You draw your child aside and say very gently and softly: 'How would you like someone to do that to you?' "

She looked around the room. "Which manner would be likely to succeed?" We were silent. The answer was obvious. *It doesn't matter as much what you say, as how you say it.*

"Now, another situation. Everybody's waiting for dinner, but a lovely aroma from the kitchen indicates that you've burned the rice. Your husband berates you: 'Why do you always do that? If you were more careful maybe we'd have a decent meal around here once in a while!' How would you feel?"

"Angry," answered one woman.

"Defensive," replied another. "I'd explain myself, like I had to go stop the baby from falling out the window, or something."

I raised my hand. "I'd feel low."

"Yes," said Mrs. Levi, "you'd feel low. Well, that's frequently how we talk to our children, isn't it?" We all smiled uncomfortably. "Now, when we consistently yell at a child like this, he might react outwardly by demonstrating self-pity, or by answering you back accusingly or in self-defense, or he could just deny the facts. But inwardly he probably agrees with the implications of your treatment: he feels that he's really just a low creature. No good. 'Yes, I'm a crumb. I'll stay this way. This is the way I am.' Has this achieved our goal?" Mrs. Levi removed her glasses and looked around at each one of us. "Hmmm? Isn't our goal to change his behavior? Now, going back a bit: you've burned the rice." She smiled. "What if your husband chose instead to say something like this: 'Darling, don't worry about it. I know how hard it is to concentrate when everyone's distracting you.' "

As the women in the workshop proceeded to discuss this issue, the scene which surfaced in my mind was of Daniel in his Superman pajamas, tonight around seven fifteen... There I am, rushing around. The house has got to look nice! The kids can't come into the living room and mess it up again! They've got to be asleep by the time the class starts! And, oh my gosh, I should have made refreshments for the guests! *I don't even have ice cubes!* I've yelled at the children to get into bed, but when I go to their room to review the troops, there's Daniel wandering off somewhere with his giant Materna Infant Formula can of apricot pits (for his pit-toss game). Something goes through my mind at this moment having to do with his willful insurrection. Whether that's really true is not my business right now: I'm in no mood for self-analysis. "What are you doing?" I shout. "I told you to get into bed!" Daniel cradles the precious collection more closely to his chest and continues on toward his Miscellaneous Drawer. "Hurry up!" I yell again. He fumbles, the can falls. Apricot pits scatter everywhere! "I told you not to do that now! You see? See what happened? Now clean it up!" Holding the large can, he drops frenziedly down on all fours to search under his bed, and the remaining pits also spill out. *Now that's the end!* I think furiously. "For goodness sake! OH! Just get into bed! I'll pick them up! Just get into bed!"

"No!" cries Daniel, in tears now. "I want to put them in my drawer!" The women will be knocking on the door any second. I feel ready to cry myself. "So do it then! Fast!" Daniel crouches down to peer again under his bed for more pits, and his position makes it convenient for me to administer a good hard smack, *just in case he didn't get the message.*

It's after midnight. I'm still too uneasy to fall asleep. What have I done? Such shouting, such hysterics. And it all started just because he was putting his things away where they belonged! Could I have made Daniel feel "like a crumb"? Absolutely. As Mrs. Levi said tonight, you don't have to explicitly say to a child, "You're no good" to make him feel it's so.

I guess you can be a very loving, devoted, well-meaning mother, and "a good person" to boot, and still make your child feel like the lowest of the low.

June 23, 1986

This morning I was rudely awakened at quarter to six. Someone was pulling on my left foot.

"Mommy. Mommy, did I miss my bus?"

I glanced at my watch. "No, Danny, it's early. Go back to bed." My eyes closed.

A few minutes later: "Mommy, I can't find my pants."

"They're on your shelf."

"No, not those. I want the pants I wore yesterday!"

"I put them in the hamper already, Danny. They're filthy. Wear the blue ones."

"Why did you put them in the hamper?" Daniel stamped his feet and burst into tears. "And I had something in the pocket!"

"Put on the blue ones, Danny, please."

"I don't want the blue ones, they're so stupid. I want the pants from yesterday!"

I raised myself up on one elbow, summoning up from within me the strength to put down this unfair onslaught so early in the morning, to meet this challenge forcefully...but all at once the good news came back to me—a strange message from last night's workshop:

It is within your power to be calm. It is not necessary to raise your voice.

I was touched by a gentle happiness.

It's easier not to yell.

It lasted all morning. Daniel waved to me light-heartedly as he ran downstairs to his bus in his dirty pants, though I wondered what his rebbe would think of me. Rachel ate two bowls of rice pudding instead of being too frantic, as usual, to eat anything. Dinah cried for only five minutes (rather than the customary twenty-five) when she couldn't find a pair of perfectly matched socks. Elisheva accepted my refusal almost graciously when she asked for corn-on-the-cob for breakfast.

Everyone left the house in a good mood.

No sooner had I rejected Elisheva's unusual request for break-fast this morning, than I regretted having done so. Why shouldn't she have corn-on-the-cob for breakfast? It was only due to some vague allegiance on my part to Mother Convention. "Start having corn-on-the-cob for breakfast," an inner voice had warned, "and who knows what will come next! We must maintain at least a facade of civilization in this household!"

So I made corn-on-the-cob for lunch.

Why does it so often happen that precisely the one I'm going out of my way to please is only made more miserable by my special efforts? The other three children are merrily chomping away, but Elisheva took one look at her corn and flew into a rage.

I don't yet know why.

I gather that something's wrong with her portion. Too small? Too hot? Too cold? The butter melted before she was able to spread it?

Ten minutes or so have passed. Her tantrum has escalated, perhaps because I'm at such a loss to help her when she's screaming like this. I cannot in good conscience give her a new ear of corn, when just last night in the workshop I listened attentively to the admonition that giving in to tantrums is not wise educational policy. Therefore, I have retreated dutifully to my typewriter, resolved to ignore her. Stay calm, Sarah, I tell myself. She will stop this eventually, so maintain your perspective. Let her know that she cannot dictate your response by behaving like this.

Stay calm. Your detachment is for her own good.

Five more minutes have passed. It's hard on the eardrums.

It's evening now, and the kids are in bed. What finally happened is that all of a sudden, like a message lighting up on a computer screen, the word *empathy* appeared before my mind's eye. Miriam Levi spoke of it last night, saying that except in certain instances in which a child is unleashing anger abusively against a parent, empathy is almost always called for.

I made my approach cautiously, watching out for flying objects.

"Elisheva?" I said softly, telling myself to tune in to her genuine misery. She ignored me. She was still down on the floor kicking.

"Elisheva?" I said, more softly. "Elisheva, something is wrong with the corn?"

She quieted down enough to find out what I was saying.

Now, very softly: "Elisheva, something is wrong with your corn?"

Struggling to get a hold of the sobbing, her complaint at last became intelligible. "IT'S DIRTY!"

"Where is it dirty, Elisheva? Can you show me?"

She arose. She had stopped crying. "THERE!" she wailed triumphantly, pointing to a brown kernel. "You SEE?"

"Yes, I certainly do." I plucked it out.

Elisheva, still red-faced, wiped off her nose and then her eyes on her sleeve, pulled up her chair and sat down to eat. Luckily, she didn't notice that her corn had gotten cold.

June 24, 1986

The children and I are all in a good mood. Could it be simply because I'm not raising my voice? Child raising has always been such a complicated maze of methods, philosophies and psychological angles. Mrs. Levi emphasizes the most obvious yet most overlooked factor: to speak with kindness and respect to our children, as we ourselves wish to be spoken to. It is our obligation to teach them to behave as we are commanded to in the Torah, and we must teach them in a kind way.

Recognizing the thoughts underlying my angry reactions is something I can hardly imagine even beginning to tackle at this point. Nevertheless, the act of speaking quietly—no matter what—goes a long way towards tempering the emotion.

The only thing is that I'm so scared of losing this calm. It's ridiculous for me to pride myself on having overcome in two days an ingrained inability to control my temper with my children. Impossible. So when am I going to break?

June 25, 1986

Rachel lied today. Dinah came running into my bedroom where I was nursing the baby, pressing her hand to a red-tinged cheek. She yowled that Rachel had slapped her in the face, which elicited my fury. As I arose to find Rachel, I reminded myself to speak quietly and calmly.

Rachel was playing dolls in the children's bedroom with her best friends Ahuvi and Perla. Upon my entrance, she looked up and quickly turned back to play.

I've always worried about Rachel. She's one of twins, and Dinah was born a year-and-a-half later. I was so busy and overwhelmed with three children in less than three years. Daniel, the ever-active boy, continued to get a lot of our attention—even if some of it was negative—but we were not compelled as much to focus upon the quiet, obedient Rachel. I fear that during those first three, four, five years, she lost out. Around the time she turned six, I suddenly woke up and looked at her: *Gee, what a lovely child.* Sensitive, mature, considerate, generous... But something had happened. She'd been hurt. Each time she'd get a reprimand, she'd sulk for hours; it was as if I were tapping into an underlying reservoir of sadness. To this day, whenever I catch sight of this part of her, I am seized by guilt and agitation: *She's suffering and it's my fault.*

Now I called Rachel aside, so as not to embarrass her in front of her friends. (She has a finely tuned sensitivity to public humiliations.) I asked her what had happened to Dinah. "Nothing," she replied.

"Nothing?" I inquired. "Did you hit Dinah in the face?"

"No." Her blue eyes looked up at me steadily. Too steadily. If there's anything I hate and fear in my children, it's the ability to lie.

"You didn't hit her, Rachel? Are you sure?"

"No, I didn't."

Miriam Levi wrote in her book that if one is sure a child has lied, it's better to confront him directly with that fact, rather than wheedle the truth out of him. This advice came to mind. I had the two friends go home, then asked Rachel to please come sit down next to me on the couch. She eyed me warily. "Are you going to hit me?"

A needle of shame and regret pricked my heart. So that's what she has learned to expect from me.

More softly now, I told her she would have to stay in the rest of the afternoon because she had not told me the truth. Though she usually chooses to stay at home after school anyway, this denial of her freedom set Rachel off like a firecracker. She jumped up and ran around the house in fury and desperation. She kicked at me and tried to hit me. I warded off her attack and continued to speak quietly, though my heart was squeezed with sorrow. I don't know how long it had been going on, but it was becoming hard to listen to this shrilly powerful tantrum. She was getting more and more distraught, and I was starting to worry about her. I got an idea.

Taking Eli from his playpen, I held him out to her. She looked up at me with swollen eyes, considered whether to accept the offer, then opened her arms. She is ever awed by the existence of this new baby. Rachel quieted down and walked with him to the couch. A smile played upon her lips as she examined his hands. Some minutes passed as she cradled him in silence. "Rachel," I ventured, "it's so, so important to tell the truth, especially to the people in your family." She kept her eyes on Eli. "Did you hit Dinah in the face?"

Now she turned to look into my eyes. "Yes."

A load rolled off my heart. "Thank you for telling me, darling. It's so good to be honest about things."

We then got into an interesting conversation about lying. A real conversation! She was really absorbing my thoughts for her consideration and offering me hers. What a lovely thing, for us to exchange ideas! Her spirits unwound. She bounced Eli on her knees with buoyant gaiety.

Miriam Levi said in the workshop that just as a heavy sense of guilt seldom serves to effect changes in our own behavior, it has an equally detrimental effect upon our children. There are two ways of protecting them from guilty consciences: First, rather than focusing on the badness of the child when he does something wrong, focus only on the wrongness of his deed. Second, don't "spare" him. If he has done something wrong, don't overlook it, for a child who feels as if he has gotten away with doing something bad isn't going to like himself for it. A child's guilty conscience is a mighty burden. So confront him, but do it gently and with respect, so as not to corner him.

It was a lovely sight to watch Rachel being freed from her

self-contempt. It reminds me how once, long ago, I saw my mother brush a load of snow off the long branch of a pine tree that was so weighted down it was touching the ground. The branch sprang up at once as if it were alive with joy.

"All right, Rachel, you can go out now," I told her in my happiness. "You don't have to stay in the house all afternoon." *No! I said to myself. If you told her that she was going to get a punishment, then you should go through with it. You're so inconsistent and confused!* I sat there kicking myself for a minute, then recognized that familiar habit I have of worried self-flagellation.

All right, maybe it's a mistake, a minor mistake. It's all right.

"No," Rachel answered dreamily. "I don't want to go."

A negative experience had turned into a highly positive one. My heart sang.

June 26, 1986

Last night the workshop dealt with praise. Giving praise, it was emphasized, is actually of less importance to a child's development than the avoidance of excessive criticism. Nonetheless, a judicious use of praise can work wonders in encouraging positive behavior and a good self-image.

What is an incorrect use of praise? First, overpraising. Let's say we've done someone a favor, and the person just doesn't stop talking about it. Don't we start feeling a trifle uncomfortable? Don't we somehow start discounting the value of his appreciation, or feel obliged to reject it? Don't we start thinking, "Well, what I did wasn't really all that great."

Children react the same way.

Yet compliments that are sensed as authentic and unexaggerated are welcomed.

Another incorrect use of praise is the praising of character rather than of deeds. It is preferable to state: "That was generous to share your toys," rather than: "You're such a generous child." Better to say: "These dishes are very clean. Thank you!" rather than: "What a wonderful boy you are for doing the dishes." When a child's told how brilliant she is for her apt comment on the *parshah* at the Shabbat table, she may feel uneasy the next time around if she has nothing to say. She might feel she's forfeited her elevated status and the admiration that came with it.

A parent needn't carry this too far, however, and worry if "What a good boy!" slips out. Such a comment obviously does less damage than "What a bad boy!"

I remember how I felt as a child when my mother would tell me, as she often did, that I was sweet. I didn't doubt her sincerity. My mother is a frank person who doesn't give compliments unless she means them. Yet that picture of me didn't quite jive with my self-image. I had all kinds of feelings going on inside me that were anything but sweet, and her polished portrait of me produced an uneasy sense that somehow she didn't know me all that well, as well as I would have liked. There's a sense of security a child gets from feeling his parents thoroughly know his faults and love him anyway. I wanted my mother to think I was sweet, and wasn't eager that she discover the truth. I thought she loved me only because she thought I was sweet. Therefore, I hoped I could continue forever to pull the wool over her eyes.

The fact is, I probably wasn't doing anything in particular to earn her love. What I know now, from being a mother myself, is that she most certainly was not ignorant of my faults. It wasn't due to some misconception on her part that in her eyes I was sweet. For no matter how awful a child of mine may appear to me at one moment, the next minute he may seem the dearest thing in this world—the incarnation of sweetness. As a little girl, I didn't know that mothers operate this way.

One thing I've always felt good about is my natural tendency to liberally dole out the praise. I am truly thrilled by my children's accomplishments; in my eyes, none of their successes are trivial. I think that basically I'm on the right track here. Now, however, I have a sneaking suspicion that the way I give praise and encouragement is rooted partially in my own insecurity—in my own excessive need for positive feedback from the outside. I'm striving to ward off in my children that lack of confidence from which I myself have suffered. Nothing wrong with that, if my methods are successful. Yet perhaps my manner of boosting them up too frequently, too earnestly, breeds some of the very insecurity I'm so anxious to spare them. Maybe it convinces them that they need the boosting.

I myself am so suspicious of anything smacking of ungenuine flattery; it's not unlikely that my children are, too. I'd better prune some of the more luxuriant bouquets I toss their way, if I would have my expressions of praise be accepted.

I'm worried about what I've done by my mistakes with this whole business of praise. My goodness, when I start learning what I do wrong, I can so easily sink into a muddy pool of discouragement. It's overwhelming.

Undoing the damage seems horrendously complicated. It's unlikely that I can really correct a great deal of this stuff, because it's so rooted in my personality and background. Miriam Levi asserts with equanimity that it is a matter of changing one's habits, and that it is possible to do so in spite of the difficulties involved. That's a polite way of putting it. It's more like dragging a recalcitrant elephant out of quicksand.

2
Outside the Frame

June 29, 1986

I told the children this afternoon that I was going to take a nap while the baby slept and please not to wake me.

They didn't wake me. It's amazing.

Instead of finding the place a complete mess when I got up, I discovered that they had tried valiantly to put the living room and kitchen in order. I think they're so grateful for having been given respect this week that they reflexively long to please me. The speed with which their behavior has altered in response to the slight change in mine is unnerving. They're like flowers that wilt or blossom according to the quality of light I'm shedding. What power I have! What a responsibility! I so want to keep this up when I glimpse the pleasure that child raising can be, yet fear that I'll break. For sure I'll break—it's just a matter of time.

It's as if I have been occupying a huge old mansion for years and have become thoroughly familiar with its dark, confusing interior. One day someone suggests that I move across the street into a sun-drenched cottage with a flower garden, and I do. The move is not as difficult as I would expect, given how settled I was in my other surroundings, and I decide never to set foot again in what I now recognize was that depressing environment. Yet each time I look out one of my gaily curtained windows, there's the old house staring at me, and its closeness is unnerving. I fear that coming home one day, out of habit, I'll walk up automatically to my old door, enter and get stuck inside without my keys.

Miriam Levi asked us what we would like to discuss in the workshop tonight, and we all agreed that children's fighting was on the top of everyone's list. But as we were about to begin, Leah made a remark that veered us off in a different direction.

"I'm in pain from a chronic illness, and even though I do try my utmost to control myself, I'm so distracted by the pain that it's hard for me to keep a rein on my reactions to the children. I can tell myself that I'm going to be quiet and kind, and a second later I'm yelling at them. I really think that these techniques you're teaching us are good when everything is basically all right in your life, but when things go wrong—major things that don't even have to do with the children, but they affect your nerves terribly..." She broke off. Then, with obvious resentment: "What good does it do for you to tell us that getting angry doesn't educate? I know that already. But how do you implement these techniques in real life when you're in pain?"

"Look, there is no doubt about it," Mrs. Levi answered, "physical pain is such a source of stress from within that it makes it far more difficult to tolerate stress from the outside. When you're not feeling well, your frustration tolerance zooms down. It's very, very hard. I know from my own experience with back pain. It is very hard. Nonetheless, it behooves us to recognize that we cling to the idea that we can't function when we're in pain, that we shouldn't have to, that it's impossible. These beliefs can be modified. We can say something to ourselves like: 'It's harder, for sure, but I can go on a little bit longer.' And it's important that we not come to regard our pain as a justification for causing other people pain. Have you ever heard yourself say, 'Oh, I feel so terrible, I just can't help yelling at the kids today'?

"Any manner of stress will do it," she continued. "Dissatisfaction with yourself, marital problems, a sick child, an argument with a friend, tiredness, money problems. There's an infinite range of situations that can crop up and make daily life harder. All I can say is that we can strive to get our tools in good working order so that we can take them out and use them when we really need them. We can make using these tools a habit. If you do something enough times, you'd be surprised how it can become habitual and second-nature. But what we're aiming for here is not self-control (though of course self-control plays a big part in life for all of us). What we're aiming at is a change of attitude toward pain. Not only physical pain, but all the pains of life. All the discomforts with which we are endlessly confronted."

She paused. "You know, a hundred years ago, or maybe even fifty years ago, people had the idea that life is a tough business. They expected it to be a struggle on just about every front, so they weren't surprised to be confronted by difficulties. Today, however, there's something in the whole environment that cultivates the conviction that a good life must by definition be a comfortable, easy one. 'I should have an easy life. I should not have all these problems. My difficulties must be eliminated.' This is an outlook that undermines our ability to lead lives guided by the Torah. In the Torah view, the goal is to fill your life with as many mitzvos and good deeds as possible. We have now in the western world an intense focus on the body's physical well-being and on the extension of our years. Life *is* of infinite value in and of itself, but a longer, healthier life is not an end in itself. A long life is desirable insofar as the longer you live, the more time you have to develop as a person. Within that framework, we should enjoy the permitted pleasures that G-d's world offers us to the extent that this enjoyment helps us to function better. Whatever can be made easier should be made easier, for the sake of freeing us to accomplish, to perfect ourselves. Comfort and pleasure can be advantageous, except—and there's a big except here—when a comfortable life distracts you so that you stop striving.

"Look at the people with a high degree of comfort in their lives," she continued. "Things have worked out for them pretty much the way they dreamed, whether on the emotional or the material level. The husband's a doll and the children are perfect little angels, the house is pretty and the family is close by and whatever. Now this could be just fine. People in such situations could very well be spending every free moment thanking *HaShem* for all their blessings and praying to prove themselves worthy of His kindness by giving to others. But it often happens that without a certain amount of pain, a person can fail to reassess. We have to be constantly reassessing, and it is pain that pushes us to look into ourselves.

"So," Miriam Levi looked around at us, "are you still with me?" We nodded. "So we should make our lives as trouble-free and as pain-free as possible, but when you do have difficulties that you can't eliminate, what do you do? If you think, 'It shouldn't be this way,' the pain you experience increases. If you think, 'This is unbearable,' your burden grows heavier. Any daily occurrence can be transformed into something genuinely torturous. People upset themselves terribly because they have problems. Aside from the unhappiness of the problem itself, they have the unhappiness of thinking that they shouldn't have the problem in the first place! That it just shouldn't be! Something's gone wrong! So the main thing to remember is that pain fits into the total picture. It's part of it all, of the whole grand design."

As the workshop continued, an image came to my mind: In a large frame was a huge painting of what life is supposed to contain, the picture of life I got growing up in America. Inside the frame is everything beautiful and happy, but anything horrible and painful is being pushed outside the frame...it must be pushed outside the frame.

Later on, I walked with Miriam Levi to the bus stop and told her about my fear: the better things get, the more intense my apprehension that I'll lose what I've suddenly found.

She replied that, given my long held, habitual pattern of responding angrily when I'm displeased or frustrated by my children, it's inevitable that I should sometimes make mistakes, and yell and hit. The trick is not to eat myself up with guilt over it. I have to get used to the idea that I'm a fallible human being. If the parents provide a generally positive environment, she said, children won't be seriously affected by occasional mistakes. In fact, the mistakes of parents serve a certain purpose. Were children to get nothing but consistent justice, empathy, respect and understanding, they could end up being poorly equipped for a world that is often insensitive. (Great. My kids are out of danger!) If the mistakes are within a normal range, the child develops the strength to handle them. I should cease demanding perfection of myself. It's unrealistic and counter-productive.

As she spoke, I wondered if that's really what I'm doing, demanding perfection of myself. I'd say I'm expecting of myself only what I legitimately need to expect and condemning myself justifiedly for failures. My failures, after all, don't occur in a vacuum: they hurt five children. I can't afford the luxury of being philosophical and lenient with myself about all my understandable human weaknesses. Doing so might make me feel better, but it wouldn't help my children any. Such cliches: "Nobody's perfect." "Everybody makes mistakes." They've always struck me as mankind's excuse for mediocrity.

Nevertheless, as I was walking home from the bus stop, for a split second, I saw a light: I'm human. I will make mistakes. I don't have to be perfect.

June 30, 1986

Rachel has a pretty doll that she has kept in excellent condition ever since my sister Candis bought it for her two years ago. The secret of the doll's eternal good looks is that it has never had its hair washed. When our real baby appeared on the scene four months ago, Rachel's interest in her doll waned, yet this past week the doll has inexplicably recaptured some favor in its mother's eyes. It has been dressed and undressed and cradled and groomed as in days of yore.

This afternoon, Rachel discovered that her doll's elegantly smooth, shiny blonde hair had suddenly turned into a ragged old mop, the telltale sign of having gone to the hairdresser's.

"Who messed up my dolly's hair?" Her sorrowful cry from the children's bedroom pierced the afternoon. "Mommy!" She burst into the kitchen. "Mommy! Who messed up her hair? Did somebody wash it? I know that somebody washed it!"

I had been witness to some strong circumstantial evidence, but suspecting what could be in store for the guilty party, I hesitated to provide incriminating information. "Yes," I ventured in what I hoped was a neutral tone, "it does look like somebody washed her hair, doesn't it."

"Yes! Yes!" Rachel jumped up and down with agony. Then she paused. "I know who! Elisheva did it! RIGHT? RIGHT, MOMMY? OOOOHHHH!" In exasperation over this frustrating world, she stamped her foot and rushed out to find her sister. I braced myself.

A few minutes later, I heard the following exchange from my post at the kitchen sink:

"Elisheva?"

"Yes?" came Elisheva's bright little chirp. "What, Racheli?"

With friendly politeness: "Did you wash my dolly's hair?"

I turned around to look into the living room. Elisheva was pouting doubtfully, obviously wondering whether truthfulness constituted the better part of valor. Rachel evidently didn't need direct confirmation. She read Elisheva's face. "Don't wash her hair again, O.K.?" Rachel cajoled in a motherly coo. "She's scared of the water, O.K.? O.K., Elisheva?" Elisheva's eyes widened with understanding, and she nodded silently.

This was a reward. The self-restraint which I've been exercising recently had been mirrored in Rachel's behavior. She didn't even force her sister to confess. My heart jumped for joy.

I took Rachel aside. I wanted to tell her she was the most wonderful sister in the world and that she'd be a great *tzadekkes* when she grew up. With mighty restraint I said instead: "You asked Elisheva so nicely if she washed your dolly's hair, Rachel. You didn't make her afraid. Now I bet she won't do it again, because of the way you talked to her."

Rachel smiled thoughtfully. "You want to see what I did?" She dashed off and returned, holding her doll up proudly for me to see. Though the hairdo will probably never be the same, it had been smoothly combed out, and the doll had reacquired some loveliness. "You know why it looks like this again?" she whispered.

"No. Why?" I whispered back.

"I prayed."

I returned to the dishes with such an exalted sense of pride, hope, gratitude and triumph that I finished off the whole sink-load without the usual grinding boredom. I had sprouted wings. Suddenly there was a scream from the bedroom—Rachel's scream. For goodness sake, I wondered, is peace never permanent? Rachel appeared a second later, clutching her doll. "Mommy!" she sobbed breathlessly. "Mommy! Tell Danny! Tell Danny!" She pulled me out of the kitchen toward her bedroom. I visualized blood, broken toys, scratched faces... What could it be?

In the corner, with a tentative grin, stood Daniel. For whatever atrocity he had committed, I was on the verge of clobbering him.

"He's looking at my notebooks!" screeched Rachel.

I tried to get oriented. "What notebooks?"

"My notebooks!"

At Rachel's first grade farewell party yesterday, her teacher presented each girl with a bound collection of the whole year's work. Daniel had evidently been caught leafing through them, but no damage had been done. Having expected something of a criminal nature, I said, "Well, Rachel, you didn't need to yell so much. You could have just told me, sweetheart."

Daniel, encouraged by my support and indignant now at having been unfairly accused, lunged at her. She landed hard on the floor, got up, lunged back. He reciprocated. My intercession had only made things worse. With this fresh affirmation of what I'd heard in the workshop about avoiding involvement in children's fights, I decided to depart, but that, too, was a wrong move. What havoc is wrought by slavish adherence to any doctrine! A few seconds later, on my way to the kitchen, I was shocked by such a stinging slap on my back that it almost took my breath away. I spun around and faced Rachel—her eyes streaming, her eyes astonished. If I hadn't shared such a tender exchange with her a few minutes earlier over the doll, I would have shouted at the top of my lungs and slapped her right back. "You didn't help me! You never help me!" She was weeping. I had betrayed her trust. "You just help *Elisheva* when someone hits *her*!"

My heart constricted with her anguish. I was crestfallen. The roller coaster ride doesn't stop long enough at the top for me to savor the lofty heights.

July 1, 1986

"What's this?"

"That's an eyebrow."

"What's this?" Elisheva smiled, knowing I did not want to talk. I wanted to finish the book I'd been reading.

"Those are my lips."

"What's these?"

"That's my forehead, Elisheva."

"No, not that. These." She drew her finger across my forehead once, then twice. I put the book down.

"What do you mean, darling?"

"What's these lines on your forehead?"

I imagined the letter I would write to my mother. What a kick she would get out of her grandchild's adorable, innocent frankness. "Mommy, you wouldn't believe what Elisheva said to me the other day. It was so funny..." But a few minutes later I was leaning over the bathroom sink, peering into the mirror, hoping that I wouldn't find what I was looking for. Yet there they were. Yes. The lines were more prominent. I resolved to get more sleep. I resolved to start taking brewer's yeast again.

I've been going around the rest of the day in grouchy sensitivity, mumbling to myself in a silent inner dialogue: How stupid to worry about wrinkles. Are you the first human being to get wrinkles? Has the scourge of aging never afflicted anyone but you? What a ridiculous waste of energy to worry about such vanity! Grow up!

But that's just it. My body is growing up. Is my mind growing up? What have I accomplished in my life to justify wrinkles and render them noble?

The children.

Yes, but anyone can have children. It's not a unique accomplishment. That's what you thought before you got married, that having children would finally do the trick. They'd legitimize your existence. They'd be your ticket to civilization as much as any Ph.D. But no one's handing out any graduation papers.

The children do ward off the darkness. They do keep at bay that gnawing sense of dim futility which used to nag at me. But only some great demonstration on my part of spiritual or emotional or intellectual self-mastery could ever mitigate the embarrassment of my physical self's helplessness before biological processes. How humiliating to be nothing but dust!

I should start using face cream.

July 2, 1986

Dinah called me bad names this afternoon because I ate the ice cream she had saved from Shabbat. When I found it in the freezer, I decided it was a hard-working mother's prerogative to indulge in somebody's forgotten delight, but somebody's memory wasn't as hazy as I had assumed.

In the past, I would have yelled at Dinah. "You can't say those things to your mother! Stop it! Stop it right now!" This time, I apologized for having taken what didn't belong to me, and quietly informed her that even though she was right, she is still not allowed to talk to me like that. She averted her eyes and was quiet, but later on started up again, calling me "stupid," "*rasha merusha*," and other choice epithets. In my heart of hearts, I couldn't blame her. I would have been mad, too, if I had saved some precious morsel and it disappeared. I told myself, though, not to let my guilt excuse her inexcusable behavior. I stayed silent now and cast her a Miriam Levi glance of sorrowful disappointment.

Some twenty minutes later I was nursing the baby in my

bedroom when the door flew open and Dinah burst in like a hurricane, screamed something, dissolved with laughter, and raced out, slamming the door behind her. It was a few seconds before I realized that what she had screamed was "I'm sorry!"

This evening, Dinah was especially loving towards me—hugging me tenderly, making funny faces for my amusement, stroking my cheek, gazing up into my eyes.

For what seems to me to be a comparatively modest outlay of effort at keeping my voice down, I'm getting disproportionately high returns.

July 3, 1986

This morning I finally went out to buy new socks for the girls. I was thinking especially of Dinah, whose dressing rituals each day drive me crazy. (If I were to take the advice I heard in the workshop, I'd tell myself instead: "Her dressing rituals frustrate me, but I can tolerate them.") I bought four pink pairs for each girl, easily distinguishable from all the mismatched whites that make everyone so miserable.

Elisheva and Rachel were eminently pleased with theirs, and immediately squirreled the socks away to guard against filching. Dinah, however, exploded in tears.

"What's wrong?" I pleaded.

"It has a hole!" she yelled.

"Oh, no, it doesn't, Dinah. They're brand-new socks."

I snatched the sock she was brandishing out of her hand to prove my point, but lo and behold...the new sock, straight out of its cellophane wrapper, sported a tidy, half-inch-wide hole on one side! I was incredulous. Just my luck! The defective one could at least have ended up with Rachel or Elisheva, but how can I fight my fate? "You're going to have to get me another one!" she ordered. "Go back today! Today! You don't even know how to buy socks!" I denied to myself that this hurt my pride and bristled at her impudence. Of course I know how to buy socks. How absurd. I shouldn't permit such talk from a child. I was certain that,

indeed, such rudeness and ingratitude should not be coun-
tenanced, but was less certain just how to stop her, other than
with a good hard smack. My faith in brute force, however, has
been damaged by the workshop. "You have to!" she was wailing.
"You have to go back to the store right now and bring me a new
one now!"

I was abashed. I wondered how this five-year-old could order
me around like this, and actually succeed in making me feel guilty.
Guilty enough to actually consider going back to the store! She
was determined to get her way, that I knew. If only I were as
determined to get my way, but I didn't know what my way should
be. How should I deal with such chutzpah? How should I mod-
erate my annoying subservience to this tiny dictator?

All afternoon Dinah simmered like a volcano, casting me accu-
satory glances and glaring at me distrustfully. "Nu? See? You're
not going back! You see? You're not!"

"Dinah, don't worry, you'll get your sock," I told her, even
though I knew instinctively that to simply satisfy her demand
would be unwise. The best way would certainly be to help her
accept that life is imperfect, mothers and socks are imperfect...*lekabel et zeh beahavah*. But how could I get this across to a
child campaigning against universal injustice and maternal incom-
petence, to a child on the verge of volcanic eruption? And how
could I be tranquil and wise when I was bobbing about on little
waves of self-doubt and frustration? The only thing I could do
safely was to keep my voice down. Whatever I said throughout
the afternoon—about respect for parents, one's need to develop
patience, tests from *HaShem*, etc.—was said calmly, but also apologetically. She had really succeeded in making me feel guilty. I was
under her thumb.

Tonight after class, I walked down to the bus stop with Miriam
Levi and told her the tale of the hole. She was intrigued by my
daughter's assertion that I was *chayav*, but the bus arrived right
away, so I was left to my own devices. When I got back upstairs,
who should be standing there at the door to the children's room
but Dinah herself.

In the workshop, it had been suggested that good communication with children is usually impossible in the middle of a stormy conflict: it's better to try after tempers have cooled. Here was my chance.

Dinah had had an accident. After I changed her bed sheets and she was cuddled under the blanket, I made my attempt.

"Dinah?" I whispered.

"Yes?" she whispered back.

"Remember today when I bought you socks and when you opened the package the first sock had a hole?"

"Yes."

"Was that Mommy's fault?"

Dinah was quiet. I saw her little face peering thoughtfully into the darkness.

"I'm sorry."

"All right, darling. Good night."

Dinah blew me a kiss. "Good night."

July 4, 1986

I went to bed last night, after my loving exchange with Dinah, full of hope for the future. Even if I don't know what I'm doing, I thought contentedly as I plumped up my pillow, I just have to communicate calmly. I needn't be so pessimistic about changing. Anything that comes up can be handled. Tomorrow's my birthday. I have made strides as a mother and as a person. I have not been wasting time. I slipped off to sleep infused with new confidence and fresh determination. I was awakened out of a deep slumber by that familiar, offensive tug on my foot. "Mommy, did I miss my bus?"

"Go see what time it is on the kitchen clock, Danny."

A minute later: "The clock says seven."

"SEVEN!" I bounded out of bed. "Get dressed!" I had twelve minutes.

When I finished his sandwich, I rushed out of the kitchen and found Daniel—standing there in his underwear. "Danny!" I shouted. "Why aren't you dressed? What are you doing?"

"I can't find a shirt."

"You have plenty of shirts!"

"No, I don't have shirts!"

"So get on your pants and socks and shoes and I'll find you a shirt! Go! Go!"

"No, first I want a shirt. And I don't want one with sleeves down to here."

My temper soared. I steered Daniel into his room, disregarding his tears and protests, and forced him to put on a shirt of my choosing. This was a matter of life or death. In other words, if he missed his bus, I'd have to spend half my precious morning taking him to school. In the workshop last night, Miriam Levi said that contrary to most contemporary child raising theories, the Torah version of the family unit is not one of democracy. So now, as Daniel balked at my authority, I inwardly exploded with indignation. How I'd suffered like a fool all these years at the mercy of this mutinous bunch of upstarts! I'd teach them who's boss! No longer would I relinquish my rightful place as queen around here! The rest of the morning I hit, I yelled, I pushed them through their paces, and like every other authentic, undemocratic queen, I thought: "If they don't mind me, it's off with their heads!"

But even as I was strutting around in my self-righteousness, within me I cried. Oh no...here I go again...

This morning was the worst one I've had in ages. It was worse this morning than before the workshop began.

My tiny first steps of improvement were illusory and insignificant compared to the Olympian feat required to actually change my ancient patterns as a mother. I feel as if I don't know where I am, as if I've been walking on sand. I thought I'd made footprints, but I look around and there are none there.

July 5, 1986

Yaacov and I would like to find a mother's helper. During his lunch hour last week, he composed an advertisement which he intended to post in various neighborhoods around the city. It went like this:

> **YOUNG AMERICAN COUPLE**
> **SEEKS MOTHER'S HELPER**
> Young woman wanted for light
> housework and babysitting.
> Room and board or part-time.
> Call 803746

I thought it was a perfectly reasonable ad, but my husband had a change of heart. The next day he asked me: "You think it's O.K. that I say we're a young couple?"

"What do you mean, is it O.K.? Of course it's O.K."

"But I'm forty-four and you're thirty-seven."

"Thirty-six. My birthday's not till Friday. I'm young! And forty's young, for goodness sake. What are you talking about?"

He dropped it, but that night he showed it to me again. He had substituted the word "middle-aged" for "young." "How disgusting," I said. "Are you kidding? Look, if you want to be middle-aged, go right ahead, but I'm not."

Yaacov mulled that over, then came up with:

> **MATURE AMERICAN COUPLE**
> **SEEKS MOTHER'S HELPER, etc.**

"Forget it," I said.

"O.K., what about 'Friendly, mature couple'?"

I smirked. "Look, there's no reason you have to put anything about our age in there. It doesn't have anything to do with it!"

"How about 'lively, mature couple'?"

"Very funny, Yaacov."

"How about this one?" He scribbled something on a piece of paper and shoved it across the kitchen table.

> YOUNG, MIDDLE-AGED
> COUPLE SEEKS MOTHER'S
> HELPER, etc.

After the children left the next morning, I went to do some shopping. I had intended to put up our want-ads, but couldn't because somehow we hadn't gotten around to editing a final version. With the baby asleep in my arms, I was gazing absent-mindedly out of the bus window as it turned onto Rechov Yaffo when I chanced to glance up at the side of a red-brick building. On it had been painted a white rectangle a few meters wide, where—in English, for my benefit—was stenciled in big block letters:

> 37
> MAY YOU BE FOREVER YOUNG

It was a left-over sign in honor of last year's Independence Day, but since yesterday, July 4th, was my 37th birthday, I took the message personally—an uncanny birthday greeting to me from on high. July 4th has always linked my destiny so clearly with the U.S.A., but I'm just one year younger than the State of Israel.

May we be forever young.

3

The Guilty Millionaire

July 6, 1986

It's a quarter to eight and they're all asleep. The morning wasn't great, but the afternoon was lovely. It was so good, in fact, that my mind was fringed with anxiety. At any moment my *yetzer hara* could rise up monstrously to ruin it all.

When the children arrive home from school tired, hungry and demanding, that's the time I dislike more than any other aside from bedtime. I always brace myself for that moment when they barge in on my peaceful scene. Today, I had just opened the refrigerator, the baby in my arms, when I found myself suddenly surrounded by all four of them. There was Daniel, and Dinah, and Rachel, and Elisheva. The baby had just spit up a sour-smelling, jagged dribble down my sleeve. A quick wave of inexplicable happiness passed through me, and I thought: my family. "Isn't it nice to be all together?" I was about to say, but was so charmed by the unusual nature of this idea that I forgot to speak.

After lunch, Daniel cleaned up the children's room without being asked, and then the living room. He did a scrupulous job. Later, I heard them all laughing and talking together, so peacefully! I patted myself on the back for being such a good mother, and went on about my business, taking pleasure all afternoon in them and in my motherhood. Could our family life be like this all the time? The prospect was exciting, but the inverse was also true: if I don't remain calm, then it's back to meaningless pandemonium. I must stay calm. I must stay calm.

Can this big improvement in the emotional atmosphere be simply the result of a consistent lowering of my voice? Speaking quietly must be affecting my subconscious assessment of my life: "Since you're not yelling," says my brain, "there must be nothing to yell about. I'm coming to the conclusion that your life must be O.K. Maybe it's even good. Maybe you even have something to be happy about."

Staying calm with my children has gotten me into the habit of speaking calmly with my husband, which in turn affects my perception of events. "If you're not yelling about it," says my brain, "then it's not catastrophic that he forgot to take out the garbage again. You can remind him calmly."

When I'm not yelling or complaining, I'm not as inclined to feel sorry for myself.

It is frequently out of guilt for some mistake that I shout at the children, to divert the blame to them.

I'm also not as tired as I usually am. "Getting all worked up" is an apt expression, for getting angry is hard work. I still have this peculiar feeling, dating back to the first morning after the workshop, that I've been relieved of the obligation to get upset. I've always imagined that staying on top of the situation in the house requires a great expenditure of physical and vocal energy. It's a job from which I can go off-duty. True power is gentle.

Tonight was the workshop. The main topic was anger and guilt. Mrs. Levi said that in essence, anger is intolerance toward the behavior of others, and guilt is intolerance toward the behavior of oneself. This fascinates me. It gives me a clue as to why anger and guilt are inextricably intertwined in a vicious circle: they are both rooted in intolerance.

"You can't be a good educator when you're upset. When you're angry, your influence is minimal, because what does a child feel when you're angry? He feels: 'She doesn't like me, that mean old witch!' and he resents you for it, because he really longs to have your approval. When you're angry at him, he will not want to do as you wish. So what can you do to develop greater tolerance? Well, you're usually angry at a child because he has caused you some trouble: anxiety because he's come home late, or extra work because he's made a mess, or tension because he's fighting with his brothers and sisters. So the first thing is to convince yourself—but I mean *really convince yourself*—that this trouble is not really all that awful. What it really comes down to is: *we can strive to develop greater tolerance for all the pains of life.*

"You know, most of us are missing a sense of accepting ourselves as human beings—*human* beings. You know, if a child fails at something, and we say, 'You didn't try hard enough! Try again!' what happens? He feels discouraged, and it will be hard for him to try again. He doesn't want to come up against those awful feelings again. But if we say: 'I know it's so difficult. You tried so hard and now you have to do it all over again,' then it's easier to summon up the courage to try again. Be understanding of yourself and of your children, for understanding is encouraging. Freeing oneself of the self-condemnation is what makes working on oneself possible."

I was six. I came home after school, pulled the toaster from the kitchen cabinet, and took butter and a loaf of cinnamon-raisin bread out of the refrigerator. I set up the toaster, pushed down the bread, then ran into the dining room to turn on the T.V.

"The Millionaire" had already started!

"Sarah?" The molasses-slow southern lilt of Alice's voice drifted in from the kitchen. "Your toast is up."

Oh no! I didn't want to miss it. Mr. Anthony was just about to say who would get the anonymous gift of one million dollars today!

"Sarah?" Alice was our maid. I didn't answer her. Oh, well, let the toast get cold. Oh, but then the butter wouldn't melt!

I forgot about my snack. After a few minutes, Alice walked into the dining room and set up the little folding table by the big armchair where

I sat. Then she set down a glass of milk and a dish with my hot buttered cinnamon toast.

"Thank you, Alice!"

"That's all right, now," she said.

The next day I came home from school, opened the cabinet to get out the toaster, and was about to set everything up when Alice said, "You go in and sit down. I'll do that for you."

Oh, goodie! I was so happy. I ran in to Mr. Anthony, or maybe "Queen for a Day" was on. Which old homely woman would get an entire wardrobe of designer clothes that couldn't possibly fit her, and a refrigerator or a new car? The one who could really cry in front of the audience and make the applause meters go crazy.

Alice brought in my toast and milk.

"Thank you, Alice."

The next day when I came home, I went over to the cabinet, opened it and reached for the toaster. Alice said, "I'll do that for you." I rushed to the television and settled into my father's armchair. The hot toast and cold milk appeared in a few minutes.

I found that all I had to do each afternoon was make a gesture of opening the cabinet and Alice would say that she'd finish the job. I made the gesture as an innocent-looking signal to her, by way of pretending that I was just about to do it myself. It became a ritual in which Alice and I engaged every afternoon that year of first grade.

And when she set the plate down on the table, I would say, "Oh, thank you, Alice!" as if I were surprised. I ate the delicious buttered toast, sat absorbed by Mr. Anthony, and ignored the flower of guilty self-contempt which had budded within my heart.

July 7, 1986

Rachel was hanging around the house this afternoon while the other children were outside. I was lying down reading on the couch when she appeared at my side with an unopened bar of halvah in her hand and a question in her smile. I had forgotten to dole it out on Shabbat, and now she had discovered it in the kitchen cabinet. "All right," I said, and then, conspiratorially, "Just for you and me." I gave both of us a piece and rewrapped the halvah in its silver foil.

A few minutes later she reappeared. I myself wanted another piece, so I said O.K. We both had seconds.

Some minutes later she returned. My sense of decency told me no—after all, it had been bought for all four children, not just one of them and me! And I should teach Rachel to be fair and considerate and not greedy... But it tasted so good.

We had thirds.

By the time she came back for fourths, I had already sneaked another portion, so I gave Rachel her fourth and myself a fifth. The halvah had quite nearly disappeared by now. I sat there on the couch feeling guilty and ashamed of myself for being so piggish, when some message from the workshop drifted back to me about guilt and feeling guilty. Granted, this little adventure in appetite was not a serious *aveirah*, but the guilt feelings engendered were worthy of a major crime. *So!* I said to myself with cheerful defiance. *Don't wallow in guilt. Enjoy that stuff to the last crumb!*

"Rachel!" I called. "Come here!" She ran out of her bedroom. "There's only one tiny piece left. Let's share it." Rachel's eyes widened with wonder at my marvelous degeneracy. As we licked our fingers of the last sweet fragments, I whispered to her with a mischievous grin, "Aren't we bad!" She threw back her head with a delighted peal of laughter at our intimacy, at our shared delinquency, gave a jump for joy like a delicate fawn into the air, and danced away out the front door.

4

The End of the World

July 8, 1986

Elisheva is four but still drinks from a bottle. For the past few years, it has been the nutritional aspect which has concerned me—that her consumption of milk ruins her appetite for other foods, so I add a half-teaspoon or so of brewer's yeast to each bottle, to compensate. Her dentist has furthermore explained to me that the lactose, sucked for hours in her sleep, works wonders on Elisheva's enamel and on our dentist bill. Yet in spite of all this, I haven't wanted to force a weaning to the cup. My philosophy has been to let her addiction take its natural course, for if she wants it, then she must need it. Trust her own system to go by its proper schedule. There's nothing wrong with drinking from a bottle, other than in the minds of unenlightened neighbors.

When she was three-and-a-half, Elisheva announced that on her fourth birthday she would start drinking from a cup. During the intervening months she often reminded us of this, as if to lessen her present indignity. On her birthday she gave it a try, and I forget exactly what happened, but that night she went to bed with the bottle. I wonder how she felt as she came up against what all of us discover eventually: that a resolution to turn over a new leaf is easier to declare than it is to fulfill.

What worries me now is that ever since her self-imposed deadline passed, she seems shy and embarrassed about it. Should we have somehow forced her to break the habit, rather than let her fail like this? When I myself turned three, my father took my bottle and threw it into the woods—an event I don't recall, but a scene I envision clearly from having heard its retelling so many times. It's one of the family legends. When I got older and was introduced to modern psychology, I relegated to this forced weaning the status of childhood trauma, and took my father to task for a lack of subtlety in his approach.

Trauma or no, I do fear the effect upon Elisheva of a sudden weaning from her friendly source of solace, especially now that a baby has appeared whose privilege it is to nurse. But what about her self-respect in the meantime? If she's drinking from the bottle when unexpected neighborhood children pop in, she startles, so afraid is she of being caught in the act. Much of the time she prefers its company to theirs, and asks me in a whisper to tell those people to leave. Furthermore, I've seen one of my other children get her to do things by threatening to publicize her babyish bottle-drinking if she doesn't comply. How can I help her? She shouldn't be subject to this sort of blackmail.

Today Rachel was upset that Dinah wanted to come along with her to Perla's house. Youngest sister that I am, my own ancient pain of being an unwanted tag-along still a live wire within me, I told her that she'd have to let Dinah come, too. Rachel flew into a fit of tears, jumping, running around like a trapped bird.

My eldest sister Andrea has told me how the oldest child is often expected not to have a child's feelings. *Empathy*, I told myself.

As soon as Dinah was out of earshot, I asked Rachel why she was so opposed to having her sister come along. I almost said, "Be fair," but caught myself in time. Fair to Dinah. What about fair to Rachel? "Because Perla will like Dinah then and not me!" cried Rachel.

I was taken aback, skeptical, frustrated. Perla's devotion to Rachel is remarkable for its persistence and intensity, so my first reaction to Rachel's reply was that she was "just making an excuse." She must know better than to think that her best friend would prefer that little five-year-old to her! Fortunately, I quickly recognized the fallacy of my self-serving conclusion here: it's a style of interpreting the children's feelings when they don't coincide with my expectations, when they're telling me something I don't understand. If Rachel was "just saying this to get her way," then how to account for her anguish? Why would she want to leave Dinah behind unless she had a good reason? But Perla hardly seems to notice Dinah! Could Rachel really believe that there's a danger here? "Rachel," I inquired, "do you really think so? That Perla would like Dinah and not you?"

My question pricked open her fear and frustration, and fresh tears streamed forth. "Yes!" she snapped impatiently.

"But darling, Perla likes *you*. She wouldn't like Dinah more than you, for sure."

This irritated Rachel all the more, and I could see in her fierce glare that she was infuriated by my utter thickness. "You just don't know! I know it! She will like Dinah and then she won't be my friend anymore!"

This insecurity of hers really worries me. It's my fault. Once upon a time Rachel must have sensed how Dinah really did get some of the vitally important, irreplaceable maternal attention that had been hers before. Though I was the youngest rather than the oldest, Rachel and I share the experience exactly: the shaky, anxious fear of losing love because of a sister.

I let Rachel go by herself. Dinah cried, desolate to have been left behind, unwanted. I recognize too well that haggard, tender yearning to be included as an equal.

The kids went to sleep easily tonight. Thank G-d.

Come to think of it, bedtime has generally gotten easier. It is no longer quite so astonishing that on workshop nights, even if they're not asleep when the class begins at eight, they still remain in bed obediently.

July 9, 1986

The girls are home now for their summer vacation, and it will be a week or so until the day camp sponsored by Bais Yaakov starts. Though I have been anticipating this vacation as if it were a mean old monster crouching just offstage, now that it's upon us there's something relaxing about it. I don't have to rush around each morning to get them dressed, fed and off to school. I don't have to squeeze every last drop out of my free time, because I don't have any free time. I don't have to rush to get the place clean before they arrive home because it wouldn't be worth it: a permanent mantle of messiness has settled over the house and I'm getting used to it. Whenever someone visits I mention off-handedly that all the children are on vacation.

Today, Dinah heard me on the phone arranging for a babysitter. Ever since, she's been sticking out her tongue at me, holding the freezer door open and waiting for my reaction, coloring over the numbers in my address book. Every once in a while her anger dissolves into tears. "Take me with you! I want to come with you!" I try empathizing. "I'm so sorry that you can't come with me. I understand how much you'd like to come." This has not gotten her off my back. So I'm just staying calm and repeating my assertion that I have to go by myself.

She just came over to me and asked me to unzip her dress. Now she's on the floor with a needle and thread that she apparently took from my sewing box and she's sewing a torn seam! I hope that I can repair whatever damage she inflicts. In the meantime, she has calmed down, and is even happy. I'm so glad that I maintained my position without losing my cool or putting her down.

She has just brought me the dress. To my surprise, the seam really looks fine. I won't have to redo it. I am proud. There are few better cures for distress than a feeling of accomplishment.

She has just brought the dress to me again for a second inspection. "I'm finished," she said with a satisfied smile.

There is such pleasure in disciplining myself. Getting into the habit of speaking calmly to the children is tantamount to getting a handle on my *yetzer hara*. Little did I know that I have been given, right in my own backyard, the perfect setup for my spiritual struggle, right here next to the kitchen sink and the laundry line. It's intriguing how we women usually define *chessed* in terms of helping the poor family down the block. Why is it that working on one's *middos* as they come to bear on one's own children doesn't catch our attention as much? Why doesn't it carry the same status in our eyes? Is it because a mother's love is considered so natural, not something you get credit for achieving? Is it because being a good mother is not something which gains you the recognition—both from others and from oneself—that going out and helping people publicly does?

I feel such joy. I have a glimpse of what it's like to rule myself, rather than be the downtrodden servant of my own emotions. Controlling myself is not something that's "over the ocean." It's an accessible feat.

My calm voice gives me a sense of security; hearing it is like having a lifeline during the times my inner self is bobbing around precariously on the waves of my feelings.

I can imagine what it does for the children as well.

Suddenly, I understand the old cliche that children want discipline. (I've always been skeptical: don't they want freedom?) It doesn't mean that in some perverse way that only perverse psychologists understand, children want to be slapped and yelled at. It does mean that they want to be kindly, firmly prevented from doing what their own consciences tell them is wrong. A mother who disciplines calmly provides her children with a sense of security.

It must be scary to have a mother who seems to think that there's always a good reason to lose control.

It's now eleven o'clock. I felt so utterly depressed tonight as the class began. How ridiculous to attend the workshop twice a week, work inch by inch to gain territory, exult over my advances, then lose it all in one fell swoop.

All afternoon the children were fairly cooperative with me and with each other. At times I got a little rush of joy for no reason other than the pleasure and challenge of being a mother. Their arguments didn't escalate into wild battles, and dissipated without my entering the fray as policeman and judge. They cleaned up their rooms without being told. I heard them engaging in long, subdued conversations (I wish I knew what they were talking about, but their Hebrew's too fast for me), then they'd break up in laughter. Dinah embroidered a duck on one of her father's old handkerchiefs. Perla visited, and Rachel didn't seem nervous when Dinah was around. Elisheva gave her doll a bath, and I didn't get upset about the spilled water all over the bathroom floor. I gave her the *sponga* stick, and she took intense pleasure in negotiating the water down the floor drain. Daniel hit Rachel and I made him sit in a chair for five minutes. He hit Dinah later on, and again he had to sit down. After that, he didn't hit anyone.

I felt like the most skilled, sensitive, competent mother around.

If I blame myself for my children's negative behavior, I also take the credit when they're happy and behave civilly. The only trouble with this, as we were warned in the workshop, is the flip side to this pleasure. If I preen myself as mother of the year when I succeed, I set myself up for the metamorphosis in my own mind into witch of the century the next time I slip. Taking care to judge deeds rather than the person—when it comes to my own behavior as well as my children's—enables me to learn from mistakes rather than berate myself for them.

There I was this afternoon, having permanently mastered discipline with love. We moved along on a gentle wave—four, five, six o'clock. On to bed, dear children. "O.K., kids, eat and drink whatever else you want now, because we're going to bed soon." They ignored me. "Kids! Danny, Dinah, finish up dinner now." Again, they kept on talking. "All right, sorry kids, I'm going to have to clear the table now." In my calm, crisp, professional mode I matter-of-factly removed their dishes. Screams of protest. "All right, then, so eat!" I snapped, falling a bit out of character. Concerted eating for three or four minutes, then again talk, argument, laughter. *They don't listen to me!* I thought. *Enough!* I swiped the dishes off the table. Cries, screams. "Go brush your teeth! You're finished eating! Come on, now, every one of you! Go brush your teeth!"

"Go brush your teeth!"

"Go brush your teeth!"

"Go brush your teeth!"

"Go to the bathroom."

"Go to the bathroom."

"Go to the bathroom!"

"GO TO THE BATHROOM!"   .

"GET INTO PAJAMAS!"

"GET INTO PAJAMAS!"

"GET INTO PAJAMAS OR I'LL HIT YOU SO HARD YOU'LL CRY! HOW DO YOU WANT TO GO SLEEP?" I screamed. "YOU WANT TO GO TO BED HAPPY OR YOU WANT TO GO TO BED CRYING? GET INTO BED OR I'LL SMACK YOU!" Then I demonstrated the parental consistency of which I've heard and matched word with deed. Daniel, who, as it so often happens, chanced to be right there as my temperature took off like a rocket, received the full force of the maternal missile. He was picking up his collection of *tzadikkim* trading cards when I entered the children's bedroom. "WHAT DO YOU THINK YOU'RE DOING!" I shouted, coming down on him with a sharp slap. "Pick those up and get into bed! Did you brush your teeth?"

"No."

I hit him again, harder this time. My hand stung. A shadow of something passed over his face—silent surprise at this abrupt resurrection of mother as enemy. It took just a fraction of a second for him to shift ever so delicately into his corresponding role. He was transformed by a subtle rearrangement of his features into the resistant, resentful child. With downcast eyes and a tiny smile, Daniel dawdled with his cards, or rather, I perceived him dawdling and saw red. "Pick up the cards!"

"I am."

"You are not!"

He began ever so slowly—or so it seemed—to gather them together. *He's trying to get me mad on purpose. He's teasing me,* I thought, lights flashing on and off in my brain. I thereupon smacked him hard, again, thinking self-righteously that this would teach him not to enrage me like this ever again. *He deserves it, he deserves it,* I thought madly. Daniel was crying. *What are you doing?* piped up a small voice within me. *Stop.* I hit his hand, the one holding the stack of cards. Pictures of the Chofetz Chaim, Rav Moshe Feinstein and Rav Elchonon Wasserman scattered onto the floor. Their presence embarrassed me. "Now get into bed!" I shouted.

The other children, as usual, had chosen to avoid Daniel's fate and were all under the covers. I checked on them like a swaggering officer carrying out inspection. All were perfectly quiet. Hiding my horrible self-hatred, I marched into the kitchen. A few minutes passed before Elisheva called out, "Mommy. Come."

"Go to sleep!" I snapped loudly.

"Mommy! Come!"

When I got to her bedside, she handed me her bottle.

"Look, Mommy."

I looked, aghast. She had bitten the nipple in two. We had no others in the house. "Why did you do that?" I bellowed. "We don't have another nipple!" I could just see her coming out into the living room crying, bothering everyone in the workshop. Elisheva's face collapsed, and she wept.

"You'll just have to go to sleep without the bottle now."

"No," she whimpered. "No."

"WHAT DO YOU WANT? YOU WANT ME TO GO OUT NOW AND GET YOU A NEW ONE? ALL THE STORES ARE CLOSED. IT'S THE NIGHTTIME. GO TO SLEEP!" It was ten minutes to eight. The class would start in ten minutes. "GO TO SLEEP!"

I wanted to cry, but witches don't.

A few minutes later, as the first fragmentary replays of my violence toward Daniel started filtering up to mind, I went to his bedside. I could tell by his breathing he was still awake. I wanted to redeem myself from the horrible feeling of being trapped in my guilt, the feeling of having done evil, of being evil. "Danny, you were trying to make me mad at you, weren't you?"

His face was turned towards the wall. "No," he replied.

"Yes, you were, Danny, you wanted to make me mad." I sat down and put my hand gently on his back. "Why? It's your own fault I got so mad at you. You should mind me." Elisheva was calling from the other room. "Just a minute, Elisheva!"

Daniel turned his face towards me, eyes swollen from crying. "I didn't!" he moaned miserably. "I didn't try to make you mad!"

"Danny, when I kept on asking you to go to bed, why didn't you just do it? And why didn't you pick up the cards quickly? You knew I was in a hurry."

"No, I didn't!"

"Danny, you knew my class is tonight, and I told you that was why I was in a hurry. A lot of women are coming here. They're going to be here any second, so you have to help me. You were trying to upset me. Why?"

Daniel was sitting upright now, gazing abstractedly into my eyes.

"Daniel." My voice deepened. "You did want to make me mad and upset, and you should say you're sorry."

"All right."

"All right, what?"

"All right, I wanted to make you mad." His face drooped. He threw himself back down and turned to the wall. I leaned over to kiss him. He averted his face. Somebody knocked at the front door. Elisheva was crying.

"Elisheva!" I whispered sharply. "Go to sleep!"

"I want my bottle."

"For crying out loud! Why did you bite the nipple?"

"So buy me a nipple."

"All right, I'll buy you a nipple in the morning."

"FWEE nipples."

"All right, three."

"No, six nipples."

Someone knocked again. Oh, my gosh! I hadn't answered the door. "All right, six nipples. Now go to sleep!"

A horrendous fact dawned on me about nine thirty, during the workshop: I had succeeded in convincing Daniel of his own bad motive. That had been my Pyrrhic victory.

I realized that if Daniel had indeed been provoking me on purpose, it had been done unconsciously. That was the only way he dared to vent his own anger at my anger. Furthermore, it was uncertain that he had in fact been "trying" to get me mad. Who knows how a child's mind and heart operate? I don't. Daniel certainly doesn't. I had defeated him by forcing him to agree to my interpretation of his behavior. I had forced him to betray himself, for the sake of my pride. I'd been so eager to clear myself of guilt in his eyes and in my own that I had been blind to the unconscious and automatic nature of his response to my own loss of self-control.

July 10, 1986

I apologized to Danny this morning almost before he opened his eyes. He looked up at me quizzically from his pillow. "Mommy, did I miss my bus?"

"No, it's still early."

"I have to do my homework. I didn't do my homework yesterday."

While Daniel in his Superman pajamas pondered 20-4 and 7x3, I felt awfully glad to see he was still in one piece. But is there any way of knowing, really? What I sometimes do to my children—out of simple tiredness or unexceptional impatience or pressure to hang the laundry—could rival the most famous tales by Freud, Dickens, Twain, et al., of traumatic childhoods. Parents in those accounts always personified for me human insensitivity of grotesque proportions, parents with little room for love in their stupid, narrow hearts. Or they had no hearts.

But I do have a heart. I want to do right by my children. I want to bring them up with kindness, justice and vision. Then what a cruel twist of fate that I should treat them sometimes so roughly, crudely, and hit them so hard.

During the workshop last night, Elisheva kept calling for me to come to the bedroom, until Miriam Levi arose and strode majestically back into the children's quarters, calling out softly, with great curiosity in her voice: "Who is that? Who is that calling Mommy?"

I held my breath, imagining that Elisheva would be frightened of this tall stranger entering her bedroom at night. I heard Mrs. Levi speaking very quietly and Elisheva's little voice in reply. I was dying to know what was being said but couldn't make it out. After a minute or two, she returned to her seat and resumed the class. Elisheva didn't call out again.

This morning Elisheva asked me: "Who is that lady?"

"You mean that woman who came into your room last night?"

"Yes. That lady."

"She's the teacher of my class. Was she nice?"

Elisheva nodded, with a slight smile.

"Did she get mad at you?" I asked.

Shaking her head slowly: "No."

"Were you scared?"

"No."

I forgot to go buy nipples for Elisheva's bottle this morning. She ran into the house about noon, after playing outside, with a wide smile. "Where are the six nipples?"

"Oh, Elisheva, I'm sorry, I couldn't get them yet. I will."

Her mouth fell open. She was trying to swallow this big, sad disappointment, looking up at me in silence. All of a sudden, I had an idea. "Elisheva," I said, "I know you'd like to stop drinking from a bottle, even if it would be so hard not to have your bottle. Maybe you can drink from a cup instead. Then, on Shabbat, we'll have a party!"

"A party?" Stars came into her eyes.

"Yes, because you stopped drinking from a bottle. We can have potato chips."

"Potato chips?" Her eyes widened. "And cookies?"

"Yes. Do you want big cookies or small cookies?"

"Big cookies!"

"And we can get apple juice."

"And Coca-Cola!"

Coca-Cola. I wondered. Should we go all the way? "All right. And Coca-Cola."

"No," she countered. "Not Coca-Cola because it makes the teeth hurt."

I tried to conceal my satisfaction.

"So ice cream!" she exclaimed. "All kinds of junk."

"Oh, yes! I'll get a lot of ice cream. And a lot of junk."

All afternoon we kept this up. Our plans for the party went up like a shining structure of crystallized sugar. Interestingly enough, Elisheva at once began sucking her thumb, a habit which I would have imagined evolves gradually, not one which is substituted instantly for a lifelong institution. Though the dentist would surely lift an eyebrow in warning, I myself considered it a reasonable price to pay for freedom from bottle-bondage.

She lay down for her nap, to my astonishment, without her bottle...just her thumb! And to top it off, she even fell asleep. Later on, I held my breath: what would happen at bedtime?

At bedtime, Elisheva crawled into bed, pulled her pink blanket over her head and was asleep before I left the room. She was certainly entitled to some rest after passing this milestone.

Yaakov was amazed when I reported that Elisheva had fallen asleep without her bottle. "Really?" he asked incredulously.

July 11, 1986

Elisheva fell asleep this afternoon on the couch, as usual, and I was so relieved to have one of them out of circulation. I was so tired. Cooking in the kitchen a quarter hour or so after she'd dropped off, I was flabbergasted to hear her cry out. When I rushed into the living room, I found Daniel at her side. He must have woken her up! "Danny!" I shouted. He dashed out. I ran to his bedroom. He was nowhere in sight. "Danny! Where are you? Come here! Right now!" No answer. I bellowed now at a higher pitch for him to come. I was in a rage. He appeared. He was about to say something when I started hitting. *You're not allowed to hit in the three weeks leading up to Tisha B'Av,* an inner voice reminded, yet my own shrill retort snapped, *He's got to know how bad this is! He'll do this all the time if I don't teach him! He'll drive me absolutely crazy! He can't do this!* I, the victim, smacked him hard on his backside. *What else can I do? Any mother would feel this way! Poor me!*

Am I depressed now? Am I smothered by guilt? Of course. So what else is new.

Even if I tell myself wisely that this response is not constructive?

Don't ask.

Back at the beginning again, here I am.

An hour or so later. I'm continuing to yell. The girls are fighting. I'm yelling at them to stop. I put the baby in his crib. Great! One down, four to go. Rachel takes him out to play. I scream, "Didn't I tell you not to take him out of there without asking me first? I just put him down! Now he'll cry if I put him back!"

It feels as if yelling is my only weapon.

Elisheva is not asking for her bottle. My husband bought all the stuff for the party and she is arranging and rearranging the bags of potato chips, pretzels, cookies and ice-cream cones on a kitchen shelf.

July 12, 1986

We had the party today. Elisheva didn't want any guests. The other children, enthralled by the unrestricted platters of junk food on the table, didn't pay much attention to Yaacov's speech about the meaning of our celebration—Elisheva's sacrifice for the sake of maturity. But Elisheva sat there at the table serene, proud, honored.

And she went to sleep tonight with her thumb.

I can't believe how easy it was. The miracle we'd been unable to bring about for fear of forcing her has now been accomplished (I hope there's no hitch) by confident straight-talk and incentives. My matter-of-fact tone in proposing the idea to her conveyed my confidence that she was certainly capable of achieving the difficult thing she wished to achieve. Apparently, this influenced her own attitude. I'm pleased with myself.

July 13, 1986

Dr. Spock says somewhere in his book on child care that it takes a knowledgeable mother to create a child's eating problem. I am one of those well-informed ladies. My own mother, fifteen years before health foods became the focus of the American counterculture, spared herself nothing to provide balanced, natural meals for her husband and children. All by herself she raised a barnyard-full of chickens so we could have fresh, chemical-free eggs—this in a sophisticated, sleek Connecticut suburb where the other mothers were more interested in country clubs than in foul chicken coops. She never bought vegetables in the supermarket; everything on our table came from her own organic garden. We drank only fresh milk that she picked up from a farm in another town. She permitted no junk food in the house. White sugar, white rice and white flour were other-worldy things foreign to our home.

As a child it never occurred to me to appreciate my mother's hard work in the garden, chicken coop and kitchen, much less to thank her for all of it. I was actually rather ashamed of her eccentricity. I wished she were like the other mothers. I remember the Milky Way that Clare's mother bought for me in the supermarket when I was a first-grader, and Mrs. Johnson's remarking upon how polite I was to eat it so slowly. She had no idea how much I treasured that sinful thing and just wanted it to last. I remember taking nickels from my mother's purse throughout fifth grade to buy wint-o-green Lifesavers. I'd leap off the school bus, that stolen nickel in my sweaty palm, and sneak into the neighborhood grocery store before walking slowly home.

In all my childhood, I never experienced hunger for breakfast, lunch or dinner.

So here I am, my brain teeming with facts about calcium, magnesium, lecithin, protein deficiencies, vitamin loss through overcooking, the empty calories of white bread, the reduced food value of canned and frozen vegetables, the chemical components of margarine...here I am transplanted in Israel, country of antibiotics, agricultural hormones, candy, cookies, ice cream, of sandwiches filled, by loving mothers, with chocolate spread. Each day a tug-of-war goes on between my inner child and the voice of my mother: "Let them have it! Don't make such a big deal over it! If you forbid it, they'll just want it more, and your food less!"

"No. It's a mother's responsibility to provide the best possible nutrition. Children have so little room in their stomachs, and such high nutritional requirements because of their fast growth. If they get empty calories such as white rice and white noodles, you're missing your chance. These are the years their bodies are being formed. Let every single thing they eat be body building. If they want sweets, keep a lot of dried fruit around the house. If they want snacks, always keep nuts on hand. If you let them fill up with things that have no food value, you're preparing them for health problems that only show up later, when their youth no longer conceals the abuse to their systems. You cannot fool nature."

What I'm looking for is *not* a moderation between the two extremes, with the scales tipped with artful subtlety in favor of health. That, of course, is the solution any objective observer would advise. What I want to achieve is just the *illusion* of balance. The children should come away with the impression that their mother is reasonable and fair-minded, while I actually aspire to the extremism of my mother. To strike this uneven balance gracefully, I'd need a balanced state of mind, and when it comes to food my mind is anything but on an even keel. Monsters lurk behind every bit of junk food I've ever allowed on my kitchen shelf, threatening ill health due to maternal irresponsibility. These hairy, healthy beasts point their paws at me accusingly whenever I fail to live up to the inheritance I was bequeathed. "You're pretty healthy yourself!" they chide me. "Why not do the same favor for your kids that your mother did for you?"

The upshot is that I urge my children, they balk, I hover, I encourage, lose my temper, deprive them of desserts, then try the opposite tack and pretend I couldn't care less. "You want cookies? Sure! Have all of them!"

Miriam Levi has said on more than one occasion: *It's not so much what you say as how you say it.* It's not so much the decision to control their food intake as it is the manner in which one carries out that control. Carrot sticks could be fun, if I only had the knack of presenting them as if they were.

Today I was feeling the effects of a stomach virus and couldn't stand the sight or smell of food. All day the children had to fend for themselves. They invaded the refrigerator, rummaged through the cabinets, emptied the fruit bowls, cracked every almond in the house, peeled every banana. My mother would be proud. I looked on from my reclining posture on the couch and was sickened as they finished off the brown-rice pudding (how *could* they?) and a whole loaf of whole wheat bread (they took turns with the toaster). They chomped on cucumbers, red peppers, tomatoes, carrots, hard-boiled eggs...and complained that I wasn't giving them anything. I apologized and explained there was nothing I could do: if I even *thought* about cooking, I'd throw up.

I should always strive for such apathy as I was blessed with today.

July 14, 1986

The main topic of the workshop last night was children's fighting. Mrs. Levi said that this is usually one of the first things mothers want to talk about.

"We have the notion," she began, "that if we were doing everything right as parents, then our children wouldn't fight. But kids are kids, and kids will fight. It happens in every home. Siblings fight for a simple reason—and it's not to get attention as a lot of people say. It's because they haven't learned a better way to settle their differences. To some extent there are things you can do to reduce the amount of fighting, but in your own mind make peace with their war. Make peace with the fighting."

"But Mrs. Levi!" I cut in. "Sometimes it may be true that children's fighting is just because they haven't learned ways of working things out. But I'm sure that at other times there *are* deeper reasons for it. It sounds like you're tossing the whole issue of sibling rivalry right out the window."

"It is not advantageous for a mother to focus on this issue," she replied. "It just makes her scurry around trying to give each child the love he's supposedly missing. Sibling rivalry is given far too much weight; I'd call it a very minor factor."

The workshop broke out with ten different voices.

"A minor factor! In my house, it's major."

"When I was growing up, we kids fought all the time and we weren't jealous at all."

"Right. People take it too seriously."

"But when I was a child, I was so jealous of my little sister I wanted to strangle her!"

"Sibling rivalry is real! If it was important enough to be in *Bereishis*..."

"That's right! Look at Cain and Abel!"

"Or Yaacov and his brothers!"

Ruth spoke above the cacophany: "I don't know about sibling rivalry, but as far as that other thing you were saying, that it's not the parents' fault when children fight, I can see right away that my kids get nervous and fight with each other more when I'm nervous myself. So it *is* my fault."

"Your moods will definitely be reflected in their behavior, yes. So it is necessary for us to exemplify the behavior we expect in our children," said Mrs. Levi. "And if it's an extreme situation of parental stress, we do have to get special help. Any extreme situation will foster abnormal problems. In general, however, parents don't realize that the fighting they see in their children is within the normal range, and they guiltily and anxiously search for the deeper causes. It is fair to say that one need not take responsibility for one's children's quarrels. You can far better restore peace and teach children that hitting isn't allowed if you're free of the nagging guilt: 'It's really my fault that they're acting like this!' "

I asked Mrs. Levi about how I find myself getting inexplicably angrier with Rachel than with the others when she's having a run-in with one of her siblings. If she exhibits any kind of mean-spirited behavior, I identify with her and see it as a reflection of my own meanness. Whenever she fights with one of the other children, I feel that I'm facing the results of having deprived her of enough warm attention in her earliest years. Mrs. Levi asked me to give an example, so I told how Rachel pinched Elisheva today. Mrs. Levi said that we'd role-play: she'd play me, and I would be Rachel.

"Rachel," she began very quietly, looking with great, gentle seriousness into my eyes. "Why did you pinch Elisheva?" I was spellbound. Miriam Levi could have made it big in theater if she hadn't gotten into child raising. "Hmmm, Rachel? Why did you pinch Elisheva?"

I felt myself turn into a seven-year-old. "Cuz I'm mad at her," I replied shyly.

"Why are you mad at her?"

"Because she called me stupid."

"Aaaah," said Mrs. Levi, lifting her eyes to the ceiling as if in deep meditation. "She called you stupid." Then very slowly and softly: "Yet we are not allowed to pinch. Why did you pinch?"

"Because my mother doesn't love me."

I was taken aback by my own words. Evidently Mrs. Levi was also. "Did your daughter actually say that?" she inquired.

"No, it just came to my mind. That's how she feels, I think. I think her hostility is my fault."

"Are you sure she feels that way?"

"I don't know. I think so. She was a twin and another baby came along right after them, so I don't think that after that she ever got enough time and attention from me. I was always so busy."

"And is there any problem as far as your feelings toward her go?"

"You mean do I love her?"

Mrs. Levi nodded. "Yes. Sometimes there are cases where that is a problem, and it has to be approached differently."

"No, no problem. I love her."

"All right. Good. So let's assume that what you say is accurate, that Rachel missed out to some degree on the attention that was due her. You may or may not be able to provide her now with the high-quality attention she would need to begin to make up for it, but don't think in terms of treating the child's supposed psychological problems, O.K.? By changing your own methods of handling her, you help her automatically. Aim to eliminate some of the negatives: try not to yell at her, try not to put her down. If you reduce the negatives, many problems take care of themselves. Very young children are flexible. They forgive and forget much more easily than older children. With the older children it's more complicated. As for this pinching business, I doubt that it's rooted exclusively in the hypothetical deficiency of love. Pinching is common among children. Fighting is universal. It's a time-honored phenomenon, no matter what the childhood background."

"But if she felt loved and secure, then she wouldn't have that anger."

"Is that so? She wouldn't get angry if she felt loved? Let's say one child has always been treated as his parents' favorite. Would that guarantee that he's never going to get angry? Isn't anger part of human nature? There you go again, Sarah, thinking that if only you had been a perfect mother, your children wouldn't have problems! Life will always present us with problems. It's counterproductive for you to indulge overmuch in feeling guilty, to have 'what I did wrong' as your focus. It's certainly of little use to

Rachel, because your sense of guilt makes you more angry rather than less."

"So what can I do?"

"Well, in dealing with this specific situation, that of her pinching her sister, you focus on staying calm, on speaking gently. You strive to impart the message that the Torah forbids us to hurt others. And as far as your imagining that your own meanness is reflected in hers, are you a mean person?"

I was on the spot. I looked at myself. Somehow, in that moment, I perceived myself with vision unclogged by guilt. "I don't want to hurt other people. I really do try very much not to hurt other people." It was the truth, and the truth was favorable. I basked inwardly in the light of this newly discovered fact. *I am not so bad after all.*

I then asked about Rachel's fear that her best friend would prefer Dinah to her. Mrs. Levi agreed that I'm right in not forcing Rachel to bring Dinah along. She suggested I keep in mind that the ultimate aim is to reduce the fear of not being loved. Sometime, when the time is right, I can have a conversation with Rachel in which we'd explore the meaning of not being loved. "If Perla were to like Dinah more than you," I could ask, "would that mean that Dinah is better?"

Having myself been so fearful as a child of not being wanted by my older sisters, I can't conceive of teaching Rachel that loss of love is not all that serious. "I don't see eye to eye with you on this," I said. "Losing the love of someone you love does make you feel less valuable. How can I tell her that it doesn't?"

"You're right, at her age you can't expect her to overcome needs which we ourselves as adults find it difficult to overcome. But let's imagine that—"

"Excuse me, Miriam, but do any of us 'overcome the need' for love? I don't even see that as a goal."

"Well, you know, it often happens that what many of us are actually referring to when we use the word 'love' is really the desire for approval. Let's imagine that when we were as young as Rachel, someone had said to us, even once, 'Look here, if so-and-so doesn't love you that doesn't mean *you're* lacking something. The important thing is whether you approve of your own behavior.' There's a chance that perhaps, just perhaps, a little seed would have been planted. A chance that as adults we would be having an easier time dealing with disapproval or loss of love when it comes our way."

"Right," I said. "I do agree with that. No amount of approval and love or even adulation from the outside is going to make one iota of difference if we're feeling the opposite on the inside."

Ita shook her head. "I think this whole discussion is much too abstract. Children need love. Period. All this philosophizing doesn't change that."

"I agree!" Tova, uncomfortable in her eighth month, shifted in her chair. "I've noticed something about your whole approach, Mrs. Levi, that doesn't sit well with me. What about giving love? You don't talk about that very much. It seems very cold to me."

"In general, I don't talk about giving love because we can pretty much take for granted that we love our children. But as we all know, loving them doesn't always keep us from hurting them with our anger. We can feel like throttling them, we can even experience hatred toward them sometimes, but we know that actually we love them tremendously."

"But that's not what she's talking about," I interjected. "The point is whether children know it. Sure, every mother knows that deep down she loves her children, but children—and actually, I'd say this is a common human trait among adults as well—register the negatives much more easily than the positives. To take an example, let's say you give a child a present every day—Monday, Tuesday, Wednesday, Thursday—but if you don't give him one on Friday, then it's: 'You don't give me anything! You never buy me any presents!' The present is a symbol of love, and the child can never get enough of it."

Miriam Levi nodded. "Yes, that's true. Children do need to be given a lot of affection—"

"That's an understatement, I think. It's more like a bottomless pit. And besides, I think it's a pretty high level you're talking about here. Is there any one of us who doesn't look for love from the outside?"

"Well, there are degrees. To an extent we can learn to give ourselves that love as adults."

Tova sat up straight in her chair. "So what are you saying, Mrs. Levi? I hope you don't think we should deprive our children of love so that they'll learn to give it to themselves!"

She laughed. "No, I'm not. If a person doesn't feel loved as a child, it's much, much harder for him to receive love and approve of himself as an adult. It's possible, but it's certainly harder."

"Then why don't you focus on it more?"

"Because in many instances women don't benefit from being told that they need to give their children more love. Whatever positive behavior may result from such advice is often short-lived because it is rooted in guilt. Tell her that she doesn't give her children enough love (even if it's true) and she usually just ends up feeling very bad and worried. So here in the workshop we focus on eliminating the negative aspects of your relationship with your child—the anger, the criticism, the sarcasm, etc. My emphasis is on the methods of discipline which will effectively communicate your love. On handling our angry responses within ourselves, and on manipulating our words and voice to ensure that our children will not feel demeaned by them."

Mrs. Levi paused and thought something over. "But please bear in mind that even if a person has received very little love as a child, he could very well end up as someone with a remarkable capacity for loving others."

July 15, 1986

During the workshop on fighting, I remembered reading something that Rabbi Nachman said about families, and to my delight I found it today:

> A man living alone can become insane. Within him are all
> the warring nations. His personality is that of the victorious

nation. Each time a different nation is victorious, he must change completely, and this can drive him insane. He is alone and cannot express the war within him. But when one lives with others, these battles are expressed toward his family and friends.

It's hard for me to write, I'm so tired. It's time for me to start getting the children ready for bed, yet the prospect of climbing this big mountain once again, as I did yesterday, and the day before...Can't I climb it once and for all? Why do I have to go through the same thing every night, starting all over again way down at the bottom, dragging each and every one of them all the way up to the top? I worked so hard yesterday to get them to brush their teeth! I wish their teeth could just stay brushed.

July 16, 1986

Tonight I was even too tired to yell. When Elisheva wouldn't stay in bed, I said very quietly, "If you don't mind me, I'm going to spank you." She didn't mind me. I spanked her, an unhysterical, to-the-point sort of thing, without comment. She turned around, took a good look at me, and seemed to perceive some justice in the fact that my unheeded warning had been fulfilled. "All right!" she said brightly, with a cheery little smile. "Good night!"

Rachel kept calling me from her bed for this and that. Water, another blanket, granola in a bag (out of the question!). I felt like screaming: "Shut up!" *Baruch HaShem*, I didn't. I just kept repeating: "Time to go to sleep, Rachel. Good night." I felt like going in there and smacking her, but fortunately didn't want to exert myself that much.

She fell asleep. As I plopped down on the couch, I felt contented. I had gotten them into bed without violating their dignity or mine.

July 17, 1986

I didn't have what it takes to write in here today. It's seven forty now. The children are in bed. They were difficult, but it wasn't all that bad, because of my calm voice. I just kept hold of that calm, low voice. They yelled, they played, they were disobedient, they laughed, cried, fought, made up...all evening. But I was convinced that whatever it was that was going on wouldn't improve if I got angry. I'm beginning to believe it: anger will get me nowhere. It's a large expenditure of energy without any returns.

They went to sleep pretty happily, their spirits and mine intact. I feel happy and at peace, greatly encouraged that it is possible. I've been so scared all this time of breaking, and I have broken, yet have not lost the lifeline, thank G-d. I can cope even when I'm as tired as I am right now.

I remember that in my first entry, when the workshop started, I said I'd have something to fall back upon in case of trouble—Miriam Levi. Now I feel I have something within my own self to fall back upon, something to which I have unlimited access: my own sure, calm voice—even if I'm falling apart on the inside, even if I'm unsure and exhausted and confused.

I will break again, naturally. I have to get used to the inevitability of that and not fall into despair each time it happens. I keep looking for a sign that I've arrived, changed for good, permanently reformed my ways—a sign preferably engraved in concrete with large indelible letters. No such final assurance is to be had. I have to accustom myself to the ambiguity of my struggle to be a good mother: in a certain sense, I'll never really know how I'm doing. I can pray that G-d is caring for them when I myself fail. When I break, if I can only bypass the bottomless pit of discouragement and just start speaking calmly again. "To get right back on the horse that's thrown you."

July 18, 1986

At the workshop last night, I talked about that evening's bedtime. I had kept my voice down, and it wasn't a big struggle to do so because it's becoming my habit. But what I was feeling and communicating with that low voice was terrific irritation and impatience, as if I were a chained animal snarling and growling through clenched teeth.

" 'He who is slow to anger is greater than the mighty; he who controls himself is better than the conqueror of a city,' " quoted Miriam Levi from *Mishlei*. "The fact thay you have acquired some control over your voice is a significant achievement. Now perhaps you can challenge the thoughts that are provoking you to anger. What is it that you are worried about at bedtime? What constitutes the tension for you?"

The answer seemed ridiculously self-evident. "That they won't get to bed on time."

"What is the difficulty there?"

I glanced around the room to see if the other women were smirking. Any mother in her right mind knows what the difficulty is there. "Well, in this case, tonight, it was because of the workshop. The workshop starts at eight."

"So?"

"So the children have to all be in bed by eight. And preferably asleep."

"And if not?"

"If not, they might come in and bother the class."

"And this would be a problem?"

"Yes, of course it would be a problem. It would disturb people, and I would feel embarrassed probably, and I'd have to miss the class while I was getting them back into bed."

"Hmm. You'd feel embarrassed."

"Yes."

"And you'd have to leave the class. What would you be thinking about having to leave the class?"

"That it's not fair, that here I am in my class and I should have that time to myself. That I shouldn't be bothered during my own free time. I need very much to have my own private time."

"Do you hear your 'should'?"

"Yes, but it's true. I *shouldn't* be bothered during my own time.

I've reserved it for myself. If I get it, it's for their good as well as for mine, because I need it."

"And you tell yourself that it's very bad if they bother you during your free time?"

"It *is* very bad if they disturb me during that time. I deserve privacy."

"But can you tell yourself something a bit different? Now you're thinking, 'I must have my own time right now. It is unfair, I cannot stand it if they should delay it for me.' Can you say something along these lines instead? 'This is frustrating. I so much want my own time to myself right now. It would be so nice. But I can tolerate waiting a little bit longer.'

"Keeping your voice down is absolutely necessary. But it's not enough unless you can also get at the roots of your anger. Challenge your belief that this, that or the other thing is so terrible that the only proper response to it is anger. Really question yourself: Is it really so terrible? Can you tolerate it?"

July 20, 1986

I must be doing something right. Rachel keeps plying me with food, a gesture of love that's new to her. Yesterday she presented me with a salad of carrot, tomato and apple. If I hadn't been nauseated already, eating this dish would have brought it on. Today she's making me crackers with cheese and crackers with peanut butter. She gets very busy in the kitchen, glancing at me from time to time to make sure I'm not looking. On a cloud of anticipation she dances over to me where I'm sitting on the couch, watches with exultation as I take the first bite, then half-flies back into the kitchen to make me more.

I have hidden the crackers behind my back until I can put them somewhere.

July 21, 1986

I think I may be pregnant.

July 22, 1986

I'm nauseated again this morning. It could be the stomach virus that's going around. I cannot imagine that it could be on account of pregnancy. The baby is just four months old! It couldn't be. But why else would I have this tiredness, as if I were treading water? And why nausea together with the tiredness?

It could be a virus. One of the women in the neighborhood told me that she and her children had it. I do think it must be that I have the virus.

But if it's not, and if I'm pregnant...I don't know how I can go through it again so soon. I had migraines all through the last pregnancy, and nausea even in my later months, and problems with my vision. That in particular was frightening. In all my life I'd never had any problems with my eyesight. I was emotionally at loose ends, constantly tired and yelling at the children, crying to my husband, angry that he wasn't understanding enough. He did help me a lot, but I still was overwhelmed. That tiredness! It's as if you're underwater. It makes me so depressed not to get the housework done.

I'll have a test done. I've been meaning to go since Sunday, but I've been too tired to drag myself into town.

Tonight is the last workshop.

It's one thirty. I went to get the test done, and they're going to have the answer at three. I can call for it.

It went like this: I gave my name. She said, "Just a minute, *geveret*." Then she got back on. "The results are positive."
"What does that mean?"
She repeated herself. I didn't understand these Hebrew words. "WHAT DOES THAT MEAN?"
"Oh, I'm sorry, it means that yes."
"YES? YES WHAT?"
"Yes, that you are pregnant."
"I'M PREGNANT?"

"Yes. Mazal tov."
"PREGNANT?"
"Yes, *geveret*. Shalom."

Later. I'm still speechless. I can't believe it. I can't believe it. It's impossible. I was so sure.

It's bedtime. I'm yelling. The children are not minding me. I've lost track of how in the world to be calm when the children are disobedient and I'm tired. I'm so tired.

5
What the Cow Does

Every night before dinner, I walked with my husband through the back streets of the Zichron Moshe neighborhood of Jerusalem. Boy, I thought, if my mother could only see me now. I really have gone back to the Old World. Men with black waistcoats hurried in and out of the shul. Little girls with braids hanging down their backs, their dresses below the knees, played jump rope. Stout women in head scarves carried home groceries, or chatted with neighbors from their windows while pulling in laundry. Little boys with long side-curls ran along the buckled streets shouting to each other and playing in the twilight. I got glimpses of high-ceilinged rooms with starkly unadorned walls painted apple green, lavender, pale blue. Utterly clean and spare. Americans were few and far between in this little universe. The girls playing jump rope caught me watching them. They cupped their hands to whisper about me. I felt so awkwardly out of place and tightened under their stares. Where do I belong? Why should I be shy of them, they're only children.

We had what I had originally thought was a charming one-room apartment to rent in this neighborhood, but now its quaintness had flaked off like the peeling paint job. I wished we had Americans for neighbors. These people made me feel simultaneously inferior and superior, jealous and haughty. They think they're so holy, I'd grumble to myself. Who do they think they are?

Yet in a way I didn't care. I didn't care about anything. Walking at my husband's side, I felt graceful and beautiful, and he was tall and handsome. He'd point out flowers and together we'd admire their intricate and quiet glory. One night, some months after our marriage, after Yaacov had disappeared into the shul for maariv, I took a stroll down a narrow side-street and discovered a tiny park consisting of one tree, two benches and an ivy-covered wall. I took a seat and looked up through the black filigree pattern of leaves and branches above me to the fair, tranquil sky and its few pale stars. A couple passed leisurely, she in slacks and he with one arm draped casually over her shoulders. Sharing a bag of sunflower seeds, he cracked some private joke and she threw back her head with a laugh. I knew how much they were savoring their little defiance of this neighborhood's unwritten rules. I knew how they relished their freedom in what appeared to them to be a ghetto, an anachronism. They're trying so hard to convince themselves, I thought dimly. Their freedom's not freedom.

That afternoon I had been at the Kotel. When I had turned around from the Wall to leave, I found myself facing a young woman with two small children. Toddlers. One in a carriage. They were doing something, the babies, acting up, or being noisy, and she was telling them in a low voice, "No, don't do that." In those few seconds, her eyes were cast downward as she shook her head, no, but after the reprimand a little smile lifted slightly the corners of her lips, and her face turned to softness. It was a smile that illuminated her face from within, an expression the likes of which I thought I'd never seen before, one of such unearthly tenderness that I almost couldn't bear it. I stood there a moment, turned to stone by jealousy and transfixed by her transcendent beauty. I'd gotten a glimpse of what it must be to have children. I had peeked into something private and utterly pure.

I turned back to the Wall. I pressed my forehead against the cool stone, ashamed. "G-d!" My throat tightened. "I want children, too! Why not? Am I so undeserving?"

Here in this tiny park now, I closed my eyes.

Dear G-d.

I looked around. Two old women had sat down on the next bench.

Dear G-d. I'm so scared to get pregnant.

The stars were getting brighter.

I'm scared of getting fat. Isn't that stupid! I'm so selfish and terrible! How would I ever take care of a baby? I don't even like children that much.

The blue of the evening was deepening.

Dearest G-d. I was scared to get married and You still let me get married. Please, I don't want to get pregnant but please let me have children.

Nine months later the twins were born.

July 23, 1986

The first hour of the workshop last night, the last one of the series, was devoted to my fear of being pregnant. Doesn't G-d want the best for the children I already have? It's as if a carrot were waved teasingly before me and then swiped out of reach just as I was about to catch hold. Ha! You thought life was going to be easy, right? You don't deserve to do well! Too proud!

I was self-conscious talking about being pregnant in front of everyone in the workshop. I'd never talked about being pregnant while in the first three months except to my family or close friends. I kept imagining what these women were thinking: "You should be happy! You should be thanking G-d, not waving your puny fists at Him! How many women would be overjoyed to be in your shoes! Ingrate! Have you no *emunah*? You don't know a blessing when you see one. You're petty and selfish and small-minded."

Most of all, I was scared that by speaking openly and complaining, I was inviting punishment. I feared (and still do) that my lack of appreciation could, G-d forbid, bring on deformity or ill health in the child. Even writing that down scares me. I tell myself that such premonitions of disaster are superstitious, alien to Judaism, yet here I am afraid to put these thoughts into black and white. I'm afraid of giving them any reality.

Miriam commended me. "It's good that you admit you're not thrilled. Many women have similar reactions but can't admit it to themselves." The praise comforted but wasn't entirely convincing. I doubt that many other religious women would be as ungrateful and self-centered as I. "Your fear of retribution," she told me, "is a misinterpretation of *HaShem*'s ways. Being unhappy about this pregnancy is not an *aveirah*," she told me, "and therefore deserves no punishment. *HaKadosh Baruch Hu* doesn't demand that we be saints."

During the hour of our discussion about my pregnancy, the most important thing I realized is this: I behaved calmly with my children because of the belief that it was possible to do so. And now, on account of the pregnancy, it is my belief that it is impossible. I see no way out of being constantly exhausted, high-strung, physically drained by two pregnancies in such close succession. I'm so frightened of the probable recurrence of the vision problem and the migraines. I dread the prospect of not being able to keep the house clean. I am so angry that I won't be able to give this baby, Eli, all the love to which he is entitled, that my full joy in him is being nipped in the bud because I'll be too exhausted to take pleasure in him now. I feel that this pregnancy is such a stupid, irresponsible mistake. (How dare I call a living human embryo a mistake?) I'm so mad that I won't be able to nurse Eli for two years, as I expected. Unless I nurse him and the new baby simultaneously, which I did with Dinah and Elisheva. But it's just too hectic and crazy that way, I don't want to do that again.

Oh, I was in such a good state of mind before this happened! Once I began dealing calmly with everyone, it was easier with five children than it had ever been with four or three. Why did this have to happen?

"Yes, it is difficult," Miriam was saying. "It is very difficult. It is *normal* for you to feel upset, and all right for you to talk about it. There is absolutely no reason to feel guilty." I sat with my arms crossed, not wanting to be taken in by false reassurance. "But you don't have to believe that you won't be able to cope. Eventually, you will cope."

Ita turned to me. "You know, I have a friend who's had eight or nine children. Whenever I go and see her, I look around and say, 'Oh, Frieda, how nice, you've had another one since I last saw you.' And so she always points and whispers, 'Oh yes, well, that's unwanted baby number nine. And over there, that's number eight. There's unwanted baby number five and unwanted baby number six...' And meanwhile it is perfectly obvious that she's in love with every one of them. Sarah, the truth is we don't know what's good for us."

The sense of control I enjoyed up until a few weeks ago, when I started getting so tired, was wonderful. Finding out that I'm pregnant—which was not what I had planned for myself at all right now—has served as an unwanted reminder that I'm helpless. I can do a great deal: I can sculpt my own self...but destiny is not in my hands. I feel like a tiny little ant that's been strutting around boasting of his great powers, and now look at me, desperately out of control and overwhelmed. If I ever do regain some of that ability to be calm, my pride will have to adjust to the reality of my weakness. I was calm only as long as the circumstances were right.

Three or four years ago, in an old neighborhood of Jerusalem, I stood with Elisheva strapped to me in a Snuggly baby carrier, waiting to speak with a certain renowned rabbi. One of his assistant's hurried out of the rabbi's house and stopped for a minute to say hello and ask me how I was. "Fine, thank you," I said. "But I'm here to talk with him about having lost control of myself a lot lately."

He squinted in the sunlight. "We so many times speak of losing control, though we never had the control in the first place. Like a car that thinks it is driving itself, or a pipe that thinks it's the source of the water that flows through it." The front door opened and someone gestured to me to enter. "Be well!" called the assistant as he scurried off. I entered a high-ceilinged, violet-wallpapered dining room, dim and cool, a relief from the summer day. Books lined the walls. I was shown into the living room, where at a table in the middle of the room sat the white-bearded rabbi. A dish of melon slices lay before him on the table. He gestured to the chair opposite him. As I took a seat, he forked a slice of melon and slid it onto a dish. "Here, please."

"No, thank you."

"You left your house without breakfast, maybe? Here." He

passed me the plate. "Of what would you like to speak?"

We were living at the time on a settlement in the Judean desert. I had indeed left without breakfast, and I doubt if anyone else had been able to eat either, so determined was I to make the eight o'clock bus to Jerusalem. "My anger, Rav Simcha. I lose my temper with my children and my husband."

"Often?"

I nodded. I was ashamed. "Yes. Even this morning, before I came here. I have four children under the age of four and it's very hard sometimes." Would he feel sorry for me? No, he didn't seem to. His eyes danced with happiness for my good fortune. "I want to change this about myself."

"It is your nature."

My nature? A weight of hopelessness clamped down upon me. "You mean I won't be able to change?"

"Can an apple become a pear?" His black eyes twinkled. "You will have this nature until you die."

Until I die? That couldn't be. It couldn't be that as an old woman I would still just be the same person I am now!

"Your Creator gave you this nature so that you would always have to work to overcome it." He pointed to Elisheva. "Can she forget you?" I didn't understand what he meant to ask, and wondered if it was his stilted English. I pulled in my chin and looked down at Elisheva's tranquil face off in some unknown baby dream. Her eyelids flickered.

"Can you forget her?" he asked again.

"Well, I..."

"She cannot forget you. Why can she not forget you? Because of her need for you. She is helpless. So in the same way did your Creator give you your nature, so that you would not be able to forget about Him. If you were always strong and perfect, you would feel that you are the creator of your own talent. It is only your weakness that brings you to an awareness of your Creator. It is your need that causes you to cry to Him. When you bump into a table, are you angry at the table?"

"No."

"No, you don't get angry at the table. So when someone hurts you or insults you or bothers you, or your little child does not obey you, shall you lash out? No. That human being is for you only the messenger. 'My dear daughter,' your Creator is saying, 'you have forgotten Me.' The rabbi's face expanded with a smile as he awaited a reply, but I had none to offer. He was amused. Was I amusing him? Getting up abruptly from the table, the rabbi shuffled his feet lightheartedly and swung his arms. "How can I do this?" he asked. *What in the world was he getting at? How could he do what?* "How is it that I walk? I walk because G-d gives me the power to walk. How do you walk?" He paused. I sat there, blank. "Because your Father in Heaven gives you the strength to walk. *He also gives you the strength to restrain your temper, to go beyond your nature.* In the moment that you hold yourself back from lashing out, G-d takes the gr-r-r-eatest pleasure in you."

I was skeptical that G-d would pay that much attention. Doesn't He have more important things on His mind? "G-d would actually take pleasure in me? Really? Or are you just saying this in order to motivate me?"

Rav Simcha nodded with a glint in his eye that said: "How much this child has yet to know," and pointed again to my baby. "Do you get *nachas* from her?" I nodded. "Your Creator is a father. He also wants *nachas* from His children. He wants you to love Him and remember Him, for *your* sake, because in this way you reach out of yourself. When you transcend your nature, you give your Creator much joy, and you shall be the happiest person in the world."

Ever on the lookout for guaranteed happiness, I was tempted by this prospect, but what if I couldn't do it? "I doubt that I'd be able to keep that up very long," I said.

"If you plant an apple seed in the evening, do you wake up in the morning to an apple tree?" Elisheva stirred in the Snuggly. "It is a happiness to accept your weakness, or G-d has to keep on reminding you again and again. The reminder is the pain."

"All right, I do think maybe I could succeed sometimes but I know I'll fall back..."

"Do not be surprised when you fall. Do not be broken. What does the cow do when she falls down?"

What does the cow do? Dear me, I don't know. If this were an exam, I'd flunk.

"She picks herself up again," he rejoined with a wave of his arm. "So must you pick yourself up again. When you fall, do not be broken, and when you succeed, do not be swallowed by pride. G-d is not in the brokenness nor in the pride."

"But sometimes I do feel so disappointed in myself."

"Who are you to feel disappointed? Did you create yourself?"

A foreign concept. My mouth fell open.

"The sweetness of life," the rabbi said with a wide grin, "is in the true struggle."

July 24, 1986

"You're blaming G-d?" Beyla Potash laughed out loud. "What a great line!"

We were on the telephone. I was having my morning cup of coffee with her. Two months ago, she got pregnant when her baby was five months old, and upon hearing the news, I had found it difficult to conceal my irritation: this wasn't fair to the baby she already had! I was secretly so thankful not to be in her shoes. "Oh my gosh, Beyla, how are you going to take care of the two of them so close together?"

When I announced today that now it was my turn to take out the maternity clothes four months after giving birth, she was tickled pink. "You're kidding me! And you were so glad to be thin again, right, Sarah? Great! Don't worry! We'll meet each other for coffee in Geulah and commiserate."

July 31, 1986

Elisheva gave me the recipe for cookies this afternoon. She said that she learned it in *gan.*

"First we take butter and then we take flour and then we take a thing that goes like this [circular motions with hands] and makes noises and it goes around and around. It's for dough. That's how we make dough and put it in the big bowl and then we just a tiny bit smash it up. So then we put a jelly bean for the mouth and we take a candy and put it inside the dough and then we take a raisin for the eye and then we put it in the oven until it's all finished. Then we take it out and we don't need to eat lunch. And then after that we eat lunch because it's more healthy."

I was taking this all down as fast as I could. Elisheva, noting my interest, paused to twist her head around and watch me write. "You want to know how we do ice cream? I know!"

I nodded.

"We take chocolate and we stir it up and then we take cheese and we stir it up and then we put it in the oven. Then we put the cheese inside the cupcakes. Then we put the chocolate on top of it and we put it in the oven."

"Again?" I asked, looking up from my notes.

"No, the first time. And then we smash it up and we have to save it until it's melting and then we smash it again and then we eat it. I have a mitzvah because I told you how to do it, right?"

"Right."

"You have to buy me a lot of money because I told you. And everything we're doing without lunch! But the ice cream we eat with the lunch. We can eat it together!"

"How wonderful."

"Now you want me to tell you how to do challahs? We put butter inside the thing and then we put flour. (It's the same thing like for cookies. Dough and dough, it goes together!) Then we take an egg and we put little things in it—you know those little things?"

"Sesame?"

"Yes. That's how we do challahs! I know!" Elisheva clasped her hands together with a single, motherly sort of clap. "And I know how to do matzah! We go to the matzah bakery! In Pesach time I will tell you how. Without lunch we eat it!"

August 8, 1986

When I took Elisheva downstairs this morning to cross the street, a little three-and-a-half year old boy who lives in the neighborhood was seated atop a pile of dirt in the front yard, playing with a toy truck. I hardly took notice of him; he's not one of my favorites. He's the sort of fellow who throws stones at cats.

A well-intentioned neighbor must have looked out her window onto the yard and turned informer, because the boy's mother suddenly rushed down the path towards our building and, running over to him, shouted: "Why aren't you in cheder!" Her son looked up, mouth hanging open, and the plastic shovel fell from his hand. She at once set in boxing him powerfully around the ears and face, hollering gruffly all the while: "Why didn't you go to cheder! Why didn't you go to cheder!"

Elisheva and I stood transfixed. I felt more than a tinge of gratification to have one of my children observe another mother in the act of losing her temper, and suspected that Elisheva was glad that woman was not *her* mommy. I tried to ignore the intense satisfaction I got from observing this woman in the midst of her uncontrolled fury. It was fascinating. She's one of those extremely organized, fearless super-balabustas with whom I feel out of my depth whenever we chance to meet and attempt a friendly chat. In her presence my sense of myself wilts. I now relished the idea that her confidence was part and parcel of her insensitivity. She might beat me at *sponga*, but I'd beat her on the empathy racetrack any day, and I marvelled that she didn't even have enough smarts to feel ashamed of acting like this in public. With sudden compassion for the little derelict under her blows, I imagined how it must have happened: how he'd had every intention of making the long, two-block journey to cheder, but had been enticed by that comfortable pile of dirt, the shade of the tall tree in the already glaring sun, the big, broken, red toy truck, the old yellow shovel. He had entered that world untouched by time which is accessible to very young children. Perhaps he did aspire to a few wistful thoughts of rebellion, but more likely he had fallen deeply, simply into his play.

Bang! Whack! His enormous, furious mother was upon him.

What effect could it have had upon his mind to have been swept so violently out of his own world? One thing is sure, it wouldn't increase his love for cheder. Nor would he start being more kind to cats.

I glanced up at the building, hoping that our lengthy pause to watch the goings-on had not caught anyone's notice, then took Elisheva by the hand and continued on our way. I felt like a Peeping Tom. We crossed the street, blew each other kisses, and I hurried back upstairs to our apartment. I felt embarrassed before my own conscience for my relief that I hadn't been the one making such a spectacle of myself. Yet my heart was light. I congratulated myself. *Gee! I'm not so bad after all, if that's what other people are doing.* As I brought the kettle to a boil, I wondered if perhaps my neighbor was also preparing to sit down by herself with a cup of coffee. Was she feeling bad now, in her own way? Was she trying not to feel bad? Perhaps she was telling herself that she'd just done what any responsible mother should, and had taught that boy a lesson he'd never forget. She had walked steadfastly along her own righteous path.

I poured the steaming water into my cup.

Is my way really better?

I took a seat and stared out through the window, across the valley to pale Ramot. My way: not as straight as hers. Strewn with useless and useful thoughts of remorse, brightened by hope and effort and illusion, sparkling with my successes, littered with rotten failures and unfulfilled resolutions. Nevertheless, when it comes right down to it, it's the way I much prefer. Were I to have a choice.

And she, having a coffee break in her kitchen a few buildings away, would, I'm sure, much prefer hers.

August 21, 1986

I haven't written in here for some time. My inclination to do so now, at five in the morning, has to do both with my having awakened without nausea and with a conversation I had with my parents the night before last.

They found out I'm pregnant through a third party. They were dismayed at the difficulties this presents me with, hurt I hadn't told them myself, astonished I allowed this to happen so fast. "I just don't know why you have to have such a hard life," Mommy said more to herself than to me. Her voice was muffled underneath the mild static of our bad long-distance connection. "It will be like having twins again. Are you taking brewer's yeast?"

Daddy came on. "Are you all right, Sarah? I was so worried I couldn't sleep last night. Are you feeling well?"

Having pummeled myself with shock, distress, disbelief and worry all these weeks, I agreed with their evaluation of my predicament. I so regretted having hurt them by not having given them the news myself, but I just hadn't been able to bring myself to do it. When we hung up, my whole being filled up to the top with sadness. I yelled at the children and continued throughout the rest of the day: I screamed at Rachel for not letting Elisheva use her glue, I screamed at Elisheva for having used hers up so fast. When Dinah cried that she wouldn't eat her toast because Rachel had touched it, it seemed I was being swept under a huge onrushing wave. *Why is my life so hard?* I smacked Daniel. *How will I manage?* I felt I was about to collapse. *This is completely ridiculous! Absolutely impossible!* I decided that I'd either go on a vacation right now or else climb into bed and let my husband take over.

Like a dog to a bone, I kept returning to chew upon the fact that just a few weeks ago (just a few weeks ago!) I was finally becoming the calm mother I had always wished to be. It had been a different world... How the children had benefitted! I gave Miriam Levi a call, to see if she could come up with anything inspiring. She listened in silence. "Your parents' reaction is a very normal one, are you aware of that? They're worried for you."

"Yes, I know they're worried. I am, too."

"Oh, but you see, you've got to be very careful not to adopt their attitude toward this situation as your own. Their attitude is that of parents toward a daughter, and when the time comes, it's quite probable that you'll have precisely the same protective attitude toward your own daughters. But your own attitude toward yourself has to be different. You have to develop the outlook that surmounting these difficulties will strengthen you. That's how you grow as a person. Your parents have done you a favor by bringing this out into the open like this, because it is this idea precisely, isn't it, that your life is unfairly difficult, which you have been trying to weed out of your mind all these weeks. That 'Poor me!' which so frequently spurs you on to anger. That's when you start thinking, 'I shouldn't have to deal with this, I deserve an easier life, this is terrible, I'm supposed to be more comfortable, this is just impossible, I can't handle it, I shouldn't have to handle it...' Hmmm?"

I grunted. Right.

So here I am at five thirty, unable to sleep. The love and concern of my mother and father have awakened my bravery, and I have started replying aggressively now to my own doomsday predictions. My retort goes like this: "Sarah! Wake up! If, G-d forbid, you had a serious illness, then you could wring your hands and weep. But this is all about another child! Look how much joy Eli has brought into the children's lives. You're still surprised each day at how much pleasure that baby boy gives everybody in the family. Yes, it's difficult. It's hard being pregnant and having to function. You would have much preferred not to be pregnant now. Yet for most of mankind, life is not something that always proceeds as planned. Planned parenthood? There's no such thing.

"You screamed at the children last night and then felt horrible and depressed and worried about them, and you were convinced that actually you had made no progress... But for most people in this world, life rises and falls. The difficulties do pass. You'll be able to become calmer again, with G-d's help. It's not the end of the world.

"It's the beginning of a world."

August 26, 1986

Tonight I didn't feel well, so when my husband arrived home he told me to go to bed and he'd take care of the children. I had made spaghetti for dinner—without even a salad on the side! A truly worthless meal, absolutely no food value. What an achievement. I waddled off to bed with a book and slid under the covers into that delicious coolness of rest.

After a while I heard them all playing dominoes. Dominoes, that mainstay of my own childhood. The children had never played before; my husband just bought it today. "Do you have a one or a four, Rachel?" I heard him ask. Exclamations, argument between Dinah and Daniel. "No, no, Danny," Yaacov was entreating. Dinah's cries: "Then I'm not playing! *Lo ichpat li!*" Yaacov's voice. Somebody's laughter. Argument.

I lay in bed, seasick with nausea, yet within me expanded a balloon of joy.

Daniel came into the bedroom. "Look, Mommy! Daddy bought me an album and I put all the rabbis in it. You want to see?"

August 27, 1986

Tonight, when the children started resisting each stage of the nighttime ritual, I put a question to them: "Daniel, Dinah. Elisheva! Rachel! Come! Tell me, what do you think I should do? Should I yell at you and hit you to make you listen? Or do you think if I speak quietly that you'll do what I say?"

I had to repeat this question a few times (restraining all my natural impulses to let them have it) before getting their undivided attention.

Elisheva's answer: "Don't yell."

Dinah: "Tell us one time very quietly and we'll keep on playing and then say it another time and we'll do it."

Daniel went off to brush his teeth.

Rachel lingered, then drifted off in the general direction of her bedroom. Slowly she got undressed and into pajamas.

I said: "Wow, children, you're right. You do listen when I speak quietly. I'm going to tell Daddy about it."

I am so glad. I have spoken calmly again, all day! I don't know where it came back from. If only in moments of black pessimism and despair I could conceive of the possibility of regaining the magic touch.

I read today in *The Divided Self*, by R. D. Laing, that life histories of schizophrenics show that as children they are often excessively obedient, "good" and unaggressive. Boy, that's encouraging! My kids don't seem to have that problem.

August 30, 1986

I'm starting to understand that having confidence doesn't mean that you're sure you won't fail. It means you accept the inevitability of failure and trust you'll be able to get up off the ground.

Someone once told me she'd read somewhere that each person's life is one specific ladder. You have to climb up that one ladder repeatedly, from birth up until your dying day.

Sometimes you think you're going up when you've actually fallen. Sometimes it looks as if you've fallen, but in fact you've been ascending.

You think that if you had made progress, you'd get to the top and go on to other things. It fills you with despair and frustration to find yourself constantly engaged in the same old familiar climb up from the bottom. But that's the challenge. To develop the strength (and the humility) to begin again.

6
My Ladder

August 31, 1986

Washing dishes, watching the dishes,
not really seeing
her hands wash the dishes, because
it's always like this, and the sun
lengthening along the floor.
                                        One,
two o'clock, and then she's done
the laundry. Get the baby crying.
Sweet baby.

Because.

There is no because.

But one day the sun hits a frying pan in soapy water
and she's holding a rainbow.
The thought flashes through her like lightning:
"G-d's creating light!" and she sees all this,
the light the water her hands herself
are miracles.

September 1, 1986

Tonight we're going to start another workshop. I called up the other participants last week to see if they were interested in an extension of the classes, and to my relief, it turned out I wasn't the only one. All came forth with tales of having regressed during this month and a half and said yes, they could use more training. All but one. "I don't want to overdo it," Sharon told me. "I think I could get overdependent on Miriam Levi."

This touched on a sore spot, though I hadn't exactly known the sore spot was there until I heard these words. "What do you mean? You started looking too much to her opinion?" I hoped she didn't pick up on the defensive note in my voice.

"Yes, you know, I think I lost some confidence in myself because I kept thinking, 'What would Mrs. Levi say about this?' "

"And you disagreed with her ideas?"

"Oh no, I think her ideas were fine. They really helped me while I was going to the workshop, but I don't know. I don't like the idea of depending on anybody. What, I'm going to keep going to her parenting classes for the rest of my life? Even if I make mistakes, I'd rather that they be my own mistakes. I don't want anyone looking over my shoulder. I think it's really pretty hopeless. I just have to get myself together to do as well as I can according to my own judgment."

I was shocked. "What do you mean, it's pretty hopeless?"

"Oh, come on, Sarah. I think you know what I mean. That I don't think I'll ever really change. Things did start getting better while I was going to the workshop. I was yelling a lot less and not hitting and the children were listening to me. It was lovely and I was excited about it, but it was really cosmetic. The whole thing has such deep roots in my personality, and in my childhood, and my whole upbringing. I've read all the books, every last one of them. Ginott and P.E.T. and all the rest. You name it, I've read it. I'm just so tired of it all. I get so excited about these great ideas, then I watch it all dissipate. Nothing from the outside's going to help me. I've just got to be my own teacher, and go by my own conscience, and do my best. What can I say."

We bid each other good luck, and I, feeling foolish for my obdurate, gung-ho naiveté and my willingness to don disciple's garb, hung up the phone. My spirit sagged. *Admit it,* I told myself, *I feel the same way.* Perhaps that pioneering sense of being a mother on the outskirts of enlightenment is an illusion. Sure, I've had some good, calm days since the workshop ended. Yet these random bright spots just remind me how much more consistent my improvement was before. I do believe in the principle of "Try, try, try again," but something about Sharon's realism had exposed a raw fear. Maybe I'm being an innocent, well-meaning Pollyanna to blithely go on organizing these workshops. Why don't I have the strength to accept the reality of my situation? Where's my pride, to look to "experts" when it comes to my own children?

Being a mother can be a spiritually elevating adventure in self-mastery and an exercise in enlarging my capacity for compassion and empathy. It can be a surprise-filled experiment in communication with interesting little people and a major source, for me, of self-respect.

Or it can be boring and depressing, a repetitive experience of disappointment in myself and my kids. Of having to face again and again the daily erosion of my ideals. Of feeling cynical about my chances of really changing.

So my first step, if I am to make a first step, is to get back the belief that changing my behavior is a realistic possibility.

This time around I hope that the belief takes deeper root.

September 2, 1986

Today was one of those calm days that give me satisfaction. Even bedtime went smoothly. I think that simply being present as parenthood was being discussed last night had a good effect on me. There's something about being a mother in isolation that breeds an unconscious sort of robot-ness; the reaffirmation of child-rearing as a vitally important affair reminded me that it's not something to be freely knocked off according to the haphazard fluctuations of my moods, in the uncritical privacy of my own four walls.

Elisheva is taking her afternoon nap on one couch, and I have sunk into the other one. I think she might be cold and I should get her a blanket, but my legs would rather not obey my sense of duty. It's forever that pull between my own highly developed affinity for gravity and the demand being made upon me to do so many things.

1-2-3-up. Here I go to get the blanket.

Something dawned on me during the workshop last night: in my great desire to be a good person, I employ my ready capacity for feeling guilty as a way of proving to myself that I'm not as bad as my actions could otherwise make me out to be. In other words, if I do something bad, my way of feeling better about myself is to feel guilty! To feel guilty is to coast downhill. As bumpy and uncomfortable as the ride might be, it's easier than the uphill climb of controlling one's temper, examining one's thoughts, establishing new habits...

September 3, 1986

This morning, when my friend Esther came over, we were talking about how parents so often have no idea what's going on in their children's minds. I told her about a nightmare I had had as a little girl: a black, hairy, many-legged spider the size of a child was scurrying about in front of my elementary school. When I awoke from that dream, I knew even then that the spider was me, and that the dream had to do with being the only Jewish child in my class, and one of the few Jews in town. Though that's how I felt about myself, to any onlooker I would have appeared only as a cheerful, friendly, happy little girl.

I suppose that this dream occurred sometime after an incident in sixth grade. My teacher had been discussing the Bible. I think he made reference to the Jewish people in the context of the ancient history of Babylonia or Egypt: the early civilizations of the so-called fertile crescent. Then he said something about there being no Jews in our vicinity. I waved my hand in the air and burst out proudly, eagerly seizing the opportunity to get everybody's attention: *"I'm* Jewish!"

My classmates looked around at me.

The room became quiet.

Mr. Knight was a kind man (you could see that on his face) and he was kind now as he replied softly, with his broad Maine twang: "Sarah..." His head tilted to the side slightly with surprise, and his bushy eyebrows strained together with the effort to understand how he could have remained so ignorant about his little pupil. "Sarah...I didn't know you were Jewish."

That was all, and after a few seconds, the class discussion carried on. But if life were structured in such a way that human beings would be notified from on high whenever they are undergoing events that are to affect their entire futures, then at that moment the bells would have started ringing and the colored neon lights would have flashed off and on. For at that precise moment, I had become aware that to be Jewish was to be different from the classmates with whom I had always felt unquestioningly at one, and that my difference was not benign. I was guilty of something; it was bad to be Jewish. Though I had no idea why this should be so, I had abruptly discovered that to declare I was a Jew was to put myself in danger. There in my Connecticut suburb, a decade after the Holocaust, the message was carried invisibly on the prevailing winds, and I was unfamiliar with the religion that would have told me otherwise.

September 4, 1986

Today, while out in the oppressive, dreadfully deadening heat wave of this abnormal September, I bought the stickers which I promised the children back in July, for supposedly having gone to bed easily and punctually on workshop nights. Now that the classes have started up again, I figured I'd better hurry and make good on my promise so that I can use the same ploy a second time around.

Their responses upon receiving the stickers were, as usual, varied. Dinah, who arrived home from school first, got her first choice, the rainbows. She was happy. Elisheva, who came in second, picked the rainbows-cum-hearts. She was happy. Daniel, who slid onto home plate dirty, hot and tired at two o'clock, accepted his stars (which I presented without offering him a choice) with a half-smile of mild surprise and transient appreciation. Then he disappeared. But Rachel, who arrived at three o'clock after having eaten lunch at Perla's, saw that everyone else had gotten first-pickings. Only the hearts with stars remained, the ones I had expected the girls to fight over. Now they were leftovers, worthless.

As Rachel began to cry, my disappointment was acute. I'd expected to take it easy on the couch all afternoon as they all played with their stickers—a guaranteed respite from conflict. Instead, the ensuing struggle was drawn out and wearying. Many unpleasant remarks passed back and forth between Rachel and me, then the argument finally petered out without a resolution. We fell silent.

Shall I brush it off as just another exasperating yet insignificant outcome to a very minor episode, and try steering myself sharply away from over-concern and guilt? My thoughts waver unsteadily. Am I being too analytical, too anxious for perfection, too worried about normal daily problems? Too much influenced by psychology and psychiatry, with their forecasts of disaster brought on by maternal insensitivity?

Or, on the contrary, am I indeed blind to the seriousness of my mistakes, which are no less significant for sometimes being so easily overlooked? Do I take for granted, as part of the normal wear-and-tear of family life, words that actually eat like acid into a child's fragile heart?

In other words, am I oversensitive or not sensitive enough? This is my underlying insecurity.

One thing is not in doubt: when I do handle these run-of-the-mill conflicts with equanimity and wisdom, the events are transformed. These small problems unite us, educate us, elevate us.

Such high ideals. Such crushed hopes.

When the fights over the stickers abated, things proceeded satisfactorily. We had a good two hours of peace. Then everyone got into pajamas, most teeth got brushed, everyone was just about ready to get under the covers, when all at once I noticed how tired I was. *How hard I worked today! How hard it was getting those stupid stickers!* I felt a pang of frustration and futility. And now here we were again, running through the eternal bedtime torture. I turned out their lights and sat down on the couch.

Dinah called out for a drink of milk.

"No, Dinah. You just brushed your teeth."

"Then water."

I yelled out: "Oh, shut up! Shut up and go to sleep!"

She went to sleep. They all went to sleep with these last words. An evening's worth of patience down the drain.

Oh, for goodness sake, shall I take all this seriously, as I'm wont to do? Or shall I trust that my children are resilient enough to overlook this minor indignity without absorbing it sadly into their innermost selves? That's what I would have done as a child. But maybe they're different. Or maybe it's not a minor indignity. Maybe it really affects them. Maybe they'll feel it's all right to yell, as I did.

Shouldn't I just consider myself a normal mother, like millions of other mothers around the globe who must be screaming "shut up" right along with me?

What I want now is some butter-pecan ice cream, a mindless magazine and a big fan—to blow away the questions.

September 7, 1986

When I told Danny to go brush his teeth tonight, he walked toward the bathroom, halted at the door and apparently thought better of it. "I don't want to," he declared.

I was too tired to pressure him so I just gave in, muttering, "All right, Daniel. They're your teeth."

Freed from duty, he got poised to run off, then paused in the hallway and made some sort of fast mental calculation. He turned back into the bathroom.

I heard him brushing his teeth.

I must try to use this approach more often! If I can only convey that what I'm requesting is usually for their benefit!

Daniel was in the bathroom a long time. The other children were already in bed and their lights were off, so I plopped down on the couch to read. Ah, that moment! It's always delicious.

Suddenly Danny bounded up to me like a puppy, and I was going to shoo him off to bed when he exclaimed excitedly that his tooth had fallen out. This tooth, the front one, had been hanging on at a disconcerting angle for a week.

I congratulated him and eagerly asked where it was.

He apparently hadn't thought of this, and his smile faded. I wished I hadn't brought it up because now he'd be looking for it for hours. "I don't know!" he exclaimed. Off he rushed to the bathroom. "Maybe it fell off when I brushed my teeth."

About five minutes passed. I heard noises from the bathroom and dreaded the scene which would now ensue if he couldn't locate the tooth. He returned. "Did you find it?" I asked.

"No." He was pensive. He swung one leg over the arm of the couch. I waited. "Right, Mommy? Right, now it's three?" Daniel opened up his mouth and stuck a finger inside, pointing at the empty gaps. "Tonight, this one. And this one fell out before. And this one, a long time ago. Right? Three all together." He gazed off, abstracted, pondering this pleasant morsel of information with a faint smile. Then dreamily, almost inaudibly, he announced: "It's fun."

It struck me with what genius children and teeth were created: that the former would take pleasure in losing the latter.

September 8, 1986

Last night Rachel climbed into bed with me, and as she sprawled out comfortably I found myself awakening against my will. I tried to keep my eyes closed, but at last I decided to get up and read. Not wanting to wake up Yaacov, I peered over at his bed in the dark. The blankets were flat. I bolted upright. Where was he?

It's all right, I told myself. He's studying late tonight, remember? I reached up to turn on the lamp.

One thirty!

The clock says one thirty!

Where is he?

I jumped out of bed and wrapped my robe around me as my heart thudded like an empty bell. Something has happened! On the way here...an accident...Somebody could have...

We never know! We never know what life holds for us around the next bend! What could have happened?

I pattered down the hall in my bare feet, and was greeted even before I got to the living room by Yaacov's shoes. His shoes, that he'd kicked off. They had never been so eloquent.

And there was he, an after-statement on the couch. He'd fallen asleep with a *sefer* in his hands. I turned off the living room light and went back to sleep.

What it comes down to is this: I have my worst conflicts with the children when I'm tired, bored or upset by something else in my life. That's when I get indignant. "Here I am, so overburdened/unhappy/overworked/underprivileged. I shouldn't have to deal now with their childish nonsense!" This indignation increases my suffering and my tension, then I proceed to come to a boil and explode—as proof to one and all that the situation is truly too much to bear.

Right now I'm tired but under none of those adjacent pressures. I'm engaged in one of my favorite pastimes of pregnancy: sitting on, or shall we say sinking into, the couch. My conscience is clear. The baby's asleep. The children have had a good lunch and are playing outside. The house is clean.

It has occurred to me to experiment. What if it were now six o'clock instead of three? Let me imagine it.

There's the pressure to get them fed and into bed by seven thirty. There's my underlying boredom with my role as the in-house lion tamer, the one who has to get everyone jumping through the bedtime hoops. There's the ache in my legs as I drag my heavy self from one place to the other, pushing the children on, pushing them on.

Now, when I have time and patience, I'm going to examine what I would be thinking, and I'm going to prepare an arsenal of counter-thoughts to strengthen me this evening when I'm actually in the ring.

1. "I shouldn't have to work so hard when I'm pregnant." Counter-thoughts: It's a universal phenomenon: People would rather relax than work, and most pregnant women don't have maids. I'm a member of the human race, and for the grand majority, life here on Earth hasn't been designed to provide relaxation-upon-demand. Life is full of difficulties great and small. Transcending them is how we grow.

2. "I'm an irresponsible mother if the children don't get into bed on time. They'll wake up late and leave without breakfast and get to school late looking like ragamuffins and their teachers will think badly of them and of me." Counter-thought: All this is true, yet not the stuff of tragedy. Staying up past bedtime was one of my chief childhood pleasures. Don't get too upset if they want to snatch the same forbidden joy.

3. "If they go to bed late, I'll be cheated out of my evening's freedom." This is a hard one. No counter-thoughts yet.

4. "I can't let the children get the better of me. I'm a weak mother if they override my authority. What have I done wrong as a mother that they ignore me?" Counter-thoughts: All children disobey their parents to some extent, unless they've been totally squashed. It's natural for human beings to resist being told what to do.

5. "I can't handle all these children." Counter-thoughts: Yes, I can handle all these children. G-d doesn't put anyone in a situation without providing him with the capacity to handle it. The less difficulty, the less growth. The more difficulty, the more discovery of one's latent strength.

It's nine o'clock. In the midst of pajamas and toothbrushes and glasses of water, I didn't have the presence of mind to observe my thoughts, much less utilize the counter-thoughts. Nevertheless, the time bombs in my mind did not go off; they'd been success-fully defused. The children all went to sleep in a good mood.

September 9, 1986

When I returned this afternoon from the telephone company, Rachel told me that the babysitter had said I'm a very good mother. "Oh, really?" I inquired casually. "She said that today?" I didn't care to let on that a teenager's opinion of me could be so thrilling.

"Yes," replied Rachel, her head cocked to one side as she scrutinized me curiously, wondering if the baby-sitter could have been right. "She said you're the best *ima* of all the *imas* in the world."

I've been turning this little news item over and over again in my mind all night, examining it from all sides. Were Danny, Dinah and Elisheva within earshot? Hope so. How was I acting this afternoon to have elicited such praise? Perhaps she always sees me only as I'm smiling and kissing my way out the door, making one of my escapes. No, maybe it's really true that I'm a good mother. Maybe I'm an exceptional, unusual mother. Or...could be this girl's mother is so cold and strict that I just look good by compari-son. Or she knew Rachel would pass the remark on to me. She just wanted to butter me up. And she succeeded. It's good to have her around. I'll give that girl a raise.

Inspired and motivated by this wonderful image of me as the best mother in the world, I was tranquil, loving and unrufflable—a saint—throughout bedtime. A few times I caught sight of Rachel looking over at me with that dubious, tentative, hopeful admira-tion. I knew what she was thinking: *The best mother in the world. My mother. Could it be?*

I wanted to live up to it.

September 10, 1986

"Do you want your children to obey you?" Miriam Levi asked in the workshop last night. "There are three things you can do to make this happen. The first is to resolve firmly that you are not going to lose your temper. If it's obedience you're after, you've got to remind yourself often that losing your temper is not going to make it happen. In the short term, certainly, you might scare them into obedience in each particular instance, but that's not the kind of compliance we should be aiming for. Consistently bringing about their obedience by getting mad at them is not something you want to depend on. It's very distressing for all concerned. It's a stop-gap measure, but many mothers use it throughout their child raising years. We usually think we're going to get on top of things with anger, that we'll get in control, but it's the opposite. When we lose our temper, we lose our authority.

"The second idea to bear in mind: Before you ask your children to do something, decide whether you're prepared to follow through. If you decide that yes, this is something that's worth the time and effort involved in teaching them, then don't give up. Even if this calls for many repetitions of your instructions, resolve to do so pleasantly and firmly. Tell yourself: They're going to do this, and I'm going to persist calmly until they do.

"And the third thing is: lower your expectations. Don't expect instant obedience. The trait of being obedient is a long-term goal. A lot of times I hear women saying things like: 'What's wrong? Here I am talking quieter than a mouse and they're still acting like monsters!' Expect some disobedience. Don't think of it as a personal affront to your honor, because then you're likely to crack. Try to remember that this is your opportunity to teach them the mitzvah of obeying their parents.

"If I were to have to pinpoint the most important thing to remember about training children to obey, it would be the light touch. Use the light touch on them, use the light touch on yourself."

On my way downstairs to take out the garbage this morning,

a small girl on her way up bumped into me as she rushed by, and glanced up with an expression devoid of apology before speeding away. Inconsiderate! I grumbled to myself as I leaned down with disgust to pick up some scattered orange peels. She should be taught!

What a curious phenomenon it is that adults are generally so astonished by children's disobedience. We're outraged by their misbehavior, as if it is the tiny people of the world who are responsible for all the irresponsibility, selfishness and inconsideration that plague mankind.

Can we bring ourselves to have a drop more patience? After all, if we're intolerant of children for behaving like children, we betray our intolerance for the children who we ourselves once were.

My parents had bought some large appliance, such as a washing machine or refrigerator, and I asked my mother if I could have the huge cardboard box standing empty out by the garbage cans. I pulled it up the hill behind our house, dragging it out beyond the old tool shed into the woods. I found a suitable space between three trees, stood it on its end, and crawled inside. Then I ran back home, got a book, grabbed an apple, and ran back up the hill to the woods again. It was my house.

A few days later it rained. I was in my box reading Little House on the Prairie, with illustrations by Garth Williams. Those pictures transported me to the pioneer world of the little girl Laura, who felt jealous, just as I did, of girls with blonde hair and blue eyes. Her parents, Ma and Pa, were everything that to my mind parents should be: all-knowing, all-American, handsome, young and Christian. I wished my parents were like that. I had a vague suspicion—which I never formulated into a clear thought—that somehow we Jews wouldn't have fit in out there on the prairie. There were no cars then, so everyone in the family stayed close together, and Laura's trundle bed was kept right underneath that of Ma and Pa, while my own midnight visitations to my parents' bedroom involved a long, frightening walk in the dark, feeling my way like a blind man through the halls. My world was endangered by atomic bombs, against which it was impossible to protect anyone or anything. The possibility of nuclear war—the mere idea of torturously slow death from radiation sickness and of firestorms reducing the whole Earth to a cinder—rendered pitifully insignificant everything mundane, commonplace and small (including me). The little house, threatened as it was by Indians, bears and other natural disasters, was a small but thoroughly protective fortress, a calm and orderly world unto itself in which everything was made by Pa's and Ma's own hands. It looked so cozy. I ached for it.

The rain drummed down on my cardboard roof, and my stash of refreshments was only half-gone. I peeked out through the window I had cut. Framed by the slightly jagged cardboard, a group of white birches beckoned through the faint, slanting lines of rain. I'd seen them before, of course, but differently now. They stood at graceful angles to each other, more silently than silence, their full silver-green heads of tremulously shining leaves all trembling beneath the whispering drops of rain. Thousands and thousands of tiny whispering drops! It was getting a little too dark in my box to read easily. The fresh, moist air held the fragrance of wet soil in summertime.

I don't know how long I'd been sitting in there when, through the soft rainfall, my mother's dinner bell rang out noisily. She was summoning me to dinner.

Deeeeng-doonnng, deeeeng-doonnng, deeeeng-doonnng. The melodious bell sang out distant yet clear.

To my surprise, I didn't jump up to run home.

Deeeng-dooonng, deeng-doonng, deeeenng-dooong. Pause. Deeeeeng-dooonng, deeennng-donnng, deeennnng-donnng, deeeeeng-donnnnnnng.

The book lay open in my lap. I was so comfortable. I peered out my window and caught the sound of the back door shutting. She must have gone back into the kitchen. A few minutes passed. I returned to my book. Then:

"Saaaaaaaaarah."

I caught my breath.

"Saaaaaaarah! Saaaaaaaaa-raah!"

In my mind's eye I saw my mother standing by the door of the back porch, hands on hips. She was looking around, wondering where I'd gone off to. Little did she know that I heard her bell, and she'd never dream I'd do this; I gave her no cause to suspect me of such a thing. Her voice didn't sound angry, she just thought I was out of earshot. The dinner she'd made was surely on the table getting cold: my lamb chop and potato. Probably carrots. Probably peas.

"Saaaaaaaraaah! Saaaaaaaaaaaaraaaaah!"

My daring amazed me. I was astonished by the ease with which I was denying her authority. Unless I chose to inform her, my whereabouts were my own secret.

A few inches over my head, my soggy roof sagged towards the middle, but the silvery, luminous green world loomed great and gentle all around. I sat a long time in the quiet box, with only the intimate, low pattering of the rain, which was abating. What a thrill to have successfully disobeyed!

I was in my own world, tailored, for once, to my size, and without giving it a name I had tasted freedom. I was at peace. I brimmed with happiness.

September 11, 1986

It took three hours to get the children into bed tonight, but since I didn't yell at anyone or hit them, there was no regret and depression when it was finally over. It does bother me, though, the idea of having spent three whole hours putting them to bed.

If I looked upon mothering as my sole purpose in life, would it bother me less on a night like this to have spent all my energy on this one mundane task? Do women brought up in Orthodox environments also experience ambivalence about their roles? Having myself grown up in an intellectually oriented, secular environment, nothing will convince me that being a wife and mother is my whole share of the pie. I keep thinking there are more important things. "Like what?" that chiding inner voice retorts saucily. "You want to go talk to Gorbachev?"

"Oh, come on, that's not what I mean. Something more along the line of going back to painting."

"So go! Who's stopping you?"

"I just don't have time."

"You have time to write in this diary. If you thought it was important enough, you'd make time for it. Nothing's stopping you."

"I can't take it seriously enough. I'm so geared now to real problems. You know, getting everyone to school on time and keeping all those ears clean, that sort of thing. The diary serves a useful purpose, practically speaking. But painting? It's not a mitzvah."

"Wrong! To make yourself happy is a vitally important mitzvah! You're uninformed, dear."

"But it's not like visiting someone who's sick, because it wouldn't be doing anyone any good but me."

"Wrong again. It would do your children good to have a happier mother. Stop your bellyaching and get out those watercolors, for crying out loud!"

"I'm not in the mood. You have to have the right mood."

"*Oi vey!*"

"No, really. Painting is just pure pleasure. That's what I said before: I'm so concerned all the time about practical things, like vegetable soup. I can't just shift gears all of a sudden."

"Is vegetable soup important?"

"Yes. That's important."

"But didn't I hear you complaining the other day how cooking bores you so? Why do you always wish you could be doing something else instead? Seems like you demean everything you do. You're always nagged by the feeling that there's something else more important you should be doing instead!"

I once heard Rebbetzin Dina Weinberg tell a story about having visited the wife of Uri Zohar to encourage her to attend a particularly good class for women. Mrs. Zohar apologized that eight o'clock at night was an impossible time. That was just when she gets all the kids into bed and starts cleaning up. "But don't you say the blessing every morning thanking the Almighty for the mitzvah of studying Torah?" asked Rebbetzin Weinberg.

"Of course I do. So I study with a friend every day when the children are in school. Otherwise, I wouldn't be able to say the other blessing, 'Who has not made me a slave.' "

In the religious world, freedom is defined as the opportunity to cultivate one's spiritual growth—no matter that you're right there in your own kitchen. No matter that nobody knows. No matter that you'll never get a degree to prove you've accomplished something...because you yourself recognize your deeds. You know that in the eyes of G-d, this has value.

In the secular world a woman's freedom from slavery, the freedom to reach beyond the clothesline to other dimensions, is expressed in terms of career or creative achievement, something through which you attain recognition from other people. It's this point of view that I've inherited. This doesn't mean I'm pining to get into my business suit and march off to the office. It does mean that I carry around with me an ever present, low-key disappointment that I'm not meeting up to a vague, hard-to-define standard of success.

What would that success consist of? The Nobel Prize would be nice. Getting into a size eight is a possibility. How about a Ph.D.? That would really make it clear once and for all that I'm worth something. I used to imagine, before I had children, that motherhood would get me that much-coveted, indisputable seal of approval from on high. Yes, giving birth would surely do the trick: from there on in I'd be an upright, card-carrying member of the human race.

Once I had those babies, though, it was gee, everybody's got one. Just count all those carriages coming down Rechov Malchei Yisrael! They're all over the place! The only contribution to the whole process of becoming a mother, the only active input that I could sort of call my own, was the he-he-he-hah breathing I learned so well in my Lamaze class. Even that (which twenty-five years ago might have branded me as an individual) is nowadays commonplace.

So the secular prize is elusive. It would have to be an accomplishment stamped unambiguously with my individuality, and would have to win me the profound respect of everyone I have known from kindergarten on up. That means Miss Eliot, my piano teacher, and those neighbors of ours, I forget their names, who always sort of looked at me askance. All those who failed to bestow upon me the acceptance that I longed for as a child. The blonde, smiling girls who made the cheerleading squad while I barely made it through gym class—they would marvel that the tables had turned. Mrs. Johnson, who failed me not once but twice in Algebra I, she'd feel sorry now for not being on my good side. Kathy and Bambi, my best friends who suddenly decided in seventh grade not to associate with me anymore...

Yet even if tomorrow morning I got letters of remorse and belated admiration from all those near, dear and not so dear...wouldn't I still have that sense of somehow not having made the grade? Their approval wouldn't touch me deeply enough. Some vaguely perceived standard-bearer would still be casting a shadow over just about every load of laundry or pot of vegetable soup that I triumphantly complete. And even, tragically, over each child to whom I give birth.

I know there are religious women who share my fragmented sense of priorities and direction. Yet I know too that many of them have succeeded in leaving secular standards of Western culture far behind, not by way of self-deceit or repression but by having acquired a different set of ideals on the deepest level. They understand that mitzvos possess infinite and permanent worth. They don't need to build monuments to themselves.

The sense of not having reached fulfillment is understood differently by such women. "The more a person feels empty, grasping and yearning," I once heard it said by Tziporah Heller of Neve Yerushalayim, "the more the person feels the *yetzer hatov.* The *yetzer hara* wants us to feel in charge, in control, independent. The *yetzer hatov* wants us to feel yearning so that we throw ourselves on G-d."

Rabbi Zev Leff of Moshav Mattisyahu said in a class last year that by the standards of modern Western culture, success is proportionate to the recognition accorded one's achievements, while according to Judaism, one's finest achievements most likely go unrecognized by one's fellow human beings. In fact, one's deeds may even acquire more merit for having remained hidden. "*Tznius,*" he said, "is a higher value than publicity." The countless small acts of *chessed* a woman performs while maintaining her family and home have far more worth than what she herself may imagine.

In another lecture I went to, in the Discovery program run by Aish HaTorah, Rabbi Noach Weinberg said that all humans are implanted with the instinct to imitate the creativity of *HaShem*. On one level of creativity are the artists, the writers, the musicians. "What is another level of creativity? It's to find someone miserable and cheer him up. To give one of your children a compliment and see him smile. This," he said, "is power. This is creativity. You will have the pleasure of bringing life."

Creativity is diminished by its usual secular definition. We don't usually think in terms of creating ourselves, creating our children, creative acts which, recorded in nothing but G-d's memory, occur without paints, pencil or piano.

So...until I do that painting of the mountains out my window, the one I'll hang right over there by the couch, I pray for a whole heart with which to cook dinner, iron Yaacov's shirts and get the children to bed on time—without yelling.

September 12, 1986

Something today made me realize the absence in the children's lives of their grandparents. At lunch Elisheva said: "My teacher is married but she has a mother." I wasn't sure I understood and asked her to repeat herself. "My teacher got married but she still has a mommy. Even now she has a mommy. She told us." Elisheva's blue eyes opened very, very wide. Elisheva's Believe-It-or-Not.

"So do I," I said, a bit startled. "I'm married, and I have my own children, but my mommy is Savta, in America. You remember Savta, don't you?" Elisheva nodded. "Well, your Savta is my mommy."

"No," Elisheva shook her head and waved her hands energetically like a policeman stopping traffic. "No, no, no. My teacher has a real mommy."

"What do you mean, a real mommy?"

"She's real! She lives in Haifa!"

September 13, 1986

Rachel and I have devised a secret signal if we want to say "Sorry," but for one reason or another would find it hard to say it aloud. The one who's apologizing tugs down on her earlobe.

September 14, 1986

I was just ironing my husband's shirts for Shabbat, feeling proud of myself for doing it on Sunday rather than pushing it off till Friday afternoon, when I noticed that one sleeve was hanging down in a suspiciously unidentifiable puddle of liquid underneath the ironing board. I snatched up the sleeve from the floor. Though it hadn't really gotten dirty, I was very irritated and happened to notice this thought go through my mind: "This *would* happen to me just when I was trying to do something good. Just my luck."

That hardly noticeable thought surfaced from out of such a deeply submerged mental cavern that it was an effort just to keep it up there in the light for examination. *Is* it "just my luck"? Each word in that expression, which I so take for granted that it hardly seems worthy of analysis, is up for question:

Just. (The arrow was aimed perfectly at me.)

My. (Of course. And not anyone else's.)

Luck. (There's something about me that makes stupid things like this happen more often to me than to other people.)

There's an inconsistency here: Luck is random and blind, yet behind "just my luck" lurks the assumption that this fate is well-deserved and perfectly aimed at me by some malevolently clever and sadistic power. It's a pagan notion.

I once heard a tape by Rabbi Avigdor Miller in which he says that even if your pen drops, so that you have to lean over to pick it up, the incident didn't happen by chance. Yet how this tiny detail fits into the grand and intricate design of your life remains, naturally, unknown. It's not that I deserve bad luck; it is, rather, that each fragment of frustration bestowed upon me is probably engineered to provide me with the possibility of change and refinement.

Antithetically opposed to this principle is the idea that the world operates by chance, and that this mechanical, randomly operated non-system of accidental events is nevertheless diabolically arranged to punish little me for the sin just of being the person I am.

Harboring this idea subliminally makes me prone to anger. It has to do with some vague negative image of who I am and what I deserve. It is antithetical to the principle of our each having been created *be'tzelem Elokim* for an inestimably high purpose.

September 15, 1986

I'm worried about Danny. He was so difficult on Shabbat—yelling, fighting, being disobedient. I was going to say he was "unfeeling," but it doesn't take much power of observation to see that he's in pain. I do think I've done wrong by him, come down too hard on him, raised him with altogether too much anger and punishment.

Why? Why should our first son have to bear the burden of our high expectations?...He should always obey, we should always love him, he must be the feather in our cap.

After his first three months in first grade, I went to speak to his rebbe. I braced myself. To my wondrous astonishment, the rebbe told me that Daniel was the best student in class in every respect: behavior, scholastic performance, zeal for davening, relations with the other boys. When I gave him the good news, my husband got tears in his eyes. "The rebbe said I should realize who it is I have in my house," I told Yaacov with joy. My greatest guilt had been replaced with my greatest pride.

Suddenly I recognized that all along, Daniel had personified for me our failure as parents. Now I thought back on the people who had criticized me for "letting him be wild," and congratulated myself for not having crushed his spirit. We might have directed an indiscriminate amount of our anger at him, but evidently we were also doing something right. I was so proud, yet I also had a sneaking suspicion that G-d had simply had mercy on us and on Daniel, and had blessed him.

That admonition to realize "who it is I have in my house" came to mind often, and as a result I treated Daniel as if he were a little prince visiting our home on sabbatical leave from the palace. His rebellious antics took on the charm of royalty's forays into commoners' territory, the lively spiritedness that differentiates the healthy rascal from the goody-goody. And magically, mysteriously, his behavior at home began to measure up to the rebbe's description of his behavior at school. He calmed down. I found myself glad to have him around.

Sometime during this period, Yaacov heard in a lecture that the most important thing for parents and teachers to understand is that self-image is the root of a child's behavior. As we reflect him back to himself, so to a great extent will the child see himself. As he sees himself, so will he behave. I was much influenced by this and tried more conscientiously to gear whatever I said to Daniel towards building his favorable self-image.

It became apparent that our greater tolerance for whatever rowdiness Daniel displayed, as well as the positive interpretation we were applying to his character in general, was affecting him significantly. I couldn't help but feel wisps of sadness sometimes, to realize how I don't usually take advantage of my power to mold my children for good.

But little by little over the next few months, something happened: we got used to what the rebbe had told us. The fact of Daniel's beautiful behavior at school no longer dazzled.

Our habit of being quick to anger with him returned.

Recently Daniel has refused to accompany Yaacov to shul on Shabbat. I very much want him out of the house at that time, because he gets bored and restless, and bothers the girls as they play mommy and baby—their favorite pastime lately. I do all I can to entice him with bags full of goodies, to no avail. Danny goes into the bedroom, closes the door and prays fervently by himself. This moves me, but once he comes out, I get frustrated that he's on my back again. *Baruch HaShem* he has the baby to love. Before Eli was born, I used to wish Danny could have a pet. Now the baby brings out a reserve of tenderness and kindness in Danny that perhaps he wouldn't have access to otherwise.

Each night when I tuck the children in and kiss them goodnight, only Danny will not kiss me back. He averts his face, or brusquely, with annoyance, sort of pushes me away. Is this just how boys differ from girls? I grew up in an all-girl family. Maybe I just don't understand.

September 16, 1986

Daniel, Rachel and Elisheva left for school happily this morning and at ten to eight Dinah, too, stood at the door, book bag strapped to her back. It takes her about five minutes to walk there, and school begins at eight. I was watching lovingly as she started down the stairs when she turned and asked what time it was.

If I had said seven fifty, she would have proceeded on her way, but when I said ten minutes to eight she stopped in her tracks. "I'll be late!"

"No, Dinah, you're not late. Go ahead, darling."

"I'll be late! My teacher will yell at me!"

Her teacher, *Morah* Zivia, had served me stern notice that tardiness in the morning affected Dinah's entire day negatively. I was glad that today the teacher would have no cause for anger. The baby was asleep...my private moment of quiet was within reach...just this last strand of foolishness stood in my way. "Dinah, you have ten minutes. Go now, you're not late. Your teacher will not yell at you."

"Oh yes! Oh yes she *will* yell at me! You don't know!"

"If you're not late why would she yell at you, for goodness sake? There's plenty of time. Now go!"

"I have ten minutes?" She looked at me doubtfully. "Oh no."

My stomach squeezed into a knot. "Bye-bye!" I exclaimed cheerfully, shutting the door. There! At last! A bit frazzled by my change of tactics, I waited for a moment to make sure she'd gone, then turned to go into the kitchen. In my mind's eye, there was Dinah scurrying down the stairs with her heavy load of books. But I heard the door opening behind me. Quick! I reached over and locked it.

She knocked. I made no move. She banged. "Dinah!" I shouted. "Go to school!" Then I heard her starting to cry.

This is not the way at all, I thought to myself. *You bad mother!*

I know it's not the way! I shot back. *Shut up! This is no time for philosophy, this child's being impossible!*

Dinah started kicking at the door now, making a terrific commotion, so I, wondering which of my neighbors were listening in, suddenly opened up. As if bursting through a broken dam, Dinah fell into the house, hysterical. "Now I'm not going to school!" she shrieked. "I'm not! Everybody will see I was crying!"

"So we'll wipe your eyes. Here." I grabbed a washcloth from the kitchen. "Here, no one will see. Your eyes aren't that red."

"They are red! You're lying!"

"SO STOP CRYING AND THEY WON'T BE RED!" I yelled. "STOP CRYING AND THEY WON'T BE RED!"

At one minute to eight, I dragged her downstairs and marched back up.

A few moments later she reappeared, petulant.

"Oh!" I moaned. "You're driving me crazy!"

At ten after, having made a deal that if she'd leave I'd let her have three orange-flavored vitamin C's, she departed, crying as she set off.

I feel horrible. And to top it off, what will her teacher say? Little does that woman know how desperately Dinah and her mother both want that girl to arrive on time.

The faith in herself that I'm trying to build, by having Dinah arrive at school on time, is precisely what I break when I behave as I did this morning.

To keep my voice down while it was going on seemed not only unreasonably idealistic, but downright ridiculous. I didn't *want* to speak quietly! When my husband came home for breakfast, I snapped at him for not having carried the laundry to the roof.

I feel drained. It's my own fault.

September 17, 1986

As the class got under way last night, I jumped up suddenly from the couch. "Oh, my gosh, I'm so sorry. I'm sure all of you would like some refreshments." The night was hot and the air in the apartment was as still and oppressive as an oven. The women shook their heads—that's all right, we don't need anything. "Oh, no, I'm sure you'd like something to drink at least. I'll get some cold apple juice." I hurried into the kitchen, got out the juice, opened the freezer...but there were no ice cubes. The drinks would be lukewarm. I reentered the living room. "Well, guess what?" I curtsied like a dainty lady-in-waiting. "Wonderful house-wife that I am, of course I forgot to make ice cubes." The women tittered at my little performance and I went back to the kitchen to turn off the light, but I heard Mrs. Levi say something to me. "What?" I asked her.

"I said, you should really watch out for that."

"Watch out for what?"

"Putting yourself down like that."

"Putting myself down? I was just joking." My goodness, I thought, that's going too far. "I didn't really mean it."

"Yes, I know," Mrs. Levi said, "but it is a put-down, and it's best to be aware of it."

I was chastened in front of my own conscience, and I got the message: *Don't feel obliged to demean yourself, Sarah.*

It seemed that everyone came with specific issues to discuss, so we dispensed with the structure of a general topic.

"The other day," said Devorah, "my eight-year-old was very disappointed because he was expecting something to arrive in the mail, and for some reason the mail didn't come at all. He was moping around and complaining far beyond the amount of time you would expect in such a situation. I spoke with him calmly about it, but it didn't work, and all his kvetching got on my nerves."

"What did you say?" asked Mrs. Levi.

"I said, 'Look, being so upset isn't going to make the mail

come, so you might as well accept it.' But he just kept right on complaining. I wanted to help him, but he sulked all day."

"It sounds as if you didn't give him enough empathy. Imagine a situation in which something you expected didn't come to pass. Let's say you were going to have a cleaning woman and she didn't show up, so you call your sister, and she says, 'Well, there's nothing you can do about it so you might as well not be so depressed. Forget about it.' How would you feel? Wouldn't you feel better if she would say something like, 'Oh, I know just how you feel. You saved this for her to do, and that, and you thought you were going to have help, then she didn't show.' When a child is disappointed, empathize. It does far more good than admonishing him to snap out of it. At a time like this, maybe you could say to your son something that conveys your understanding. Sometimes that's all a child needs to help him come out of his dejection."

I rose and went into the kitchen for a lukewarm glass of apple juice. When I returned, Rena was saying, with a look of embarrassment, that her six-year-old daughter calls her "*rasha*," and now the younger ones are following suit. Mrs. Levi suggested telling the little girl that we're not allowed to speak like that to Mommy, and if she persists, one can say very quietly, showing friendly concern in one's voice: "Since you're speaking like that to me, I won't be able to talk to you right now."

"Try not to lose your temper. Anger will not convince her that it's wrong for her to speak like that to you. All it will accomplish is to show her that she's gotten to you."

"But what if it does hurt me? Isn't it right for her to know that?"

"Well, it's all right to show a child once in a while that she has hurt you, but in general it's not the right tack to take. It instills too much guilt. What you want to convey is the wrongness of the deed, that the Torah forbids it. You don't want to emphasize too frequently that her actions cause you pain."

"Aren't you suggesting that she bottle up her feelings, though?" Rena inquired.

"Look, we have been brainwashed by pop psychology that anything short of 'letting it all hang out' is 'bottling up' our feelings. There are ways to communicate our feelings without causing pain to others. Of course, if what you're modeling to your children is a lot of anger, impatience and intolerance, then you *are* going to have a hard time teaching them how to communicate kindly.

"When a child does something wrong on this score, you don't have to give a whole speech. You can be very gentle, just a word or two is sufficient. But don't ever simply overlook disrespect. Two things happen if you do that: First, the child ends up feeling guilty, even if this is unconscious. And second, it confuses him to sometimes be reprimanded for disrespect and sometimes not.

"Speak quietly. The quieter you can be, the more successful you'll be. In fact, the more important something is, the more quietly you can say it." Mrs. Levi paused and thought something over. "How are you in general with your children, Rena?"

She lifted her eyebrows in a smirk of tired resignation.

"Do you notice the expression on your face? Is it possible that you show that face to your children sometimes?"

She shook her head, once again with that same quiet exasperation. "We have to watch our facial expressions, too, if we can become aware of them. Because a child looking at Rena's face will conclude that there's just no hope. She'll start feeling something like, 'I'll always be bad.' Are you a bit too heavy-handed with them, perhaps? Or impatient? Perhaps your daughter's getting back at you for something?"

"Yeah, well..." Rena muttered sadly.

"Would you like to call me in the morning, Rena, and we can discuss this some more?"

Rena nodded.

"The main thing," Mrs. Levi told us later on in the class, "is to be firm but kind."

September 30, 1986

It has suddenly come about that I'm going to America! My parents invited me, and Yaacov said I do need a rest, so he'll take care of the kids and I can go during the Sukkos vacation! I'm taking just Rachel and the baby.

I'm so excited about doing this with Rachel. For years I've had the sense that she needs time alone with me.

Thank G-d.

Rachel is treating the other children with nothing but kindness, ever since I told her.

7

The Magic Gate

October 15, 1986

I'm on the El Al plane to New York. I cannot believe I'm getting away with this. There doesn't seem to be a good enough reason for so much money to be spent and for us to travel so far, just because I need a rest.

I am so thrilled. First I'll be staying with my mother-in-law in Brooklyn and then I'll go on to my parents. I'll see my sisters, Candis and Pigeon, and my Aunt Sophie and my Uncle Bob, and I'll drink Tropicana orange juice and Maxwell House coffee.

I wonder what in the world I'm doing, leaving the family at Sukkos. I feel a hollow sort of gulp in my stomach—guilt mixed with gratitude for Yaacov's willingness to do this for me.

The stewardess just installed our bassinet. I'm so happy. Rachel is trying to attach the dinner trays to our arm rests. There's a couple with a baby seated to our right. Their baby is staring from his bassinet at Eli in his bassinet, and the mother and father are obviously busy comparing their baby to ours. I recognize that look of disdain as they glance over. Of course they're mistaken. Eli is by far the more adorable specimen. Rachel has figured out how to get the trays on. I can't wait for the food to arrive.

This is so much fun.

I am so anxious for Rachel to feel loved by everyone.

Daniel gave me one of his dearly departed teeth to show the relatives in America.

Rachel and I left at midnight for our 2 a.m. flight. Next to each child's pillow I left a bag with three presents: among other things, I gave Elisheva a little doll, Dinah a string of fake pearls and a Mickey Mouse digital watch, Danny a pair of binoculars and a digital airplane watch.

I pray the children will feel all right.

We've been on the plane for about six hours. Aside from the fact that the baby doesn't fit into the bassinet, this is so relaxing that I can't relax. I think my brain's so tightly strung that unwinding makes me light-headed. It's disorienting not to have any pressures on me. I don't seem to have the mental equipment one uses for doing nothing.

Eli has finally fallen asleep. So has Rachel.

I feel proud when I realize how busy I am in my daily life. I've always seen myself as lazy little Sarah, who made her bed about twice a year, probably washed dishes five times between kindergarten and high school graduation, and in general was of no help at all to anybody. I used to find my mother asleep on the couch sometimes, a book or newspaper loose in her hand, and it would puzzle me that she'd want to sleep in the middle of the day. I realized it must be because she worked so hard. I remember her telling me that she felt uncomfortable sitting down to read because she should really be doing things. I was awed by her goodness. She was so industrious that a small respite from her continuous labor made her feel guilty! How selfish I was in my own eyes!

In my life now, thank G-d, my natural laziness has been overwhelmed by the demands of caring for my family, but my self-image remains the same. I could be taking care of ten screaming infants, washing the floor and stirring a pot of soup—all at the same time—yet it wouldn't seem authentic. Deep down, I'd still be little Sarah who never lifts a finger to help her mother.

Here on the plane, in these my first hours in so long of

freedom from responsibility, being lazy is sweet. Doing nothing is thrilling.

I'm in Brooklyn now at my mother-in-law Helen's house. Everything is as I imagined it—her big smile of welcome, how much I feel at home, the great pleasure she takes in Rachel and the baby, the Tropicana orange juice, the pink-carpeted bathroom, the Italians on their front stoops, the phone calls of welcome from Mommy and Daddy, Aunt Sophie, and our family's close friend Dori, the phone call from my beloved friend Diane, the delicious feeling of getting between the sheets of the big, comfortable bed after the all-night flight.

I'm proud of Rachel. She helps me with the baby and is eager to help Helen.

In spite of the severe arthritis that makes walking painful for her, Helen's good humor is natural and unforced. A few days before my wedding, she told me, "You've got to take the bad with the good." It struck me at that moment that behind her casual, unpretentious manner she was handing over one of life's major secrets. It is only as years pass by that the well-worn phrase takes on more and more meaning for me. How hard it is to take the bad with the good! If you can do just that, you've covered a lot of ground.

After I slept for a few hours, Diane visited us. I was so excited to see her again. She is like my sister. I've known her since I was fourteen. Over the din being produced by her crying baby, she said: "You must be such a good mother to have such calm, happy children, *beli ayin hara.*"

I was tempted to let her take this incomplete picture home with her, but Diane is much too close for anything less than truth.

October 16, 1986

I'm having such a good time doing nothing. My mind is going on the blink. I don't feel like writing in here.

October 17, 1986

Looking at yesterday's entry, I'm reminded of the time Yaacov called from the yeshiva at eight o'clock.

"Are the kids in bed?" he asked.

"Yes, they're all asleep."

"Isn't it peaceful?"

"Yes," I replied, realizing that it was peaceful.

"I just love that moment when all the kids are asleep. It's good to be a father just to be able to really appreciate what peace is."

Rachel and I have been having fun together. She loves sleeping with me in the big bed in Helen's room, over which hangs a 1930s portrait of Helen and Benjamin at their wedding. He died the year before Yaacov and I married. Rachel is amazed that the pretty young girl is Grandma.

I take pleasure in visualizing what I would be doing at home this Friday morning. The standing, the grating vegetables, the checking cabbage and the yelling and trying to control my temper and hurrying and washing dishes and pushing myself onward while I'm pining to sit down. The pressure on the back of my legs from the pregnancy. Peeling potatoes and taking down laundry and mashing hardboiled eggs and crying over the onions and begging the children to play downstairs. Dropping matzah balls into the soup and watching as they disintegrate...How in the world will I ever get back into all that?

Today I read the *New York Times* and went shopping on 86th Street with Rachel. What a lovely discovery that I have in my daughter a wonderful companion. I'm so thankful I brought her. This is precisely what I dreamed of being able to share with her, and I see her delicately blossoming like a rose that's been taken out of the shade and set in the sun. When I see how much Rachel benefits from being with me without tension and pressure, I'm struck by a sharp pang of regret: what about Daniel, Elisheva and Dinah?

I bought stockings, two maternity dresses at LaMama, pajamas for Yaacov, take-out chicken, fake pearls, gloves for Rachel and Dinah and nineteen silver bracelets for one dollar.

America! America!

I called Yaacov last night. One of the first things I wanted to know was how they reacted when they found the presents on their pillows. Well, turns out the pearls I gave Dinah are Sukkos decorations, not children's jewelry, and she hated the Mickey Mouse watch. Elisheva's doll suffered an involuntary decapitation within a half-hour, and no, it's not the kind that can be popped back into place, and yes, Elisheva cried. Danny likes the airplane very much and also the binoculars.

Everything's fine.

I've been worrying again about how it will be with the new baby. To what extent will Eli be deprived of the good care and great love he now receives?

October 19, 1986

I'm amazed that during the rare moments of disagreement between Rachel and me, the same kind of thoughts arise as do at home. It doesn't matter as much how many children you have, as how your mind works. Here I'm under no pressure to speak of, yet when Rachel fretted this morning that she didn't have a pretty blouse, and nudged me repeatedly this afternoon for a cookie before lunch, I thought: "How unfair that during my vacation, when I'm supposed to be having a complete rest, she's bothering me! Isn't it enough that I brought her with me? I deserve to get my trouble-free relaxation, unhindered!"

At such moments, anger flickers through me like fire, though for lack of adequate stimulation it then vanishes back into the darkness whence it came.

How peculiar. That inner voice often replays the plaintive line: "I don't deserve this unfairness/imposition/aggravation," while under similar circumstances at other times, the same voice intones caustically: "Just my luck! Just what I deserve!"

I had a wonderful Shabbat doing a great deal of nothing and

sleeping. Every once in a while, a sorrow passes over me—fear, worry and guilt in one dark stroke. How will I be able to take good care of Yaacov, Rachel and Daniel, Dinah, Elisheva, Eli and an infant? It will be impossible to do right by each of them.

There is no doubt that Rachel is benefiting from this precious period of special attention. As far as our relationship is concerned, the luxury of this vacation is a necessity.

October 20, 1986

We're staying with Aunt Sophie in Manhattan for two days. Uncle Sam died a year ago, and her manner is more subdued than it used to be, but Sophie's strength of character has not faded in any way, neither with age nor with her loss. She works for AmericasWatch, an organization that helps writers living under totalitarian regimes.

Sophie has always balanced motherhood with a career. As soon as her children were old enough, Sophie worked as an editor, first in one then in another publishing house, eventually becoming the director of whatever department she landed in. Her job brought her several times to Moscow, where she organized international book fairs.

I asked over the fish and baked potatoes if it was still difficult without Sam. "Yes," she said, "it gets very lonely. But I'm all right."

"Do you usually make dinner like this?" I said, uneasy to have put her to the trouble of cooking a big formal meal.

"I cook like this every night. It's very important for me to do it for myself now, just as I used to do it for the family. It's very important for me to keep my life structured. That's why I'm so grateful for my job."

I told her that at our seder this year in Jerusalem, I had been swamped by memories of the large annual Passover seders that we attended at her house throughout my childhood. Our own celebration, by comparison, with a few guests we didn't know that well, lacked the emotional richness and sense of security of Sophie's. I found myself trying to imitate her.

"You know," she said, "I realize now that those seders were the most important thing I did in my life."

These were astonishing words, coming from Sophie. The most important thing for her wasn't sending both sons through college, or her successful career, or her good marriage?

She sat thinking. "All of you kids, and the families, have connections to each other that wouldn't exist if not for those seders through the years."

It was at the seders that my grandfather donned his yarmulke and recited the haggadah in Hebrew. We children laughed at the nasal sound of those indecipherable words, and I see now that our laughter was our shield. There was something larger than us, something unappealing and threatening in those little pamphlets with their ancient texts. It was embarrassing. It made us vulnerable, to what I didn't know. Everything about it was weighted down with shame and fear, so we cracked jokes.

What was it to be Jewish? The seders were one of my only links to that identity. How could something of which I knew so little loom so large, and disturb so powerfully? What Sophie said is true, that those seders forged my deep connection with my relatives. Yet they were forging also, unbeknownst to me, my connection to the Jewish people. To my Jewishness.

"This year," she went on, "a lot of people told me they were coming. Pigeon was coming down from Boston, and Michael and Bobby were coming with all the kids, and Uncle Bob and Alice. By the time it was all straightened out, it came to around fifteen." Sophie's face was savoring something funny. "But the fish didn't come! The guy didn't get the shipment on time. He told me it'd be here the day before but it never arrived. Anyway, to make a long story short, there I was the night before the seder and I couldn't sleep. I couldn't sleep because of that fish!" She burst into laughter. "So there I was at dawn and all of a sudden I asked myself: 'Why are you so upset?' That was when I realized that I was upset for me."

She leaned towards me, wondering if I got it. If I really understood the punch line. "All those years I thought I was cooking for everyone else. But it wasn't for everyone. Without knowing it, all those years I was doing the whole thing for myself."

October 21, 1986

My sister Andrea, whom everyone in the family calls Pigeon, is on her way down on the train from Cambridge today. She's a psychologist at Brown University. I always find a way of mentioning casually (as I am here) that she has a couple of Ph.D.s from Harvard.

Last week she called to say she couldn't make it next Sunday, as we had arranged, because of some other obligations. *She doesn't care about me,* I thought. *She cares more about her friends! What kind of sister is she? She doesn't really care about seeing me!* "All right, if your friends are more important to you than I am," I burst out loudly over the telephone, "then forget it! You can have your stupid friends. Here I come all the way from Israel, all the way to America, and you can't tell your friends that you're sorry, but your sister just arrived from Israel? Then forget it, Pigeon, just forget it!" I started weeping. I had been caught in an unanticipated flash flood. She started to say something and I couldn't stand the idea of her making excuses to placate me. I slammed down the phone.

I stalked into the kitchen intending to boil up some water, and took down a Lipton tea bag from the cupboard. Helen, with a look on her face of purposeful absorption, was setting things out for Rachel and me to have for lunch. She didn't want to show that she'd heard me. I was ashamed. "I was talking to my sister Pigeon in Cambridge."

"Yeah," said Helen, making herself busy.

"I thought she was coming next Sunday, but she can't."

"Oh."

"That's why I was so upset over the telephone."

"Yeah, I understand."

Feeling crazy, I wandered aimlessly back to the bedroom and sat down on the bed. I looked at the phone, felt sorry for myself and cradled my face in my hands to cry. Then I dialed her number.

I was so glad to hear her voice. "Pigeon?" I said.

"Hello, Sarah dear."

"I'm sorry."

"Thank you, sweetheart. I'm sorry, too."

"I just want to see you so much!"

"I want to see you, too."

"You do?"

"Of course I do. I wanted to tell you that I arranged to come Tuesday when it turned out I couldn't on Sunday."

"Then why didn't you tell me?"

"You didn't hear me because you were yelling."

Today's Tuesday. I'm waiting for her to arrive.

Married, mother of five with one on the way, and still the child feeling like an unwanted tagalong to her older sister.

When Pigeon first saw Rachel, whom she hadn't seen for four years, her tears welled up. "She looks so much like you when you were that age," she told me. My elder by eight years, Pigeon has clear pictures in her mind of my childhood, a whole movie that for me is largely erased. Rachel must have been for her a living reincarnation of the past.

It's Sukkos. We took a walk to once-elegant Washington Square Park. The trees weren't orange and scarlet and violet and yellow, as in the autumns of our Connecticut childhood, but we were presented with a passably magnificent representation of a cool, sunlit fall day in New England. I felt such satisfaction to share this with Rachel. We found a bench and watched the Frisbee players. Eli was the only carriage-age baby in sight, though once in a while someone would drift by holding the hand of a child. I didn't notice any families. A few yards away a sensitive looking, petite woman of about forty-five sat in a wheelchair, looking around with a strained smile. Something was incongruous. One wouldn't have expected to see her in a wheelchair. Two chassidic boys strolled by, holding *esrogim, lulavim* and *hadassim*, on the lookout, as is their practice, for Jews to whom they could teach the blessings of Sukkos. The woman in the wheelchair called them over.

So. She was Jewish.

She caught me staring, and I abruptly redirected my gaze. She wheeled herself closer. "Hi, where are you all from?" We had the standard introductory conversation of strangers, and fell awkwardly silent. "Those boys don't really know what Sukkos is all about. Most religious people don't," she said to us, shaking her head. I winced inwardly. "My son isn't like that. He's not religious, but he really took it upon himself to find out what the deeper meaning of it is." I wanted to say something knowledgeable and patient, but words failed me. "Those kids don't know what religion's all about. There's a certain kind of people that go for it, and they aren't the ones who really know." For the next five minutes or so she spoke about the various approaches one can take when searching for the meaning of life. I can't recall her words. Abruptly, she pointed to the wheelchair. "This thing's recent."

My stomach tightened. I was uncomfortable with my curiosity, wanting to conceal it even as I showed my interest. "It's recent?" I tried to sound casual, not to betray pity. "How recent is it?"

Her reply was vague, or else I was too uneasy to pay proper attention.

"It'll be just a few months?" I asked her.

Somehow or other her indirect reply got across that no, this was not a temporary condition. I looked over at the Frisbee players dashing in and out of the sun and the shade and didn't know what to do with my face. I wanted to turn to Pigeon, who sat quietly next to me. Rachel was pushing Eli here and there, in circles.

"I'm really enjoying life," the woman said with abrupt enthusiasm. "I've got all kinds of time nowadays to do all the reading I never had time for before. I've got a great life. I live in an apartment over there—" She pointed off somewhere in back of us. "I come down here every morning. I just love it here. He's my boyfriend."

She turned and smiled warmly at a mustachioed, muscular man in an undershirt seated with folded arms, quite close to us, on the next bench. I was startled. I hadn't noticed him. He gave us a nod, then stared stoically off into space. His forearms were covered with tattoos.

"He's great," the woman said. "He takes good care of me. He takes me down here every day, and I've just got everything I want. I'm free. I can do whatever I want." She smiled expansively and continued expounding upon how different types of people approach life differently.

"Well," I announced casually during a pause, stealing a glance now at Pigeon. "I guess I've got to get the baby to sleep now. We better go back to my aunt's apartment." Giving Pigeon's arm a squeeze, I rose, Pigeon rose. Rachel merrily set off with the carriage. "Good-bye!" I exclaimed brightly, aching to hit the right note, but wasn't that her face falling? Why should I feel guilty?

I didn't glance back. The air was fresh, the sky a fragile blue, the sunshine gentle as we passed under yellow oak trees. I felt as if we were escaping. "I couldn't stand that anymore, Pigeon." My sister peered over at me and touched my hand. "I have such stomach cramps now. I'm so glad to get out of that conversation!" We walked along in the sun. I pressed my hands against my big stomach.

"Why do you have stomach cramps?" Pigeon asked.

"I don't know." I watched the cracks in the sidewalk pass under our feet.

"Could it have been her denial of her pain?"

We walked a few more steps, and I then had a distinct sensation of a knot in my stomach unraveling. I even dimly visualized that knot coming undone. The cramps vanished. "Yes, that's what it was!" I said. I could have picked up my feet and run in the sun.

I hated standing downstairs in front of Sophie's apartment house saying good-bye to Pigeon. To be doing so was to be facing an unmoving wall of fact: our lives are proceeding on through the years and we do not share them with each other. My having chosen to live in Israel has denied us access to the profound, unforced intimacy unique to sisters. When I was a child, Pigeon's beauty, popularity and academic success placed jealousy in my way: now I want to reap the fruits of our sisterhood.

I watched my sister and my daughter hug each other. Pigeon waved and smiled through the back window of the taxi as it sailed off toward Penn Station.

My sister Candis called me tonight from Oakland. She's a child psychologist. She has always been solicitous toward my children, worrying about them from afar, ever reminding me to give each one enough individual attention. Since discovering that I was pregnant, I haven't looked forward to telling Candis about it. I've imagined with mild dread that moment in which she asks: "So how old will that make Eli when the baby is born?" I resolved that the best tactic would be to head her off at the pass: before she'd get a chance to express her concern, I'd voice my own.

"I hear from Mommy and Daddy that you're pregnant, Sarah," she told me after a minute or so on the long-distance line.

I was doodling on an envelope addressed to Sophie. "Yes, I am."

"I've been trying to get pregnant for so long. I'm frightened that I won't be able to because I'm forty-one."

"Oh, Candis, I'm sure that—"

"I'm scared now that I made a mistake to put it off."

"No, really, there are a lot of women who get pregnant at that age. They just had to wait a while. A lot of women in Israel have children after forty."

"They do? Really? Their first, though?"

I rummaged through my mind. "Yes, I know two like that."

"Really?"

"Yes. It'll just make you appreciate the baby when it comes."

There was a pause. I assumed that she was concealing the other side of her thoughts now. "Candis," I ventured, "are you mad at me for being pregnant again so fast?"

"No."

I couldn't believe it. "But Candis, Eli is just seven months old. Isn't that ridiculous?"

"No, it'll be all right. A lot of people have children close together, and it's all right. Look at me. Mommy didn't want to have another baby, and look how wonderful I am." We laughed.

"Candis! You really think so? I can't believe you're not mad at me."

"No, I'm jealous."

"*Jealous?*" My astonished heart melted with gratitude. "Candis, you don't think it will be bad for Eli to have someone so close behind him?"

"It depends on how you handle it, and I really think you'll do all right. You'll be fine. It'll be difficult for a while, but I trust you."

I felt like crawling through the telephone cord to Oakland. "Candis—thank you so much!"

"Sarah, I'm scared that maybe I'll never have children. It's so hard for me to imagine not ha—"

"No, I'm sure you will. I'm sure of it."

"You think so?"

I resolved to pray, and to ask the children to pray. "Candis, hearing all this from you is so strange for me because I've always felt so inadequate next to your being a doctor—"

"Psychologist."

"Psychologist. The fact that you actually have patients come to you and that you have your own business and do well. And that paper you wrote for the Congressional Committee." Candis was quiet on the other end. "Candis? Did you hear me?"

"Yes. I heard you. I just want to be at home with a baby."

October 22, 1986

Yaacov's sisters and their families came to see us at Helen's house. Fran and Lewis's little boy Justin asked Rachel to teach him Hebrew, and he says he wants to come visit us in Israel. Rachel luxuriates in her membership in this large family. She's always seen her Israeli friends with all their relatives; now it's her turn to feel that she really belongs. She ran around the house playing with her cousins, shimmering with pride.

October 23, 1986

Last night we arrived in Los Angeles. I was so tired after the flight; it was one o'clock in the morning New York time, but I got a second wind. As my mother cooked dinner for my father, there I was standing by the stove, telling her about the time a few weeks ago that the baby had choked on something. I had yelled out, "The baby's choking!", swept him up off the floor and run with him to the couch. I stuck my finger down his throat—a maneuver which comes to me instinctively since that's what Mommy used to do with us—but this time it wasn't working. I grabbed him and tried nursing, to wash it down, but he couldn't. "He can't nurse!" I cried out, dimly aware that Daniel was reading on the other couch and that the three girls were standing there watching.

Something white suddenly appeared in Eli's mouth. I dug it out aggressively, Eli's normal expression was restored and he at once wriggled off my lap to go on to higher things. Falling back into the couch to relax, I looked up. There were Elisheva, Rachel and Dinah in wide-eyed silence. Danny arose and looked at the baby. His eyes were pink, his cheeks were wet.

"Danny!" I exclaimed. "You were crying?"

He shrugged.

"Because of the baby, Danny?"

He smiled bashfully and went back to read.

"Isn't that something, Mommy?" I said, my account finished. "You can just see from that how much he loves the baby. The baby brings out all his gentleness. Tough little Danny! He's really so tender!"

My mother was looking at me closely. She had stopped stirring the soup. "Sarah..." she said in a hushed voice. She put down the spoon.

"What?"

"I just realized that you look so run-down."

I was taken aback and annoyed. "I am not run-down."

"No, you're so thin."

"I feel great!" I countered with a disdainful flick of the hand, thinking with a little rush of fear: And I do not want to be told otherwise! She could make me believe it!

She kept looking at me. "Yes...you see...you've got big circles under your eyes. I've got to build you up while you're here."

It occurred to me that maybe she was really thinking that I looked older. Maybe in the fluorescent glare of the light over the stove, the lines on my forehead were starkly emphasized. I took a little step to the side. "It's two o'clock in the morning for me, for goodness sake, Mommy! That's why I look tired. I'm exhausted, that's all! I do not feel run-down!"

My mother picked up the spoon and stirred the vegetable soup. "Sarah," she said softly, "please try to stop nursing while you're here."

Anxiety again. This was one thing where I couldn't let her influence me! With this other baby rushing along in his wake, the least I could do for Eli was to give him the closeness of nursing, as long as possible. "I've always nursed when I'm pregnant, Mommy."

"But I can see that this time you're depleted. You can't fool your body."

I changed the subject. We conversed a while longer, but I felt disturbed and distracted. *Do I look old? Am I depleted? If I think of myself as weak, I'll become weak.* I was really scared.

I kissed Mommy good night, and for a moment, as if angels' wings enclosed me, she held me in a tender embrace. In the darkened hallway to the guest room, I groped for the light switch and pressed a series of buttons. Various living room lights went on and off, then the light in the study, then, through the window, the outside light over the front door, and then several others that didn't seem to be connected to anything. At last on came the lamp in the guest room. There was Rachel, ensconced on the huge, king-size bed, arms and legs flung out as if in flight. I got ready for bed and was about to sink into sleep when I heard the doorbell ring. Who could be coming over so late? I was curious. I got up and opened the bedroom door a crack.

"...don't believe anyone here rang the alarm, Officer," my father was saying.

"Well, someone rang it all right," a Midwestern voice drawled cordially. "We got the signal down at the station."

"I'm sorry to have troubled you, Officer, but everything's all right here, thank you very much."

"O.K., then, as long as you folks are all right, I'll say so long. G'nite!"

I waddled guiltily off to bed. Enough for my first night in L.A.

October 24, 1986

My father took Eli on his knee this morning. The baby eyed him warily, and the two of them looked as if they were trying to behave as grandfathers and grandsons should. After a few minutes of this staring at one another, Daddy looked around, conscious that his performance was being scrutinized and perhaps evaluated. With an apologetic grin he handed him over. "The glory of babyhood somehow eludes me," he said.

With Rachel, however, my father is in his own league. He engages her in lengthy, comical conversations, Alice-in-Wonderland-style. Rachel waits patiently for the punch line, and he is clearly gratified when she throws back her head and lets go with a long giggling stream. I can tell that she doesn't understand everything he says, but she knows when she is supposed to laugh.

She observed him cheering and moaning over the World Series. "Why does it matter who wins?"

Oh, how far her culture is from America! This tickled all of us. "It doesn't matter at all, Rachel!" laughed my father.

I once heard someone say that mankind wants to think of G-d not as a father, with his duty to discipline and admonish, but as a grandfather.

October 26, 1986

Candis has come. She's been with Rachel virtually non-stop during her visit, which gratifies me deeply, though I do kind of wish I could spend some time with Candis alone. In a luxuriantly drawn-out ceremony this morning, she washed Rachel's hair, introducing her to such niceties as hair conditioner and blow-driers. Then came a gentle combing out of the locks. They talked a lot throughout the grooming session, and whenever I passed the bathroom door I tried unsuccessfully to eavesdrop. After more than two hours, Rachel emerged with head held high, hair swept elegantly up in back and tied with a ribbon. She had the air of a princess coming out to accept the admiration of her public.

Rachel follows Candis around everywhere and has little time for her grandfather now, brushing off his comic overtures with polite smiles, skipping off in search of her aunt. I see myself. This is what it was like having Candis for my older sister: she made life sparkle. She organized my birthday parties, made me cinnamon toast with a lot of melted butter, she was Peter Pan, she was Mary Poppins, she was the Pied Piper. When I was thirteen and she left for college, life fell in on itself, deflated and faded. Every winter vacation during my four years of high school, I took the train out to Ohio to stay with her in her dormitory at Oberlin.

What if my parents had decided to exercise planned parenthood?

I see Rachel playing now inside that same magic playground which Candis somehow sets up. I can't enter it. A whole Disney set has been constructed in my parents' living room, but it's invisible. It's a place where for once someone is respectfully communicating with Rachel as an adult, at the very time she's being appreciated most as a child.

I grabbed Candis and pulled her off to a side room to talk when she was preparing to go to the airport. We had a forced, unsatisfying imitation of a deep talk. Suddenly she glanced at her watch and was astounded to see that she had twenty minutes before the plane took off.

"We can do it! Don't worry!" my mother proclaimed as she ran out the door. "Get in the car!"

On the thruway to Burbank Airport, I sat in the back with Rachel and braced myself as Mommy made her terrifying foray through the traffic.

We pulled up in front of the departures terminal and Rachel lunged at Candis with a passionate kiss, a kiss of adoration. I pecked her cheek sadly, Mommy said "Go, fast!" and off Candis ran, smiling and waving back at us.

October 27, 1986

I spent the morning in my robe, leafing through old copies of the *New Yorker* at the kitchen table, looking for the cartoons while my mother did her cooking. I came across one by a female cartoonist (with what sounds like a Jewish name) entitled "Mom-O-Grams." You see a series of three pictures of a behatted, sixtyish woman bearing a somber expression, her mouth wide open. She's delivering a singing telegram that goes like this:

You are too thin.
You look so pale.
This is the path
that leads to jail.

I showed it to Mommy. For the rest of the day we kept erupting into laughter when our eyes met.

October 28, 1986

To my surprise, I'm glad that my mother is helping me to stop nursing. She spikes the baby's bottles with brewer's yeast and blackstrap molasses. I expected much yearning and frustration on his part, much ragged remorse on mine. But there is neither of these. I nurse him only when he wakes up during the night, and take him into my arms as if we have been separated for a long time. The sweetness of those reunions.

My mother serves us fresh papaya, fresh fish, whole grain cereals and cabbage salads with sweet red onion, bean sprouts and red peppers. The baby's gotten plumper and Rachel's cheeks rosy. Though I was unaware of feeling worse, I find myself feeling a great deal better.

Fifteen years ago, my mother asked, with bewilderment at my

naivete, whether G-d really cares if I use a meat or a milk fork. Now she goes to great lengths to accommodate me respectfully, without comment.

We were sitting on the couch tonight talking. I closed my eyes at one point to assign to memory that unique feeling of Mommy's hand and arm in mine—something resonantly familiar to me in my mind's most darkly buried places. By the touch of that warm skin and by the look of those fingers and fingernails, the wedding ring, and that thumb, I was transported—as if in an archaeological dig of the self—down through a tunnel of echoes towards the beginnings of my own history.

Is it possible that one day I'll be for my children anything approaching what my mother is for me?

We said good night, and as I groggily made my way to the guest room, I was stirred by the conviction that family is the only worldly possession of value. Life is so fragile and unpredictable, and framed all around by the unknown. Groping through the dark hallway, my heart hurt with new gratitude that I have my own family. I thought of Yaacov. I thought of Daniel and Dinah and Elisheva, so dim and faraway in Israel. When I opened the bedroom door, I bumped noisily into a chair and the baby woke up. I held him close to me, wanting just to soak up the beauty of having my baby in my arms.

October 29, 1986

Taking care of two children filled up my time today as much as five do at home. It's analogous to the way gas entirely fills up a room, no matter what its dimensions.

I agonize over my loss, and the loss my children suffer, in not living close to our relatives. Yet in Jerusalem we are spared much of the amorality of the modern world. Living there is no protection against the eternal hazards of human nature, but the children are shielded from contemporary American society's craziness. They are like flowers growing in natural light.

October 30, 1986

I've undergone an emptying-out of the brain and have been lazing around the entire day.

I think of the children with bemusement. Am I the mother of those people? It's peculiar that the closer one is to someone, the greater the sense of unreality upon separation. I wonder what they feel about my leaving them. Who can claim to know what's going on in a child's mind?

I suspect that upon being reunited, I'll snap back into my established ways of relating to them. How depressing. I wish that the emotional distance could be sustained long enough after I'm home for me to juggle around with my old patterns and familiar perceptions. The power of habit!

In the middle of the night last night, I started worrying about the way I always push Danny to go play downstairs. I know that mothers the world over do the same; it's natural to want a restless, inquisitive, troublesome little boy of seven out of your hair. Yet if someone were constantly, impatiently urging me to go enjoy myself outside, wouldn't I get the idea that I wasn't wanted? I wouldn't think, oh, in general they love me, it's just right now they don't want me around.

For me as the mother, an incident like this appears insignificant. It's nothing; I just want to have a moment's peace! For a child, however, small things can be big things. He has absolutely no way of knowing, as I'm pressing him to go, about my underlying feelings for him. Little rejections frequently repeated can make him feel unlovable.

Rather than shoo him away, I should organize something creative for him to do at home.

But will I? When I'm tired and fed up, my only reality is the desire for relief.

October 31, 1986

When I get annoyed with Rachel, it's an uncomfortable flashback to a foreign world. This morning she seemed to ignore me when I told her to please move so I could make the bed. "Rachel!" I repeated sharply. "Get up!" She jumped. I saw a book in her hands and realized she hadn't been consciously ignoring me; she had been engrossed in her reading. I apologized for getting mad.

"Oh no, you didn't get mad," she replied.

"Yes, I did, darling," knowing from her face that she had certainly felt my anger. "I was nervous and got a little bit mad."

"No, you didn't. It's all right."

She seemed tolerant in a motherly sort of way. Grateful for my overall lack of tension, she's choosing to overlook my lapses.

November 1, 1986

It appears that my relationship with Rachel has mended, yet it seems too good to be true; it could be a fabric that will rip open when we return home. Could the solution be this simple: three weeks alone together, with competition neither from her siblings nor from my household responsibilities?

One thing will surely remain: her discovery that she is a member of a big family, and that her aunts, uncles, cousins and grandparents are securely connected to her.

November 2, 1986

I woke up this morning from a worried, convoluted dream. Upon opening my eyes, something told me that I should check the date. I wandered into the kitchen and found my parents up early as always—my mother concocting some powerful egg-yolk-and-whole-grain brew for my father's breakfast and Daddy glancing through the L.A. Sunday *Times*.

"What's the date today?" I asked groggily.

They looked up, startled by my sudden appearance at the doorway. My father found the day's date on the paper. "It's the 2nd."

"IT IS? I thought Monday was the 2nd! My plane to New York leaves in two and a half hours!"

My mother stood silent for a second, sizing up the extent of the challenge, set down the spoon and exclaimed: "All right! Let's get going! I just want to give Daddy his cereal."

"But Mommy! I was going to spend all day packing! I have so much to do! Our stuff is all over the house!"

"So hurry! Get the children in here for breakfast!"

"But it takes forty-five minutes to get there! It's L.A. International, not Burbank!"

"Yes! We can make it! Go get dressed! Get the children dressed! I'll make a bottle for the baby!"

Off we set, my mother and I, on the mad rush to collect belongings, take clothes off the line and stick them in the drier, squeeze things into suitcases already crammed chock full, search wildly for string to close boxes that wouldn't close...Rachel dashed around being helpful. The baby gurgled.

It was easier under these circumstances to say goodbye to Daddy; we hardly had time to look each other in the eyes. My mother sped us to the airport without mentioning my mistake. When we screeched up in front of the departure terminal, I swung open the car door and assaulted a porter. "I'm on flight 002, and I think I have to pay overweight!"

Tall and plump, as a porter should be, he took my ticket calmly and cocked his head. "Lady," he said genially, "you don't have time to pay overweight. Gate number fifteen."

I waved goodbye to Mommy, swallowing back a sudden sob. Please, G-d, I entreated, let me see them again soon.

Helen welcomed us all over again, yet this time her joy upon seeing the children was greater. Bouncing the baby on her knee, she said to Rachel, "It was too quiet around here! How are you? Nu, did you have fun? I missed you! It was too quiet around here!"

During these, my last twenty-four hours in the *goldeneh medinah*, I'm consuming as much Tropicana orange juice and creamy American ice cream as I can manage. I should have gone to sleep early tonight because our flight leaves tomorrow morning at seven, but I've just gotten off the phone with Fran, Yaacov's sister. We talked for two and a half hours, mostly about disciplining children. She told me that Bob, the husband of my other sister-in-law, never raises his voice or uses physical punishment.

I wanted to make sure I got the story straight. "He doesn't yell?"

"I've never heard him yell in nine years."

"And he doesn't hit?"

"Never."

"So what does he do? Punish them when they disobey?"

"They don't disobey him. He doesn't really need to punish them because they know he means what he says. If he says that if they don't do such-and-such, they'll get penalized in such-and-such a way, they believe it. He always follows through."

November 3, 1986

The El Al stewardess has just handed us some bags of roasted peanuts. Rachel was embarrassed by the mess around our seats, so she's leaning over now to clean up the tissues and spilled food, lost baby toys and used diapers. Eli has confiscated the earphones for complex dental exercises, so I'm gladly sacrificing my last movie opportunity for a nobler cause.

I'm apprehensive about going home. I dread feeling swamped, I'm worried how I'll react walking into a messy house, I'm already getting depressed envisioning myself nervous and pressured, and I'm wondering how the children will be, and most of all, how Yaacov is after his long stint. I have no choice but to acknowledge the visible improvement in our health after staying in my mother's house. I rebel so against the American belief that we humans are first and foremost physical bodies, with a generous smattering of spirit and emotion thrown in for good measure, that I'm resistant to the fact that food does significantly affect our feelings and behavior. "We aren't what we eat!" has always been my rallying call. To accept that what we eat has a lot to do with the way we feel and behave is to accept the tremendous responsibility that a mother has. It's a job that requires concentration, time, effort, dedication. Dear me.

The baby's left eye, which is often crossed, even straightened out somewhat while we were in Los Angeles. A general strengthening of the body, my mother says, will naturally affect all the organs.

Not counting several fleeting moments of fitful, weird dreaming with my eyes open, I haven't slept during these past ten hours on the plane, and I dare not even try to determine if this is our night or our day. (Let's see, we were in California yesterday, or was that last night, but by New York time I'm still asleep, so is this tomorrow already?) The baby keeps standing up unexpectedly in his bassinet, and only constant vigilance can prevent disaster, so every time I start to nod off, my eyelids snap open to attention. As far as I know, Rachel hasn't slept either. She has been as concerned about Eli falling out of the bassinet as I am.

I love her.

Being in this first row has given us the advantage, in addition to the dangerous bassinet, of unmovable armrests. This means that we gaze around from upright positions at all our fellow passengers who are stretched out for sleep on two or three seats. Thank goodness we have been saved from their indignity!

Rachel had finally gotten the baby to sleep after hours of his confused, exhausted crying when the pilot's muffled announcement that we will land in a half-hour exploded onto the loudspeaker. Yes, El Al, thank you! That is my little boy you hear screaming again.

Now we're making our descent, so they're entertaining the bedraggled clientele with "Havah Nagillah." As the familiar tune blares tinnily through the cabin, passengers glance at other passengers. We give the timid little smiles of strangers compelled to acknowledge (at the end of twelve impersonal hours stuck uncomfortably together) the intimately complicated knowledge of each other we share. Yeah, I'm Jewish, those shy, quickly suppressed little smiles are saying. You're Jewish, too, aren't you. We are now taking our leave of the modern, sanitized, safely nondescript international ambience to which all savvy air travelers aspire and are approaching the land of our own passions. Like a family that has kept up appearances out in public, now we can let go. Admit it. We're home. The seats are emptying out as women form long lines at the back of the plane for their turns at the lavatory mirrors, and I, too, am eager to put on lipstick and my brand-new "Superlash" mascara. I sit here studiously reading the wrapper, as carefully as I would a box of breakfast cereal. I can't wait to improve myself with the "NEW! Self-regulating applicator!"

November 6, 1986

We arrived in Sanhedria HaMurchevet at 11:30 a.m., which made it 4:30 a.m. New York time. Because of a delay at Heathrow, we'd been up all night and then some. I argued with the driver about the fare all the way from Ben Gurion Airport to Jerusalem, because in good Israeli fashion I was sure I was being cheated, but as he pulled up in front of our building, I don't know what happened. I realized that he was right and I was wrong. My pride battered, I meekly shelled out the cash in dollars and shekels, and the cab screeched off furiously, leaving me standing there with seven ragtag suitcases and a big torn box, wondering how I was ever going to climb up to the fourth floor with all of it. My clothes were dirty, the children looked pale and messy, and I feared we weren't giving off that certain glamorous *je ne sais quoi* which one should radiate upon arriving home from one's overseas vacation. As I stood there in a mute stupor, one of my neighbors greeted me cordially with a warm smile of welcome and this horrible greeting: "*Bruchim habaim!* Oh, your children missed you terribly. It's been so difficult for them without you!"

"Thanks a lot," I almost snapped. "Is that your way of making me feel good? Or do you already want me to feel guilty?" But I restrained myself. (Rav Simcha, is G-d taking gr-r-r-eat pleasure in me?) We smiled sweetly at each other and she hurried off to catch a bus. "Rachel," I moaned, "maybe Daddy didn't leave for the yeshiva yet. Go upstairs and see." I stood there with the baby in my arms, noticing suddenly how heavy he had become and how much my stomach had grown. A minute later, Yaacov appeared. A stranger. Was that Yaacov? Yes! "I didn't know when you were coming!" he exclaimed as he walked hurriedly towards us and picked up a suitcase. "I've been waiting to hear from you! Go upstairs, I'll bring the bags."

I'd been rescued. Yaacov! My family! I cried inwardly with joy. My family! *I'm so lucky to have a family!*

When I walked through the open door, the apartment looked unfamiliar.

What a nice apartment! And it's so clean! What a beautiful view we have! I'm home!

November 7, 1986

It's Friday and I shouldn't sit down to write, but I just have to say that these three days at home have been wonderful, even though I've had to get up each night with Rachel and the baby around two in the morning.

When we arrived home on Tuesday, Rachel went right to sleep, and Yaacov encouraged me to lie down too, but I, being Mommy (it still surprises me), had to get everything put away and make lunch and dinner. I floated through the day, my motor running purely on spirit, and was up again that night at one. The next day, after the children went to school and the baby fell asleep at ten o'clock, I sank into bed. I've just got to have a nap, I thought. I'll clean up later.

I awoke with a start, like a drunken sailor who'd gone down with the ship. Staggering into the kitchen, I took due note of the breakfast dishes overflowing the sink, then looked up at the clock.

Three thirty.

Three thirty?

IT MUST BE THREE THIRTY IN THE AFTERNOON! The children! Where are the children? Didn't they come home at one o'clock? I ran to the door, opened it with a bang. No sign of them!

Down the stairs to my neighbor! She explained that yes, she'd heard the children buzzing our doorbell and knocking and banging, and since I wasn't home, she took everyone in to her house for lunch. Now they were downstairs playing.

I was grateful to have such a good neighbor, and was so glad that the children had been taken care of, but...there I was, once again, caught being a horrible mother. She's so wonderful, that woman, she puts me to shame. And to top it off, she would be so sorry if she knew that this is how her kindness is making me feel. She's such a good person, she really wants to help everyone, any way she can. My children love her and trust her and admire her. I feel like a horrible person in comparison.

Poor kids, I thought sadly. They must think Mommy's already left them again.

Those five and a half hours Wednesday morning were the longest stretch of sleep I've had in six days, but my nerves are in good condition. I'm doing fine, even though at this point my head is tethered to my body by only the flimsiest filament of dream-fiber and my body itself is on the verge of floating entirely away. But I'm all right. It is with amazement, pride and gratitude that I see myself carrying on calmly, happily. That's what a real vacation can do for you.

I feel guilty being so lucky. Any one of the women I know could have used a vacation as much as I, if not more.

Miriam Levi once said that she'd like to hand out anti-guilt pills. I must tell her that I'd order a carton.

November 9, 1986

It is happening. I'm getting into the habit of speaking quietly even when I'm not feeling that way. My emotions can be taking off like crazed chickens, but a quiet voice brings them down to earth. A quiet voice makes all solutions feasible, if not possible, and uplifts us to a higher plateau where it's no longer an issue of who shall win and who shall lose, but rather: who has the self-restraint to avoid hurting others, who can be helpful, who can make everyone happier.

I'm experiencing feelings of love, even in busy moments, and I think that's happening because I like myself right now.

Keeping anger under control appears to me now to be the key to so many other things. A life bent out of shape by hitting and shouting loses an essential beauty. It's devalued. My father used to speak about the desensitization that occurs as a result of self-destructive behavior; since to yourself you're not giving enough respect, you can behave with a half-unconscious cruelty to the people who are closest to you. Daily life in this world has to be accorded the proper dignity, it has to be seen as the infinitely valuable possession it is, for every minute moves us along inexorably toward death.

How I pray that the habit of speaking calmly takes root in me.

I'm not as frightened as I used to be of breaking, because I've broken so many times and yet caught hold again of the lifeline.

Sometimes I can see how behaving in a calm manner modifies my perceptions. For example, when I told Daniel to get into his pajamas last night, he started clapping his hands, singing at the top of his lungs and strutting around the house. It was that American Indian-style war dance of his that has always just set me off. I look at him prancing around like that, disobeying me, and I think: "Wild boy! He's trying to upset me! He's defying my authority! He's taunting me!"

Last night, these weren't the thoughts that arose. There was Danny, clapping and marching around, and I beheld a precious little boy exulting in his vitality, in his boyhood, and yes, exulting in this small demonstration of rebellion against his mother—that woman who has all the power on her side. I thought: "It's good we haven't crushed that spirit of his," and told him in a quiet voice to please go brush his teeth. He changed direction. Singing and clapping, Daniel strutted into the bathroom.

Normally by that time, he would have been spanked.

On Friday afternoon, with a million things still left to do and the children pulling at me and the baby crying, I found myself remaining calm. It astonished me. The force of habit was making its appearance! One part of me stood off in surprise as I heard my voice, soft and gentle amid chaotic pressures. I was so proud of myself.

At one point I was at the sink peeling potatoes, worrying about the chicken not defrosting on time, watching absently as the brown bits of peel dropped onto the dirty dishes, when within my heart a tender joy suddenly warbled up like an unsummoned songbird. Happiness usually flees the minute you take note of it, but this little critter stuck around even though I was looking right at him. For an hour or so...the musical bubbling of a tangible joy. *Dear G-d!* I said in silence. *I've been looking out there for happiness all my life, and now it's come upon me unexplained as I stare into my kitchen sink!*

Still at the sink sometime later that afternoon, a dreamlike sequence (a side benefit of severe sleep deprivation) played itself out like a tiny home movie before my inner eye. The entire film probably took no more than five seconds, but it had a luminescent clarity:

I have been led down a certain path, farther and farther along—a rough and uncomfortable descent through brambles and underbrush. The discomfort gets worse and worse and worse until I think I can't stand it anymore, then I find myself before an old white gate. The gate swings magically open. I pass through. I enter a garden. The garden is richly brilliant with deep, bright colors, and surrounded by a white picket fence.

Somehow it's apparent that I have come upon my own property. I recognize it though I can't remember when I was here before. A joyous confidence comes over me: this place is mine. There's no way it can be taken away from me, no way it can be lost or ruined. It belongs to me eternally, though I might not often be able to find my way there.

I have come upon it now by surprise, but it's always there.

It is my own self.

8

The Message of the Sparrow

November 10, 1986

I always wanted to touch the sky,
to be tall enough to touch the Why.
Giants walked all around—alas, not I.
I was just a child wondering why.
A Jewish child, I knew I was.
But what's in a name if there's no because?

Still that child, I grew to be tall.
I learned so much but learned nothing at all.
Someone gave me two candles and I covered my eyes.
A weak human being, I touch the skies.

All right to be nothing, all right to be small.
All right to know almost nothing at all.
I'd found my name, I was holding hands
with Jews of many eras and lands.

A Jewish woman. So that's what I was.
I had yet to find why, but I had because.

November 11, 1986

At four o'clock this morning I was at the kitchen table with Rachel and the baby, enjoying what I thought was a wonderful little extension of our private threesome. Their schedules are on the way to normality, but anyway, there we were. The baby was fooling around with his dish of mashed banana when Rachel announced: "Now, in Israel, you have to give me love because in America you didn't give me any love."

I thought I'd heard right, but could not believe my ears. "What did you say?"

"You just played with the baby. Everyone just played with the baby and not with me."

I was speechless. Perhaps thirty seconds of silence elapsed as my head instantly got all jumbled up in a mental traffic jam with a number of contradictory thoughts simultaneously: "She knows better than to say something so ridiculous. I gave her all my attention and love in America! Everyone did! She doesn't mean it, she's just trying to get my attention." "No, she means it but it's no big deal. Some feelings of not being loved are inevitable, regardless of what the reality is. It's a sign of emotional health that she's able to express it to me." "Oh my gosh, what did happen in America? Maybe I really did ignore her, because I was so secure I was doing the right thing simply by bringing her along. Maybe everyone did give the baby a lot of attention and she felt that only by filling the role of Mother's Little Helper could she catch everyone's eye. Maybe it was I who cast her in that role, because I wanted to display what a good mother I am to have educated her so well. I did so at the expense of the real Rachel." "No, now wait! What nonsense! She did indeed get love and attention. It's plain old human nature that's to blame here, for humans are insensitive to what they have and sensitive to what they lack. No matter what, if it's theirs, it's crumbs. Wow! She's impossible! The ingrate! This is horrible. The whole point in bringing her with me was lost! All that money for nothing! The trip failed!"

In half a minute I had filled right up to the brim with a

horrible depression, and I felt so peeved with Rachel. *Nothing was gained after all.*

"Rachel," I implored, thinking that maybe she'd been trying to crack a joke. "Are you teasing me? Do you really feel that way?"

"Yes!" she shot back. "I really KNOW it!" She started to cry. I was astonished all over again. *This is a bad dream. The whole thing was futile.* I was so confused, suddenly I didn't have the will power to look for the right thing to say, and before I knew it we were engaged in a nightmarish dramatization of precisely that which she needed least: an argument. I threw up my hands in exasperation and told her she was wrong. She complained more loudly. I ordered her to be quiet or she'd wake up the whole house, whereupon she went into the living room and noisily kicked a cabinet. I spanked her. She cried.

I snarled, "Shut up now or I'll hit you! Go to your room!"

She went to her room and closed the door behind her. I went back to the kitchen, and the baby smiled ecstatically to see me after my minute's absence. For goodness sake, his blind adoration of me!

As the sun rose I was still sitting at the table with a hollow heart, holding Eli in my arms, when Rachel appeared at my side, in silence. I was so glad. A moment went by. She asked, "What are you thinking?"

"Rachel, I'm just feeling so bad that you think I didn't give you love when we were in America. I'm so sorry you felt that way!" She stared at me. "Sometimes people don't realize it when other people love them, Rachel. Do you know that?" She stared, still silent. "I didn't expect to get mad at you before," I continued, groping. "I was just so surprised. Tell me more about this, and I'll try to understand."

She stood there a minute. Then she pulled on her left ear. My heart jumped, I pulled her close to me. We hugged.

November 13, 1986

My life has an underlying sense of order and purpose, but I'm still nagged by a host of sundry dissatisfactions, because I'm looking for perfection everywhere. All humans are seekers of perfection, each after his own fashion. The Coca-Cola ad plugged into this drive shrewdly when it advertised "the real thing in the back of your mind." What is the real thing? If it's not Coca-Cola, could it be a new Peugeot? A husband who will do the dishes? Will G-d never grant me, outright, His seal of approval? Can I never get that sense that I've finally made it?

How interesting this imperfect world would probably be— with its multitude of wondrous and imperfect phenomena— if I were to cease demanding perfection here and now. I want the perfect marriage, the perfect children, the perfect communication with the perfect friend, the perfect figure (fat chance, now that I'm in my seventh month). I want to be the perfect mother who makes perfect whole-wheat banana-nut bread, and I impress upon Yaacov that he has the perfect wife. Then I put the darks in with the lights, and his undershirts come out pink.

Perhaps my quest for perfection is simply another natural manifestation of that longing for the Creator which is implanted in each and every one of us. The enigma is this: essential to finding the strength to continue striving is the acceptance, which deepens with time and with one's failures, that the goal of worldly perfection is unattainable. The banana bread might come out just right next time—neither burnt nor heavy, nor wet at the center—but Dinah could very well declare it's icky anyhow. Perfect moments pass. Perfection is not part of human life. Yet our all-pervading human imperfection is an integral aspect of the perfect creation that is this world.

November 14, 1986

Dinah was the only one home at one point yesterday afternoon, and we were in the midst of one of our familiar tussles. She was upset that I had touched her food, or put two different kinds of food on her plate, or she saw me put salt in the pot—when all of a sudden she burst out: "When we were getting the rug and I got lost, you didn't look for me!"

I didn't know what she was talking about. "What?"

"When we got THAT RUG!" She pointed to the carpet on the living room floor. "And it was SO CROWDED!" Her face now crumpled up like paper crushed in a fist, tears poured out in a flash. She glared at me fiercely. Yes, I remembered. Carrying that carpet rolled up in brown paper under my arm, I had turned left out of the rug store on Rehov Yaffo and called to the four children to come along. I'm not sure whether I realized she wasn't with us and turned around to look for her, or whether it was only when a crying child pulled on my coat that I wheeled around. In either case, I recall nearly knocking over a passerby with the unwieldy roll of carpet.

The store owner's son was at Dinah's side. He saw her reunited with her mother and disappeared back into the crowd. Perhaps a total of five minutes had elapsed since we'd left the store.

It happened right after we moved to this apartment two and a half years ago. Dinah must have been about three and a half, but this was the first time she'd mentioned it.

"You didn't look for me!" Her eyes now were as big as they could be, remembering this discovery that despite appearances, her mother was capable of betrayal.

"But, Dinah..."

"Oh no! Just for Racheli!" she whined sarcastically. "When Racheli got lost you looked for her!"

I didn't know which incident that was, but it didn't matter. "I did look for you, Dinah." *Is that a lie?*

This set her in a rage. "YOU DIDN'T! I went back to the store and the man asked me where is your mommy, so he told his boy to help me find my mommy and we couldn't find you for a long, long TIME! Then I saw you walking away! When Rachel was lost you looked for her but for me you didn't! You didn't!"

Rather than go on trying to prove she was wrong—and I wasn't sure she was—it dawned on me to empathize rather than deny. "So you thought I didn't care that you were lost?"

"Yes!"

"But that when it happened to Rachel, that I loved her and wanted to find her?"

"Yes! And with me you didn't." Dinah cried now in silence. More tears and more tears.

"Dinah, that's not what I felt at all..."

Her eyes blazed into mine. "OH YES!"

"Dinah...Dinah darling..." I tried to touch her face but she pulled away. She was aflame, what could I say?

I spoke almost in a whisper: "Dinah...I'm so sorry that you felt like that. I just didn't know that you weren't behind me when I went out of the store." I reached again towards her. She jerked away. I asked if she looked for me for a long time.

"A LONG, LONG TIME! And it was so crowded!" She wept.

"So you got scared?"

Something went through her mind. She stopped crying. "Were you going to get on the bus?"

"Yes, but a taxi came first so we took a taxi."

"What would you do if you got on the bus and you saw I wasn't there?" Her lips were parted and her eyes narrowed slightly.

"I'd scream for the driver to stop, and I'd throw the stupid rug down and make him open the doors, and I'd run out of the bus to look for you." Dinah was watching me carefully with her red eyes. "I wouldn't stop looking for you everywhere until I found you. I would never go back home until I found you."

She gazed at me in silence. Her focus was not upon me but through me.

I reached over to her and cupped my hands around her face, then drew her curly brown-haired head towards me. She let me. I stroked her little head and held her close, and took her on my lap. We sat like this and rocked back and forth for some minutes, without talking.

Suddenly she sat up straight, brightening. "Mommy, look. At my birthday party—right? We're going to have one for school?"

"Right."

"At my party I want a cake like this." She drew a big circle in the air. "One cake on bottom and one tiny cake on top."

"What do you mean, a tiny one on top?"

"You know, a tiny one on top of the big one. Like this." Now her hands drew a small circle. "O.K.?"

"Well..." I decided it would be wise not to get into it right now.

"And a picture of a guitar like Shlomoh HaMelech's, on the big cake. You make it with those little candies with all the colors. Riki's mother did it one time. All right, Mommy?"

"We'll see, Dinah."

November 16, 1986

A few minutes ago, I noticed a strange warmth in Rachel's ordinarily frigid bedroom. I touched the radiator. It was hot! *The steam!* I exulted. The steam is on! I rushed into the living room, to my bedroom, from one radiator to another. Yes! All of them are hot!

I had started thinking that our cold apartment was but one more indication that it was my destiny to suffer. Just our luck! I darted out now to ask the next-door neighbor if they had just gotten heat, too, for the first time, and she said yes. I hurried back in to make sure all the radiators were properly opened.

Those first rattlings and stirrings of warmth in our house made me want to dance and clap hands. All's right with the world! What a comfortable life I lead! I'm one of the blessed ones! I returned to Rachel's cozy room and leaned against the wonderfully warm, the deliciously warm radiator. Chin in hands, I set my elbows on the windowsill and looked out.

Out there to my right was the Ramot Forest mountain, off to the left the buildings of Sanhedria HaMurchevet, away down there on the street a scattering of teeny anonymous people. A bus roared.

The playground next door was empty save for one child. He climbed up the ladder to the slide, entered the barrel positioned at the top, emerged head first, slid down the slide and ran around to start again.

A large, black crow leisurely flapped its way in slow motion from somewhere out of the mountain, and then, on an unseen breeze, floated across my view of the late afternoon clouds. The sun would soon be setting. The horizon was stained faintly pink.

I realized that it had been a long time since I had gazed out of a window like this. It's thanks to the radiator, I thought to myself.

Appreciate the moment!

Seize the day!

Suddenly, an old, familiar sadness passed through me like a cold shadow, the shadow that once dimmed my world when I was an adolescent and young adult: the thought that life is going by and I don't know how to live it adequately, that death—so strange and threatening—could be just around the corner. That death could arrive, mine or that of the people I love, before I've really touched life and held it close to me. That nothing I'm doing is of genuine worth.

A small, tidy, brown bird, with black eyes like tiny glass beads, appeared out of nowhere to alight on the window box. It pecked at a purple blossom, cocked its head and ruffled its feathers like an intricately complicated mechanical toy. What a wondrous creation!

The children.

No. With the children I am not walking on shifting, ever-vanishing sands.

With the children there are footprints.

9

It's Not to Thailand

November 19, 1986

I was folding laundry in the children's room this afternoon when shrill cries of grief emanated from the adjoining *mirpesset*. I leaned over to peek through the door. Danny was in there building a little house of Lego, and Elisheva was down on the floor kicking up a storm. Her eyes were shut tight, the tears were already a torrent, her face was red.

I went back to the laundry. I felt that I should find out what was going on—maybe she'd been hit—but I wanted so much to get the laundry all put away. I didn't feel up to jury duty. I did the towels, waiting for the nerve-rattling, ear-piercing screams to peter out. But they didn't. After ten minutes, the laundry done, the air-raid was still going full blast.

I entered the *mirpesset* and asked what had happened. Above the din, Daniel came stridently to his own defense. "I'm using the door on my house, and Elisheva wants it for HER house. But I need it!"

"Did you take it away from her?" I asked.

Danny jumped up, frantic. "No! No! I just FOUND it!"

Elisheva rose to her feet, hysterical. "Oh YES!" she bellowed. "Oh YES! He DID take it away from me. It's for MY house! He's a liar! He's a liar!" She lunged at him. I caught her.

Rachel appeared quietly and whispered something in my ear. "What, Rachel? Say it out loud."

"Elisheva had the door, and Danny took it away."

Danny started crying. "She's a liar! She's saying *lashon hara*! I found the door! It belongs to MY HOUSE!"

It was pretty clear that everyone was telling the truth as he saw it. My role was to establish justice. Without listening to or believing *lashon hara*? The prospect was somehow so daunting and it just didn't feel right to once again, as usual, compel Danny to surrender, so I walked off without comment. The thunder and lightning did not abate. It was difficult to bear. I felt guilty for not coming to Elisheva's aid, especially when Danny started mimicking her wails and moans, which sent her to greater heights of frenzied misery. I knew I should somehow restore law and order, but I felt so pregnant.

Some minutes later, from the living room, I heard Danny's quiet announcement: "All right. You can have it." It took a few more minutes for Elisheva's sobs to wind down. Then, all was quiet.

I guess he didn't like the noise either, or he took pity upon her, or he didn't need the door anymore. In any case, I intended to compliment him on his voluntary act of kindness but forgot, as other issues arose in this one's place. I was so glad to have left them to their own devices.

November 22, 1986

On Friday, once again having slept hardly at all, I was able to work steadily and remain calmly quiet in spite of the pressure. I thought of the line from *Pirkei Avos*: Who is strong? Not he who conquers a city, but he who conquers himself. I felt I had attained life's supreme victory.

After lighting candles, I sat down on the couch, observed that everyone was happy, and I rejoiced.

November 23, 1986

Sometime yesterday afternoon, Shabbat, Yaacov was on the couch holding the baby, who was screaming. I was busy in the kitchen. Elisheva, crying about something, had thrown herself over Yaacov's knees, and Daniel and Dinah were arguing about the Lego. Rachel was skipping back and forth across the living room from one wall to the other, seeing how high she knew how to count in English. It went like this: "ONE!" Skip across. "TWO!" Skip across. "THREE!"

"I'm counting all the way to a thousand!" she yelled.

I came to the kitchen door and Yaacov and I exchanged glances. I knew there was some apt phrase for this scene, but couldn't put my finger on it. *Ah! I found it*: The Indians have their bows and arrows drawn. One cowboy, hands up in surrender, says to his colleague, "Well, partner, looks like they got us covered."

I delivered this line to Yaacov, who seemed to understand. He lifted one eyebrow.

November 24, 1986

I heard in a *shiur* by Rabbi Leff last night that a Jew's capacity to leave home and family to live in Eretz Yisrael is derived from Avraham Avinu's strength in obeying *HaShem*'s command, *lech lecha*.

One would think, given my scorn and distaste for so much of United States culture, that it would be easy for me to leave it. How could I get credit for leaving something I don't miss? I do suffer keenly from the separation from my family, and I am moderately sad to have left the physical beauties of nature in Connecticut, but I don't experience much pain about anything else. So does Rabbi Leff's statement apply to me?

Yes. Because "Queen for a Day," "The Millionaire," "To Tell the Truth," "Lassie," "The Mickey Mouse Club," "Father Knows Best"...these creations of ABC, CBS and NBC are imbedded in the crevices of my heart. Macy's, Grand Central Station, the New Canaan Shop Rite...their architecture is imprinted on my brain cells, and the Beatles pull at my heartstrings at unexpected moments. With love, hate or indifference, I carry all of it within me, it's part of me forever, and I have to make *aliyah* all over again every time I'm reminded of my past.

November 25, 1986

I'm trying to change one of our bedtime traditions, one that's always driven me to distraction: when the children are in bed, they ask me for apples. According to our dentist, apples and carrots are natural toothbrushes; that's how this habit started. Now I want out.

A few days ago, I said I'd let them have water from now on instead of apples, but I was soon at work changing the sheets that got soaked from all those overturned cups. Now it's my ambition to eliminate the whole business.

Tonight Danny asked for a glass of milk. "No, Danny. And then you'd have to brush your teeth again. No. You can't. Go to sleep."

"Mommy, please!"

"Go to sleep!"

Danny started making the weirdest noises at that point, like a hyena on its last legs. I resolved to ignore it, but Dinah called out to me that she couldn't go to sleep.

"Be quiet, Danny! Stop that and go to sleep right now!"

He continued.

Entering their room, I saw that Elisheva's eyes were flickering. What a mess it would be if she woke up! I felt like screaming at Danny to stop that noise, but instead I proclaimed in a voice not far above a whisper that because he was disobeying me, I would not be speaking to him right now. Then I walked out. The hyena got more strident and awoke the baby. This really made my fists clench. "You woke up the baby, Danny!" I snapped on my way to the crib in the next room. I changed Eli and prepared a bottle as Daniel's cacophonous symphony reached a crescendo. Then the noise subsided. Five minutes passed in silence.

Once Daniel's head is on the pillow, it takes him only a few moments to drop off, and I didn't want him to fall asleep while we

166 Growing With My Children   December 2, 1986

were still at odds with each other. I tiptoed into the bedroom. There was Danny, to my relief, his eyes open. He was looking up at the ceiling, his arms folded behind his head.

"Are you ready to say something to me, Danny?"

He said nothing. I walked out.

I fed the baby, put him back in the crib, and passed by Danny's room again. He was lying there in the same position. His pride wouldn't let him apologize, but he couldn't fall asleep. I came in and sat down on his bed. He tried to suppress a smile. We looked into each other's faces.

"I'm sorry," he whispered.

I kissed him and held him. "All right, Danny. I love you."

Seconds later he was fast asleep.

December 2, 1986

While putting the children to bed tonight, and right after the thought had crossed my mind that I was so tired, I heard the distinctive sound of the plastic pitcher falling to the floor, bouncing noisily two times. I asked myself: Now, was that pitcher empty or full? And the answer was: Danny was just in the kitchen squeezing oranges…a pitcher full of orange juice.

"Mommy!" Daniel called from the kitchen. "Look what happened!"

For the next twenty minutes I yelled so much that I got a pain in my side. I recognized that I wanted Danny to feel as guilty as possible, but was getting too much satisfaction to stop my harangue. "Don't you know how hard it is for me to do *sponga* now?" I shouted. "I'm not supposed to be leaning down like this! I can't! You should be more careful!" and "Look how sticky this orange juice is! The ants will love it!" and "How ridiculous! How absolutely ridiculous! I can't DO this! I'm pregnant, Danny!"

Daniel walked off to his bedroom, sobbing deeply.

With all my anger churning powerfully, I scrubbed the floor with all my strength. And pulled something in my back.

"Oh, for crying out loud! I shouldn't be doing this! I knew it! Danny! Come here!"

Danny appeared at the kitchen door, his eyes swollen and red.

"Danny! You're going to have to clean up this mess yourself. I hurt myself. Here. Do it yourself!"

In quiet eagerness, and chastened, Danny took the mop from my hands.

For the next hour, long after the other children had gone to bed, he worked. "Mommy! Come see!" he called out, and he stood in proud silence as I came in to inspect. He felt good. The floor was quite lovely. Then I let him make another pitcher of orange juice.

December 4, 1986

Dinah was in the bathtub and I was sudsing up her hair, when the bathroom went dark. I heard Daniel's muffled giggle on the other side of the door. My guts clenched. "Danny," I called out in a low-pitched, artificially friendly manner. "I can't touch the light switch because my hands are wet and it's dangerous. Please turn on the light right now and don't do that again."

Dinah and I looked at each other in the dark. The light came on.

"I'm sorry, Mommy," said Danny through the door.

So nice. What pleasure I got from that unprodded apology.

December 9, 1986

I spoke on the phone tonight to the mother of one of Daniel's classmates. She asked me if I'm going to the parents' meeting on Sunday. "A lot of the parents are very upset about the rebbe's hitting," she told me. "They think that the only way he'll listen to us is if we get together as a group. For misbehavior, I can see a teacher punishing a kid, but for not knowing the right answer? Once he pushed Shmuli's head down on the desk and hit him on the neck. Now, I know that Shmuli can get fresh sometimes. He knows how to get an adult's goat, but I still don't think the rebbe should act this way." I didn't tell her what I was thinking: that she was grossly underreacting.

This was not the first time I'd gotten wind of this problem.

Danny had told me that his rebbe hit some boys on their hands with a ruler—a tactic my grandfather once told me that his own rebbe had used (to no benefit) in a Russian cheder. And Daniel had, unsurprisingly, become more answer-oriented and scared of making mistakes than he had been in first grade. Yet Daniel was still loving school and doing well, and never had I gotten a report of this kind of violence. It came as a shock.

Yaacov and I agreed that their idea of forming a delegation could backfire; the rebbe would probably feel unfairly cornered by a bunch of overprotective, worrywart Americans, and unless the parents were to go all the way and have him fired, or remove their children from the school, the only thing they'd accomplish would be to arouse his resentment, which he might take out unconsciously on their children later.

I scolded myself inwardly for never having gone to meet the rebbe, even though a trip to the school when I'm this pregnant knocks me out for the rest of the day.

"If I were you," I wanted to say, "I'd get my little boy out of there fast," but if this was my advice, then shouldn't I take Danny out of the class, too, as an act of solidarity? Although Danny himself had been spared the worst, shouldn't I act on principle?

December 11, 1986

I went to meet Danny's rebbe today. My intentions were modest: harboring few hopes of converting him to American democracy, I just wanted to get on his good side and make sure that Danny never got punished the way Shmuli did. The rebbe was physically smaller than I had imagined, and he inclined his head forward to listen with an unexpected humbleness.

I had brought along my Hebrew-English/English-Hebrew dictionary. First, I told him how frantic Danny gets sometimes while doing his arithmetic homework. "He's so scared of not getting the right answer," I tried to explain, "that he can't think straight. Please understand that he's more sensitive than he might appear." I thumbed as fast as possible to the S's. Sensitive. "*Hu meod ragish,*"

I said with as much charm as I could muster.

The rebbe smiled. *"At ima mesuderet,"* he said, gesturing to the dictionary. *"Zeh tov."*

Mesuderet. Let's see...this took me longer...*mem, samech*, or is that *shin?*... Ah. I'm an organized mother. I was flattered. I told him that even though he had never hit Danny, Danny was scared that if he gave the wrong answer, it would be his turn to get it.

"I only hit to keep them a little scared, so that they'll study hard," the rebbe told me. "It's good for the boys."

My mind reeled. He was that untouched by twentieth-century philosophy? I looked into his sincere, gentle countenance, and then at his long, black coat, his long *peyos*, his black hat. Of course. A traditionalist from the old school, a Yerushalmi who truly believes in the educational efficacy of hitting. It dawned on me that there was no use: he and I would never see eye to eye.

We talked on for some ten minutes or so. Since I had timed my visit to take place during the morning break, this must have been his only chance to get something to drink and relax, but he gave no sign of impatience. He listened closely, told me carefully how Danny was doing in each subject, and when I prepared to depart, called Danny over.

"Danny," he said, pinching Daniel's cheek affectionately. "Do you see what a good mother you have, that she came to talk with me about you?"

Danny smiled shyly.

Walking to the bus stop I knew I had made a good impression and that the meeting had been a success, for the rebbe knew that as far as Daniel was concerned, someone was keeping tabs. In spite of my disagreement with him, the man struck me as a warm, devoted teacher, endeavoring to do his best. He's not malicious, I thought to myself. His attitude toward physical discipline is that it's right, and mine is that it's wrong. Nonetheless, we both end up in the same boat sometimes, and from time to time go overboard.

I'm magnanimous enough to forgive him his human fallibility. As long as Danny is never on the receiving end.

An organized mother. I liked that.

December 14, 1986

On Shabbat afternoon we were all taking a walk. Yaacov and Danny were up ahead, and I was lagging behind leisurely with the girls. "What are you thinking?" Rachel asked. She could tell my mind was elsewhere.

"About how Candis wants to have a baby."

"I'll pray for her to have a baby," she said.

"I will also!" said Dinah.

"Also me!" said Elisheva. Their serious faces turned inward as they took upon themselves this duty. Dinah's lips moved. If I weren't afraid of sounding like a missionary, I'd write Candis that she has three pure advocates.

A close friend, an older woman whose friendship matters to me, just called. "Sarah," she exclaimed, "why did you write 'eight' on the check?"

I didn't know what she was talking about.

"You know. The check you gave me last week for the dishes. You put eight shekels instead of seven!"

"Oh. I'm sorry, Bluma."

"Sarah, what's wrong with you?"

Having been in an open, unguarded mood, my heart buzzed with an electric flutter of adrenaline.

"Oh, wait," she was saying on the other end. "Oh. It's O.K. Sorry. Never mind. My mistake. Look, I have to rush to the bank before it closes so I'll call you later. Bye!"

I was left with the receiver at my ear. My friend evidently had no idea how those words "What's wrong with you?" had hurt me, and part of the pain came from her not even giving it a thought.

Haven't I sometimes said to my children, when aggravated, "Why did you do that? What's wrong with you?"

December 15, 1986

Yaacov and I went to parents' night at Danny's school. He got the same impression as I had, that the rebbe is really a sweet man and a caring teacher. At the end of our talk, Yaacov brought up Danny's refusal to accompany him to shul on Shabbat. The rebbe shook his head with a stern, melancholy air and said, "This is not good." This instilled us with anxiety—of something very wrong and the need to correct it.

December 16, 1986

Yaacov checked today and found out that by Israeli law it is illegal for a teacher to strike a child.

December 22, 1986

Tonight I found myself having a pleasant experience putting the children to bed. It was like riding a chair lift to the top of the mountain instead of making the grueling uphill march.

Danny met me in the hallway on the way to his bed, and he reached up happily to kiss me. He's been doing that lately. It confirms this faith I have in natural processes: remove the negative (the yelling, the hitting), and much of the positive (love, obedience, happiness) will arise of itself.

Whenever they did something tonight which made me nervous, I took note of the gripping sensation within me and said to myself: "I don't need to tighten up like that inside myself just because out there they're fighting…Yelling is not going to help…This is a normal problem…Breathe in…Relax…Now, whatever you say, say it softly."

When Yaacov came home, Danny ran out to hug him, Rachel called out for a glass of water (I said no), Danny said he wanted an apple (I said yes. The inconsistency!), Dinah said that then she wanted an apple, too, and Elisheva jumped out of bed and said: "Why is Dinah getting an apple? I want one, too!" Then Rachel cried, "Why are you giving everybody an apple but to me you say no?"

I gave in, muttering and grumbling and feeling frustrated and angry about my loss of control over everyone.

Dinah ran out into the living room. "Not a green apple! A yellow apple! I don't want a green apple!"

I started yelling. "You see, Danny, what you started? Why do all of you get up when Daddy comes home? Back into bed! Back into bed!"

Then I remembered how Daniel had met me in the hall and reached up to give me a sweet kiss. I switched off the yelling and lowered my voice, felt the control coming back, saw the children wind down, quiet down and get under the covers.

December 23, 1986

A half-hour ago I looked up from the typewriter and beheld Dinah crouching on the kitchen counter, pulling the miniature squeegee over the wet surface to wipe off the water. I wished that she weren't up there with her shoes on, but she looked so intensely self-satisfied to be accomplishing her mission that I didn't interfere.

She sensed my eyes on her and lifted her face. "Look, Mommy, I'm cleaning the counter. Come see."

She was on all fours, working from the left end of the counter toward the right, and was almost finished, but her shoes were leaving a trail of dark, dirty water behind her as she progressed. Dinah turned around to show me what she'd accomplished, but paused in surprise at the sight of that long, muddy puddle. Then, appearing to have come up with a satisfactory explanation for it, she started all over, working back in the other direction again. "You see how much dirt there is here! I bet you haven't cleaned it like this for a LONG long time. Right?"

"Right." My lips were already parted, about to dispense advice, but I suspected that whatever I said might injure that fragile spirit of helpfulness which only recently Dinah has begun to exhibit.

She stopped scrubbing for a moment and sat up. "So much dirt!" It puzzled her that I should be such a negligent housekeeper, yet it pleased her, too, that her labors were necessary.

"Yes," I agreed meekly. "That's wonderful."

Ten minutes passed. She was working hard. She stopped to unbuckle her shoes.

"Why are you taking off your shoes?" I asked.

"Because I don't want them to get the counter dirty."

She had figured it out herself! Thank goodness I hadn't given any advice. Dinah proceeded to finish off the whole counter.

"O.K., now, darling, thank you so much! Have you done your homework?"

She clasped her hands together with the excitement of an idea. "Mommy!" she exclaimed with a warm smile. "You want me to do *sponga* on the *mirpesset*?"

Oh no. This I really didn't want. It would mean a lot of work for me. "Not tonight, Dinah."

"Why?"

"Because it's such a cold night."

"So what?"

"You have a cough. I don't want you to get cold from the water."

"So what! I'll wear my shoes!"

"But your shoes will get wet."

"Mommy! Please!"

Don't crush that spirit, Sarah. Let her do it. "All right, but just a little bit of water, O.K.?"

"O.K.!"

Dinah sprang into action. A few minutes later, she was on her way through the living room with a wet *sponga* rag, mop stick, floor brush, broom, dish soap. I felt tired.

Dinah cleaned up the *mirpesset*, without using too much water. She did not make a mess. I didn't have to clean up after her, and the *mirpesset* looks nice.

January 1, 1987

Tonight I went with the girls to Geulah to get a birthday

present for Yaacov. I decided on a biography of the Chofetz Chaim. Elisheva got lost at one point, and while Rachel and Dinah dashed here and there along the crowded sidewalk looking for her, I imagined that perhaps she had been kidnapped, and I started to cry.

The three of them appeared. I told Elisheva that I had cried when we couldn't find her.

"So did I," said Rachel.

"So did I," said Dinah.

Elisheva, her eyes still red, smiled broadly, her head tipped to one side. She put her thumb in her mouth and we continued on our way.

January 4, 1987

Since Daniel and Rachel's birthday is fast approaching, today was my last chance to make Dinah a birthday cake for school before we start celebrating theirs. We did have Dinah's birthday party at home in October, but I always seem to prepare the one for her class a few months late.

As I ran up the hill to go shopping for the ingredients, I was thinking how disorganized and incompetent I am to be celebrating Dinah's October 26th birthday in January. Then I caught myself. *No*, I retorted to that put-down. *What a good mother I am to be going to so much trouble.*

January 5, 1987

When I say goodnight to Danny nowadays, he looks up from his pillow with a big smile, reaches up to encircle my neck with his arms, and draws me down for a sweet kiss on my cheek.

Thank G-d I'm not screaming at him and hitting him as I used to!

It's after ten at night. Elisheva woke up a little while ago, having fallen asleep after dinner in her clothes, as is her habit. Noticing that she had wet her stockings, I pulled them off. That did it.

She had such a tantrum, a wild tantrum, that I felt sort of scared. It's the second time recently that she has awakened and gone into a tailspin. Had she had a bad dream? How helpless I feel with this heavy abdomen jutting out in front of me. I kept thinking automatically: "Yaacov will be home in a few minutes," but he wasn't due back till eleven. "Yaacov will take care of it," I thought again.

I tried to embrace her, but she thrashed and kicked, and I instinctively kept turning my big belly away from her. What can I say I was feeling? Such agonizing weakness. Quite suddenly she quieted down. "I want a cup of milk. HOT milk." I hurried to make it and returned holding the cup.

"Yuck," she said, scowling. "The milk isn't good." I smelled it and yes, it was sour. Oh no, I thought. Now she'll start up again.

"Then give me water."

She took a few sips, pattered into her room thumb in mouth, curled up like a little squirrel and fell back to sleep.

January 6, 1987

Dinah told me this afternoon that she's so glad she has exactly the mommy she has, because Chaya's mother yells all the time. How gratifying for me to come out on top. A little while later I sprinkled sugar on her cereal. She grabbed the spoon. "No, Dinah," I said, "I'm going to do it."

"I want to do it myself!"

I didn't want her to load up with an overdose. "No, Dinah, I'm going to do it."

No sooner had I taken my stand than I realized it was a mistake: more and more, I have to grant Dinah autonomy, if not a separate state with her own flag. She seems to need, more than my other children, to exercise power over her own life. I was considering changing my mind about the sugar when Dinah burst out: "I want to kill you!"

I saw myself in my mind's eye slapping her in the face. *She shouldn't get away with such a thing!* I didn't slap her but I did fly off the handle, pulling her to the door, threatening to put her out of the house. Then I stopped. My goal, I reminded myself, can't be to stamp out such behavior on the spot, but to change it over time. The important thing right now is just not to overlook it. I'll have to await an opportune moment to speak to her about it.

Somehow or other, the scene passed.

After tucking her in tonight, I sat down on the bed and hoped to come up with the right words. "Dinah, remember the wrong thing you said to me today?"

She looked me in the eye.

"You have to work very hard to stop your mouth from saying that, because it's very wrong to say it to your mother. It's wrong to say it to anyone, even when you're angry."

She giggled very gaily and mischievously. "No! I'm not going to work very hard to stop!"

"You know what your *yetzer hatov* would say? It would say: 'Even though it's very difficult, I'll try to stop myself from saying things like that.' "

The line of her mouth lifted crookedly with a grin. "I'll try to stop saying things like that."

"O.K., darling. Good night."

She closed her eyes and fell asleep.

January 8, 1987

Yaacov and I don't know how to handle Daniel's refusal to go to shul on Shabbat. His rebbe seemed to think that this is something we cannot allow, but how can we force him? I don't want prayer to be associated in Danny's mind with coercion. That would negate what prayer is. So should we ignore it and let time take care of itself? But he gets so bored every Shabbat morning and has nothing to do but bother the girls and get in my hair. If he would only try going, we're sure he'd enjoy himself more than he does at home.

Yaacov suggested I call Miriam Levi. She said that until his bar mitzvah it is our job above all to cultivate his joy in davening. "Does he pray by himself?" she asked.

"Yes, he loves to," I answered. "He goes into a room and prays very happily, but doesn't like anyone to look at him."

January 12, 1987

The children have left for school. I've straightened up the living room, put in a load of laundry, made the beds and eaten a tuna fish sandwich. (I longed for something and I thought it might be tuna, but it wasn't.) The baby's sleeping, and I just don't feel like starting the kitchen yet, so I'm wrapped up cozily in the soft white blanket that my mother gave me and have closed the doors to the bedrooms so I don't remember them, and now, I can drift.

I can feel the baby inside me stirring and kicking little liquid kicks.

When I took my typewriter to write in the journal, I thought: Oh. There's nothing to write about.

I mulled this over, staring out the window.

Then I thought: Untrue.

Every interaction with the children is significant, yet unless it's so lovely or horrendous that it catches my attention, it is instantly washed out to sea with the tides of passing events—one more small, unconscious moment, forgotten almost as it goes by. Only were I to record everything that takes place (an impossible feat) would the underlying meaning and importance of each interaction reveal itself.

When I was staying those three days with my aunt Sophie, the Tuesday science section of the *New York Times* featured an article in which child psychology theorists were reported to be changing their minds about what most affects children's personality development. The accepted theory used to be that it is the "major" or "traumatic" events in a child's life which determine the direction his personality will take. Now, the article explained, child psychologists believe that it's the tone and quality of the everyday communication between him and his mother (or main caretaker) which make the major impressions. I had two simultaneous reactions to this. One was: "How stupid. It took them this long to find that out?" The other was: "I'm right, after all! Hurrah!"

Since during the vacation my mind had gone off-duty, I wasn't inclined to figure out what this exultant sense of vindication was all about. I recognize now, though, that it had to do with an interminable argument being conducted out of earshot in some subterranean chamber of my inner self. It goes something like this:

"Oh, come off it. Stop taking every little thing so seriously."

"But you never know how that might have affected them."

"You're guilt-ridden. What will affect them negatively is if they pick up on your own uncertainty. It doesn't matter so much what you do as whether you do it with confidence. Relax."

"But if I relax and just go according to my nature, I'll do all kinds of very damaging things, and might not even realize it."

"For goodness sake, where's your *emunah*? You're going to make them into withering lilies, shrinking...shivering lilies—however that expression goes. How will they get along in the world if you're so overprotective?"

"Children are sensitive."

"So what else is new. Aren't we all? We have to learn to survive, and we do. That's what makes us strong."

"No. Not all of us. The mental hospitals are full of people who don't survive pain with flying colors."

"Those are the exceptions. Those are the ones from families that are completely messed up. Alcoholic parents, the fathers who take out the belt when the kid sneezes, the mothers who scream profanities all day long. Don't be such a worrywart! You're doing all right. You're even *too* kind. You're *too* guilty about acting as any normal mother would, at least any mother in her right mind. Give yourself a break. You think you're doing them a favor by worrying so much? You're just giving them another kind of insecurity, believe me."

"But people in mental hospitals didn't necessarily get obvious maltreatment. Being consistently misunderstood or undervalued is enough to drive a person over the edge, or at least to severely desensitize him. One sort of person cracks, another kind grows a callus over his true self. I don't want to force my children to go either route."

"With your excessive sensitivity you're making *them* unnecessarily sensitive. Your antennae are so high-frequency, they pick up on things that the kids of a normal mother wouldn't."

(With grudging admiration for her critic's self-confidence, and intimidated by the cutting remark:) "What in the world does that mean, too sensitive? If you ignore your natural sensitivity in one area, you simultaneously stunt it in all the other areas right down the line. Sensitivity to beauty, sensitivity to happiness, sensitivity to other people. There are plenty of people who are desensitized, and yes, they function very well in the world, you're right. They learned at their mothers' knees that feeling deeply wasn't in their own best interest, that sensitivity is not necessarily of practical value. But are their lives enriched by this sort of practicality? Does it bring them to become better people? It doesn't make them patient or creative or generous or spiritually oriented, or kind. In most cases people give back to humanity precisely what they have received."

"That sounds good, but you know what's very intriguing? You have plenty of neighbors far less philosophical about child rearing than you are, far less worried—women who aren't trying to be saints but who do raise normal, strong, good kids. Kids who grow up to be *menchen*. And the funny thing is that without all this heroic introspection, they actually end up yelling at their kids a lot less than *some* people I know."

"That's just because they're not honest enough to talk about it. Or my walls are thinner."

"Very possible, but at least when they do yell, their kids know not to take it so seriously. Oh yeah, by the way, wasn't that you I heard screaming this morning when Elisheva wouldn't put on her red sweater?"

(Stung by this low blow:) "But...I'm improving."

"Look, sister, my advice to you is this: lay off the parenting books for a while. Instead of the workshop Tuesday nights, catch up on your sleep. Take it easy, for crying out loud, your kids are fine! Don't examine every little thing to death—it's unnatural. Your kids'll be better behaved, mark my words, and you'll spare yourself an ulcer."

(Armed with no less an authority than the science editor of the *New York Times*:) "Now you listen for a minute, you overconfident Mack truck! The scientists are starting to confirm that every little interchange between mother and child does make an important impression on a child's mind. Each casual put-down, each slightly sarcastic remark, each unconsciously critical glance...each leaves its mark on the child's self-image, though the child may seem to weather these apparently insignificant discomforts and insults quite well. Quite well, that is, until the next generation comes along and then we have a replay. It's right to strive to reduce one's own sensitivity to affronts to one's own honor, it's right to reduce one's own vulnerability to other people's opinions and words, but it's not right to take that attitude towards other people's sensitivity. *And that includes your own children.* It's strange: The world doesn't question that adults deserve respect, that their sense of personal dignity is an inborn characteristic. Tread on it at your own risk. But children! They're resilient! They'll survive! Don't baby them! You'll weaken them by being too careful! Yet children are the ones who are the least armored!"

(With a tolerant smile:) "Is that all?"

I nod.

"Honey, look, your motives are great, but everyone would benefit more if you only had a little bit more faith in yourself. And in G-d. He runs the world, not you."

"But the scientists say..."

"Oh, come on now, please! Scientists schmientists!"

January 14, 1987

Last night, Danny and Yaacov planned out how they would meet at the yeshiva this afternoon and go get haircuts together. But Yaacov called me this morning to say I should expect Danny home at the regular hour; the two of them hadn't confirmed their appointment in the morning, and Danny would probably forget.

Danny arrived home late with a stonily expressionless face.

Once inside the door he exploded. "Daddy is so stupid! He wasn't there! He told me to go to the yeshiva after school, and he wasn't there! When he comes home tonight I'm going to HIT him!" Danny's face was red, his fists were clenched and he had started sobbing. He took his briefcase and slammed it against the wall.

What's wrong with my son that he should have such incredible anger? I thought. *There's something very wrong with him!* I was about to reprimand him when I recalled something from the workshop: if a child gets angry, it doesn't mean there's something wrong with him, or that he's basically unhappy, or that he has a psychological problem—any more than your own anger necessarily means these things about you. Nor does it indicate that you have failed as a parent. It does mean that he hasn't learned to tolerate frustration, and if he gets angry often, it means he has developed a bad habit. You can help him change this habit, but don't try to do so in the midst of one of his outbursts.

So for the moment I refrained from comment, yet was taken aback by the man-like depth of his rage. Daniel was utterly broken. I worried: *Why should this situation convince him that Yaacov has betrayed him, forgotten him...unless he already suffers from an underlying sense of rejection?* "Do you want to go to the barber with me, Danny? I can take you."

"NO!" he lashed out. "I want to go with Daddy!"

A quarter-hour later, Yaacov called to check that Daniel had arrived home, and I told him what happened. "Danny!" I called. "Daddy wants to speak with you."

Danny ran out of his room with a little smile. Before coming to the phone he dashed to the mirror and arranged his hair with the palms of his hands, and looked closely to see if his eyes were red. Then he took the receiver.

"Daddy?" he said as softly as a lamb.

Daniel nodded his head.

"Yes." He nodded again.

"Yes."

"Yes."

He smiled.

"Bye-bye."

Later on this afternoon, I found a quiet moment. "Danny, you are not allowed to say that Daddy is stupid. A mistake happened. He didn't want to hurt you or forget you."

Daniel looked at me and didn't say anything.

There are other things I wish I had said, but didn't think of, such as: "Next time you feel hurt and angry, can you tell me about it without screaming?" Or: "This is what's called a misunderstanding, Danny. It happens between people often, and it will happen in your life many, many times." Or: "How disappointed you must have been, Danny. Maybe you even thought Daddy didn't care, G-d forbid. I understand! Daddy cares so much. He just thought you weren't coming."

Later this afternoon, Chaim, the son of our upstairs neighbors, came to tell me that Danny had kicked him. Not having gotten over my fears about Danny's temper earlier on, this got the red lights in my brain flashing all over again. In my heart of hearts I wondered frantically if Daniel's anger is actually exceptional, the mirror image of my own temper...the result of too much parental pressure through his early years. "That may very well be so," Miriam might reply, "but knowing it, and feeling guilty about it, might not be of much help to you when you're on the spot, faced with the problem. Guilt and agony won't better equip you to help him. Better to develop your skills in the present than to engage in psychological research, for we can never really know, after all, why a child behaves as he does."

I sent Dinah downstairs to get Daniel, but she returned with the message that he didn't want to come. My anger and fear flared up higher. I envisioned dragging Danny to Chaim's mother to apologize, less for the sake of Danny's education than for my own reputation as a responsible parent, and sent Dinah down again. When Danny finally appeared, he seemed to shrink upon confronting my seething presence. "What happened, Danny? Did you kick Chaim?"

"Yes, but he kicked me first."

"He did?" I asked hopefully.

Danny nodded. I looked now at Chaim. "Is that so, Chaim? Did you kick Danny first?"

Chaim bent his head shyly to the side and nodded.

He kicked Danny first, he kicked Danny first! Thank G-d!

And all the bluebirds sang.

The children are now asleep.

After dinner, Dinah, Rachel and Daniel were playing "gumie" in the living room, an Israeli form of jump rope in which, in this particular version, a long elastic band (the kind used to gather skirts) is held at either end by two children seated on the floor. They wave and shake the elastic back and forth for a third child, who has to jump over it without touching.

Elisheva, thumb in mouth, was watching from the sidelines as the three of them played. Daniel turned to her. "You want to play, too?" he asked, so kindly that my heart fluttered like a butterfly. *He's so kind and sensitive. What a beautiful little boy.*

January 18, 1987

Today I bought four books about *tzadikkim* for Danny and Rachel.

I was in my bedroom straightening up the closet, anticipating Daniel's return from school so I could see his face light up when I gave him the books. All of a sudden I heard a tremendous banging and kicking at the front door. Oh! I hadn't heard the buzzer! I ran to get the door, whereupon Daniel flew into the house like a hurricane. Again, his wildness, impatience and capacity for rage threw me into a tizzy of worry and introspection. What could he be thinking? That I'm ignoring him because I don't love him? That I'm persecuting him? Or is he just exhausted and hungry? I should have said, "It's hard to wait for a few minutes at the door until I hear, isn't it?" but I didn't say anything. I was abashed.

He had something to eat and disappeared. Some minutes later

he came across the bag of books. "Whose are these?" he said.

"Yours and Rachel's."

He looked at me, smiled, ran to get an apple and took a seat. He's been reading now for an hour and a half. He just got up to get a rice cake, and I was about to remind him that the children aren't allowed to eat that sort of thing in the living room when he made an about-face. "Mommy, you know what?" He smiled so happily. "I was JUST going now to sit on the couch and eat this when I remembered that you said not to bring it in here!" His face lit up with pride at having remembered and obeyed.

I am so proud, and grateful for this good behavior. His wildness completely subsides when he has a good book. I feel like rising before the audience and proclaiming to one and all: "You see! You were wrong! I don't have a problem child! I've done very well as a parent! It's just that we have here a classic case of what the pedagogical scientists call low frustration tolerance. And he's so brilliant that he needs a lot of intellectual stimulation. He can't tolerate boredom because he's so smart!"

I wait for the envious murmurs of admiration and the polite applause, but the only people out there in the audience are Yaacov and I.

Daniel hugged me around the neck after two hours of reading, then ran out to play. He must not have found any of his friends, though, because he returned a few minutes later and started flitting around the house in his usual manner, like a lost moth bumping against a lamp shade, looking for light. I caught myself before suggesting that he read one of the new books, which would have been tantamount to saying: "I got you new books. I thought that would get rid of you!"

So often, the process of improving my communication with the children is less a matter of finding the right words than of just eliminating the wrong ones.

Now he's getting on my nerves again, with his restlessness and his boredom and the resulting aggressiveness toward his sisters. Shall I now go ahead and conclude, as it comes naturally to do, that I *have* failed as a parent, that he *is* a problem child? That he does have a deep problem and that it's my fault? Why, just five minutes ago he was the apple of my eye and the feather in my cap!

The reality is that Daniel Binyamin experiences a wide spectrum of emotions and manifests many different kinds of behavior, like human beings throughout time. Like me. He has a lifetime of self-correction and growth before him, as do we all. Yet I hold this seven-year-old child up as my mirror, and search there for my own perfect self-image.

It's bedtime. I'm so tired. I've started yelling. Please, Sarah, stop.

Later. I did stop. I think I'll go put on lipstick. That'll make me feel more organized.

January 19, 1987

This afternoon I was on the phone when Elisheva burst into the house sobbing so hard that she couldn't catch her breath. Though her words were mostly indecipherable, I gathered that some girl downstairs had refused to play with her.

Elisheva's sorrow struck a responsive chord in me—that submerged but still live experience of having been excluded, and of having believed that it was because I was different, unlovable, somehow horrible. There are children who strike back at such rejections, either with words or with fists, and there are children, like me, to whom striking back never occurred. It was obvious to me that the rejection had happened on account of my own deficiencies, and I never told my parents about it. How much of this was because I was aware of being the only Jewish child around, I don't know. We lived not in an apartment house but in an isolated old house surrounded by woods, so I never really got immunized against the cruel rough-and-tumble of normal childhood society. A gesture of rejection like that which my daughter suffered today would have been for me of long-term significance.

"Come downstairs NOW!" Elisheva cried, pulling at my dress. "Come NOW!"

Yaacov spoke up from the couch. "Don't go, Sarah. It's not necessary." For a few weeks I've had a sciatic pain in my left leg that makes walking here in the apartment difficult, let alone up and down the four flights of stairs, while he himself is incapacitated by a foot injury. We've been extending to each other the courteous, exaggerated solicitousness of fellow invalids. But heroine that I am, I shrugged off his concern and set off on my journey downstairs.

"THERE SHE IS! You SEE? THAT GIRL THERE!" Elisheva towed me along behind her, pointing to a diminutive blonde perhaps a year younger than she. One of the boys tapped the little girl on the shoulder, to warn of the mother's approach, and she spun around, her delicate face set in a pose of defiance and anxiety.

"Shalom," I greeted her cordially, kneeling down to speak eye-to-eye.

She didn't respond.

"Do you know, it hurt Elisheva's feelings so much when you wouldn't let her play with you." My voice sounded admirably warm and gentle to my own ears. She was quiet. She listened intently. I went on. "And do you know that it's written in the Torah that we are not permitted to hurt other people?" This sentence caused me some problems because I don't know the Hebrew infinitive for "hurt." She still said nothing. Three or four kids had gathered around us now, and out of the corner of my eye I glanced at Elisheva. She was following the proceedings closely. I hoped they all thought my childlike Hebrew was a sign of my willingness to speak on their level. The little girl gazed at me fearlessly now. Had I made a mistake in grammar?

At this point Elisheva took it upon herself to demonstrate how this child had prevented her with outstretched arms from playing with the others. The girl responded with a rapid stream of complicated self-defense, of which I understood not one word. I nodded my head emphatically. When she finished, I remained silent for a long moment, as if to weigh her words, then issued my verdict: "But if someone *had* told you not to play with everybody, wouldn't it hurt your feelings, too?"

For a split second she stared at me. Then, with a little grin, declared: "No!"

The children, including Elisheva, all giggled.

"No?" I asked quietly, "It really wouldn't hurt you?"

"NO!"

Now the children, including Elisheva, doubled over and squealed with laughter. I rose, gathering up my dignity like rumpled skirts around me. Sensing that somehow or other my mission had been accomplished, I undertook majestically the laborious ascent to the fourth floor. Elisheva stayed downstairs to play with them and returned home in a half-hour, her spirit intact, with fresh concerns and new complaints.

January 20, 1987

I was just on the phone with Bluma. I mentioned that I'm keeping a journal about being a mother. "Sarah," she told me, "then I'll tell you: you don't know how to discipline."

Why did this get the adrenaline going? She wasn't telling me anything I didn't already know. "Well, the journal's all about how I'm trying to learn how to discipline with a woman who's been giving classes about it. I know I don't know how. That's what the journal's all about, trying to learn how." I heard myself being redundant.

"Oh, I see," she said apologetically. "I see. Very good. But you know, Sarah, a friend is not someone who just goes along, yes, yes, with everything you do and never says anything. Right?"

I braced myself. "Right."

"So I'll tell you: you give too much attention."

I bristled with a strange fear. "I don't agree. Every mother has to go according to her own personality and background. What you say might have been right for you and your children but not for me and my children."

It gratified me to retort, yet I was unsteady. I wanted to dismiss what she was saying as the trademark of her strict Swedish upbringing with its aversion to overtly expressed affection. Yet here was another case of my peculiar vulnerability to anyone who comes along and implies that I'm spoiling my children. What is this universal disdain for the emotional neediness and vulnerability of children, and why am I so susceptible to its arguments? I respect this woman too much to simply ignore her opinions and conveniently change the subject; her words had already slipped in, and my self-confidence had been wounded. Deep inside lurked the fear that if I lack equilibrium in relation to my children, it is because I lack equilibrium in relation to myself. Dear me, I thought. For me to change the quality of attention I give my children would be like trying to change the wardrobe of my soul. There was something true in what she said that rang a bell, but something else that constituted danger to the whole course I wanted to travel with my children. I felt awfully defensive, but wanted to be open-minded so that maybe I could learn something. She had touched on a raw nerve.

"I'll give you an example," she continued. "Let's say you have a retarded child, six years old but he acts like three. So if he does something, then you have to praise him very much. 'Ooooh! How nice! How wonderful!'"

I recognized her imitation of me, and my back went up. Why was this so annoying? "I know what you're going to say. That you don't have to do that with a normal child."

"Exactly."

"Yeah, I know. If you overpraise a child, he won't believe you. And also, he'll depend on the praise too much."

I could tell by her pause that she was mildly surprised I knew the right answer. "He won't believe you, right," she went on, "and yet he also becomes addicted to it like a drug. He starts clinging to his mother because he can't get that drug from anyone else, not his father and not his friends."

I was angry now. That key word: clinging. It refers to anything from a two-year-old's fear of strangers, to a newborn crying to be picked up, to a ten-year-old who climbs on his mother's lap. *Don't swallow it whole!* I warned myself. *It's that ancient put-down! It's her rigid upbringing. Don't let this advice affect you! Don't let her throw you off balance!* She might be sincerely trying to help, but she has certain prejudices against showing love. There was something right about what Bluma was saying...but there was also a lot wrong.

"You know what it is?" I said. "Before, when I was yelling at the children too much, I'd praise them to compensate for my mistakes. Now, it's getting more balanced. I don't feel very guilty these days, so my praise is also leveling out. But I disagree with you about the retarded child thing. I think all children need to be encouraged much more than we think they do. Don't we all yearn for love and encouragement much more than we admit? *So why not grant it to each other?* Especially to children! Why the taboo? And if it's done in an honest way—and I can tell you that I really do feel as enthusiastic as I sound—"

"All right. Maybe you're right." I could just see her on the other end, nodding her head with patient tolerance for her young American friend's half-cocked ideas. "Every mother has to decide for herself."

"*Too much* encouragement can be discouraging and inhibiting, it's true," I conceded, now that she had laid down her arms. "Anyone with a little brains can tell when he's being patronized, when somebody is being overly encouraging, but that's when it's not authentic. It makes you feel stupid—the exact opposite of what a mother wants."

"Look, Sarah." Bluma sounded weary. "I can look back now and see the mistakes I made with my children. I was very good at two things: discipline and not making them jealous. Even if one was very, very good at something, I never said anything to make the others feel jealous. But in other ways I made mistakes."

"Like what?"

"Well, I didn't give them enough love."

Amazing. An amazing confession. "You mean attention?"

"Attention...well, yes, attention and love. My children tell me today that they didn't know what I felt. They never could tell if I liked what they were doing. Oh, well, I just didn't know."

January 21, 1987

This morning, with Yaacov at home on the couch with his injured foot, I was showing off for him, doing a lot of housework in spite of the pain in my leg, and feeling proud of myself for making myself function. Before going up to the roof to hang laundry, I pulled on a pair of warmer stockings and had to pause. *What's that?* I was incredulous, I was horrified, to see that some bluish veins had appeared on my calves.

WHAT? ME? LITTLE SARAḤ? VARICOSE VEINS? THAT'S GOING TOO FAR! IT CANNOT BE!

I looked again, more closely. Perhaps it was something else.

No!

My self-sacrificing zeal to exert myself dissolved. Who *cares* about mind over matter! Who *cares* about impressing Yaacov that I'm putting up the laundry! The only thing that matters is saving my legs! What an injustice! I shall never accept varicose veins! I'll get into bed until they go away.

ME? Varicose veins? No. It shall not be.

No. No. No.

January 22, 1987

After lunch, Daniel bid us a hasty farewell and rushed out to play. Yaacov hobbled as fast as he could to the door. "Danny!" he called out. "Wait!" Danny stopped on the stairs, impatient as a colt restrained from the pasture.

"Danny," Yaacov implored sweetly, with just a hint of anguish, "you want to help Mommy and me by doing us a big favor and taking down the garbage, because Mommy and I are both having pains in our legs and we can't do it?"

"No! I can't!" Danny answered breathlessly, as if the herd were leaving without him. My goodness, I thought to myself, what in the world is going on in this family if we're reduced to begging for help from our children.

"Please, Danny," he entreated patiently.

Danny heaved a sigh of excruciating frustration, raced back up to our door, grabbed one of the three bags I'd set in the hallway and flew downstairs.

Around an hour later, after a brief visit home to grab an apple, Danny was speeding out the door when the same exchange began again. "Danny," called Yaacov, "you want to take just one more bag, honey? It would be a mitzvah because Mommy and I can't do it." Danny looked with disgust at the two bulging bags. "You can take the lighter one," said Yaacov.

At this, Danny paused reflectively. "I'll take both," he announced, taking a huge stuffed bag in each hand and making his way to the stairs.

"Gee, isn't that nice," I said. "I've got to write that down in my diary. You said he could take the lighter one, so he felt good and took both. What a nice way to inspire a child to help."

Yaacov limped back to the couch. "Well, just don't draw any general conclusions from it. If you took a hundred kids and told them all the same thing, 'take the lighter one,' you think they'd all take down two? Even with our five kids they'd probably all react differently. Even Danny might do something different if I said the same thing tomorrow." Yaacov cast about for a comfortable position. "Each child's different." He stretched out cautiously. Two of the sofa cushions are lower than the third because some springs are broken. He placed his foot ever so carefully on an arm rest. "Each day is different."

January 24, 1987

It's not to England that I'm traveling.
It's not to France.
It's not to Thailand I am going.

I am going
to clean off the stove
and wipe the milk off the fridge. I'm going
I'm on my way
to the emptiness
of the house after the children have left for school,
when I and my coffee cup
will murmur nothing, and we will gaze
at the bright, cloudy blank of the window.

Up, up and away.
I'm in a hurry. I've said goodbye. I've said so
long!
All by myself, I will be here
in myself, with the refrigerator humming.
I'm letting go.   And I shall sail

my sails getting fuller
my sails are filling out in the soft breeze

into my own

it's my very own

whiteness

10
The Beginning of a World

January 25, 1987

We went to a *bris* this morning.

This mystifies me: When a baby is born, everyone is so happy. Everyone treats the mother like royalty, as if she had just brought the sweetest possible blessing into the world. She's a heroine, a lucky heroine, for she's been deemed worthy of the highest honor and privilege: the gift of a tiny, important, pure human being to care for. It's the cause for such celebration!

But by the time that kid is four or five (unless he's an only child, in which case he stands a good chance of retaining his royal status) the celebration has pretty much fizzled out. Now he's a nudge, she's fussy, he's stubborn, she's got the terrible twos, he doesn't listen, she always wants me to carry her, he's acting like a baby, we love her when she's asleep, ha ha. Another baby comes along, and all over again, we are enchanted, we are grateful, we thank G-d. Maybe this baby will be our new lease on life. (With the others we made so many mistakes.) We make of the *bris* or *kiddush* a lovely *simchah*, and everyone understands: something great has happened. We have been entrusted with a soul.

A few weeks ago I attended one of Miriam Adahan's EMETT classes. I hadn't been able to go for a long time, so many of the faces were new to me. One woman was worried and unhappy with herself for being impatient with her seven-year-old boy. "He's a wonderful boy. I don't know why I get so mad at him for such silly things, like losing his pencil. He's always losing his pencils, and I'm always getting mad at him for it. It's so ridiculous. I mean, what's a pencil? For that I crush him. I see that I'm very good with the babies. I have a lot of patience, and I can give a great deal of love and be tolerant of all kinds of discomfort that they put me through. But then, as they get older, I get progressively more critical."

Her words, and her disquiet, have been on my mind. What is it that gradually, stealthily, robs us of our awareness of the gift?

Tonight on the phone with my friend Angie, I wondered out loud about it. "Oh, well, an innocent little baby doesn't bring out the bad in us. We want to give and be kind and gentle to this helpless little chicken, and we like ourselves for being so good. But as soon as he starts being a person, as soon as he starts bringing out the bad in us—our not wanting to give, our wanting to control, and our self-centeredness—we're disappointed in ourselves and get angry at him for being the cause. We're angry at him for making us feel what's inside us."

January 26, 1987

Last year, Rachel's first-grade teacher gave birth the day after I did. She must have noticed that I'm pregnant again, because this year she's Dinah's teacher, and we see each other from time to time. I find myself daydreaming about her: Does she remember that we gave birth together last year? Does she admire me for being fast at the gate? Does she wonder how I manage? Is she (I wish) envious? Or does she consider herself lucky not to be in my shoes? The daydream slips my mind, then later on I find myself going through a rerun. Such a waste of my mental energy! I don't know what it is that keeps me hooked on this ridiculous fantasy, when I'm surely not getting equal time over there on *her* brain waves. She doesn't give a hoot if Dinah Shapiro's mother is or is not pregnant again, especially in Jerusalem, where every other passerby looks as if she should be on her way to a maternity ward.

As I was thinking about it again today, a peculiar thought crossed my mind: "How boring it must be to have one baby and not be pregnant. Too easy. I'm lucky to have been given such a challenge."

January 27, 1987

Yesterday afternoon, Elisheva had the longest tantrum of her career. From start to finish, it must have lasted an hour and a half. It had its onset in a shove. Daniel had left his dish of noodles on the table for a few minutes, and when he came back to finish, Elisheva was in his chair. He pushed, she fell with a hard bump, she started crying, he yelled something, she cried more loudly, she started kicking, wailing and screaming.

I observed this from the couch through half-closed eyes, put out of commission by the pain in my leg. The best approach appeared to be to ignore it all, a course chosen not for reasons of child education but because I was so, so tired.

My friend Honey is here for a vacation but has ended up helping me. She's gentle and soft-spoken. She leaned down and tried to lift Elisheva to her feet. Limp as a waterlogged rag doll, Elisheva continued crying. "Elisheva." Honey spoke her name quietly and stroked her forehead. "Elisheva." Elisheva grew more hysterical. I hoped fervently that all this wouldn't wake up the baby, who had just gone to sleep.

After fifteen minutes, it occurred to me that maybe if Danny would say he was sorry, Elisheva would feel better. He was willing to be of assistance, but somehow misunderstood. Thinking I had asked him to bring her over to me, he dragged her on the floor from the kitchen to the couch. During the ride over, her head hit a table leg. My heart winced. How I wanted to just go over there and pick her up in my arms!

Once by my side, she began kicking the sliding glass door to the *mirpesset*, which infuriated me. I propped myself up on one elbow, reached over and gave her a spanking, which naturally only made matters worse. Up until then, I had been hoping to impress Honey with my serenity under trying circumstances. Even though we've been close friends for twenty years, I was getting more and more embarrassed to have her see us like this. I was a good case for the proposition that no one should ever, ever get pregnant. "I should have had lunch ready when they came home," I explained to Honey, implying that under normal conditions I have everything under control. "Elisheva's blood sugar level must be very low right now."

Honey leaned down to whisper in Elisheva's ear. "I'll read you a story if you'd like, while you eat your lunch." Elisheva cried and kicked.

I was concentrating on not feeling what I was feeling. If I got upset, I feared that out of my weakness and discomfort, I would end up screaming. Over the din, or shall I say under it, I said: "Elisheva, I'm getting up now, and I'm going to go into your room to sit down on your bed. I'm going to wait for you there. When you want to come in and talk, I'll be there waiting for you." I wanted to convey two messages: that I wasn't going to listen to this tantrum anymore, but that I do love her and care about her and want to help. It was to *her* bed that I was going. I reached over to the end table, wanting something to read in Elisheva's room, and picked up the book *Gesher HaChaim*.

I brought myself carefully down the hall, my hand against the wall, and took a seat on Elisheva's bed. Clothes and toys were lying around messily. I longed for the simple, mindless, remarkable well-being that would have enabled me to whisk everything up off the floor and restore order in a few easy seconds. Elisheva was still crying. I was helpless. I opened the book.

"It is man's ability to choose freely that is the greatest single factor in the shaping of himself and his life. Every deed, every word or thought wrought from every turn, influences one's character, the effect being cumulative. Moreover, every resulting change in character will itself bring about great changes in one's manner of living and in the events of his life...One may well ask:

What power does man possess? He is a puny creature on Earth, his life confused and brief. How can he become a meaningful partner in this system of Creation?" I looked up and lost my place. Elisheva was still hysterical. Perhaps she hadn't heard what I'd said? I opened to another page. "The measure of a man can be taken by his love for others. To the degree that he fulfills 'Love your neighbor as yourself' we know that his love for himself is to do G-d's will. If he hates his fellow man, it indicates that his self-love is pure egotism, the physical love characteristic of the animal world. Even if he does love certain other people, a relative or someone who does him favors, this is merely a manifestation of his self-love. True self-love is to love the next person as well, for such is the way of the Torah."

Elisheva's shrill screams and shuddering sobs got louder. I leaned over to peek out the door. She was propelling herself along by her hands, dragging herself towards her room on her stomach. It struck me that I would never forget that image, of Elisheva on the floor, in the pits of grief, reduced to crawling toward me on her belly. At the door, there on the floor, she said something that I could barely make out, ragged as her voice was with sobs: "I want you to pick me up."

Elisheva knew she was asking for the one thing I can't do. Whenever I lift anything, that needle-like stab of the nerve shoots through me, an electric laser. Much has been made lately of Mommy's inability to lift, under any circumstances. Dr. Shupak forbade it. "I can't pick you up, darling, because my leg hurts me, but if you come over to me, I can pick you up on my lap."

She shook her head vigorously, crying. "NO! I want you to pick me UP!"

I held out my arms as invitingly as I knew how. "Come, darling."

More kicking and screaming. Then, through the noise, another sound: of the baby crying in the other room. She had woken him up. How long had he been screaming? A wave of dim, dark tiredness came over me. I thought of the baby on its way, and of my leg, of Elisheva, of Eli. I thought: How am I going to get through this. I looked into Elisheva's eyes and got frightened. She was really suffering. Oh, G-d, please help me. How will I ever take care of them all?

Suddenly Elisheva's point of view dawned upon me: Mommy holds that baby Eli but she never holds me, and now everyone says another one of those babies is coming, because Mommy's pregnant, and that's why she can't pick me up...Will Mommy never be mine again?

Don't be a fool, I imagined Yaacov warning me. *There are other ways of giving her love. You can hurt yourself.* I offered again to take her on my lap, but she cried. No, she wanted precisely that gesture granted only to babies, that which was to her denied. She probably wasn't conscious of what it was she was testing, but knew that only this would prove...would prove...

I leaned down, braced myself for that shooting pain, and arose with Elisheva in my arms.

There was no shooting pain.

She was still thrashing around, hysterical. I told her to wrap her legs around my waist (what's left of it) and she did. I patted her head, held her close, rocked back and forth. A moment passed. Her arms lifted up and encircled my neck, and her head came to rest on my shoulder. She was trying to catch her breath.

Slowly, for the first time all afternoon, she grew still. We rocked. I pushed the door shut so we'd be all alone.

Then I sat down on the bed.

We rocked.

After a time, she picked up her head and ventured in a small voice: "I want you to feed me noodles." (She has never allowed me to feed her.) I rose with her in my arms and carried her down the hall to the kitchen, hearing, as I passed an open door, Honey in calm conversation with Rachel and Dinah. I was glad no one was around to tell me I should be more careful. We sat down on a kitchen chair and began, bite by bite, the noodles that could no longer have been hot. Elisheva did not complain. She didn't mind the congealed butter. After each spoonful, she turned to me, her tear-streaked face exhausted with grief, looked into my eyes, and smiled.

"Yesterday there were three big pussycats downstairs," she said.

"Is that so?"

She had gotten what she needed. I'm so very happy that I disobeyed the rules.

January 28, 1987

This afternoon I called Yaacov at the yeshiva. "I think you better come home now," I said. "It's better for me to give up." I must have fallen asleep as soon as my head hit the pillow. Sometime during the night I awoke and felt something angular and hard protruding a little uncomfortably from my abdomen. I turned over and passed my hand over the spot. It had already moved away. What was it?

A leg. An arm, maybe.

Boy, there really is a baby in there, I thought, startled.

I'm going to have another baby.

In my half-dream state, I panicked. How am I going to take care of this baby and that baby, and the others?

I fell asleep again, frightened.

January 29, 1987

Yesterday Dr. Shupak informed me that aside from the problem in my leg, I also have bronchitis. The coughing aggravates the sciatic nerve. I gave this information to Yaacov, who had taken off from the yeshiva to watch the children during my appointment, as if I were delivering a precious gem. Bronchitis! Boy, that's nothing to sneeze at! That's a reason to get into bed! Which is precisely what Yaacov told me to do. Yippee!

I climbed into the bed, pulled up the covers, blissful. Dinah and Elisheva peeked through the door.

"Hello," I said.

They smiled. "Are you sick?" asked Dinah.

"Yes. You want to visit me?"

With their eyes glued upon me in this strange state, they sidled in hesitantly along the wall. "Why are you sick?" asked Elisheva.

"I guess I must have gone outside without my coat," I answered, thinking I might as well make of myself an object-lesson. I adjusted my pillows, coughed impressively and sank down deeper into the covers, forgetting to conceal the pleasures of being ill. "Oh, these blankets are delicious."

"Delicious?" Dinah looked puzzled.

"Yes, delicious."

"DeLICious?" Dinah squealed.

"DELICIOUS?" Elisheva giggled.

"Yes, delicious."

The two of them sputtered, giggled and guffawed, then jumped onto my bed and rolled in their laughter all over the blankets. They held their sides and threw back their heads with scorn and delight at such a ridiculous idea, while the baby looked on from his crib in benign confusion.

January 31, 1987

Shabbat was our ninth anniversary. I forgot.

On Friday, Yaacov did all the work for Shabbat and I stayed in bed. I heard him gradually getting nervous, as one by one the house filled up with the kids returning home from school. I wanted to be alone, I didn't want anyone to even make a peep at me, and barked whenever my door opened up so much as a crack. By the time Shabbat came in, both Yaacov and I were in a horrible mood, glaring at each other fiercely, snapping at the children. I was so depressed. I thought: "What kind of home is this for these children? There's nothing here for them." I felt drained, emptied of any spirit.

We were having a horrible, tense Shabbat, until Yaacov took all of them for a walk in Sanhedrin Park. They came back buoyant and excited. Yaacov and I exchanged small smiles.

February 1, 1987

Today is my mother's birthday. I wish I could be with her.

Last night Dinah cleaned up the kitchen and living room. It was really a help to me because I was so tired. Just now she put away the groceries and fed the baby his yogurt. Then, as I went upstairs to the roof to take down laundry, she called out after me: "If the water boils over, I'll turn off the fire."

Oops, I hadn't remembered that I had started cooking a pot of noodles. Wasn't it dangerous to let her turn off the gas? But should I deny her this opportunity to demonstrate maturity? "O.K.!" I cheerily replied, eager to encourage her helpfulness. But as I pulled the clothes off the line, I had a scary fantasy that she'd turn the wrong dial and there'd be an explosion, and would Yaacov ever speak to me again, and for the rest of my life I'd never be able to live with myself...*What a fool I am for saying she could turn off the stove! That's going too far!* I hurried downstairs. Dinah was holding open the apartment door. "The water didn't go over the top," she told me. Then, as I walked in: "You know why I opened the door?"

"No, why?"

"I heard you coming down the stairs and I knew you couldn't open it yourself because you're carrying the clothes. So I opened the door for you!"

"Oh, thank you!" I dashed to the stove. Sure enough, the water hadn't boiled over. In fact, the pot was almost empty...I'd forgotten to put the noodles in. How ridiculous.

Without knowing that I could use a compliment at that moment, Dinah then proclaimed: "Mommy, you know you're the best mommy because you let me do things that other mommies don't let their children do. Miriam doesn't let her children touch the stove."

This evoked pleasure and guilt at once. Pleasure, because that's that neighbor of ours whom all my children idolize. Guilt because of my pleasure, and my jealousy, and because Miriam is probably right.

February 2, 1987

I yelled twice at Rachel during bedtime tonight, but she wasn't crushed by it as she used to be. I am so happy for that. I think it's because ninety to ninety-five percent of the time now, I'm speaking quietly. We've reached what I consider a normal plateau, where the children can more easily assimilate my lapses and failures.

February 3, 1987

Yaacov stayed with the baby today while I went to Misgav Ladach Maternity Hospital for a checkup. I took Rachel with me. I knew she'd enjoy seeing the newborns in the nursery. While there, I saw my friend Judith. I didn't know that she's been there for the past four months, assigned to bed because her cervix has opened prematurely. She has had a miscarriage in every one of her pregnancies. "Today is our twelfth anniversary," she told me. "Shmuel and I have been waiting a long time for this child." She is due about the same time as I am. I felt guilty and spoiled. Here Judith was going to such lengths to save her pregnancy, while I...

When Rachel and I went down to the maternity ward, I ran into Bracha Goetz, who was my inspiring, encouraging neighbor when I lived on the *yishuv*. Bracha is known for her capacity to be happy under any circumstance. She has a five-year-old boy and had very much wanted another son, but she was holding her newborn, her fourth girl, with something like ecstasy. "I feel like I'm running a girls' school." She looked down at the baby's face with a wry smile and shook her head with wonder. "Five children. Amazing. The circle's getting bigger."

It's the coughing that finally got me to go for this checkup today, because each time I cough there's a shooting pain along the sciatic nerve, and my legs seem to be coming unhinged. Poor me! The doctor (I chose a woman, because I thought she'd be more compassionate, ha ha) hardly showed any astonishment at all that I was suffering so. Why, she acted as if discomfort during pregnancy is normal! She informed me that everything is all right with the pregnancy, that it would be about six more weeks, that the baby is a small one, and last but not least, that I should get back into bed for three or four days to effect a full recovery from the bronchitis.

Once again, I carried this information home to Yaacov, gift-wrapped carefully in my pleasurable anticipation, and presented it to him on a platter of vindication. See? I'm not just complaining! I fell into bed and slid between the sheets as if into a marvelous pond.

February 5, 1987

After one day in bed, I told Yaacov he could return to the yeshiva, hoping he'd admire my self-sacrifice. By seven thirty this evening, however, my strength had ebbed. At bedtime I started yelling and spanking.

"Mommy! Look!" It was Danny calling me, Danny whom I had just spanked. I turned around to see what he wanted and he reached up to hug me around the neck and kiss me. Then he stroked my cheek and smiled. He had empathy for me even though I had hit him. He understood that what I needed was to be calmed down with love. How beautiful.

February 7, 1987

Sometimes I think that the most important thing to come of my attendance at the workshop is the effect it has had upon me as a wife. My having developed the habit of expressing worries, complaints, objections and disagreements in a low voice to my husband has elevated the marriage, and the whole household along with it.

Last week he showed me this excerpt from the ArtScroll biography of the Chofetz Chaim: "It is told that the Maggid of Dubno was once asked: How is it that the Vilna Gaon was never heard speaking any stern words of rebuke to his students and disciples, and nevertheless they were men of great piety and deep reverence towards G-d? He replied that the best way to improve another person is to improve one's own self to such an extent that the other must be influenced."

I have tried for years to tone down my anger. I wonder why it is that Miriam Levi got through to me. Is it the simple exposure to her personal example? She speaks so quietly that sometimes I can't even hear what she's saying without leaning forward in my chair, but she claims she's not naturally soft-spoken; she had to become so.

Steering oneself away from guilt goes hand in hand with expecting a lot of oneself. We all claim to believe in the Torah, yet excuse ourselves from living it.

In a workshop once, Miriam Levi presented us with an imaginary situation: you come home and find that the white wallpaper in your living room has been written all over with red magic marker. You can scream, "WHAT DID YOU DO! HOW COULD YOU DO THAT!" Or you can speak quietly and communicate precisely the same thing, minus the implication that the children are bad. In a very low tone you can inquire: "What on earth did you do? How could you do that?" I remember how one of the women in the workshop broke out in a bitter laugh. "What do you expect us to be—saints?"

That's it! I thought. That sums up what prevents us from becoming who we could become: that cynic within who calls high goals overly idealistic, unrealistic, unattainable. It's all right for the Chofetz Chaim, but for us it's only an inspirational story. We plead helplessness before our own natures.

Some months ago I had a conversation with Menuchah, who was in her ninth month. "I'm always screaming at my children. I'm just at the end of my rope!" she told me.

I told her about the workshop that was going on.

"Oh, yeah, I've read her book and I liked it when I read it, but I'm telling you, when you're pregnant it's a whole different ball game. It's all very well and good to tell someone to keep her voice down and think all these nice, calming things when the kids are tearing the place apart, but when you're pregnant you just can't. You're so tired, and you have all these hormones going full blast that make it impossible to stay in control of yourself. Maybe someday when I'm not pregnant I'll go to one of those workshops, but now, forget it. It wouldn't do any good."

This conversation took place when I was in upheaval over my own pregnancy, and only now do I realize how frequently that discussion has replayed itself in my mind. She had spoken with such matter-of-fact conviction that any idea to the contrary seemed like a romantic illusion. Already well indoctrinated with the belief that pregnancy makes staying calm impossible, her words had reinforced it.

This past Friday, when I was lying in bed listening to Yaacov grow progressively more nervous with the children, I noticed a change in my attitude. I wasn't condemning him. "Oh no, here he goes," I thought. "He's getting tired. I know just how he feels. That's just how I get. He's tried to keep it up, he was talking quietly for so long."

Under similar circumstances in the past, I would have thought: "Why can't he just control himself!"

Lower my standards...raise my standards higher. To change anything in myself, I have to do both.

February 8, 1987

I think that writing in this journal helps me to behave more admirably, because it makes me feel I'm being observed. In the back of my mind, when I start criticizing or hitting or yelling, I feel like a phony if I don't record it. Also, the journal gives me the feeling that I'm striving towards a goal. My efforts are not lost, my mistakes are not insignificant, my progress is actual and visible.

If recording my deeds in this journal affects me positively, how much more could I benefit by realizing that all my words and actions are, indeed, always recorded. If I truly understood this, my behavior would change in the twinkling of an eye.

February 10, 1987

Both legs are hurting so much. As soon as I say that, I wonder what "so much" is. I mean, they do hurt me, but human beings suffer far, far worse pains than this in life. So: my legs hurt me, I want to lie down, I have wanted to call Yaacov at the yeshiva all afternoon to ask him to come home, but didn't, and I'm glad. I kept on going. I feel happy. The children are playing. I can't put them to bed because of my legs. I made a good dinner for them, which relaxed them and put them in a good mood. I feel good about myself tonight. I'm not miserable in spite of pain, and this makes me happy with myself.

Miriam Adahan's statement that "every act of self-restraint is an act of self-esteem" has become especially meaningful tonight.

The poor baby, he spent most of the afternoon in his crib because I didn't want to chase him around the apartment anymore. But he was all right.

It's a challenge to describe what's going on in this apartment right now. I told the children—begged is more like it—to please, please get dressed in pajamas by themselves, quickly, because my legs hurt and I couldn't help them. Which is to say, I couldn't yell because of the bronchitis and I couldn't push anybody around because of my legs. That was about an hour ago.

Or was it two hours.

I grabbed the apple juice concentrate out of Elisheva's hands and said I'd make her a drink, but only after she was in pajamas. This ignited one of her tantrums. I asked Rachel for help. She tried to get Elisheva into pajamas, without success. Danny said I should give her the apple juice, and then she would get into pajamas. I refused. What finally happened, after I don't know how much time, is that Daniel did give her some juice, and Rachel tickled her into helplessness, and together they were able to get her into pajamas. Daniel came over to me and whispered confidentially: "We know how to make her happy."

And right now they are all engaged in an absolutely wild

procession through the house, holding hands and singing: "*Mitz-vah gedolah lehiot besimchah, lehiot besimchah tamid.*" They are so tremendously happy, without reason, and are giving each other such love! It's so wonderful! I'm rejoicing. It's as much of a celebration as if there were a wedding going on.

Whoops, Elisheva just fell down and hit her head on the floor, and is crying.

Good. Rachel picked her up.

At least they're all in pajamas, and as far as bedtime is concerned, we're not entirely off course: it's eight thirty.

I remember Miriam Adahan saying, "One of your jobs as a mother is to bring as much happiness as possible into the home." We're right on target.

February 15, 1987

We are looking for a new apartment. Ever since the baby was born, the four and a half flights of stairs have held me captive in our present home, and not having an open porch also makes me feel walled in and out of touch. What has precipitated our search now is that my sixteen-year-old niece Becky is going to be moving in with us, G-d willing, so we need another bedroom.

After seeing nine apartments, we saw one that for me was love at first sight. It was a penthouse with a good kitchen and a huge porch with plenty of room for a roof garden, bicycle riding, rope jumping, a laundry line, a hammock. The apartment was perched on top of the world. The view of the mountains, of various neighborhoods near and far, of our immediate neighborhood down below, of the clouds rushing over us...It made my heart race to imagine living there. What space! I'd put a swing out there, we'd be able to have an outdoor, roomy sukkah, I'd be able to put the babies out in the sun without worrying...Over where my stove would be, a window looked out on the terrace, so I'd be able to keep an eye on the children while cooking. Last but not least, the other side of the apartment overlooked my favorite park in Jerusalem, wooded with pine trees and flowering bushes and quiet, secluded corners underneath the leaves...a place to get lost in, as I used to as a child.

The price was right: we could sell our old apartment and borrow $5,000 to make up the rest.

Sitting on an empty wooden crate in the empty living room, our living room, I wondered what in the world I had done to deserve such kindness from *HaShem*. The children were dashing around from room to room, deciding which room would belong to whom. They loved it as much as I.

My husband was surveying the apartment, measuring tape in hand. I looked upon him with good-natured condescension: what possible difference do inches make when you've come upon your destiny?

"You can see they added on that fourth bedroom themselves. This is not really a four-bedroom apartment, you know," he informed me gravely, coming into the living room.

"What do you mean it's not a four-bedroom apartment? There are four bedrooms. What difference does it make if they did it themselves?"

He shook his head solemnly. "Did you notice anything unusual about that room?"

"Like what?" I said, guessing that he meant there were no windows in it.

"It doesn't have a window."

"So what. There's a skylight. It would be lovely for the babies."

"I wouldn't put a baby in that room. I wouldn't put anybody in that room. Do you know how hot it will be in there in the summertime with no ventilation? That skylight can't be opened up."

"Oh, for goodness sake, we could have a window put in."

"No, we couldn't. I looked at it."

"Oh, Yaacov. We can't let something like that stop us from getting this. Yaacov! It's perfect!"

He pursed his lips and tilted his head to one side.

"Yaacov! You do see that it's perfect, don't you? A window is nothing to worry about."

He went back into the bedrooms again, opening up the measuring tape. I and my huge abdomen stayed put on the crate, and I gazed out the tall glass doors of the living room. We would have to live here. We would live here. Yaacov's questions were irrelevant. I could hardly believe he took them seriously. We had come upon our shared dream.

"Sarah," he said in a low voice as he returned some ten minutes later. "The bedrooms are smaller than the ones we have now."

I was getting anxious. But this would be our house. I was sure. It was just right. "It's all right," I calmly smiled. "We'll manage. They're not that small."

"Well, if you're thinking about putting Becky in that one without windows, I'm not going to do it." I liked the sound of this more. It sounded like we had gotten to the point of just arguing placement. "And I counted the steps. It's eighty-one steps up. I can't do that, Sarah. How would you do it? With two babies you're going to go up and down five flights of stairs? It's hard enough being on the fourth floor where we are now. Now the fifth floor?"

I waved aside his objections with an impatient flick of my wrist. "It's not on the fifth floor. It's the third floor."

"From Rechov Ophira it's the third floor. But you know we'd be using the Yam Suf entrance."

"The address is 12 Ophira."

"But Yam Suf is the way out to the kids' schools and the buses and the stores. Let's face it."

"So we'd just decide to go around to Ophira."

"All the way around from Yam Suf to Ophira?" He eyed me skeptically. "I wouldn't. Would you? Really?"

"Look, I've already accepted that with two babies I'll be stuck at home for the next two years anyway. The whole difference is that in this apartment, there's this big *mirpesset* where I can be outside when I want to. I won't feel cooped up! And the children can be outside. We won't have to go up and down all the time the way we do now."

"Sarah. Think it over. Let's not jump into this thing blind."

I had not the slightest wisp of an inclination to think it over. If this was blindness, I liked what I saw. The apartment was ours.

Yaacov took the children and me back home. I was in a heavenly kind of dream, and when he instructed me sternly not to offer the man anything above $85,000, I was quietly ecstatic to see that he had overcome his own objections. Later that afternoon, Yaacov called to say that a real estate agent had informed him that the owner had been trying to get rid of that apartment for two years. "The real estate agent says they'll come down on the price," Yaacov told me. "They're desperate."

"So it's all right with you if I go ahead and call now?"

"Yes."

I called the owner with excitement and confidence. And to demonstrate to Yaacov that I was no pushover, I offered eighty instead of eighty-five. The owner refused me. I wasn't worried.

The next Shabbat the whole family went for a walk in Sanhedrin Park. As we passed the apartment on our way towards the path leading into a congregation of pine trees, I glanced fondly up at our future home. Every flower in the park was already mine. This park will be like my own huge yard, I speculated with intense pleasure. We'll be able to come here every Shabbat. What did I do to deserve this? It must be in my parents' merit. It must be Yaacov's merit, that he devotes himself to his studies so seriously.

On Wednesday the real estate agent who had shown us the apartment called. "I'm sorry to have to give you bad news, Sarah," she said. My mind jumped. What could she be talking about? "I know how you feel about the penthouse on Ophira, but it was sold yesterday." She paused. "Sarah?"

"Yes."

"I'm sorry to tell you. I know you liked it, but these things happen. Well, I guess this means that it just wasn't *bashert*."

On Friday, after candle lighting, I put the baby to sleep early and sat on the couch until Yaacov came home from davening. Somehow or other, to my mind it was because of him that we had lost the apartment. If he had just loved it as much as I had!

When he walked in I didn't say "Shabbat Shalom." The children were unruly during kiddush. It was a horrible time.

February 17, 1987

Adina called me this morning, then Menuchah. Adina said she's depressed because she's so bored by housework. Menuchah said her brother and sister-in-law are coming from England in a few weeks, and she's depressed because the house is such a mess.

What's the way out of this depression over the duties involved in being a wife and mother? If you can't afford a full-time maid, if your husband is helpful, even very helpful, like Yaacov, but doesn't want to switch places with you, if you don't want to pack up and leave it all behind, if listening to interesting tapes as you work doesn't compensate sufficiently for the fact that no matter how hard you work, your accomplishment will not last long, the floor will get dirty by nightfall...What do you do? Watching all your labor being endlessly undone, how can you keep yourself from unraveling?

What's the answer? Even for those women who protest that the whole system is society's conspiracy to keep the woman sub-jugated, responsibility for their households still seems to fall on their shoulders. It's almost always the woman who has to keep the humdrum mechanism of her household spinning around, even as it is unspun. There must be a good reason things are this way, because this is the way the world has been designed, and I don't believe that it's a male-chauvinist plot. There must be a good reason. There must be a good solution.

Tonight I was feeding the baby yogurt (an attempt on my part to cure his persistent diarrhea) when Elisheva came home crying again about being excluded from some children's play. I couldn't go downstairs this time, because Yaacov's not home with his injured foot anymore, and I can't leave the baby alone. I'm worried that Elisheva will conclude something negative about herself, or get into a pattern, if this happens often. The "guilty" child's mother is my neighbor Miriam, an exceptionally kind, giving woman, so I picked up the crying baby, who didn't want the yogurt, and went to solicit her assistance. With a big warm smile she told Elisheva, "Come," and held out her hand. "I'll play with you."

Elisheva's sobbing ceased. I was grateful and relieved, but then my insides fell flat. Why can't I do that? I wondered. I hardly even relate to Miriam's children, and she's such an expert with mine. What's wrong with me?

I trudged up the half-flight of stairs to our apartment, my robe splattered with yogurt, and opened the refrigerator. Standing there with the baby holding on to me side saddle, I tried to figure out what else to give him. *Miriam has her talents,* I told myself. *I have mine.*

But I wasn't deeply convinced.

February 21, 1987

No matter what happened during last night's Shabbat dinner, Yaacov spoke quietly and calmly. When the children made noise during kiddush, he waited in silence. When they all yelled and whined that everybody else got bigger pieces of challah, Yaacov didn't let it bother him. When Elisheva piled her plate high with three times as much coleslaw as she can eat, he made no comment. When he had to repeat five times that they get into pajamas, he did so without getting nervous about it. When my leg hurt and I had to abandon my hard wooden chair for the nice sinking couch, Yaacov declared that everyone was going to serve Mommy tonight. I felt so honored and loved as Rachel shoved a chair before me to serve as a little table, as Yaacov set down soup and salad, as Dinah massaged my neck. (Of course, it would have been nice if she had massaged the back of my neck instead of my throat.) Elisheva stood watching me, thumb in mouth, pillow in hand. Daniel got into his pajamas without further prodding and sat down to read.

On Shabbat morning, when Daniel refused to go to shul with Yaacov, we didn't comment or urge. When the children made so much noise during the meal that we couldn't hear what the guests were saying, I took note of my embarrassment, got a hold of my anger, and merely dragged Danny off to a corner and informed him through clenched teeth that if he wanted to make noise he could go outside. It was raining so hard that this was unrealistic, so he stayed, and toned it down. All in all, our Shabbat was so lovely and sweet. It was nourishment for the soul.

Our two guests, a brother and sister from Argentina, twenty-three and twenty-two respectively, have been in Israel for just two weeks. She told me that when her brother first spoke to her about a group organized in Rio de Janeiro by Yeshivat Aish HaTorah, she had told him that he was a maniac. "Are you crazy? What do you want, to be a rabbi? I don't want to speak to you anymore!"

She's here in Jerusalem's Aish HaTorah women's yeshiva. Their father is a wealthy architect, their mother a psychologist. The father doesn't think it's correct for a woman to work, so for the last seven years he has not permitted his wife to practice her profession. They have two full-time maids, plus a man who comes once every two weeks to wash windows.

I kept mulling this over. Two full-time maids! Wow! Why don't I go to a place like that? What do I need all this housework for? If there are women who are enjoying such freedom from drudgery, maybe I deserve it, too. "So what does your mother do," I asked, "if she's not working and not doing housework?"

The young man shifted uneasily. "It's a problem."

"She's bored," said his sister. "She goes shopping, or she gets her hair done, or she plays cards with the other ladies. She walks on the beach."

"My mother and father, they have a nice life together," said the young man.

March 1, 1987

On Shabbat I broke. The bottom of the ladder again. I felt depressed and worried.

On Shabbat morning I went to see my friend Rose, whom I haven't seen in many months. Halfway through my visit, she said, "Your children have changed, Sarah."

"For good?"

She nodded.

"Are they calmer, or what?"

"Much calmer and much happier."

I was thrilled. "Rose, that makes me so happy. It's because I haven't been yelling and hitting the way I used to. But last night I did. It was just horrible."

"It's been a while?"

"Yeah."

"So. It's just human to go back to that. It's just human."

March 2, 1987

I was sitting at the table this afternoon engaged in conversation with Rachel, dimly aware that Elisheva was calling me from the porch to open the sliding glass door for her. I ignored her, knowing she could go around through the bedroom. Then *crack*.

I recognized that sound perfectly, though I hadn't actually heard it before. I have anticipated, have awaited that particular sound throughout the time we have lived in this apartment. Elisheva had kicked the sliding glass door and at last the inevitable had occurred. She stood up, turned around to look at me, and smiled sheepishly.

There it was, radiating out like lightening from the point of impact, a long, jagged crack. Fortunately, I recalled at that moment the account someone had once given in a workshop of exactly the same thing—her five-year-old son had broken her glass living room door in anger. This served to tone down my reaction considerably, for I thought: Other children do it, too. My next thought: How much will it cost?

Elisheva watched me with scared eyes as I now opened the door. She waited for my explosion, which did not take place. "Elisheva..." I said softly, letting all my sadness draw my face down into sorrow. "How could you do that? Do you know how much money it will cost?"

She burst into tears. "It's your fault! I told you to open the door for me and you didn't!"

"Elisheva, when the door is locked, I don't have to come open it for you. You can go around through the bedroom."

She argued this point for a few minutes, then, thumb in mouth, surveyed the damage thoughtfully.

I wasn't about to tell her this, but that broken glass was an appropriate *kapparah* before the birth of our next child. Disturbing as it is to have this seventy or eighty shekel problem on our hands, I can't complain about the course of events. I didn't scream. Elisheva learned something.

March 3, 1987

I heard somewhere that the reason pregnancy takes nine months is that it takes that long for a woman to get used to the idea of having a baby. That seems to have happened to me. I feel excited now, not as scared about having two babies to take care of. I'm just worried that, G-d forbid, there will be something wrong with it. I don't care if it's a girl or a boy. I just want it to be normal.

March 4, 1987

Why do I have this critical, never-satisfied voice carrying on inside my head? If I do the dishes and go to bed, I think I should have done the laundry, too. If I stay up late to finish the dishes and the laundry, I fret that I should have gotten the sleep instead. And if I go to bed early, I feel like a stick-in-the-mud: Life is so short! What a bore to spend it sleeping!

March 8, 1987

The birth must be coming any day. I expect it minute to minute. My due date's March 17th, but I'm experiencing the most curious sensations all the time, as of ice floes breaking up, or earthquake tremors. Somewhere along the line, my distress over those violet varicose stains on my right calf subsided. Now I experience a sort of pride, as if they're my badge of honor: I've become a woman, I've gone through the difficult things that all mothers go through.

My change of heart occurred, I think, after getting a letter from my mother.

> Dear Sarah,
>
> Last Sunday we received a call from Sophie telling us that Aunt Martha died. She was the next to youngest of the five sisters. Esther was the youngest. Martha was house-bound—and I think bed-bound—for the last few years, with nurses around the clock, and according to Sophie, her mind was quite confused. She died at the age of ninety. Daddy was glad he went to the funeral, even though New Jersey was in the middle of a blizzard, because Martha was the last of her generation...I thought it was important for you to know that a generation has now passed out of our lives. Daddy is now the oldest male in the family. You and Candis are giving birth to the new generation. Life goes on.
>
> Love and kisses,
>
> Mommy

The profound effect of this letter upon me was incalculable. It gave me a perspective on the general situation: our family tree, like most Jewish family trees in America, is not growing as fast as it is dying. I was named after Sarah, Martha's sister. Thank G-d I am having a family. Thank G-d I'm having another baby so quickly. I don't have forever to do the planting.

I like the people my family tree produces—I don't want our family to vanish. May we be fruitful and multiply in spite of the hardships. This is what matters.

Every Thanksgiving, all the relatives came, a lot of them. There were dozens of cousins whose names I always forgot, but we ran around outside together and all over the house—upstairs, downstairs, screaming, laugh-

ing, chasing each other. My great aunts would catch one of us as we zipped by. "Take a look at that face," Aunt Florence would murmur to Becky and Martha as she held a child's upturned, impatient, polite face between her hands. "Did you ever?"

Aunt Becky came each year with her kosher turkey wrapped in silver foil, along with her own plastic forks and knives, and I'd wonder a little. Strange. Old-fashioned. Wally and Ruthie, who always arrived first, brought kosher food as well, so I speculated vaguely that Paul, Judy and Laurie, their three children, must be kosher, too. Families Goldbloom, Silberberg, Kantor...there weren't any names like that in our roll call at elementary school, that's for sure.

Sitting off to one side, my great uncle Benny always spent those five or six hours of Thanksgiving afternoon looking on in silence at the noisy, lively crowd. To anyone who would come over to make humorous banter or conversation, he would nod solemnly and utter some few words. Hands on knees, with his great, imposing, suspendered stomach that seemed to start at his collar, Uncle Benny sat up eternally erect, still, chin slightly uplifted, peering down at all of us through his exceedingly thick glasses as if from a distance. On his big, bald head rested a big, black yarmulke.

To my mind, Uncle Benny seemed to preside over our annual festivities like a confused king...no use for him anymore.

One year, he had taken up his post by the door to the ping-pong porch. On one of my excited excursions through the living room, I saw that people were starting a round-robin game out there. A lot of laughter, a lot of joking around. I ran to join them. But Uncle Benny lifted one finger as I was about to go through the door. Come here, he motioned.

I sidled over. He beckoned me nearer.

Obedient, I came up close. There was his gray mustache. There were his thick glasses as he gazed down upon me. How big and round his gray eyes were, magnified through those glasses!

"Don't marry a shaigitz," he intoned.

I wondered, what's that. I waited.

Nothing more.

I ran to the ping-pong game.

March 9, 1987

I went to a shiur by Rabbi Noach Orlowick. Some of the things he said:

—Don't look at your child as if through a microscope, checking for serious faults. One of his children used to take cookies from the cookie jar, though he'd been told not to. Rabbi Orlowick went to ask Rabbi Chaim Pinchus Scheinberg, Rosh Yeshiva of Torah Ohr, about it. Rabbi Scheinberg laughed at the "problem" and said, "Your son wants cookies. That's all."

—If a child is given encouragement by his teachers the first couple of years, he is far less likely to be adversely affected by whatever mistakes his teachers may make when he is older.

—G-d helps people who recognize they need help.

March 10, 1987

I made Dinah's bed tonight with a pink sheet I had bought for Rachel. Rachel pulled it off. "Please, Rachel," I implored. "I haven't done the laundry yet and don't have another sheet." She refused to hand it over. I felt like slapping her, and lifted my hand, but stopped.

A while later I found her sulking on the couch, as she used to. "You went like this to me!" she exclaimed, imitating the gesture I had made to slap her. I was about to launch into some speech about how she just cannot be allowed to be so selfish, when I recalled what Angie told me years ago: only a precious few of us humans want to give, want to do *chessed*. It is *HaShem* Himself who has given us our selfishness, so that we will have the opportunity to rise above it with our own free will.

So instead of wagging my finger at her, I said: "Rachel, you're no different from anyone else. I, too, don't always want to share, I don't always want to give of what I have, but I still have to try to do it. *HaShem* made us like this so that we'd get the *zechus* of giving even when we don't want to. Come into the bedroom, darling, and listen to the story I'm going to read." At first she didn't budge, and I anticipated one of those familiar, long, drawn-out struggles, yet then, to my surprise, she came in and sat down beside me in the bedroom.

Later I put the pink sheet back on Dinah's bed. Rachel made no comment.

March 11, 1987

A few minutes ago, my friend Esther Lomnitz called. She told me that her mother is arriving for a visit from South Africa tomorrow and that since seven o'clock she's been working to clean the house and cook. "Being a mother," she said, "is like a being a Jewish slave in Mitzrayim, because the Egyptians used to destroy what the Jews had built. It must have been torture not to see anything from all the work. All day long I've been cleaning, and the children—it's just that they want to play, G-d bless them—they undo my work."

This reminded me of a remark Beyla Potash once made some years ago: that housework is similar to spiritual work on oneself. No matter how much you do, the *yetzer hara* returns, and your negative characteristics reappear. We're not granted a sense of permanent achievement, and that's probably the way it's supposed to be.

March 12, 1987

Why is raising children so universally difficult? Whether one has a single child or a brood of ten, no parent is spared his share of trouble. But child raising could have been designed to bring nothing but pleasure, had G-d seen fit. If it was designed to be difficult, then God must have known that that's the best thing for us.

But I ask myself, how could these difficulties be the best thing for me?

Well, first of all, there's the general principle that a human being is ennobled and purified by hardships (unless he's getting embittered and callous instead). The difficulties of parenthood can elevate us. Furthermore, people appreciate what they pay for, and the price we pay for our children is the pain we experience through their upbringing. Still another way of seeing it: to the degree that we suffer over a child, we feel a bond with him.

The answer that holds the most meaning for me, though, is this: mysteriously enough, all the elements required for my personal growth are contained within motherhood. Children provide precisely those irritants which best bring to light everything in my personality that I would prefer to keep under wraps. Their incessant needs, their emotional dependency, the artless innocence, vulnerability, misbehavior, irrepressible self-centeredness...all this is perfectly calibrated to reveal my own pride, intolerance, impatience and lack of *emunah*. Had I not been forced by my motherhood to confront these characteristics in myself, I wouldn't have imagined they would ever describe me.

The awful discomfort of constantly bumping up against my flaws, however, is mitigated by this kindness: I have been fitted out with the maternal instinct. The switch was thrown and the instinct started operating on full power around thirty seconds after the twins were born, and it's so high-voltage, it can offset almost any selfish impulse. The instinct to guard my children's well-being keeps me striving to rein in my own destructiveness. It's a built-in antidote to the *yetzer hara*.

Nothing else in the world could motivate me as well as motherhood to rise above my nature.

March 13, 1987

This morning a terrific rush of impatience and frustration surged through me like electricity. Rachel had neglected to put away her clean laundry, and on the floor next to her bed I found all the clothes I'd washed and hung up to dry. I thought: "What a spoiled child! I cannot let her get away with this anymore! All my work! What's wrong with me as a mother that I haven't succeeded in teaching her?"

Wait. I told myself. Maybe it's possible to look at this differently. She has a bad habit which I can teach her to overcome, with time. This is a normal problem. She's such a fine girl. "Rachel," I called, "come, sweetheart, and we'll put away your clothes." She answered but I couldn't hear.

"You're speaking so softly, Rachel, I can't hear you."

She came into the bedroom. "My head hurts me."

I repeated my instructions quietly, and started picking up the laundry myself, folding it and putting it in her drawer. "You do it, too, darling." She joined me listlessly. I was irritated by her unwillingness. Don't expect her to be happy about doing it, I reminded myself. It's normal for a child not to want to do what you ask, but she must do it anyway.

Around ten minutes later, I found her crying by the bedroom door, and she wouldn't tell me why. For some reason I felt as if paying a lot of attention to this right now would be pampering her unnecessarily, and I went on about my business in the kitchen, making pancakes. I waited for her hunger to get the better of her, yet to my surprise she sat down on the couch, still crying. Finally, after a half-hour, when the other children had finished eating and she was still seated on the couch with uncharacteristic stillness, I went to her.

"Why are you crying, Rachel? Did something happen in school today?" She shook her head. I was glad she wasn't sulking too deeply to respond.

"Was it something I said to hurt your feelings?" She nodded. "About the clothes?" She nodded. "Rachel," I said sternly and gently, "all of us have to take care of our clothes."

"That's not why!" she burst out, with tears now. "You didn't believe me that my head hurts me! My head hurts me so much!"

I felt Rachel's forehead. She had a fever.

Oh, such a mistake I made.

March 15, 1987

This morning my niece Becky came over. We were watching the baby as he staggered like an exuberant drunk across the living room rug, when she commented that he looked so happy. "In that book *Is There a Chance for Love*," she told me, "it says that babies are happy because they're still just their *neshamos*, before they get older and get burdened with all kinds of things that make them feel heavy and bad. And that we, all of us, are actually still like that. Inside us, even if we don't know it, we're our pure, happy *neshamos*."

We have found another apartment with a huge *mirpesset*, one flight up, on the opposite side of Sanhedrin Park. The apartment itself is strangely laid out, but the big *mirpesset* makes up for it, and it's only one flight up. The *mirpesset* is underneath the trees, and almost everything that I loved about the other one is present here, except for the feeling you got there of being in the clouds.

Last night I was feeling so happy because Yaacov and I had agreed on it. Then, this morning, he informed me that there are legal problems with the apartment because it's not registered correctly. I was buckling Elisheva's shoes when I got this news, and I fiddled with them impatiently. "Elisheva!" I snapped. "Stand still!" My joy-ousness had collapsed like a cardboard house, but later this morning, upon hearing Becky's words, I remembered how lovely it had been, having such a light heart when I thought I had what I wanted.

Maybe I can be happy just like that now.

Maybe I have every reason to be that happy, even if we don't get that apartment.

Be happy! Why not?

March 17, 1987

Tonight Danny was noisy and troublesome in a strange way. It's hard to describe, but it seemed as if he was acting angrier than he actually felt. I was talking on the phone and asked him to turn down the Mordechai ben David tape. Danny squinched up his face like a bawling infant and roared. "You're making me turn off the tape recorder!"

He kept on with this sort of thing for the next couple of hours. I didn't get furious and that's probably because I wasn't ascribing this behavior to some deep unhappiness on his part, or to some malicious urge to upset me. It looked, rather, like the antics of an overtired, bored child experimenting with his own voice and his mother's limits. There was also something there, hard to put my finger on, of his harking back to our history. It's not that it's so quiet around here nowadays that the peacefulness grates. (I wish!) But his mother is screaming and yelling and hitting so much less that perhaps he was fooling around with me a bit, seeing if he could provoke me into becoming that familiar old witch. He doesn't miss the witch, but he would like to know where she's gone.

While he brushed his teeth in front of the bathroom mirror, he paused to roar again, with those same noisy, annoying dramatics, sort of like a lion mimicking himself to himself, curious what he looks like in full savage regalia. I asked him if he was finished brushing, he made a squinched-up face and yowled that I was yelling at him, which I wasn't in the slightest. I lost my temper and slapped him on the arm.

Tucking him in this evening, I leaned down to kiss him good night but he stiffened and averted his face, as he used to. I feared that I had turned back the clock. Would I get back into the habit of hitting Daniel when annoyed? Sin crouches at the door...Open it a crack and you're lost.

"I'm sorry that I hit you, Danny. I hate to hit you. Hitting doesn't help anything."

His face was still turned away from me. Had I erred to apologize for something so normal on my part? After all, I can't be expected to be endlessly understanding! Was I lowering myself, when he should have been the one to say he was sorry for having needled me? Am I bending over backwards too much? I started to rise from his bed (in sadness) when Daniel sat up abruptly and caught me around the neck in a hug.

It's all right to apologize to him, I thought happily. It's right to admit mistakes.

March 18, 1987

The baby has not been well today. Maybe it's an ear infection.

Maybe teething. I hope to take him to Dr. Shupak this afternoon. All morning I have been engaged in little else but holding him, comforting him, trying to figure out what he could eat or drink. At one point there he was in my arms, thumb in mouth as usual, and it occurred to me how strange it is that I don't mind it when this little person takes up all my time. When he's asleep and I can do other things, I'm so relieved. I tiptoe around, dreading the moment of his awakening. Then when he wakes up, I hurry in to get him and sometimes observe myself curiously, how I burst into song like an opera diva when our eyes meet, sweep him up out of the crib, raise him aloft over my head, swing him around, hold him close and dance. For all the world, it's as if I haven't seen him in years.

March 19, 1987

I'm in the taxi on the way to the hospital. It's 6:45 a.m. A contraction just started. I'm so happy that I was able to say goodbye to each of the children. Yaacov's going to get them off to school and then meet me at the hospital. I'm rushing to write this. All except for Elisheva, the children sent me off with excited happiness. Elisheva stared at me. My friend Malka is going to take care of them today.

It's now 7:18. I'm having a contraction. I want to time it.

It seems to be happening every eight minutes. It's now 8:10. I've been sitting here on a chair waiting to be checked. Writing lessens my impatience. When I arrived here, and the nurse asked me, "May I help you?" I announced with a proud smile, proud of my calm demeanor, which I thought must be unusual: "I'm about to give birth."

She smiled back, yet without the full measure of enthusiasm I expected. I thought she'd present me with a bouquet of red roses. Channy Stark, the midwife who delivered me last year, whom I liked very much, said hello some time ago and told me she'd be able to check me in a few minutes. Just now she came by and said, "Sarah, I haven't forgotten you," which made me feel sad and sorry for myself. Have I been forgotten? People should be taking care of me when I'm like this, shouldn't they?

I'm so glad it's not Shabbat this time, so I can put on lipstick. It makes me feel less vulnerable, like a personality to reckon with.

It's now 9:20. Channy told me to go for a walk, so I've just gotten back from a little market where I got some bagels and oranges. I pitied the other customers and the man behind the counter for their ignorance that right next to them was a woman about to give birth, a woman in the midst of one of life's major events, much more important than bagels and oranges and money. I took my little bag of food into the hospital dining room and was delighted that the women there were all speaking English. One gave birth to her first child last night, another I don't know when, one is under observation, and one is in her sixth month, I guess also under observation. This little hospital specializes in problem pregnancies. I asked one of the nurses about Judith, whom I saw when I came here for a checkup last month, who had been in bed here for four months, who had just had her twelfth anniversary without children—she gave birth to a baby boy six weeks ago!

Now it's 9:27. I'm going to time the contraction. It is stronger now.

I will be so glad to see the baby normal. Am I really going to have another child soon? I can't believe it. I called home and spoke to Rachel, Elisheva and Dinah. Daniel had left for school already. They're all happy I'm here and wanted to know when it will be.

Now it's 9:37.

Now it's 9:45. I keep forgetting to time my contractions.

We have had a baby girl!
A baby girl—she has brown hair and I think brown eyes like Dinah. That's just what I wanted, a girl with brown eyes and brown hair, though all through the pregnancy I condemned myself each

time I found myself thinking it. How stupid to ask for such a thing. You better just pray that the baby's normal, you ingrate. But G-d gave me what I wanted anyway, in spite of my stupidity, and in spite of all that I felt about being pregnant. She's normal, then I got icing on the cake. I can't believe it. I'm so glad it's a girl. *HaShem's* not out to punish me, just to lavish kindness upon kindness.

The birth was the loveliest of all my births. For how could I be relaxed and happy to bring a child into the world unless I felt that my other children were all right? Now I feel I'm doing a good job with them. Though my current worries are about Elisheva, I feel that they're all all right. Elisheva is going through a rough period because I get impatient with her when she does things out of jealousy of the baby. I have to work on that now. But as I worked on the thing with Rachel and have, thank G-d, *baruch HaShem*, seen such improvement in my relationship with her, I think now I can begin to focus on Elisheva. It will be so much easier not being pregnant, not being incapacitated, sitting on the couch unable to move, and on top of that unable to scream and yell because of bronchitis. It's over! Yippee!

Physically, this labor was pretty identical to last year's, yet my attitude toward it was so different. This time I didn't object to tricking myself with whatever happy, calming thoughts I could summon, whereas last year I was skeptical about such mental antics, and I took great care to squeeze forth from the suffering every last drop of honest agony. This time, when I started thinking, "When will this end, I can't stand it, is this the way labor is supposed to be, only I have it this hard, something's wrong, my labor must be different...," I'd answer myself with: "These pains are cleansing my record. By the time I get through with this I'll have a clean slate." And: "Other women do go through this. You've been through it five times yourself! Why, what could possibly be more run-of-the-mill than childbirth? Every human being on Earth is a testament to the fact that some woman somewhere has done it!" And: "Each contraction is bringing the baby closer, bringing the pregnancy to an end. I will survive this. I will soon be on the other side of this, I really will. This pain will be a thing of the past. This is how it happens for all womankind, and they survive, they get over it. Unbelievably, women do walk around on the street without screaming about their labor pains."

Though I wanted Yaacov to be there, close by, within myself I wanted to be alone with the pain, not to communicate. I felt like a child who in a short time has grown up, and his mother has no way of knowing how much he's changed. "I'll do it myself, thank you." That's what I wanted to say. "Be there. But I'm doing this by myself. I want all the credit." He picked up on this one way or another without my explaining and stayed in the next room, in silence, except when I'd call out, "Yaacov!" Then he'd come in and say, "You're doing very well, Sarah," and bring me tea and fruit and give me homeopathic remedies when none of the nurses were around.

I was lying there in a torment, my insides being tightly clamped and squeezed by that cold metallic hand of labor, when Channy told me she could see the baby's head. I was stunned. "YOU SEE THE BABY'S HEAD?" *But how can it breathe?* Tears sprang into my eyes. For a split second, I felt purified. *A living child was inside me!* I wanted to ask, "What color hair does it have?" but dared not ask something so trivial and unimportant at a time like that. The only thing was to wait and see if the baby was normal.

"All right," she said. "Now."

WHAT? I'd gotten there? I was going to give birth now? "NO!"

Channy smiled softly and nodded.

"No! I can't! Wait!" Suddenly, like a terrified wild bird released from a cage, a scream flew out of me. Such an embarassment, that wildly animalistic voice! No other choice now. I couldn't run away from this, but the baby would not be born until I agreed.

The baby burst out like a wriggling, squiggling fish, and cried. My new child crying!

"You have a girl," said Channy.

"IS SHE NORMAL?"

"Yes, she looks just fine."

"SHE'S NORMAL?"

"Yes, she's normal."

"LET ME SEE." I bolted upright, intent, unbelieving. A nurse held the baby up to me. Her squashed, pewter-grey face, her fast, piercing, insistent wail, WAAH! WAAH! WAAH! WAAH! Her firm teeny legs drawn up tensely in discomfort and shock. Is that what normal looks like? I lay back. Thank you, thank you. Unbelievable, she is all right. Minutes later, Yaacov came in. "Mazal tov, Sarah. We have a girl."

There wasn't any room in the delivery room for me, so they put me in a small corner room by myself, a little bedroom that looked nothing like a hospital room. A Van Gogh sunflower print was on the wall, the bed wasn't a delivery bed at all, just an old wrought iron thing, a bird in a tree was singing outside the partly open window, the walls had old-fashioned cornices...I was thrilled to have landed in the perfect place. A little room near the sky, like my yellow bedroom in Connecticut with the wallpaper on the ceiling.

So that's where I am now, in this small, old-fashioned chamber. The birth must have been about two hours ago. An attendant just told me brusquely to move so she could adjust the intravenous equipment. Even her brusqueness didn't faze me. As I sat up, my reflection moved in the little mirror opposite my bed. My eyes, full of warm, wise light, met mine and greeted me. I'd earned that light. I looked beautiful. I thought: It's all right to be thirty-seven. It'll even be all right to get gray hair.

I don't know how long I've been lying here. There's a gold-framed photograph in the hallway outside this room, of a carefully coiffed, majestic, Italian-looking Jewess in her sixties, who must have either founded this place or donated a lot of money to it. As I lie here trapped by the intravenous machine, I daydream about her. How many labors did she undergo? How many children did she bring into the world? She was a mother. She must have ached with love for her children, as do I, worried over what they ate as do I, and over what they said, worried that they become good people, as do I, agonized later over their search for husbands and wives...

To be a mother.

How great. How great.

That's life.

11

The Garden Beyond

March 21, 1987

This morning I was holding the baby—whose name is Avivah—and I remembered how throughout the pregnancy I was frightened that I would be punished for not having wanted this child. Yet she is normal. She is perfectly fine.

I opened the ArtScroll Tehillim book some moments later and noticed a commentary at the bottom of the page concerning David's fifth psalm. "Malbim contrasts David's attitude with that of the heathen. The idol worshiper visits his temple only when gripped by fear, lest he be punished by the wrath of his deity. As he gazes upon his lifeless idol of dead wood and stone, his terror slowly subsides and departs. Not so with *HaShem*, the Living G-d. David enters His Temple out of love and yearning for G-d's kindness. He witnesses only endless love in every facet of creation and so he happily draws close to the Creator. Then, as he enters into G-d's presence he is seized with trembling. Not with fear of punishment or harm, but with awe before G-d's greatness."

March 23, 1987

This morning Yaacov told me that Eli has the measles. So

that's why he was so out of sorts yesterday, throwing away his bottle and crying constantly. Eli, my poor baby. I wish I could be taking care of him.

I called Miriam Levi to tell her I'd given birth, and she said she'd already heard because she called to ask how I was. She said: "Care more about yourself than you care about others right now. Care about yourself, for their sake as well as for your own. Let people help you and accept their help graciously. For six weeks that's the best thing you can do for everybody."

March 24, 1987

I've gone to a convalescent home for mothers after birth—a hotel, really—outside of Jerusalem. All the babies are kept in one huge nursery illuminated twenty-four hours a day with a million fluorescent lights, and are fed bottles of Materna to ensure the mothers' resting hours. I find it incomprehensible that these nurses don't understand how the nursing process is established: that during the first days after birth, the infant needs to drink only minute quantities of breast milk, and that this modest amount of sucking is what stimulates the mother's milk to come in on the fourth or fifth day. Giving the babies bottles of Materna can disturb, if not eliminate, the natural, miraculous synchronization between supply and demand.

Avivah. It's a beautiful name but it hasn't quite jelled. The baby doesn't fit the title. She looks to me sort of like a tiny Eskimo baby. I should call her Wigwam. Or Igloo.

Do I love her? It bothers me that I don't yet, but it's reassuring to remember that when Rachel was born, I was astounded and scared that I didn't love her, either. She was the image of my grandfather at the age of ninety-four, and I feared that she would stay that way. How was I to know that most newborns look peculiar? I looked askance upon Dinah, as well, in the days after her birth. She too had Avivah's Eskimo face, with those tense little lips tightly pursed as if she were enraged to have been shot out into the bright, cold world. And Elisheva also, come to think of it.

I remember thinking that she looked like a Polish warlord or a prizefighter—forehead puckered up, facial features clenched like a fist. *What's wrong with her?* I wondered. *Did she catch my anger from within the womb? Why don't I love her? If it were a boy, would I? How terrible! If it were a boy, I wouldn't care if he wasn't beautiful.*

I don't remember exactly what I felt towards Eli, but I must have been going through some sort of guilt and doubt with him as well, because I do clearly recall thinking what a coincidence it was that I started to feel something just a few hours before my milk came in. I thought, "How poetic. My love is coming in along with my milk." This indicates that it must have been only after four or five days that I started to feel affection for him.

I just now went to the nursery and explained to the women on duty there that my milk has just come in, so if I don't nurse, I'll become engorged. I've had enough experience in these matters (why do I feel like such a phony when I say that?) to know that if I tell them I want to nurse for the sake of my child, they'll laugh at me and say: "You have the next twenty years to worry about her! For a few days you can rest!" They nodded sympathetically and assured me that they'll call me when she cries. But I wonder how in the world they'll even notice if Avivah cries, lost as she is among what seems to be hundreds of bawling newborns.

I just went in to the nursery to check on the baby. Those women are so busy in there, the last thing they need is an insistent mother bothering them out of schedule. Sticking just my head in the door, to demonstrate my respect for their regulations, I raised my voice delicately: "*Slichah!*" I directed my announcement politely to that amorphous personality: to whom it may concern. "You told me I could come here when my baby cries so that I won't get engorged."

A nurse looked up from diapering. Above the din she shouted: "What's the number?"

"Ten!" I called back

She scanned the room. "Ten's not crying!"

I returned to my room.

It's forty-five minutes later. I just went in to check again. I saw carriage number ten over on the left, among the sea of identical carriages, and the little dark head was lifting itself up jerkily on its wobbly neck, and falling, and lifting and falling. How long had she been crying? I stuck my head through the door with what I hoped was the right balance of determination, self-assurance, modesty and deference. "I need to nurse my baby. You told me to come and get my baby when she cries."

Two nurses whom I hadn't seen before eyed me skeptically. "Which schedule are you on, A or B?"

"I'm nursing. My baby's not supposed to get a bottle." From their annoyed expressions, I saw this tack wouldn't succeed. I'd have to emphasize my self-interest, rather than that of my child, whom they all believe can get along quite well without pampering: the infants should have enough gratitude for having been born at all to give their poor mothers a chance to rest. "I'll get engorged if I don't nurse. *Nora koev li.*"

One of the nurses waved me on in, frowning.

So now. With Avivah, whose name does not fit...Here I am feeling strangely alienated from her at the same time that I'm fighting with the nurses to let her stay here in the room with me between feedings. What is it about a newborn infant that elicits from certain nurses in every hospital an almost aggressive roughness toward mother and child?

Yesterday, since Eli has the measles, Yaacov couldn't accompany me here on the trip from the hospital, so I asked my friend Robin if she could help me. She rearranged her schedule and arrived shortly. Robin and I don't see each other often; throughout my pregnancy, she visited perhaps five times. So she had a vivid experience of how my body expanded over the nine-month period, and now, suddenly: the miracle of this living child.

As I got all my stuff together in the hospital, Robin watched a nurse dress the baby. I came into the nursery just as the nurse was pricking the baby's heels with a sharp metal device, a standard blood test all infants undergo. Robin stood there, forehead furrowed, mouth open, aghast. Over the years I have protested the brutality of this harrowing procedure, to no avail, so this time I decided to spare myself, keep silent and bear it callously. The nurse squeezed the baby's heel harder because not enough blood had been collected. I whimpered. My hand shot out. "Why do you have to—?"

The nurse reprimanded me. "It's nothing. She doesn't even feel it." Avivah was screaming. This is only an infant, the nurse meant to explain, so what if it hurts a little, the baby doesn't know anything and won't remember anything. Such a small body can't have important feelings.

When we got settled in the taxi, blankets and tote bags all around me, I looked over at Robin. "Robin! What's wrong?"

"When I have my children," she announced, chin uplifted defiantly, eyes brimming, "I'm not going to do it in a hospital. The nurse dressed your baby as if she were a sack of potatoes! The baby was shivering and her arms were flailing around all over the place. Your baby was being knocked around, Sarah! And she had this look in her eyes like this!" Robin imitated an expression of absolute chaotic bewilderment. "Couldn't the nurse do it gently? Sure, I know, I guess that the nurse sees so many babies and she probably isn't a cruel person, she's just so used to all these newborns." Robin turned her head towards the Jerusalem Forest drifting by on our right. "But the most precious thing in the world is a newborn baby. What in the world is more precious than a newborn baby? They're the ones who need the most gentleness, more gentleness and tenderness than anyone else. But instead—" She broke off and looked out the window. In the half-light of the car her face took on a statue-like determination. "This world is so cruel. It's unbelievable. I looked at some of those newborns in the hospital and they seemed to me to have already gone through lifetimes. Look at your baby now. When I first saw her, her face was so peaceful. Now she's all tense and her mouth's like this—" Robin imitated Avivah's tightly pursed lips. "She's been hurt already. She's been damaged."

My insides clenched up. "I don't think it's that serious." I looked down into the baby's face, refusing to contemplate such a horrendous possibility. Primal experiences cannot do you in: G-d is too kind for that...besides, He has other things in mind for this soul. I scanned ahead through Avivah's future. *Gan.* School. Fighting with sisters and brothers. Marriage. Mid-life crisis. Old age. For goodness sake, in ten years this will be as nothing. In ten days. In ten minutes. "She'll get over it, Robin." I sounded like a hospital nurse. "She did have a frantic morning and you're right that it affected her, but she's got a whole lifetime ahead of her of painful things that she'll endure, like all human beings. And you know that I'm going to be just like that nurse towards her sometimes? A lot of times! I'll be insensitive and busy and impatient. In order to do my job, I'll diminish my own sensitivity. And when you're a mother, Robin, sometimes your own human nature will get the better of you, too, and you also won't always be so kind to your child!"

I felt defensive and anxious, as if my fists were up. Robin was right, that from the first moments of life, the desensitization begins. But no...she's wrong: even were a child to be shielded from all ungentleness, that child would one way or another get his fair share of pain and suffering. It's built in. You have to have more faith in the whole life process. It's true that in response to someone who's helpless, needy and vulnerable, mankind's reflex is so often not one of tenderness but one of callousness. This must be looked upon as a given.

"She'll get over it, Robin. With enough of the other side of things to balance things out, she'll be just fine." It was so nice to have a friend who cared about my child. I was grateful to her for being overly worried; it helped me to not worry so much myself.

Robin gazed upon me as I spoke as if she were far away, as if she were looking upon cruelty's own apologist. "Well, that could be, Sarah. I hope she'll be O.K. Good. I'm glad she'll be O.K." She closed her eyes and lay her head back against the seat. "But I'd like to know why that is, Sarah. Why people are cruel to people who are weaker."

March 25, 1987

I have just staggered forth from the dining room, so full that my stomach hurts. After finishing the delicious grilled liver with onions, the barley soup, the beet and cucumber vinaigrette and the marinated peppers, I arose, fetched from the smorgasbord my dessert of apricots in sweet syrup, finished it off and prepared to make my exit.

Then they brought out the main course.

Consuming the large, crispy drumstick and green peas, I was myself consumed by guilt. What were Yaacov and the children eating? It's so much fun to eat delicious food, and I don't offer them a fraction of this. I have such a load of guilt about my preparation of food for my family. I always compare it to what my mother does.

The same general principle holds for my cooking as in other areas of my behavior: the guilt itself stands in the way of changing.

I asked one of the women at the table if she had any other children at home. "Yes, thank G-d," she said. "I'm the proud mother of three monsters."

March 28, 1987

I've come to the conclusion that tonight, my last night here, I will let them feed the baby Materna and I will sleep. And I will take pleasure in demonstrating thereby that nursing has not become for me another religion.

Now that I know the ropes here, I'm having a wonderful, wonderful time. Yaacov said yesterday that if I would like to stay another day, it's all right with him, but our conversation on the phone tonight convinced me otherwise. Eli is still cranky and not eating. "Give him a banana," I suggested.

"I don't have any."

"So buy some."

"But I can't take him with me to the store because of the measles."

"So ask someone to stay with him while you go."

"Well, somebody offered to, but then when I asked her to do it she said she couldn't."

"Ask her again."

"I already did, twice. That's enough."

So I must go home. I want so much to be holding Eli in my arms. He's the only one I miss, I think because he's the only one I'm really worried about right now. The other children sound fine, thanks to Yaacov. What a terrible thing for that baby, to come down with measles just when I disappear. He must be so baffled and miserable. I love him so much, that baby.

I must have faith that that's how I'll feel one day about Avivah. Today I did feel a drop of something.

When I got off the phone with Yaacov I rushed into the dining room to grab up my fair share of the loot. It was a smorgasbord. The woman next to me asked how I stay so slim, which made me ridiculously happy. *Is she blind, or does my robe hide it somehow?* She was actually just telling me what all of us want to hear. I'm so self-conscious, I feel as if I'm the only one who's pregnant without being pregnant. Does everyone feel like that? Why in the world do we expect our stomachs to flatten up as soon as the cord is cut? Why do we expect to be teenagers? "Are you kidding?" I said. "My stomach is just as if I'm seven months pregnant. There could be another baby in there."

She looked relieved. "Yeah, me too. My doctor examined me and said that my stomach muscles were a bit weak. I felt like saying, 'Oh thanks, I needed that.' I've just decided that this time I'm going to stay in a robe for six weeks until I can fit into my clothes."

I also found out at dinner that this place runs on contributions from Americans. This whole thing's just one big mitzvah, not a successful profit-making business at all. There are only fifty-two women here tonight, and the food is outrageously copious and sumptuous. It's a reflection of Judaism's respect for mothers. Knowing that I'm here because of some unknown people's *chessed* makes me feel cared for and valued.

The wind was blowing hard late this afternoon, and I was looking out a large window. Mrs. Benjamin, a calm and self-contained woman from Meah Shearim, who just had her thirteenth child, stood next to me. She pointed to a bird who was trying to travel against the wind. He was mostly just staying in one place, bobbing up and down with outstretched wings, floating. "Look at that bird," she said. "You see that? He doesn't push himself against the wind when it's this strong. He just waits. He knows he can't always do what he wants."

March 29, 1987

I have just arrived home. Danny looks like such a lovely boy. Rachel looks so beautiful. They're eight now. They're growing up. I feel so proud of them. I feel deeply relaxed. All my reflexes are slowed down, as if I'm making my way like a turtle through gentle underwater tides. I'm so happy to see Eli again. He was asleep when I arrived, and when he finally awoke I hurried in to him, picked him up out of his crib and held him for I don't know how long—the moment I'd been waiting for. Then I sat down on the couch with him, wondering if he knew me still, suspecting that he recognized the sensation of being held by this lady, her face and smile must have been comfortingly familiar even if the identity was foggy. Out of the corner of my eye, Yaacov seemed to be watching. I imagined how moved he must be by this tender scene of mother-child reunion, and I started getting pretty moved myself by this poignant little movie. Then I looked up and saw that Yaacov wasn't even watching, he was balancing his checkbook. Ah, well.

It took me till nine o'clock to get everyone into bed, both because of my slowed-down reflexes and because Avivah woke up when I was in the middle of making dinner. I made a great demonstration (for the children's benefit) of serving them their pancakes before getting the baby. Compared to her long bouts of hysteria in the convalescent home, this slight delay was nothing. Then I nursed her at the kitchen table while the four of them were eating. (Eli had just fallen asleep when Avivah woke up. Thank

G-d, they keep missing each other like ships passing in the night.) Sitting down with the children while they eat is something that normally I wouldn't do. Ironic that it takes another baby for me to have time for it. They sang some long song together, something they must all know from school. And we all talked together. It was so nice. They're getting older. What a good thing it is to be compelled to sit down and shoot the breeze with all of them.

I remembered Mrs. Benjamin's words: "What you *can* do, do, and don't think about what you're unable to do. If the situation becomes difficult, *you* have to be as strong as iron."

March 30, 1987

Now Elisheva has measles. Mázal tov! That's just what we were scared of, because it's dangerous to newborns. I'm going to take a lot of vitamin C so it will be in my milk. My mother told me that vitamin C diminishes the effect of measles.

This morning Yaacov opened up a handkerchief to blow his nose and held it up for me to see. It was more hole than handkerchief. He pretended to sneeze and blow his nose, and stuck his whole face through the hole. I cracked up laughing. Then he put on his sweater and counted exactly ten holes in it, so I sat down and sewed them. Impatient thoughts went through my mind such as: "I could be cleaning up now," or "I could be writing letters," or "Eli's making hungry noises from his crib, I should give him breakfast." Each time such a thought made its insidious way through my brain, I reminded myself of something else Mrs. Benjamin had said: "I always put my husband first."

As I sat there at one point rethreading my needle, Yaacov said he had something to tell me. I looked up. He was standing there with a big smile and tears filling his eyes. I thought he was going to thank me for finally sewing his sweater. "I don't know how to say this." I waited. He was still smiling and crying and he looked like an angel. "Thank you for Avivah."

April 1, 1987

Manifestations of Elisheva's jealousy toward Eli have subsided, perhaps temporarily. It must be because now it's the newborn who's always in my arms.

Daniel swept the floor this afternoon and did the dishes. When his friends came over to play a little while later, it was apparent that he felt a special self-possession and calm pride, and as a result was especially kind to everyone.

April 2, 1987

Last night I was so nervous about Pesach that after being woken up by Daniel, who got frightened at three in the morning, I couldn't go back to sleep. I got up at four thirty and eagerly set in cleaning. I was really in the mood. I'd do the two living room cabinets. I got water and soap and settled down comfortably on the floor, but no sooner had I set my hand to it than the baby woke up and I had to nurse. I panicked. *How in the world will I ever finish the Pesach cleaning?* Seething at this ridiculous situation, I leaned over to the bookcase and pulled out a book by Miriam Adahan, and flipping through the pages, I came across the proverb from *Mishlei* 3:7: "As a man thinks in his heart, so it is." Miriam Adahan writes: "We all tend to place an artificially low ceiling on the amount of discomfort we can bear, as, for example, in deciding that unless we get a certain number of hours sleep, we will 'collapse' or 'go crazy.' We seize fragments of events and make conclusions about the whole. And most important, we tend to think that our feelings are facts."

This calmed me down until Eli woke up crying for his bottle at six thirty. I was diapering Avivah, when I had a sudden rush of self-pity. "How in the world can I be expected to take care of two babies?" I went in angrily to wake up Yaacov. In spite of my nervousness, he was serene and understanding. "Yes, yes, Sarah, I'll help you, sweetheart," he cried, leaping instantly to his feet still half-asleep, looking like something out of a Harpo Marx routine.

This had an enormous effect on me. For the rest of the day I spoke calmly and gently and had an especially productive and happy day. Even now, I'm still surprised and grateful that my horrible expectations of the early morning were not fulfilled.

April 3, 1987

I was diapering the baby this morning and hadn't yet managed to get her clean. Eli, entertaining himself with his ongoing contest with gravity, was staggering from one side of the bedroom to another, stumbling excitedly towards each wall in turn as if into someone's warm embrace.

As I studiously worked over Avivah with the Handi-Wipes, her teeny-tiny legs, skinny as toothpicks, wavered about jerkily. I must have then done something to hurt or startle her because suddenly she exploded. Wow! That peculiar high-pitched, strident, rhythmic shriek of the newborn! It's a sound well designed to be absolutely compelling: no matter how many times I hear it, I respond as if to an emergency siren. I'd do anything just to make that noise stop. I fumbled hurriedly to get her wildly jerking legs into the Baby Gro. Eli catapulted himself over to the bed where I was sitting, and not having learned yet how to apply the brakes, charged right onto the baby. Her wail picked up again, spiraling a horrible octave higher.

As I concentrated tensely on the last snap, Eli suddenly grabbed hold of one miniature leg and pulled. My hand shot out just in time to save her, light as a feather, from being swept powerfully off onto the floor. Shocked by this first physical contact between the two of them, I gently disengaged his fist, but then his other hand caught hold forcefully of a teency-weency arm. Help! My free hand! I caught her again.

Aghast, I took a look at him now. Eli's whole body had become abruptly hushed and still. With head cocked ever so slightly to one side and eyes riveted upon the baby, he was observing her, those madly bicycling legs, the tiny clenched hands. Her shrill siren wailed.

Registered plainly in his eyes was an expression I had never seen in him before. For the first time since I got back home from the hospital, Eli had *noticed* Avivah, and was being struck by an awesome revelation: THIS OBJECT IS ALIVE.

A shiver of fear fluttered coldly through me.

What's that? I wondered. *Strange, what am I scared of?* But it was gone so fast that the identity of the fear eluded me. Was it the prospect, which indeed elicits a subtle panic, of my having from this time forth to guard the baby's very life, on a daily basis? Of the need for superhuman vigilance if I am to ward off terrible accidents? The fear of my enormous responsibility?

Yes, it was that, but it was something else as well: In Eli's eyes had been a certain glint, something that hinted at the existence of a mature, aware person secretly hiding in the garb of a baby's body. Someone at once both highly intelligent and primitive. As he stood there stock still, entranced by that screaming infant, I glimpsed in his wild and innocent eyes such a tender, mature human sadness that my heart, reflecting it, broke like a fragile mirror. Eli seemed to have discovered in those seconds that the big mommy he needs and loves more than anything in the whole world was taking care—could it be?—of someone else.

The moment passed and Eli drummed both hands playfully on the bed, banged on the pillow, then moved on down the line with a toothy grin of pleasure, absorbed once again by the amazing universe of lifeless objects: a discarded sock, half a crayon, Rachel's Fisher-Price roller skate.

Did I imagine that fleeting darkness in his light blue eyes, eyes as pure and translucent as a sunlit sky? Or was I privileged to witness in this child the historic first stirrings of jealousy—that ancient and powerful, most bitter and primitive of human emotions?

April 5, 1987

During my pregnancy I was so worried that the new baby would rob Eli of attention. Though this might be prematurely optimistic, it seems that Avivah's entrance into our lives has increased rather than diminished everybody's love for him. The two babies live in two separate orbits of human experience, and the contrast between them has heightened our awareness of both: Big, funny baby who walks, sings, sort of, and has begun to sense his rights. Delicate newborn, uncommunicative as a flower, wisp of weightless spirit, helpless, tinier than some of the girls' dolls. It's so surprising now to see Eli do things. A baby who laughs? What a joy! A baby who smiles at us? How astounding!

April 7, 1987

Since we started cleaning for Pesach, I've found it difficult to write. Each time I go towards the typewriter I feel guilty for wasting time. It's six days until the seder. The closer it gets, the more I feel squeezed between the two babies, diaper to diaper. One goes to sleep, the other wakes up. And when Eli's up, there's no baby-proof place for him to run around. He opens cabinets, pulls down books, plays with the telephone, stuffs his mouth with Lego and I stick my fingers in to dig it out. I must redesign my house to give him the free run that he so passionately needs. But how? This is crazy. I need an open *mirpesset*.

I dream of the apartment with the big porch, but there are so many legal problems with it. I pray that we don't lose that apartment.

I've lost my habit of speaking in a low voice. I pray that I can get it back, that this is only on account of the extraordinary pressure of Pesach cleaning. When the children don't obey me now, I jump, I bark, I bite, I slap. Danny especially, dear boy. The slaps are not nearly as hard or as frequent as they once were—yet they are enough to make him wild, frustrated and nervous again. These days, he doesn't kiss me or smile into my eyes, nor does he entwine his arms about my neck when I lean down to kiss him good night.

April 10, 1987

Three more days until Pesach. Eli opens a kitchen cabinet and

I yell at him, "Get out! Get out of there! Yaacov! Put him in his crib or I'll smack him!" Yaacov lifts his head out of the hollow cabinet he's scouring under the sink and throws me a look like a knife. I thought getting mad would elicit his love and sympathy. "Why do you look at me like that!" I snap. "Can't you see I can't stand this anymore, Yaacov? It's too much! Just too much!" The two of us get into an argument. We yell at the children. The children fight with each other. I can't stand the way the children say horrible things, like "shut up," to each other, so I scream at them: "Shut up or get out of the house!" Elisheva takes a swipe at Eli. I spank her. She shrieks, starts crying. I go back to work. Unattended, Elisheva consoles herself with her thumb, her pink pillow and her pink blanket, and curls up in a corner to sleep.

I feel no love for the babies, neither one of them. The thought crosses my mind that it's no good to have too many children. I can't do a good job. I feel absolutely not a drop of love for anyone. I feel frightened for the future.

April 11, 1987

Yaacov reported that Rebbetzin Chait asked how I'm doing, and he replied that it's difficult, that having two babies is like having twins again.

"Tell her that it's worth it," said Rebbetzin Chait.

April 24, 1987

It's now four in the morning. This is the first time I've picked up this notebook to write in what seems like a long time. It has not been a good time. I feel so depressed that it's hard to express myself.

Isn't it a bit late for postpartum depression? I'm all right physically, aside from some tiredness, but I feel as if I'm on a treadmill that's going too fast. I speed from one baby to the other, speed through dishes, speed to bring laundry up to the roof, throw something down on the table as a meal, put in another load. I never go out and don't know where I'd want to go. I want to scream sometimes: "Stop! Stop! Babies: be quiet. Children: stop it. Yaacov: stop. Stop. No more. No. No. No."

I have no time for myself. I have lost myself.

That's it. I have lost myself.

April 25, 1987

Miriam Levi called to say hello. We decided that, G-d willing, the workshop will start up again a week from this coming Tuesday. When I told her how I'm feeling, she suggested I keep in mind that it is, after all, right after Pesach. People are exhausted from that month of work, and now there's more work to do getting everything in the house back to normal. It's a pressured time for everyone.

Eli just woke up. He's cooing and singing to himself. He doesn't seem as happy as he used to. I remember the way he used to throw back his head and gurgle with pensive pleasure, for no apparent reason.

The possibility that my depression is as much post-Pesach as postpartum makes it less frightening. Hard to believe, but maybe I'll come out of it.

April 26, 1987

I have to maintain constant vigilance over my reactions. Rachel spilled some rice pudding this morning and I had to do some quick thinking. "It's all right," I said to her.

"I knew you'd say that," she answered. "You're a good mommy."

I feel encouraged to continue trying.

April 27, 1987

Rachel, her best friend Perla, and Perla's ten-year-old sister Bila are at this moment on the *mirpesset* conducting Elisheva's birthday party. She is five years old. Elisheva has anticipated this event for weeks, and in the last few days her excitement bordered painfully on ecstasy: she almost couldn't bear it.

It's up for debate whether anyone's having fun, other than the three masters of ceremony themselves, but no one could deny that if there was ever a well-organized affair, this must be it. Nine little girls are assembled on chairs lined up neatly against the wall, along with one boy, a downstairs neighbor, who was allowed to attend only because of a special relationship to the birthday girl: his mother and I shared the same maternity ward in Bikur Cholim Hospital five years ago.

Each participant has been asked to rise and give her name and address. Perla's three-year-old sister was spanked for jumping up and down on her chair. Daniel and his four curious friends were chased out of the house. Dinah was warned not to make noise while Bila was talking. Dinah has now quit altogether: she is upside down on the living room couch, kicking her feet up against the wall and shouting insults back into the gathering. "Stupid! You're so stupid, Perla! Bila's so stupid!" Every once in a while Rachel rushes out to plead with her in hushed exasperation to stop it.

When Elisheva herself ducked out of the festivities with tears in her eyes, and whispered to me with trembling lips that Rachel wouldn't let her touch the birthday cake, I realized that I had let things go too far. I summoned Rachel discreetly with one finger. "Rachel," I whispered, "You don't have to act like a policeman. Let Elisheva and everyone have fun. It's supposed to be fun for them."

"*I know!*" she whispered back in anguish. "We *know* how to do a party, *really*! Bila knows *so well* how to do a party. *Please!* Don't come in!" This plea was as earnest and heartfelt as Elisheva's. I sank into the couch and watched now, wondering. Elisheva wiped her eyes on her sleeve and ran back to her chair. Dinah stayed where she was, upside down.

Ten minutes have passed. This celebration bears no comparison to the pitifully meaningless pin-the-tail-on-the-donkey free-for-alls of my youth in the Old Country. I'm beginning to see the merits of Bila's genuine Israeli approach, for this thing is shaping up as a no nonsense party with structure, interest and purpose. Each girl has risen to give a blessing to Elisheva on this great occasion. "May you be a *tzadekkes*." "May you have many children." "May you marry a *talmid chacham*." "May you live to see the Temple rebuilt in our days." "May you be like Sarah, Rivkah, Rachel and Leah." "May you go straight to Gan Eden."

As Rachel and Perla hover over all, keeping order, Bila runs everyone through cheerfully military, carefully orchestrated songs and games. In one presentation, each girl recited certain phrases (that I couldn't catch), which elicited, in turn, specific responses from the others, in unison. In another, all of them recited a poem wishing Elisheva happiness and righteousness until 120. The one they have just completed was a performance worthy of the Mickey Mouse Club: against the background of a suspenseful, drawn-out humming, which grew gradually louder, each girl sweetly sang out a number, starting from one and on up to eighteen, whereupon they all burst out: "*CHAI!*"

It's now nine o'clock and the kids are finally in bed. The party was, in its own way, a smashing success, but for Dinah it was a disaster. There weren't enough bags of goodies to go around, and who ended up as the one who had to go without? Dinah, of course. Things like this always seem to happen to her more than to other people. One could blame it on the fact that she was upside down on the couch when Bila was handing out the bags, but that would be missing the point. Dinah is not one to submit to senseless indignity, and that's good, but it means that neither does she reap the benefits of conformity.

The rest of the afternoon and evening was uncomfortable for the whole family. Dinah yelled and cried for hours and hours, and though I offered her money to buy herself some junk food tomorrow, she was inconsolable. There was not much I could say, for she was right. She had suffered an inexcusable injustice. Rachel tried to comfort her but missed the mark. "It's your *mazal*, that's all, Dinah," she said.

"Be quiet, Racheli! You're so stupid!"

Rachel wandered off into her room. Dinah sobbed.

Some time later Rachel reappeared. She handed Dinah her own bag, which had not been opened. "I don't want it!" cried Dinah, at wit's end. "I don't need it! I want my own!" This showed me that Dinah's pain was not at having been deprived of the lollipop, pretzels and candies in and of themselves. Dinah was after something else, something more sublime: a recognition of her equality. Since the reality was that *there were no more bags,* how could this wound to her dignity be healed?

As I tucked Dinah in tonight, I noticed that for a six-year-old, she really looked pretty haggard. It had been a long, hard day for her, a day of real suffering. I dared now to suggest, hesitantly, that perhaps it was because G-d loved her that she had been given this special test, not to have what everyone else did. What else could I say?

To my surprise, she accepted this point of view. "That's right," she said hoarsely, her little head on the pillow. "Maybe *HaShem* did it because He didn't want me to eat all that junk."

April 29, 1987

It's hard rounding up the kids for dinner and bedtime these days because of daylight savings time. They've been going to sleep night after night past nine o'clock, and they go off to school groggy. So tonight, when Daniel rushed into the house at ten of seven to go to the bathroom, I locked the door behind him and put the key in my pocket. "Mommy!" he called out happily, "we're going to the forest!"

I braced myself. "No, Danny, it's seven o'clock. There's school tomorrow. You're all going to have dinner and go to bed."

His face wrenched up in agony. He looked at his watch. "No! It's not seven! It's six forty-eight! I'm going!" He ran to the door, gave a pull, realized it was locked. With clenched hands, red face and a furious light in his eyes, he shouted and cried and jumped around like a caged tiger. "But I promised them! They're waiting for me!"

"No, Danny," I repeated quietly.

He grabbed a handful of pecans and threw them across the room. They smashed against a wall. Avivah started crying from the bedroom. "Avivah woke up," Rachel called out from somewhere in the apartment. I told Danny to pick up the nuts. He wouldn't. I wondered: *Maybe I should just let him go. Maybe I really should. He's so upset. Is it that important to have him home right now?* But Miriam Levi's words came back to me: If a child cannot tolerate no, then you better tell him no more often.

Danny was weeping deeply. I wondered again if I was mistaken. *Springtime...friends...a little boy's play...*Danny ran to the window bars to look down at the other boys walking toward the Ramot Forest. "Mommy! Mommy! Please let me go! I promise I'll be back in one minute! Please, Mommy!"

"No, Danny," I said again, quietly. "There will be many times when you want to do things and I'll have to say no."

He sat at the window, legs dangling out, forehead pressed against the bars. Several minutes passed. "Mommy," he said, turning his head around to me and pointing at the window box. "If I don't take my eyes off the flowers and I keep looking at them all the time, right, I'll see them open?"

Thank G-d. Now I just had to get him to pick up the pecans.

And yes, Daniel, it is possible to see flowers opening.

May 3, 1987

Bedtime tonight began to resemble bedtime as I used to know it. I was yelling, pushing, spanking, threatening. They were talking back, running away from me, fighting with each other. It was torture. I felt myself suddenly injected with apprehension: is it going to be like this again every night?

This fear, laced with adrenaline, shot a warning through my system: Danger! Stop! Wrong way!

I must have lowered my voice and brought down my temperature, for the atmosphere cleared. The children began to mind me. They went to bed a little after eight, in a good mood.

It's later on, around ten thirty. I was just thinking about my anger yesterday and today, and I think it's because of my frustration and boredom at being consumed by the two babies. In between the rush from one diaper to the next, one meal to the next, from dish load to laundry load, crying child to crying child...running to catch up all the time, I have lost sight of the underlying meaning of it all. I'm sure there is a meaning, but I'm too drained to look for it. Aren't I supposed to be happy and awed by the wondrousness of a new life? Instead, I'm sensing the shadow of that familiar old fear—that life is slipping away from me, that I'm not accomplishing anything, or at least not seeing it if I am. To not see it is to not take pleasure in it. My accomplishments are: the changed diaper, the wiped nose, the clean floor, the laundry dry on the line, the child smiling. These accomplishments are subject to instant disappearance. The next time I look, the job has been undone.

I wish I could acquire a better perspective on the larger picture. The long-term achievements.

I probably have everything a person in this world can have, but if you don't know you have it, it's as if you have nothing. If I just had the key to appreciating what I have, I'd be rich.

May 6, 1987

Last night Miriam passed out optional questionnaires at the workshop. I was so depressed, I whipped out my pen and scribbled down the first thing that came to mind. It went like this:

PRESENTING PROBLEM

1. Describe the problem in general terms in no more than three sentences. Mention, if possible, when the problem began and how long it has existed. My anxiety about giving the children good food, along with my dislike for spending my time cooking. I'm insecure and unimaginative and blocked when it comes to figuring out menus, because I used to hate eating the healthy meals my mother served me as a child, precisely because they were healthy, I think. I wanted the instant soups and frozen corn and desserts that I saw in the homes of my friends. I had to finish everything on my plate before getting up from the table.

2. *Present a typical incident involving the problem behavior.* I'll make a separate meal for each child, according to what each one is willing to eat!

a. *What are your thoughts about the behavior when it occurs?* This is ridiculous! What bad children for making me go to such unnecessary bother! I'm so stupid! Change!

b. *How do you feel as a result?* Angry.

c. *How do you then react?* Impulsively lash out at the children.

I had no intention of passing the sheet back to Miriam for discussion; this was not the place for such deep problems, and I would expect any listener to say something like, "Sorry, lady, you don't need a workshop. What you need is a psychiatrist." But the woman sitting next to me spotted my sheet sticking out of my notebook a few minutes later and asked if I'd forgotten to hand it in. Since everyone was looking, I was embarrassed to refuse.

When Miriam Levi read mine to the class, I defensively announced that we didn't need to spend time in the workshop going into it. "It's too deep a problem, I think."

It was with a tentative little smile of apology that she disagreed. "I do think that there's a solution to this. Can you describe the problem more fully?"

"Well," I replied, "for one thing there's the fight over whole wheat bread or white bread. All their friends eat white bread so my children are ashamed of eating the weird dark bread. They say it's icky. If I forbid the white bread, it becomes more desirable. If I let them have it just occasionally, they develop a taste for it and want it all the time."

"What I would suggest," said Miriam, "is not to force them. Put both white and whole wheat bread on the table. You can have a talk with them about it. Don't be afraid to indoctrinate them. You can say something like: 'You know, children, you may think that your friends are lucky to be eating white bread, but it's really you who are the lucky ones, because to make that bread white, they take everything out of the wheat that *HaShem* put into it to make it life-giving. It's so silly, isn't it? But you can decide yourselves, children, which bread you want to have today.' "

"I do try to give them a choice sometimes," I said. "But I can't carry it off. For instance, a few days ago, Rachel said she wasn't hungry for lunch, so I said the opposite of what I was feeling. I told her, 'O.K., Rachel, you don't have to eat.' I thought she'd get hungry and change her mind. A while later, thinking about how tired and kvetchy she'd get later on in the afternoon, I called her into the kitchen, and she called back: 'But you said I don't have to eat.' I got so indignant and frustrated, looking at all that uneaten food I'd prepared, that I yelled, 'Come in here right now and eat!' "

Miriam advised me to decide on a course of action in relation to these questions, to make some hard and fast decisions, and then stick to them. I would have to think it over carefully, she said. For example, am I going to let them have white bread? Never? Sometimes? Just in their snacks for school, when they're with their friends? Just on Shabbat? Also, rather than thinking how terrible it would be for them to have the white bread, that they have to have the whole wheat otherwise I'm not a good mother, perhaps I could think something like: It would be much better for them to have the whole wheat bread all the time, yet isn't it counterproductive to make an issue of it? What can I do to find a harmonious solution?

I got a flashback of standing in the kitchen of pretty, blonde Donna Worral in New Canaan, Connecticut. I was there for a slumber party. She opened up her refrigerator, and I remember experiencing an almost physical pain of sad awe that right there, right there at Donna's fingertips, available for a taste whenever she wanted, was a long, hefty, red and white aerosol container of Redi-Whip, the whipped cream topping for ice cream and cake. To my amazement, Donna took something else out of the refrigerator and closed the door. Wow...if that were my house I would have secretly taken that thing outdoors somewhere and tasted it and tasted it as many times as I wanted. She was so lucky! How I wanted my mother to be as ignorant and lenient as Mrs. Worral. I ached with yearning and envy.

"Miriam," I said, "whenever one of the kids has a birthday, I engage in my own private popularity contest—hoping my children will look upon me as the best mother who serves the most junky, fantastic cake of all the mothers."

"What would be if you don't succeed in winning their favor over this?"

"Well, I remember being so angry and sad that my mother didn't give me what I wanted."

"You don't want your children to be angry at you?"

"Right. I want them to love me."

"It's inevitable that our children will dislike us at times. Look, perhaps you can steer away from this problem. Instead of thinking, 'I must give them only healthy food all the time,' you can think, 'I will try to give my children healthy food.' The main thing is to do it lovingly, not angrily."

Miriam reiterated her own personal preference for putting food on the table in big dishes in the middle, letting each person take as much or as little as he wishes. "Good meals can be so simple. Some fresh, raw vegetables, a few slices of whole wheat bread, some yogurt or cottage cheese—and there you have a balanced, healthful menu."

May 13, 1987

Last night at the workshop I brought up my problem with Dinah. When Dinah started first grade, she was so excited about learning to read and write that she used to burst through the door after school, throw her books down right there on the floor, and start her homework before I could get her to eat lunch. But a few months after the school year began, she came home one day and said she wouldn't do her homework anymore. I finally got it out of her that her teacher—whom Dinah loves so much that she calls her the best teacher in the whole world—had reprimanded her for not writing her homework neatly.

From that day on, Dinah has followed through on her new resolution: she does her homework only if I remind her, and finishes it with distaste, just to get it over with. My anger at the teacher is not insubstantial; she should have known better. But when I went to the school to discuss it with her, she was receptive and eager to correct her mistake. "I thought that Dinah was starting to be careless, and I didn't want her to start bad habits," the teacher explained. "I'm glad you came to tell me this, and I will try to give her encouragement now."

It's such a pity, it's such a pity, I keep thinking in bitter futility. *Dinah was in love with reading and writing!* But I can't ignore the fact that this development cannot be laid entirely at the teacher's feet. For what must be a year or so, Dinah has manifested an unaccountable inner tension which erupts over what appear to be trifles: someone touches her food—she pushes away the dish; if her socks don't match to a T, she explodes; if her popsicle breaks, she throws the whole thing away; if she's one minute late for school, she won't go at all.

Miriam Levi said that it sounds as if Dinah is a child who demands perfection of herself. This expresses itself in her desire for external perfection, and manifested itself also in her excessive vulnerability to that one criticism. Dinah seems to feel that any failure totally wipes out any success. If she loses favor in her beloved teacher's eyes in any respect, then she loses her sense of worth as a person, and there's no use trying.

With all due respect to teachers, she continued, and to the educational system, we must bear in mind that failure and success in school is not the yardstick by which Judaism measures a person. Sometimes a child is made to feel that failing an exam in school is a terrible offense. We can remind our children that although it's very nice to do well in school, their worth as human beings does not depend on their scholastic performance.

It seems to me that we have to tread a thin line between the need to inculcate respect for teachers and the need to develop a child's healthy self-respect. Teachers can make mistakes. Even a teacher as competent, sincere and sensitive as this one can, with one ill-advised comment, inadvertantly destroy a little girl's zeal and joy in learning. Teachers are human. We expect them not to be.

During the workshop I sat on the couch holding Avivah in my arms. It's so hard to believe it was eleven months ago that I sat in that very same spot announcing my pregnancy. The microscopic, itsy-bitsy speck of whatever it was that produced a positive result in the lab test bears no relation that I can see or feel to the baby who came along later. The reality of the child is unassociated in my mind with the nausea, anxious imagination and bewilderment of last July. My pain and fear, so tangible then, now appear like the passing shadows, the nothingness and emptiness before the creation of a world. From out of *tohu* and *vohu* a human child appeared. "In the beginning...when the earth was desolate and void, and darkness was upon the face of the murmuring deep..." Creation out of nothingness.

May 14, 1987

Candis called this week. She's in her seventh month. She asked a lot about Elisheva. The last time Candis saw her, Elisheva was two.

Since our conversation, I have found myself focusing more on Elisheva. The whole year of Eli's life, she has gotten a lot of: "No, Elisheva! Put him down!" "Let him crawl by himself! That bothers him!" "Elisheva, did you hit him?" Some time ago, I resolved to work on that, but didn't change things significantly. Now, again, I hope to restrain myself from such remarks unless his safety is at stake.

Yesterday I asked Elisheva to draw a picture of a person. "I don't know how," she said.

I was horrified. "Of course you know how, Elisheva! Somebody's just made you think you don't know how. However you like to do it, that's the right way for you."

She looked at me wide-eyed. "But the legs I don't know how to do, and the nose and the arms."

This was ominous. Has she that little faith in her own perceptions? And it's my fault for not spending time with her drawing—teaching her that she doesn't need to be taught.

I did convince her to do a drawing. She did a clown and a house. It's adorable.

May 15, 1987

I have found that the only thing that works with Dinah in the morning is to encourage her gently and fortify her self-confidence that she is the sort of person who arrives on time. I also have to confer occasionally with her teacher so that she knows we're trying.

It's vital, also, to let Dinah's independence express itself at every opportunity. Then, when she must submit, she is apt to do so more willingly.

I don't know why it is that almost every time I buy her something, even if she's right there doing the choosing, she will discover something wrong with it when we get home or a few days later. And sometimes, there does seem to be a real problem! Why is that?

The other day I bought shoes for Rachel, Dinah and Elisheva. Perhaps it was because they all had decided to get the same shoes, but on the bus ride back home, Dinah whispered into my ear: "Mommy, when I get home I'm not going to say I don't like my shoes."

May 17, 1987

This morning as Eli was happily splashing and kicking in his bath, gurgling, sputtering bubbly non-words of surprise at the wet, funny water, I realized how I myself, to some extent, turn into a one-year-old in the process of relating to him. Each time a woman has a child, it's an opportunity to begin her life journey anew. "Oh, I wish I could do it over again," people sigh with regret. But they can.

May 18, 1987

If yesterday was manageable, then let's say that today was...was...an impossible dream. I gave both babies baths early in the morning so that they'd sleep a long time. They were awake all morning.

I have been running all morning and afternoon without cease, like a madwoman, trying desperately to get through the house-work. It's six o'clock in the evening now, and the sky is bright. Avivah just woke up again. I am beside myself with frustration, seething with boredom. Rachel took Eli downstairs, thank G-d.

My friend Rose just called, and I poured out my bitterness to her—and she herself is suffering from not getting pregnant. I feel much lighter of heart now, having told someone and not being condemned for it. The worst thing, I realized, is my guilt for being an ingrate. YOU SHOULD BE HAPPY! a vicious witch screams at me in silence. YOU TERRIBLE WOMAN WHO DOESN'T APPRE-CIATE G-D'S GIFTS!

Avivah just began crying again. I guess that seething is not going to help lessen the demands upon me, is it. Smiling might help. Speaking calmly might help. Say to yourself, "Sarah, it's all right, be calm, take good care of the children."

May 21, 1987

It's ten thirty at night, and the whole time I've been cleaning up, I've been thinking how much I want to sit down and write what I'm feeling. On one hand, I feel constricted and hemmed in by the endless tasks: wash the dishes; organize the food in the refrigerator before you wash the dishes so that you can wash the pots in the refrigerator; stop washing dishes and throw out all the leftovers in the refrigerator so that you can organize the refrigera-tor and find the pots; oops, garbage cans are full, take out the garbage so you can throw away the leftovers, but first empty the laundry hampers and start up a load in the washing machine so you can make room in the laundry room for the garbage cans...On the other hand, as the kitchen begins taking on light, and order, and cleanliness, I start getting a little exhilarated by the gradual clearing away of confusion. This was the night I was going to go to bed early because I've been so exhausted, but the solid satisfaction of having these silent night hours to work while the children sleep is like seeing my own personal dawn, of my own making, break over a dark, jumbled countryside. To get something done. It feels so good.

The task of sitting down here to write in the diary is more intimidating. Will I ever be able to get it all down? Time is piling up and piling up and I forget things that happen. Life gets swept away by the endless flood of intricate, forgettable throwaways of daily existence. Life gets thrown away in the garbage unless I can force myself to sit down here and catch things before they disappear. Where is the meaning? Where are the million tiny meanings and the big, colossal meanings, the small and fragile glimmers and the big chunks of stuff that I want to catch before they're swept out to sea? The only way I can do it is to keep this journal. Dear Diary. Dear dear diary. As a child I wondered why Anne Frank addressed each entry in her diary "Dear Kitty." Now I can imagine—her diary was her friend.

I have been so depressed during these weeks of never being able to get my head above water. I figure that if taking care of the babies is a full-time job, and cleaning the house is a full-time job, and keeping everyone else dressed and out of the jaws of starvation is another full-time job, then when in the world will I have time to breathe in and enjoy it all, or even just notice that I'm here, let alone record it so that it's not lost to me forever?

May 24, 1987

Avivah laughed today.

Sometimes I daydream that maybe this child is the one I'll be closest to, but that's a false, melodramatic way of revving up love for her. I don't need to make comparisons in order to feel something. The fact is, every one of them is the child I've always dreamed of. Each one is the child without whom I can't imagine living.

I'm so tired. I'm so tired. I'll do the dishes and then go to bed. Why do I always have this critical, complaining, nagging voice in the back of my mind? "Don't go to bed. That's a waste of time. You could do something better..." Then, if I do stay up, it's: "Fool. You'll be exhausted tomorrow."

It depresses me to imagine that one day I will yell at Avivah and Eli the way I do at Dinah, Rachel, Daniel and Elisheva. It must be possible to keep that sense of awe you have for a newborn. If you were to treat all children as gently as you do an infant, then the awe wouldn't vanish.

Avivah just started crying. She sounds like a rusty seesaw.

Oh, no...and Eli is making noises, too.

I feel constantly that I need and want to boost myself up out of all this, over the wall...to get a peek into the garden beyond.

And that garden is my own life, that I myself am living.

12
Lost and Found

May 31, 1987

On Friday morning I went to the bank while Yaacov stayed with the children. It was a fair, clear, breezy morning and as I rushed along through Mea Shearim to catch the bus back home, I realized two things: one, I was happy; two, I was reining in that happiness as if it were inappropriate.

The baby might have woken up and is probably crying, I told myself. *I have so much cooking to do, it's not right that I should have to come to the bank on a Friday. Dinah had a tantrum today and I lost my temper. Elisheva is so jealous of Eli, she needs more attention. I haven't been in touch with Mommy lately. Oh! Yaacov needs an ironed shirt for Shabbat. Eli looks pale. I have to remember to pay the maaser money I forgot last month. Do I have on lipstick?*

The leaves of all the trees along Rechov Malchei Yisrael rustled in the sunlight, and the fair, blue sky sailed peacefully overhead, but nagging at me were all these things, all these imperfections of myself as wife, mother, daughter and Jew. I saw a momentary image of myself at a Shabbat table, pulling at the corners of the tablecloth to straighten it out—here, there, over there...this unending desire for order, peace and perfection.

So live with imperfection, I thought suddenly. Live in happiness with imperfection! Coexist with it, for imperfection's the name of the game, forever, in oneself and out there in the world. Let yourself be happy in spite of the problems...No! Not in spite of, but with the problems. The definition of life is the ironing out of problems.

A sunflower of happiness burst within me. Hold on to that happiness, I told myself. Make it stay!

Ah...no...for happiness is also imperfect...it comes and goes.

To live with imperfection, the imperfection that's within me, the imperfection in which I am submerged, like a fish in the sea. To not expect the ocean to be free of crosscurrents, mud, stones, sharks, fish, seaweed...

June 1, 1987

I sent Dinah and Elisheva to the store today and Dinah lied to me about how much change there had been. I saw the evidence: they had bought gum. When I asked her, she denied it, and flew about the house with a great show of cheerfulness and *joie de vivre*. I called her over. An embarrassed, awkward smile curled over her lips.

"Dinah," I said, "chewing gum is not the thing I'm worried about. It was that you lied to me." She turned her face away. "It doesn't make you a bad person, but it was a very bad thing to do." Her face went through some subtle changes. "Do you think it makes you a bad person, G-d forbid?"

"Yes! I'll go to *gehinnom!*" she cried angrily.

"No, Dinah." I put my arm around her. "*HaShem* knows that all children lie sometimes when they're scared. Were you scared?"

"Yes, that you'd hit me!"

"Maybe I would have hit you, but you still can't lie." Now, in a very soft voice: "Look at me." She turned her face tentatively. "Dinah, we can't lie."

She gazed into my eyes, cuddled up, then planted a kiss on my cheek—a warm, lovely kiss—and whispered wetly in my ear: "I won't lie, Mommy."

Case dismissed.

June 2, 1987

Elisheva and Eli have been playing together on the *mirpesset*. Tonight is Shavuos, and everyone else is sleeping in preparation for the long evening.

Every few minutes, Eli squeals in pain, then I catch sight of Elisheva retreating with a pensive little smile of satisfaction. Her power! She must feel like a giant with vast powers to cause him misery. A few times I've admonished her gently to cease and desist, but to no avail. Her poking at him, her needling, the illicit little jabs and stabs...A few minutes ago he sat down finally on the floor and cried, beside himself with despair and confusion. I gave him his bottle and blanket and took Elisheva with me to the couch. She fought me off, but I held on. "Elisheva," I began softly, "you can't hurt him like that." She stared at me. "Elisheva, you know, I had a sister who was bigger than me, and since I was smaller, she could hit me and I couldn't hit back. I was so scared."

Elisheva had stopped fighting off my embrace. "Who?"

"I can't say."

"It's *lashon hara*, right?"

"Right. But when she got older she apologized for doing it. She told me the reason she did it was because I was the baby and she wanted the attention that everyone was giving to me. I understand that so well."

Elisheva leaned her head against me and stuck her thumb in her mouth. A few moments went by. "*Motek* Mommy," she said, and stretched up to kiss me.

June 7, 1987

Dinah went eagerly to school on Friday morning because she was wearing her new sandals, but this morning she stalled again. I felt like pummeling her but restrained myself by thinking: "Be patient. It won't help to get mad, it'll just make things harder. After all your efforts, don't ruin it now." Becky gave her an eraser, saying that it was for going to school on time, but after Becky's departure, Dinah cried that the eraser was purple, not pink like Rachel's. This made me so angry that I glared right into her eyes and declared: "If you had a pink eraser, then tomorrow you'd probably find something else about it that you don't like. Right?"

Her face got an unusual expression. She was clearly taken aback. I had spoken to her as I would to any adult who was playing tricks on himself. Embarrassed to have been exposed—to herself as well as to me—Dinah smiled shyly.

When she was finally on her way out the door at five of nine, she turned back with a frightened look. "But if I come late, my teacher will yell at me."

"Yes. She might. I guess that tomorrow you can try again to leave on time." She was silent. "Dinah, do you want to be on time? Is it important to you?"

"No!" she shot back.

I didn't reply. She stood there.

"Bye-bye, Dinah." I smiled and closed the door. A few moments later I heard her little footsteps going downstairs.

June 8, 1987

I have just finished reading *Heroine of Rescue*, the account of Recha Sternbuch's rescue work during and following World War II. It infused me with a desire to stop complaining. I complain to my husband, to my children and to myself about how tired I am and how hard I'm working, while what that woman accomplished is just unbelievable. It proves what motherly love—which was, I believe, the power behind her efforts—can do. Unlimited love, unbounded motherly love, drove her to save thousands of individuals from the Nazis.

So here I am with my six children, my husband, our home. Is what I'm doing with my life of less significance in the eyes of G-d than what she did? The setting is less remarkable, but I am sure it would be possible for me to achieve as great a good with just these eight souls.

I shouldn't feel sorry for myself for having a burden; I would be worthy of pity if I had no burden.

I feel dwarfed by such heroism, yet her sister-in-law is quoted as having said that before the war, Recha Sternbuch didn't manifest the great strength which war brought to the surface. This makes me feel better; it could be that I, too, am latently in possession of a similar power. I have only to recognize the compelling nature of the challenge which faces me: to transform this home into a magnificent microcosm of G-d's kind and good world, to create an environment that will bring beauty out of me and Yaacov and the children who are growing up here.

If my job is sometimes too much for me, good! That means there's plenty of room for me to grow. Let me carry out my duty graciously, for goodness sake, and wisely, and be someone the children can emulate. Just to change my own *middos* is a giant task. To move from selfishness to generosity is in itself a gargantuan struggle. I can lift my eyebrows cynically to hear myself aspire suddenly to the greatness of Recha Sternbuch, but why not? We only live once. Why not try to be heroic?

Well, actually, there are plenty of reasons why not. I think I should probably just aim to stop complaining.

June 9, 1987

I got Dinah up at six today, but it was no use. At nine o'clock she was still here, and by the time I took her to school myself, I was drained. What happened is that I lost my temper terribly, spanked her and dragged her downstairs. She ran away from me when we got outside, and I stood there on the sidewalk bereft, immeasurably depressed, embarrassed before the light of day to find myself standing there like an idiot at the mercy of my six-year-old. It reminded me of the time I looked on with satisfaction as my neighbor beat up her little boy for not going to cheder. What would I be thinking if I were peeking comfortably out a window now at the scene which I myself had just been playing?

I had turned around in hopeless defeat and headed back home, when out of the corner of my eye I saw Dinah running towards me. "I'm not going to school!" she cried. Weary and speechless, I took her hand. In a fit of helplessness I started off with her up the hill to the left. School was to the right. She fell into step. "Where are we going?" she inquired after a minute.

"Up the hill." Where can I go with her, I wondered. I thought of going to Geulah to get milkshakes, but Yaacov would be leaving in a half-hour. Besides, I didn't have my purse with me. Ah, I could charge some stuff at the supermarket and have it delivered! "I'm going shopping. You want to help me get some things?" She smiled faintly and looked away. Her eyes were red. She, too, was exhausted.

On our way up the hill, we paused a few times to examine and smell the flowering bushes, and we took our time in the super-market, buying a lot of treats I knew she'd enjoy: vegetarian hot dogs, white rolls, sunflower seeds, pita bread, crackers, matzah, strawberry jam. We had both calmed down by this point, but I was still worn out. All of a sudden, on our way down the hill towards the school, she halted. Tears sprang into her eyes. "I'm shy to go."

A bench up ahead looked inviting. We sat down.

"My teacher's going to yell at me," she said.

"So...if she yells at you, Dinah, that doesn't mean you're bad. You were scared to go because you didn't do your homework— right, Dinah? Is that why you didn't want to go?" Dinah looked off in the distance to the Ramot mountain. She nodded and smiled. Her cheeks were wet with tears.

We looked together at a large, soft, pink blossom past its prime, drooping from the bush behind us, then rose and continued on, and entered the Bais Yaacov holding hands. Twice Dinah stopped in her tracks, and I urged her gently on. When her teacher opened the classroom door, she was about to ask Dinah why she was late but I signaled with my eyes: shhhh. Not now. As Dinah, her head held high, walked quickly to her desk, I whispered, "Please just give her encouragement today, Zivia."

Dinah arrived home from school happy.

June 10, 1987

This morning I began to lose my temper with Dinah, but the

hint of depression that crept up within me was enough of a warning to get a hold of myself. Fortunately, Yaacov came back for breakfast at ten of nine and promised her a shekel if she'd go to school on time for the rest of the week. Dinah lit up, and readied herself for departure...very slowly...playing with Eli and conversing with us. She changed her stockings (she said they weren't a pair).

I bit my lip.

June 11, 1987

Dinah at this moment is standing on a chair looking at herself in the mirror. Now she has gone back to the kitchen, where she has a buttered matzah and a cup of tea waiting for her on the table. It's ten o'clock in the morning. She should be in school. I decided to let her stay home today and have yet to see if my instincts are right. It became evident yesterday that nothing Yaacov or I have done to solve this problem is working. Her inner tension—from who knows how many sources—has tightened up into one grand knot within her, and any attempt on our part to untie it elicits nothing but more protests and resistance. On Shabbat I told her to change her dress since it had gotten dirty, and she flew into a rage. Sunday, the tantrum was set off when she couldn't find barrettes. Monday, her shoes didn't fit.

Yesterday, I came to the conclusion that something serious is going on here, and though we hadn't recently discussed it, Yaacov declared last night: "Dinah has a problem."

So this morning, when Dinah said she wasn't going, I said nothing and did nothing—not out of apathy: it was a throwing up of the hands. I no longer know what to do. Strictness, laxity, rewards, punishment, benign neglect, malign attention, empathy...everything has failed. Now my instinct is to let her be. I want to lift the pressure from off her little shoulders.

She spotted the unopened box of matzah we bought in the supermarket together the other day, and though it's worthless as far as nutrition goes, her relaxation is more important now. Whereas every other morning she must rush through breakfast, it was at her leisure that she carefully buttered two pieces. *How is this morning different from all other mornings?* Then she requested tea. *Forget about the caffeine, Sarah. Let her have it.* For several long minutes she watched the glass of hot water as the spirals and tendrils of auburn tea unfurled and uncurled from the tea bag. To be hurried is to Dinah anathema.

It's eleven o'clock, and Dinah is beginning to get dressed, by herself. All in all, she has accomplished in three hours what normally she must do in twenty minutes. Her cure, I believe, must be to be left alone for a while. I have faith in the capacity of her own self to effect a cure.

Looking back through the years (which is difficult to do accurately; the past is a series of such dim, undeveloped photos) I think I've been both too hard on Dinah and too soft. Ever since she was born, I've always adored her so passionately, and trusted the goodness of her character so deeply, that I have tended towards indulgence. I felt obligated to get angry just for the sake of balance, overconfident that it wouldn't hurt her because she got so much love. Besides, with jealous Rachel looking on, I was eager to demonstrate an even-handed policy. The upshot is that I have been short on discipline, which has made her stubborn, which has evoked my inconsistent anger. Nonetheless, she must have sensed my great love, which has contributed to her confidence to think and act independently.

I think now that it's of the utmost importance for me not to lose my temper with Dinah. At the same time, I mustn't give in to her tantrums. Tonight, G-d willing, I'll call Zivia and request her continued cooperation.

June 17, 1987

Last night we went to the wedding of Sender and Sarah Tannenbaum. In the hours preceding our grand departure, my time was swallowed up by the two babies, so the children had to bathe themselves, choose their own clothing, find matching socks, brush their own hair and keep the peace unaided. I felt pride and satisfaction to see how well they managed. It gave me confidence in the future. It made me think there's nothing better for children than a mother who's too busy to do everything for them.

At the wedding, Dinah said, "Mommy, the bride is so sweet. When I get married, I want to be a bride just like that."

June 21, 1987

Dinah has just gotten off to school. It's quarter to ten.

She was bumbling along at her usual turtle's pace this morning, and I was gritting my teeth with impatience, telling myself that after all I had done to relax her last week, I didn't wish to ruin it. I had clearly succeeded in reducing her anxiety and could trust now that her teacher would try to be patient. As she prepared her own lunch, combed her hair, finished her homework and wiped off her new sandals with toilet paper, she kept up a running monologue, to which I would nod my feigned interest.

"Mommy," Dinah chirped, "you know what?"

"What, Dinah. Did you get your shoes on, sweetie?"

"Do you know that you're a little baby?"

"A little baby? Really?" I glanced at the clock.

"Yes," she replied lovingly, with a mischievous little smile. "For *HaShem* you're just a tiny little baby, even though you're a mommy." Dinah gazed at me affectionately, awaiting my delight.

"Hmm. Isn't that lovely. Get your shoes on now, O.K.?"

Dinah sat herself down on the couch. With excruciating slowness she buckled the right shoe, then the left.

"O.K.! Bye-bye, darling," I called merrily, opening the door. "See you later!"

She paused to check what I'd given her to eat. "Challah!" she exclaimed. "Why did you give me challah? I want bread!"

"But Dinah, you love challah. It's white bread. That's what I gave Rachel, too, today."

"I don't care! I'm not like Racheli!"

"Oh, come on now! That's the only bread I have in the house! Take it! Take it and go!"

"I'm not eating it! I'm not eating it!"
"Oh, go to school now, for crying out loud! Go! Go!"
"I don't want you to be my mommy!"

June 29, 1987

I let Dinah stay home again from school this morning, and I'm so afraid that she'll think of herself as someone who runs away from difficult situations. I'm worried that she'll dislike and fear school for the rest of her educational career because of this long, bad experience in first grade. On the other hand, would it be right to physically force her to go? Both extremes are damaging, and I have only three more days until the end of the year. Perhaps I should really just keep hands off, stop all my efforts in this regard and let Dinah regain her own initiative. But even as I write this, I disagree: I should indeed see to it that these last three days in school, Dinah feels she is a success. Perhaps I should take her in hand and walk her there myself at eight o'clock.

I brought it up at an EMETT group a few days ago. "When people try to get rid of various negative traits in their children, they often do so by shaming them, and usually end up reinforcing that very behavior," Miriam Adahan said.

At the end of the class, Miriam said: "Whenever you're in a difficult situation, you can ask yourself: 'How can I use this situation to improve myself?' You can say to yourself, 'The more distress I feel, the harder I will work to look for things I can be grateful for.' When the situation is very serious, you cannot realistically expect an immediate lightening of the burden, but you can find reasons to be grateful. If a suitcase with all your clothes gets lost, be thankful that it wasn't the plane. If your husband is angry at you, be thankful you're not alone. If a child is ill, be thankful that it's not a really serious disease. If your neighbors are nasty, be thankful the disturbance is outside your home rather than inside.

"Rabbi Dessler says that the true service of G-d is built on a foundation of gratitude. That is our work from the moment we say *modeh ani* each morning."

July 2, 1987

I've worked for weeks on restoring Dinah's relaxed, happy attitude toward school, but this morning—the last day of first grade—I shattered the whole thing. When I looked up at the clock and saw it was quarter to nine, I shoved her out the door with a great show of impatience and frustration, and uttered words I refuse to record for posterity. After her subdued, melancholy departure I spent a frantic half-hour cleaning up the house, so depressed that Dinah's last day of school should be stained with misery, wishing I could run to school and take her hand. But I'm not that crazy. I'd need to find some excuse...and I found it! I'd make a "Farewell Kita Aleph" cake!

An hour later I was on my way to the Bais Yaacov, sweaty with exertion. I had asked my neighbor Miriam if I could leave Eli with her, and off I went with the cake balanced precariously on one hand and Avivah in the crook of my other arm. I spotted Dinah outside on the playground, solemn and quiet, observing a game of jump rope. Our battle had clearly taken its toll.

"Why did you bring that?" she asked when I approached her. I felt sheepish, and keenly disappointed. I had expected a bright smile of surprise.

"It's for your last day of school!"

"We don't need it," she stated with a shrug. My spirit went flat, as if she'd let all the air out of me, but when I handed her the platter, a crowd of chattering girls clamored around her instantly, trying to catch a glimpse of the spectacle I had created. Dinah looked up at me. What was in her eyes? She wondered how the loveless woman of the morning had turned into this fairy godmother bearing gifts. Atop the cake was a candy house, cookies for the roof and doors, and smoke rising from the chimney, with *"Shalom Kita Aleph!"* printed in careful chocolate letters inside a red heart. Morah Zivia was pleased.

Dinah, a celebrity, cut the cake judiciously and handed out the pieces to an enchanted public. She cast me a warm look of love.

I hurried back home with a bright star for a heart. By the skin of my teeth, I had corrected my mistake. Dinah's last day at school was a triumph, after all.

July 8, 1987

Tonight Dinah spent an hour or so preparing a sandwich and a bag of cucumber and sunflower seeds for dinner downstairs. She went out, but returned five minutes later. "Mommy," she whispered, "I'm embarrassed to eat downstairs because that girl Shoshi is there. I don't want her to see me eating."

Shoshi, about eleven, intimidates the younger children in the neighborhood and bosses them around. (I've also heard the girl's mother give Shoshi the same treatment.) Dinah is really scared of this child and on more than one occasion has come home in tears after a run-in with her. I was almost ready to encourage Dinah to overcome her discomfort, but realized that I sometimes feel the same way about being watched as I eat. "Oh," I said, "I understand."

"But she likes Rachel," Dinah added sadly.

Again I made sympathetic noises. Dinah looked at me. Her eyes widened, getting a little dreamy. With a small smile, she said: "I want to get married to you."

I was genuinely flattered. "You do, Dinah?"

"Yes. I'll be the *kallah* and you'll be the *chassan*." I smiled my consent. "Right, Mommy, I'll be more nice than you?"

"You mean prettier than me?"

"Right. Boys can't get dressed up so nicely."

"Right."

She stood there in silence a moment. "I'm going down now. Bye-bye!" I heard the door close behind her and she went to eat her dinner.

July 13, 1987

Candis called me from America last night. Her baby is four days old. She has come home from the hospital, but her baby has to stay in the incubator because he has jaundice.

"The baby is just beautiful," she told me. "You know this already, Sarah, but I see now how wonderful..." Her voice broke. "Just how wonderful it is to have children. I was scared that he wouldn't be normal. I was scared I wouldn't like the way he looks. But he is just beautiful. He has this tiny little mouth and a little nose. Even though he was a month early he was six pounds. We're so lucky! He's just fine. Just fine. But I'm crying all the time."

"Why, Candis? Because he's still in the hospital?"

"Yes. I spend around five or six hours there with him every day, but when I'm not there...the nurses are good but they don't comfort him when he cries. I just don't know why he has to start life like this." I heard a muffled sob. She caught herself. "I don't want him to be in pain."

I had all kinds of emotions as Candis spoke, but what I noticed, and was ashamed of, was my jealousy. *Jealous of Candis, my precious, beloved Candis? How can I?* How awful, but there it was. I was jealous of her for being a new mother, unjaded, a mother of her first child, her maternal instinct untarnished, pure. Their oneness as mother and child is perfect, their oneness is the loveliest thing on earth.

July 14, 1987

Elisheva stayed home from day camp today, so she was alone with Eli. I saw that having the two of them by themselves is a partial solution to her aggressive animosity towards him. She should have plenty of opportunities to take pride in herself as The Babysitter, The Big Sister, rather than just suffer the shame of being the jealous bad one. She really had fun playing with him, though from time to time she'd give him a good shove when she thought I wasn't looking.

In a workshop, Mrs. Levi said that jealousy is as pervasive as the common cold, but parents are horrified by it.

July 16, 1987

I was busy in the kitchen when the front door slammed and

Dinah rushed into the house. "Mommy!" she yelled, running towards my bedroom. "Where's Mommy?"

"I'm in the kitchen."

"Mommy! You know what?" She stood before me, eyes shining. Something very, very good must have happened. "Shoshi told me downstairs...I was downstairs sitting, and she told me I had to stand up, and I said no. And she told me I had to go stand in the corner because I wasn't doing what she said, and I said, 'I don't need to do what you tell me to do.' Then I ran away to tell you!" The most radiant smile broke over Dinah's small face.

"Good for you!" I clapped hands.

Dinah glowed.

July 19, 1987

Now that she doesn't have to rush to go to school in the morning, and doesn't have to worry about homework, Dinah is being reincarnated as herself the past few days, with her odd thoughts and whimsical spirals of imagination. Tonight she kept jumping on my back and laughing, "Sweet Mommy, sweet Mommy." Though I told myself that this is what I've been waiting for, for Dinah to be affectionate and playful again after her long winter of discontent, it got on my nerves to have her jump on my back like that, and at last I pulled her off. She kept on jumping, I kept pulling her off. "You'll always be my mommy," she told me, her arms around my neck, head thrown back as she gazed up pensively at the ceiling. "No. You're not going to be my mommy always. You're not my mommy now! *HaShem* is my mommy."

Dinah is back. Thank G-d.

July 20, 1987

In an EMETT class tonight, Miriam Adahan said that the noiser it is on the outside, the calmer you can tell yourself to be on the inside. So...the more frustration, the more need to learn patience. The more boredom with the mundane, the more need to create. The more disappointment, the more need to unearth joy. The more craziness (provided by crying children, dirty diapers, noisy fighting), the more genuine inner sanity one needs to develop.

July 21, 1987

A few times recently, I've been in the middle of yelling something when I remember: *whatever the problem, yelling is not going to make it better, it won't make me stronger.* So my sentences come out like this: "DANNY! STOP STANDING ON the broom, please." "ELISHEVA! GET YOUR hands off the tape recorder."

July 23, 1987

Speaking respectfully to one's children is a delightful experience, once one gets the hang of it. It's like switching channels to a higher frequency (nearer to heaven).

July 25, 1987

I was feeling really on top of things this morning, singing as I worked, zipping my way through the dishes and the laundry, pondering happily all the while how well I've been doing lately, anticipating more and more improvement and more and more rewards, when suddenly from the living room there came a shriek. Eli. I ran in. Elisheva had taken away his new little toy car.

My good mood was already lost and it was *her* fault! I rushed over to grab the car, and my hand shot out and slapped hers. So fast, before I even had a chance to think, "Let's see now, how shall I speak to her, come darling..." Then, of course, I had to deal with two crying children instead of one.

It's as if there were a tightly coiled-up jack-in-the-box hidden within me, operating quite autonomously and unconnected to my willpower. Whenever my pride of achievement starts getting mingled with cocky self-assurance, that tricky little toy pops out mindlessly and surprises me, reminding me that I'm not really in control of my actions after all.

On the other hand, it's precisely those times that I'm on guard, humbly aware that I'm not the all-knowing master of my soul, that I do stand a chance of exercising dominion over that mighty little jack-in-the-box within.

December 17, 1987

I'm at Elisheva's Chanukah party in her *gan*. I tore myself away from house cleaning to come here. I usually dither here and there (just the laundry, just the dishes) and arrive late to such affairs. This time, I told myself sternly that the possibility of her being disappointed and anxious for even one minute was not worth the pleasure I would get coming back home to a clean house.

At this moment she's in the Chanukah play, holding a candle and singing along with all the others—something about turning to *HaShem*. If I had my way, I would burst out into a torrent of noisy sobbing. Whether I could sustain the glorious emotion long enough to explain it to anyone is unlikely, but I suppose I'm moved and amazed that just as Rachel and Dinah once participated in almost identical productions, it is now Elisheva's turn. Soon enough, she will be in first grade.

Time flies. Mommy used to say that.

December 18, 1987

We moved apartments some months ago. That's the main reason I haven't written in here for so many months.

We lost the apartment I wanted so badly, the one with the huge *mirpesset* under the trees; the owner sold it right out from under our noses. I called him up. "How could you do this to me? You knew I was just waiting for the legal problems to be worked out."

"But *geveret*, the legal problems have not been worked out. I knew your husband would not agree."

He was right about that, but I loved that apartment. I couldn't imagine any other place that would be on the first floor, by a beautiful park, with a huge porch. It hadn't been love at first sight; those oddly laid out rooms had grown on me slowly and surely as I envisioned our future there; I even dreamed one night about the ugly purple tiles in the bathroom and decided they were just what I wanted. If I had only known someone else was ready to buy...I could have done something...something! "But I told you to let me know if you ever got another buyer who was serious, and you said you would! You gave me your word!"

"*Geveret*, what are you getting so worked up over? If, G-d forbid, you had lost a child, then you would have a reason to cry, but an apartment? An apartment is *mazal*."

This shut me up fast. I'm always an easy mark when it comes to being shamed. But when I spoke about the conversation in a workshop with Miriam Levi, she objected to his remark. "No," she said, "that was not right of him to say that to you. Of course he's right that the loss of a child is a tragedy and the loss of an apartment by comparison is not a terrible, terrible thing. But it is a legitimate cause for sadness, and there's nothing wrong with getting upset about it."

I called my parents to tell them that the apartment I had been raving about had been sold. "Sarah," my father told me, "don't worry about it. You'll find another apartment that you'll like even better."

"Oh, Daddy, I can't imagine that, but all right. I just don't know how long it will take for me to find another one I like that much."

"You'll find it soon. Don't worry."

Well, that's just what happened. Three days later I found the place we're in now, and I like it much, much more than either one of those other two apartments I was so infatuated with. Those were nothing but the *shidduchim* to help us recognize our real home when it came along. Does it have a huge *mirpesset*? No. It has a normal-sized one, but it's open to the sky—unlike the one in Sanhedria HaMurchevet. I found out that I can be completely happy without having all my dreams come true.

That man was right: my *mazal* was waiting for me, and it was my good fortune that the other place had legal problems.

December 20, 1987

Yesterday morning at the Shabbat table, I was just about to vent my resentment toward everyone for not helping me enough with the Shabbat preparations, when I inexplicably shifted gears. "Yaacov," I announced, "I want to tell you how much everybody helped me get ready for Shabbat. Becky made the coleslaw yesterday, and Thursday night she cleaned up the whole kitchen. Elisheva folded towels. Rachel took out both babies so I was able to clean up the house. Daniel swept the *mirpesset*. Dinah went to the store to buy the challahs and milk. The only people who didn't help me were—"

"Eli!" smiled Danny.

"Avivah!" said Dinah.

"Right!" I exclaimed, and we proceeded to have kiddush, all of us buoyant and happy. Once I had said it, I was surprised to realize just how much everyone had, indeed, pitched in.

December 23, 1987

One night last week, after Dinah had brushed her teeth, Yaacov sat down on her bed. "You know why you're having such trouble in the morning?" he asked her in a confidential tone.

I paused at the door. This was interesting.

"It's not you," he said. "It's the *yetzer hara*. Every morning the *yetzer hara* wants to cause you problems and make you sad, and it makes him *so happy* when you cry and go late to school."

Dinah's eyes narrowed. "Why?"

"Because then you miss davening and you don't learn as much Torah." Yaacov motioned for her to come closer, and spoke now in a whisper: "So let's fool him, Dinah! Let's get all your clothes and everything ready tonight, then tomorrow you can get dressed very fast! When he comes to bother you it'll be just like you're giving him a big punch in the nose!"

Dinah giggled.

Yaacov helped her to choose her clothes and lay them out at the foot of her bed. He's been doing it every night.

December 24, 1988

Eli came across a dreidel this morning as I was doing housework, so I kneeled down to spin it for him. He became still, and his mouth fell open. The dreidel slowed down, wobbled, tipped over. I spun it again. Eli lifted his face toward mine and looked up at me with gratitude. I gave the dreidel one more spin before going into the kitchen, then glanced back in time to see him dropping suddenly to the floor. Stretched out on his belly, motionless, his eyes were fixed upon the dreidel spinning two inches from his nose. He was entranced.

A few moments later I was summoned to the living room by hysterical crying. I thought he'd gotten hurt, but it turned out that the dreidel had stopped. I spun it for him and Eli's face bloomed with light. He was beside himself with excitement. It stopped and he leapt to his feet and jumped up and down with misery.

I spin the dreidel and Eli drops to the floor, limbs outstretched, squealing with wonder. The dreidel stops and darkness covers the earth.

How will I get the dishes done?

January 1, 1988

I am beginning to get a perspective on a process. When I first encountered Miriam Levi, my initial reaction was despair. I got a glimpse of how many mistakes I had made throughout my children's lives, and how many I was making every day. The goal seemed too high an ideal to reach. Then, in a matter of days, just by lowering my voice, I found that I was operating on a whole different plateau. Over a period of weeks, that one relatively minor adjustment affected a wide spectrum of changes in our lives.

It was only the first step, yet without that, little else of value was likely to be understood or attained. For another mother, it could have been some other seemingly minor adjustment that was called for.

I expected that once I took this first step, my steady progress would be assured, but no. Unlike the baby, whose first step does signal that he'll be on his own two feet within a few days, I kept finding myself back at square one. Though it sounded so easy, just to speak calmly, the combined power of habit and personality constituted a tremendous stumbling block. What unexpected emotions, what depth of feeling children arouse!

Before me loomed an infinite array of challenges—how to instill in the children a sense of responsibility, how to deal with their fighting, how to build their self-confidence, how to get a handle on my own thought processes...To start listing the problems that can arise is nonsensical, for they are as endless and varied as life itself. Yet for the first time in my career as a parent, I felt that I had access to something practical and specific that opened the way. Something uncomplicated that worked even when the issues and feelings themselves were far from uncomplicated. I felt as if I had caught hold of golden keys.

Yet golden keys—like everything precious—can get lost, and my abiding premonition that this terrible loss could come to pass kept me in a state of nervous anticipation, until, of course, I did drop them. Then it seemed as if my acquisition of the keys had been an illusion, and that I had really grasped nothing.

It happened again and again. I dropped them. I picked them up. I dropped them. I picked them up.

To this day, when I'm in the midst of behaving badly, I'm convinced that, after all, I'm lost. When I find my way again, I think: "I've got it! Now I've gotten a hold of the secret, and I shall not let go!" Then the disillusionment arrives.

I see that when you try systematically to change a particular habit, it is easier in the beginning than it is later on, when the discouragement resulting from repeated failures weighs you down. You look back at your original enthusiasm and it seems unrealistic and naive. Successes that initially thrilled and inspired are later taken for granted. Formerly unrecognized problems, some of them subtler and more insidious, now make their appearance.

It is possible to change one's habits, but they will not stay in place where you want them without paying them attention. That's the rub. That's the disappointment. It is continuous work.

But the work can become absolutely joyful.

January 3, 1988

The skill I'm honing these days is that of stopping in my tracks. Something upsets me and I have already started yelling, hitting, criticizing, feeling sorry for myself, but instead of continuing on, I'm practicing the "short stop." This is a valuable skill, for the likelihood of complete emotional disarmament is small, and there will forever remain the possibility of a sudden attack from within. When it does happen, I have found that there's a way to halt the onrushing calvary rather than let it barge on in with full regalia.

This is how it goes: here comes an angry stampede of horses. I'm feeling self-righteous. The object of the attack, a guilty and bad child, deserves no mercy. There's no going back, I've come this far, I might as well let him have it. Having lost my temper, I must prove I'm right. Loyalty to the course!...But if I can just catch myself, if I can just take one second to peek into that inner maelstrom and ask if the situation really calls for such agony and pain...because (and here's the surprising part) all those big, powerful horses vanish magically into thin air at the mere sound of a soft voice.

January 4, 1988

Tonight I was so tired, so incredibly tired. Eli had diarrhea all day—a diaper change every half-hour, and for one memorable hour every ten minutes. On top of that, he has discovered Avivah again. Discovered that she sits in his high chair (I have to get another one, fast!), that she is nursing, that the children play with her, that when he cries she is often in my arms. Avivah kept crying. On top of that, I couldn't get the housework done. On top of that, on top of that, on top of that...By evening I was so tired. Too tired. Dinah didn't want pancakes. She wanted to make herself an omelet. I wanted to refuse but was too tired. She made it carefully. It came out beautifully. On the way to the dish, it slipped to the floor.

January 5, 1988

I have just made a whole series of serious mistakes tonight. Really bad ones. I am ashamed to write them down. What a mess! I have hit bottom and taken my children there with me. I don't feel worthy of asking for G-d's help.

What a fall! It's later, three in the morning now. I can't sleep, so I got up and went into Dinah's room, found a painting of a strawberry she'd done and installed it in a little pink wooden frame that I'd been saving for the right moment. Put it by her bedside.

What happened is that Rachel and Daniel are having their birthday parties tomorrow, and since Dinah's was a month ago and she and I still had not found her a present, we went out in the afternoon to get her one. So we got her a tiny Fireman computer, which she has wanted since the age of five. A good present. Got home. Rachel and Daniel wanted me to go get them junk food for their parties. Went out to a store on Rechov Shmuel HaNavi. Took a lot of time for them to decide what they wanted. Got back. After bedtime already. The babysitter was mad because she had to study for a test and I had left Avivah with her for longer than expected. By the way, Yaacov's birthday is on the same day as the twins'. When I was out shopping for Dinah, I was disappointed and frustrated that I couldn't find him anything. Spoke to him on the phone when I got back and heard in his voice that he thought I'd forgotten his birthday. Started making dinner and Rachel said she wanted to cook her own eggs.

BANG!

WHAT DOES SHE THINK THIS IS? A RESTAURANT? AM I SUPPOSED TO MAKE TEN THOUSAND MEALS AROUND HERE! SELFISH CHILDREN! SPOILED! HERE I AM BENDING OVER BACKWARDS AND NOBODY REALIZES IT! I'VE HAD ENOUGH OF THIS! I yelled, "NO, YOU'RE NOT GOING TO MAKE YOUR OWN DINNER! YOU'RE GOING TO EAT WHAT I MAKE! I'M THE BOSS AROUND HERE, NOT YOU!"

The scene which ensued was something *True Confessions Magazine* could do well to print in its entirety, but I myself shall refrain. At one point, in the midst of the yelling and the crying and the hitting, I thought: *I have lost control. I have no control. They don't obey me! Bad children! Bad mother!* "Bad girl!" I yell at Dinah, grabbing her Fireman out of her hand.

She bursts into tears. "Go away! I don't need you, you bad mommy! GO AWAY!"

And it is these words of Dinah's that finally make me shut up and stop.

Stop.

I spent the rest of the evening apologizing for my cruelty, my submission to the *yetzer hara*. Wasn't it only the night before last that I wrote in here how I no longer have long, extended outbursts, that I catch myself before exploding? Wasn't I feeling so proud of myself, a veritable expert in the short stop? Aren't I clever! So here I am at four in the morning. My apologies were heard, accepted, returned. Whatever damage I did...may I correct it. I haven't had an outburst like this for a long time, and I don't want to start again.

January 6, 1988

Spoke to Miriam Adahan this morning about children's anger. (I wasn't in the mood to talk about my own.) She said that Ramban wrote that the one case in which one should get angry is in response to injustice. The anger of children arises because they do, so frequently, genuinely interpret situations as unjust.

So when a child gets angry, I can empathize with his feelings of having been unjustly treated, whether or not there really was an injustice. If none has actually occurred, my job is to help him focus on solutions. And if there has indeed been an injustice, my job is to teach him how to communicate his indignation in a respectful, non-hurtful manner.

As I was putting Eli in his crib just now, having double-diapered him for the night, I found to my dismay that I'd have to change him again. OH! I thought to myself. It's so hard! Dinah's downstairs on the couch with a fever, Avivah is crying to be nursed, Danny is waking up Dinah by drumming on the plastic laundry basket, I've got to get something together for Yaacov's dinner, Elisheva is wandering around with her pink pillow, threatening with heavy eyelids to drop off to sleep before I get her fed, Rachel has just done *sponga* in her bedroom to clean up after her birthday party and Eli walked in and got his pajama-feet wet, so I had to get him ready for bed all over again, and NOW I HAVE TO CHANGE ELI AGAIN? NOBODY (meaning my mother) WOULD BELIEVE HOW HARD I WORK! NOBODY WOULD BELIEVE IT! BRINGING UP THESE CHILDREN IS SUCH HARD WORK! OH! OH! I would have liked at that moment to shout: "HEAR YE! HEAR YE! I QUIT! THIS IS TOO HARD!"

After burning myself to a crisp with these thoughts, it occurred to me that perhaps the injustice I perceive is not, in fact, an injustice. Maybe most human beings have to work hard. That's how human life has been designed: to be difficult. I remember Rabbi Yitzhak Berkowitz saying that every ounce of suffering is a gift. G-d could have arranged things differently, but He knew that being subjected to difficulties is the best thing for human beings. I'm not the only one. The only one? How ridiculous even to think...Images of poverty-stricken *National Geographic* Mexican peasant women flash into my brain. Of course, they work far harder than I do. But...but there's also the image of All Those Other People Out There Just Enjoying Life...attending concerts, going out to dinner. Now it's the advertisement section of the *New*

Yorker. Evening strolls along the avenue. Fifth Avenue. Park Avenue. Vacations. Maids. Whose life is it exactly that I envision? A famous journalist's? A movie star's? That sublime actress-politician who flies across country in her own special jet, the one who's applauded and admired by countless adoring audiences? Is that what I want? I thought I threw such foolish notions onto the garbage heap ages ago. What a joke. Even she's got it rough in her own way. She's probably in hell most of the time. Who am I jealous of? Who has it easier?

January 7, 1988

Out of the blue, Rachel was rude to me this morning. When I asked her what she wanted for breakfast, she replied curtly: "You don't need to know." I was disturbed and astonished. We enjoy such a sweet and trusting relationship now, thank G-d, that I was pretty sure we'd work out this little snag in the end, whatever it was. Yet my feelings were hurt, and I was angry.

Later this morning as I was doing dishes, I remembered that almost my first words to Rachel this morning, upon waking her up for school, were: "Rachel, did you take the plastic covers for the tapes that I put on the little shelf in the kitchen?" She had just opened her eyes. She stared at me sleepily, trying to identify what I was referring to. "The tapes that were on the little shelf by the kitchen window. Did you take some of those plastic covers and use them on some children's tapes?" She nodded. I thought so! "Why did you do that! Now I can't find them, and I have to give the tapes back to Happy today!" *I can't keep anything from these children!* I thought to myself. *What if I can't find those plastic covers?* "Those tapes don't belong to me," I went on. "They belong to Happy Klein's Avigdor Miller tape library. Now what will I do? I've told you not to go into my things! Haven't I?"

"But you were in the kitchen when I was doing it. You saw me." Now that she mentioned it, I did vaguely recall seeing her fool around up there with the tapes. I had thought it was a positive thing for her to be organizing them. "It doesn't matter whether I was in the kitchen!" I declared. "Just don't go through my things, do you hear me?" Her eyes were closed and she turned over onto her stomach. "Hmm, Rachel, do you hear me?"

An hour later, I was so involved with breakfast and packing sandwiches and finding shoes that the whole scene slipped my mind. How could I have been so callous?

No great mystery that she was rude and cold.

I called Miriam Levi, and she agreed to start another workshop in my home. I told her that I had been losing control of myself lately.

"So you need some reinforcement, that's all. You know, the same thing happens to me sometimes."

"You lose control?"

"Sure I do."

"That's so nice. That makes me feel better."

"Of course. And also, for my back pain, I have to learn the Alexander Technique over and over again even though I keep on hoping that I'm finished studying it. As a matter of fact I mentioned to someone the other day that I might have to study it periodically for the rest of my life, and he said, 'Oh, I wouldn't want to be so dependent on anything.' But what does that mean, you don't want to be dependent? It's pride, and it's also the fear that maybe you won't have access to it forever, and you think, then what? Which is really rather silly—to deprive yourself of the benefits of learning something for fear that you won't always have that teacher. When the time comes for something else, in all likelihood you'll be provided with other sources."

"It's the fear that because you need something, that means you're lacking something as a person," I said. "And so what if you're lacking something, so what else is new? Who doesn't lack something?" But beneath these brave declarations lurked that very embarrassment and disappointment: *I should have mastered this by now. What's wrong with me?*

"No," she replied. "I wouldn't say it indicates you're lacking something as a person. It just means that there's something you need to learn."

January 10, 1988

Dinah has been home for three days with an undefined illness: fever, stomachache, headache. The worst has passed, but I kept her home today because she still seems a little weak. At the onset of the illness, she was in school and was afraid to tell her teacher that she felt sick. She is so scared of that woman! I wish I could switch her to another class.

It has been delightful having her here. I'm sorry to have to send her back to school tomorrow. I dread her nervousness about homework, about missing the bus in the morning, etc.

My bad mistake of a few nights ago has apparently been overcome. Not that it happened automatically! I had to wriggle my way back into her heart.

January 13, 1988

I don't know what's happening with Dinah. Each night she's been preparing her food and clothes for the next day. She's been doing her homework conscientiously, though she frequently lets out yelps of frustration while at it. She's been getting up early so she can make her bus. She's been combing her hair with pride, and admiring herself in the mirror. She's been painting brilliantly colorful pictures, three of which I have now had framed. A few times I've noticed her even taking pleasure in surrendering; for instance, if I tell her to lend Daniel an eraser, first she'll refuse, and then with a little smile and a shrug, she'll say, "Oh, all right." Dinah, *beli ayin hara*, is like a flower in the delicate, slow process of blooming. The changes are perceptible, and I am thrilled and grateful. Is it because we've made a point of giving her more opportunity to feel in control of herself, less dictated to whenever possible?

Maybe it's just a gift, the gift of time. If you're not busy crushing your children, they will be busy blossoming.

I have inexplicably shifted out of my screaming mode. Don't ask me why, it's as if the weather has changed: I can only guess what brought on the more favorable climate.

Tonight while I was breaking off stalks of celery for the children, I realized with horror that perched atop one leaf was...was...a lizard? A lizard! I screamed. The children came running.

For the next forty-five minutes Daniel, Rachel, Dinah, Elisheva and I watched spellbound as a teeny-weeny chameleon picked its way slowly from one leaf to the next, precisely the same shade of green as the vegetable. He was not really heavier than the celery leaves! With those magical rotating eyes, did he see our giant faces looming up around him like Mt. Rushmore? He must have. Incredibly small, daintily perfect toes, like delicate fingers, moved him along ever so carefully over the stalks, as if on a fallen tree trunk. An outrageously exotic, otherworldly creature, like a Steven Spielberg animated cartoon, but real, alive. If he were a hundred times larger, he would have been a terrifying dinosaur. Dinah said it was good I didn't put him into the refrigerator. When Yaacov came home, he showed Danny how to make holes in a shoe box, and we now have a pet. His name is Celery. A commercial for G-d's unlimited powers of imagination.

February 1, 1988

Yesterday was our tenth anniversary. "Is today the 31st?" I asked Yaacov as he finished breakfast.

"I don't think so," he replied. "The 30th."

I checked a newspaper from last week, and counted the days up till now. "It is the 31st, Yaacov." I waited for him to say that I should get a babysitter, we're going out tonight. He put on his coat. He's forgotten, I thought bitterly. What a great symbol for our tenth anniversary. As he stood at the door ready to take Elisheva to *gan*, I decided to take the initiative: "Let's go out tonight, Yaacov."

"I'm sorry, Sarah, I just don't think I'll feel up to it. I don't feel so well." He bid farewell. He just doesn't want to go! I muttered to myself, furious and sad. If we don't go out tonight, we'll never get around to it. What a great symbol! Our tenth anniversary! There, alone in the kitchen, which was an utter mess, I began to cry. Twenty minutes later, as I was storming around cleaning up, Yaacov walked in. "I took Elisheva, but after that I had to turn around. I think I'm coming down with what Rachel had." And off he went to bed.

Our tenth anniversary! I've always prided myself that unlike the commonly stereotyped silly female, our anniversaries have never meant all that much to me, but this, a decade! We have to do something to establish clearly that our marriage is a success, to prove that we're happy! I continued to storm around, crying, thinking all kinds of depressing things, when I got an idea. I ran to the store, got some eggs and chocolate chips, ran back, made a cake and decorated it with a big heart, wrote "10" inside the heart and all around it our names and the names of Becky and the children.

The rest of the day, and during the wonderful party that we all had together last night, I looked proudly upon my having changed my own mood and my own fate. I had created my happiness, and everyone else's. It was a wonderful symbol for our tenth anniversary.

February 10, 1988

Esther Linder came over today. We were talking about internalizing the principle of *gam zu letova*. She said: "I used to be a teacher in the States and as a teacher I know what it is to create an educational environment according to what each child needs. This is what *HaShem* is doing. He has created for each one of us, in our particular life situations, a therapeutic educational environment engineered to constantly move us along toward the goal of self-actualization. Toward our own best selves. I heard a tape by Rav Mannis Friedmann, in which he says that when people think: 'If only I had something else,' it's blasphemy. Because the situation in which you find yourself belongs to you. Let's say you think you really should have been given different parents, or more money, or a different house. Or let's say you want a better husband and you decide to get a divorce, well, *HaShem* will let you do it, but then when you're single, it's: 'Oh, if only I had a husband!' It's impossible to bypass your destined test in life. We've got to live without the 'if only's.' " She grinned. "We think the purpose of life is to be found somewhere out there in the future, but the purpose of life is *right here*. Right here where we find ourselves. My purpose in life is to be found by coping with the situation that's right there when I wake up in the morning."

February 15, 1988

I was just downstairs with my husband. He's organizing the closet. He wanted me to hold a plastic bag for him so that he could put our leftover rolls of wallpaper into it, and I was so impatient. I didn't want to help him; I wanted to be up here writing in my diary. "Do you really need me to be holding this?" I asked.

"All right, I'll do it myself."

As I dashed back upstairs, I felt guilty. My help, in this instance, is not really that crucial, but just as I would like his help when I ask for it, I'm sure he would have liked mine, if only for the company. Then I realized that an amazing and wonderful thing happened even before I got to the top of the stairs: an involuntary, instant rejection of the guilt had gone into action within me. I've developed an allergy to guilt!

This is not to say that I condone my selfishness. I would feel better, I think, if I had found within me the patience and generosity to help him even though I didn't feel like it. However, if my actions are not going to be changed by remorse, if I'm going to be selfish anyway and if the repercussions of that selfishness are not serious enough to get upset over, then feeling guilty will not change matters. And it won't make me less culpable. Recognize my selfishness, be aware of how I could have transcended it, feel whatever regret I feel, but accept myself. Reject the self-condemnation, then move on. Terrific!

February 21, 1988

Rachel has been in a bitterly sour temper the past few weeks, and since I have such confidence in our relationship I didn't take it seriously until Malka mentioned it. This morning I arranged with her to meet me outside her school at ten o'clock in the morning. We'd go on an outing together. I even left the house a mess in order to be on time—which meant that the rest of the day I've been trying to catch up.

It was worth it. Those two and a half shared hours of privacy, in which I was strict with myself about thinking only of her, not about various errands that needed doing—were reminiscent of our trip to America last year. I'm so glad that I didn't wait any longer. How important to catch things in time!

February 26, 1988

In one of the workshops recently, putting a dash of black pepper on the tongue was proposed as a possible remedy for insults and dirty words. "A lot of people might object to something like this, and I'm not particularly enamored of this method myself," Miriam told us. "But some people use it and say it works. If you do try it, don't do it aggressively. All you need to make your point is a grain or two of the pepper. You can even put it on your own tongue first, as you explain what it's for: to remind the tongue not to say words that hurt."

The next day, I made an announcement to Daniel, Rachel, Dinah and Elisheva. "Children, from now on, since even though I've told you that it's wrong to say bad words—you know which ones..." Chortles, guffaws. "From now on, I'm going to take a little bit of black pepper and put it on your tongues to help them remember."

This declaration was met with thoughtful silence, then Dinah said: "Oh no."

"Yes, Dinah," I stated quietly, "I will do it." She ran to the cabinet, found the pepper before I could even get up from my chair, and dashed off with it. I caught her, grabbed the pepper away and put it on a higher kitchen shelf.

Later that day Daniel used a forbidden word. I pretended that I hadn't heard, and went on about my business. Cooking, with Avivah on one arm, I was tired and not up for a wrestling match, but then he said it again. I looked around and knew I had to follow through. He jumped under the table and cowered there, grinning expectantly. O.K., here we go! Grab the pepper! Deposit Avivah! Avivah starts crying! Catch Danny, wrestle with him! Take two grains and stuff them into his mouth!

He scowled, stood up and pondered the taste. "It's not so bad," he said.

Later on the same day, Dinah tried her luck. As soon as the dirty words were uttered, I went to the cabinet for the pepper, but it had disappeared. "Who took the pepper?" I demanded. "Come on now, where's the pepper?" Dinah and Danny smiled. I didn't really like this method. It was too strenuous. "Dinah. Danny. So what shall we do? What would you do if your children said bad words?"

"I'd put sugar on their tongues!" Dinah grinned. This reminded me that someone at a workshop once related how she and her girlfriends used to say "Sugar!" instead of the word they would have preferred.

No harm trying. "What if you think of some other words to say when you're mad instead of the bad ones?" I asked.

Elisheva, who had wandered in now, thumb in mouth, pillow in hand, volunteered a choice morsel and exploded with laughter. There I was, trying to give a sermon, and the whole subject just seemed hugely entertaining to all of them. "How about worms?" said Dinah.

Now, whenever Dinah is annoyed, that's what she says. "Worms!" she exclaims when she can't figure out a problem in subtraction. "Worms!" when the elevator leaves without her.

Miriam Levi referred in the last workshop to a *baal teshuvah* mother who was worried because her bar-mitzvah-age son was not saying the blessings over food. The mother, said Miriam, had a problem because she'd gotten too much on top of him about it, watching him, waiting to see if he'd recite them properly, reminding him, asking him if he had. "A mother can mention such a thing to her child, but it's not her job to police him. This is really something that's between him and *HaKadosh Baruch Hu*."

Two days ago, Rachel arrived home from school and found five white rolls on the table. An unusual event. I usually buy only brown bread. Right off the bat, she took a bite and at once I got that fearful, self-critical telegram from my inner world: *You have failed as a religious mother.* "Aren't you going to wash, Rachel?" I asked. She averted her head. It looked as if she were ignoring me. I opened my mouth to go on. To go on with what, I didn't know, but I was groping for a suitable reprimand. STOP, I told myself, and turned back to the stove.

Rachel put down the bread, washed, and said the blessings.

March 2, 1988

This morning Elisheva had her bride costume on, all ready to go to the Purim party at *gan*, when I saw that it badly needed ironing. I knew I'd have to hurry because Yaacov was going to be leaving the house with her at eight, so I rushed to set up the ironing board. "Elisheva! Come here and let me take off your costume! I need to iron it!"

"No!" she cried out, running away from me into the living room.

"Elisheva!" I yelled. "Daddy has to take you in a few minutes! Come here right now!"

"No!"

I grabbed her and started to unzip the dress. She struggled to get free. "Stay still! Elisheva! Stay still! I will not let you go with the dress looking like this!" She curled up tightly on the floor like a snail on strike. I struggled to get a hold of the zipper.

Yaacov was standing to the side. "Don't yell at her," he said in a low voice.

I adjusted my volume, then spoke again, quietly: "Elisheva, let me take off the dress." She didn't uncurl. "Elisheva," I said in a near whisper, with a confidential air, "a bride wouldn't wear a dress that's not ironed."

She got up. "All right, Mommy."

March 3, 1988

Cleaning out a drawer today, I came across an article that I had cut out from the Sunday *New York Times* of October 23 (we can get it here in Israel every Monday) in which eight scientists were asked to describe "some of the most perplexing unresolved problems in their fields."

> Hans A. Pethe, physicist and Nobel laureate, writes: "How is the universe constructed on the large? Apparently there are big regions in which there are no stars at all and then there are clusters of galaxies. And why is that? We have no idea. And another problem, which is even farther away from a solution: There is good reason to believe there is a lot more matter in the universe than we can see. What is the so-called dark matter? And how does it come about? This has something to do with physics. Maybe it has something to do with the very early universe right after the big bang. Nobody knows.

I'm still not accustomed to the pleasure (and I hope I never will be) of being able to step from the living room of our new apartment out onto the porch, and be outside. Tonight I was standing there, looking up, when Daniel came and joined me. I pointed out the Big Dipper to him, saying that when I was a child in Connecticut, my mother used to do just the same for me.

"They see it in America?" he asked.

How far is the world of a child from the world of an adult... "Yes, Daniel. The same stars. Do you know, I was just reading how there are millions and millions of other stars up there that we don't see."

He stared up into the darkness. "So why did *HaShem* make them if we can't even see them?"

My heart stirred. "I don't know. Nobody knows."

"I know why," he said after a few minutes.

"Why, Daniel?"

"So that we'd ask why."

13

To Be a Mother

March 5, 1988

Rabbi Avigdor Miller says on one of his tapes that for a man, the joy of Shabbat and Yom Tov is enhanced by meat and wine, for a woman by new clothing, and for a child...what else...the pleasure lies in sweets. So yesterday I decided to surrender to Purim. I went to sleep in the afternoon and left the children in charge of all the *mishloach manos*, which is to say I left the cats to watch the milk. Other years, I tensely guarded the hoard, gripped with the horrendous responsibility of keeping them from eating too much junk food. This Purim, I resolved to let the holiday serve as catharsis: a day of junk food without limits. I hoped that by removing all the tension, the forbidden fruit would lose some of its mystique.

My last glimpse of the children as I went up to my room was of four people in the throes of practically unbearable ecstasy. Rachel, intense as Silas Marner counting his gold, was taking inventory of her toffees, chewing gum, chocolate bars, *hamentaschen*, cookies, cakes and candies. Dinah hardly knew what to do with herself: so much of her life is structured around the conflict between her wanting and my forbidding junk food, and now here she was surrounded by piles of the stuff, more than she could bring herself to consume. She nodded hello to me with the goofy, gap-toothed smile and half-closed eyes of a happy drunken man, and I felt pleased with myself for having lowered the guard-rails: they'd be so mired in sugar, why, they'd hate it by day's end. As Daniel licked a chocolate bar, he hummed along to a Purim cassette going full-blast out on the porch, and Elisheva was chewing something and standing on tiptoe. Then she sat on a chair, turned upside down, and with sublime elegance reached for a toffee that had fallen from her hand. This was heaven. This was a child's dream come true. It hardly occurred to me to offer them lunch. I let go.

So it came as a mild surprise when Dinah said, as the sun set: "It wasn't even Purim." I guessed what was coming, and feigned disinterest. "It wasn't even Purim!" she repeated emphatically, annoyed that I hadn't reacted. "You didn't even let us have junk!"

At the close of Shabbat, Yaacov, Daniel and I were in the house by ourselves. Daniel has been embarrassed to go out on Shabbat ever since we moved, and only if he has a long book to read does he survive Shabbat without excruciating boredom and restlessness. This Shabbat, Yaacov stayed calm, cool and collected, no matter what the provocation, and this was reflected in Danny's behavior. "Was I a good boy this Shabbat?" Danny asked as the three of us sat reading. He dared ask only because he knew what our answer would be. "Yes," we both told him. "Very, very good."

He smiled. "Tell Becky, then, because she said that if I'm a good boy during Shabbat she'll buy me the Walkman earphones." I didn't approve of bribing him with the "good boy" label; after all, I'm now a disciple of the praise-deeds-instead-of-character school. But it worked, and perhaps this is how to help him get his footing. Maybe I should use such material rewards more often, to inspire him. The more frequently he exercises self-control, the more that will constitute his self-image.

March 13, 1988

I have been cleaning for Pesach, the first year I have done so on schedule. Hurrah! I feel terrific about it.

A few weeks ago Yaacov went to see Rabbi Feldman, who wrote *The River, the Kettle, and the Bird*. "I've been studying *mussar* for years about the control of anger," Yaacov told him, "but nothing has really helped me to accomplish it for long periods. What do you suggest?"

Rabbi Feldman said that to break a habit, one should go to the opposite extreme for forty days.

Yaacov has taken this upon himself. No matter what happens, he doesn't show nervousness or raise his voice. During kiddush these past two Shabbats, when everyone's at his most vulnerable on account of tiredness and hunger, I have watched Yaacov restrain himself. He announces to the children that he is going to say kiddush, invites them to the table rather than ordering them, and ignores whatever noise they make while reciting it. The result is that if they do come, they do so of their own volition, and if not, they say "amen" from where they are. We try to disregard the imperfections of this approach for now, with the knowledge that for all of us it will take time to get it right. Except for Elisheva, who is going through a raucous, exuberant period in general, they also make less noise.

These past two Shabbats, the problem with Daniel's behavior has virtually vanished as well, so we must conclude that his misbehavior was a reflection of his parents'. He is still embarrassed to go outside, even to play. I am sure that if we continue to take it easy about this, and abandon, absolutely, any show of force or impatience on this score, it will pass.

I notice that I've become more confident as a mother. Among the areas in which I'm currently shaky are: knowing how to respond when the children insult me, getting them to take responsibility in the house, controlling myself when they hurt each other, and knowing how to handle it when they reject the meals I prepare.

One of the things I'm grateful for is the fact that my extreme busyness causes them to become independent. They do things that at their age I couldn't, like babysitting and cooking scrambled eggs and omelets and vacuuming and washing dishes. One afternoon last week, Dinah was bored and asked me if I was planning a trip that day to Geulah. The answer was no. "Then I'll go to Geulah myself," she said.

Geulah, a shopping center, is a fifteen-minute walk or a five-minute bus ride from here. I knew that Dinah would be scared to go there by herself, and didn't feel called upon to discourage her. "All right," I replied.

"I can go?"

"Yes, if you'd like to."

She was sitting, face cupped in her hands, elbows on the kitchen table. Silence for a minute or two. Then: "I'm scared to go."

"All right, when you're ready to go, you may."

When Daniel and Rachel came home, she made a proposal. Would they like to go with her to Geulah? They asked for permission, I let go of my worries (will they cross with the light? will they get off at the right stop? will they come home before dark?) and agreed. After a slow start, during which they seemed to be gathering up their own courage and resolve, they set out. I gave each a shekel and a half to spend as he or she wished.

When they returned, they were ten feet tall.

With her money, Dinah had bought me a chocolate bar.

This morning, Eli spied the potty in the bathroom (he has seen some of the older toddlers using one in his *gan*). He pointed to it. "Pee pee" he said, and he pulled at his pants. "Pee pee." I didn't like his timing, having just gotten him all dressed and ready to leave the house, but I undid his diaper and helped him to sit down, feeling proud of my patience. The important thing was to encourage his taking the initiative. It's so frequently more convenient to discourage independence than to foster it. How much easier to keep that diaper on! How much faster and less messy to wash his hands myself! But the short-term gain is a long-term loss.

Meanwhile, Rachel asked me to feed her yesterday, and I did so with love. As the eldest child, she needs to act like a baby sometimes. Growth needs to be balanced by the comforts of going backwards.

I may not have been remembering to water the plants lately, but I do think I'm doing a good job with the children. One of the things I learned from Miriam Adahan's EMETT classes is to allow myself to feel happiness over my successes, and that's just what I'm doing now: I feel good about what I'm doing. I pray for more strength.

Danny and Rachel are cleaning their rooms for Pesach. I didn't ask them to do it. Another startling development: Eli and Avivah play with each other! They crawl around on the floor together! But she needs non-stop protection. I constantly have to keep my eye on them because every once in a while Eli just sits down right on top of her and pushes her head to the floor. I can't imagine what it's like to be at Eli's mercy. Must be very scary.

When Eli sat on her this morning and she started crying, he stood up, perplexed by this loudly crying baby, ran to get a bottle, and threw it down on her head, which naturally didn't help. "LaLa!" he shouted at me, pulling my skirt, pointing to Avivah. "LaLa!" "LaLa!"

"Help that baby! She's crying!" he's telling me.

March 28, 1988

During these weeks of Pesach cleaning, Yaacov and I have been fighting. I'm so worried about how it affects the children. When we're mad at each other, I get mad at them. In moments of faint objectivity I can conceive of the possibility that it's due to overtiredness, overwork and nervousness, and will pass, but at other times, I am imbued with despair and fear for our future.

I see myself as a daughter, I see myself as a mother, but I don't perceive myself as easily in the role of wife. I have the image before me of how good a wife my mother was to my father, and, child of the sixties that I am, resist it. My feelings about everything I do as a wife are conditional, and that condition is Yaacov's behavior toward me. If he thanks me for the meal, then I'm glad I made it. If he doesn't seem to like it, I'm resentful over the time and effort I spent. And I'm like this right on down the line, be it the ironing of his shirt or the measure of love I give in my welcome when he comes home at night. I spoke to Tova Porush about this, and she said, "Do it for yourself, do it to feel right about yourself. As a religious woman, you do feel a responsibility to G-d, don't you? Do what you have to do to make things right between you and Him."

"You mean, cook dinner for my husband for my own sake?" I asked her.

"Yes, no matter what his reaction. Have the pleasure of knowing that you have done a good job. Being a wife is a career."

This brings to mind what Aunt Sophie told me: "All those years, I was doing those seders for myself."

April 10, 1988

Pesach has come and gone. It was hard.

On the last night, we had a guest named Linda, who brought with her a gift of white wine. She and I almost finished off the bottle, while Yaacov and her fiancé looked on. I hardly knew I had taken flight until Linda's eyes met mine and I recognized a fellow space traveler. Within a matter of minutes I had changed from an incredibly tense, absolutely fed up police officer into a self-indulgent and indulging pleasure seeker, lazy, laid-back. I saw my husband through faraway eyes, and couldn't imagine why he was in such a hurry to get the children into bed on time, for it was obvious that the only thing of vital importance was having fun. I would have felt lonely on this elevated plateau had I not realized with surprise that there were indeed quite a few people around who were precisely on my wavelength: the children.

Gosh, so this is where they're holding all the time. Amazing. Now I understood! For them, the world is an infinite smorgasbord offering up all manner of fun and funny phenomena. Busy, stern adults are threatening and incomprehensible and are best kept at bay.

April 11, 1988

This morning in the grocery store checkout line, I was putting the cheese and the bread and the milk and then the ketchup into bags when the ketchup fell magically, of its own volition, from my fingers. Just as in a car accident it seems that slow moments pass during which the nose of the other vehicle gradually approaches and you accept the unacceptable reality of the inevitable collision—yes, this is happening to me—it took a long moment for the ketchup bottle to reach the floor. There will be a crash. Yes, there's the crash. And the splattered mess of ketchup and shattered glass, and the sight of the cashier's tidy little shoe sitting in the midst of the ketchup, and worse: the fact that I would have to get down on my hands and knees in a moment and clean it up somehow...it was all just too much, for I was too tired. I must have emitted a loud yelp or moan or some such animalistic protest, for when I looked up, my fellow customers standing to my left in the checkout line all smiled at me kindly, and a child stared.

The cashier, too, must have perceived my overwhelming despair over this catastrophe, for she nodded to me comfortingly, lifted her chin and called out in an operatic soprano: "MuHAAAAAAMet!" She was calling the Arab delivery boy. *What? You mean I won't have to clean it up even though I was the one who did it?*

"MuHAAAAAAAAMet!"

Oh, no, I shouldn't let an Arab clean up my mess. Yet how nice, how nice to be waited on...if you can just take all the guilt and hide it away somewhere.

All my misgivings in relation to Arabs working for Jews fell aside. Even before Muhamet appeared to clean up my mess, I had escaped the scene of the crime and was home free.

April 12, 1988

This morning I put the kettle on for my morning coffee. A few minutes later I ran to answer the telephone. "Hello?" There was the dial tone. I stood there, receiver pressed against my ear, gazing at the thunderclouds of steam escaping from the kettle, forgetting, somehow, even what I was waiting for...until I realized that when the kettle had whistled, I had answered the phone.

April 13, 1988

I caught Eli a few minutes ago by the cuff of his pants, having gotten a whiff of something suspicious when he passed me by. He squealed with laughter and wiggled from my grasp, though not before I managed a swift spot-check on his diaper. Clean! Hurrah!

When his diaper is full, my heart sinks.

April 17, 1988

I got sick. It started on the third day of Pesach, a cold, and for the first time in my life it didn't get better after a few days. I kept on pushing myself onward, noble soldier, until I lay in bed one night and realized with horror that for goodness sake, all the children had gone to bed without eating anything. I had been too tired to think straight. I took my temperature and it was 101°. It was a lovely surprise to be able to officially declare illness.

My parents called. My voice was so hoarse that I could hardly talk, but the next morning I was up again. There was so much work to do, how could I stay in bed? I felt like someone in one of those jungles that closes in on you if you don't keep cutting away the underbrush, but as hard as I worked I couldn't make a clearing. I couldn't fight off the ever-accumulating responsibilities, nor did I have enough conviction to announce: Ladies and gentlemen, I cannot go on.

At last I called Dr. Shupak, who paid me an old-fashioned housecall, smiled whimsically as he took my blood pressure and said: "Terrible. Terrible. 90 over 50. That's why you're dizzy. Your blood pressure is so low that I can't give you antibiotics. Get into bed for ten days."

"How can I do that, Dr. Shupak?"

"Ten days," he repeated, packing up his little bag.

It was a thrilling prospect, but I didn't know how Yaacov would react, for the mantle of motherhood would fall upon him and no other. As it turned out, he wished me *refuah sheleimah* and bid me farewell as I left the house to spend Shabbat at my friend Happy's house. All Shabbat I stayed in bed, so dizzy that even the lines of the ceiling wavered as if underwater. I took careful note of the pain in my throat, grateful to be ill enough to do nothing. My head banged under the hammer blows of a headache. I lay there I don't know how long, then put my face in the pillow and wept. What would happen now? How would we manage?

April 19, 1988

The phone rang at my bedside in Happy's house. "Sarah, don't be shocked. But I'm going to give you some news," said Becky.

My heart contracted. "If it's bad news, don't tell me!"

"No, it's good news! Guess who's on a plane here!"

"WHAT? Are you serious?"

"No! I mean yes! She's on the plane! She'll be in Israel in a half-hour."

"Put Yaacov on."

"Hi, Sarah."

"Yaacov! What do you think?"

"Well, I think your parents love you."

Mommy has been here two days now. I've been eating three times as much as usual, taking vitamins and drinking blackstrap molasses for iron, and I'm beginning to feel better. Daddy called this morning. I heard Mommy say, "Well, complete rest is just impossible for her, Norman. There's so much to do, and these children—"

"Tell him that I lean against the wall every once in a while," I said.

"She leans against the wall sometimes, Norman. I said, she leans against...Never mind, she's getting better. She looks much better this morning."

April 20, 1988

Mommy drove me to the phone company today to pay my bill. I haven't paid until now because the sum was outlandish and I was sure that they had made a computer error, as they did two years ago, when they finally agreed to reimburse me for two hundred dollars. "Did I lock the front door?" I asked her as we were pulling out in her rented car. We looked at one another and tried to remember. "I'm going back to check."

"No! I'll go back," she said, pushing open her door.

"No! I'll go back! Stay here!"

Up in the elevator. The door was locked. I opened it without thinking and stood there a minute looking into the apartment, wondering what I was there for. Back on down. As I ran past the mailbox, our neighbor Rabbi Chions handed me a letter that the mailman had put into his box by mistake. Seeing that it was from the phone company, I tore it open as I hurried along. I couldn't make out what all the separate headings were—a lot of Hebrew words I didn't understand. But the sum at the bottom was almost double the other bill I had just received. "You see, Mommy!" I exclaimed as I slammed the car door. "They don't know what they're doing in that place! I just got another bill from the phone company and it's four hundred shekels and something. That's double the other bill! They're loo-loo over there! They just let their computers go wild!"

At the telephone company, the line inched forward. I had nothing to read so I spent the time worrying about whether Mommy was having a hard time with Avivah in the car downstairs and wishing she had parked and come on up with me, so at least we could have been enjoying each other's company. When my turn finally came, I sat down with an air of pained indignance. "*Ani lo mevinah,*" I protested as I shoved the bill in front of a girl with heavy black eyeliner behind the counter. "This bill is impossible! I could never have made enough calls to warrant such an amount of money! Once before you had to give me my money back because I went ahead and paid, but this time I'm just not going to do it! We only made something like two long-distance calls in two months!"

She waited to see if that was all I had to say, then handed the bill back to me. "*Ani lo mevinah,*" she told me, one eyebrow lifted in a tired arch.

"*ANI lo mevinah et ze GAM KEN!*" I exclaimed, slapping the bill back down before her on the counter. "I don't understand it either! That's what I'm telling you!"

"But this is—"

I would take no static. "I want to speak to the office manager!"

"But *geveret*—"

"I want to speak to Yossi. He'll remember me from the last time this happened." She motioned for the next customer to come forward. "Oh no, this is my turn!" I protested. "You can't do that! I've been waiting in line for forty-five minutes and I want you to please get me Yossi right now!" I was standing, fingertips daintily upon the counter in what I imagined was a pose of forthright self-confidence.

"But *geveret*," she said wearily, holding the paper up for me to see. I dimly felt the people in back of me edging closer to peer over my shoulder. "This is not from the phone company. This is your bank statement."

April 21, 1988

Yesterday the P.L.O. leader Abu Jihad was assassinated. When I read the news, I found it hard to believe that this was *the* Abu Jihad of whom I'd heard for so many years, the one behind so many of the terrorist acts against Jews and Israelis worldwide. The assassination is widely believed, by virtue of its finesse, to have been perpetrated by the Israeli Mossad, though in some quarters it is thought to have been done by a rival Arab organization.

This morning I became abruptly aware that for some time there had been a roaring of jets overhead. No sooner had I stepped out onto the balcony than four more screeched over the building in formation. "Mommy," I called, "there are a lot of jets going over this morning."

She came out to the *mirpesset*. A helicopter rumbled loudly by, sounding like a huge tractor, followed not a minute later by three little World War II types. To the east, far off on the horizon, a few tiny, silver blimps appeared. The noise of their jet engines lagged behind a moment, then came upon us. SWOOSH! Mommy and I turned to each other. Her eyes searched mine, her hands were clasped under her chin. "Sarah—"

"It really is a lot of them, isn't it," I said.

"Does this happen often?"

"Not really. I mean, I don't remember anything like this for a long time, not since we lived on the *yishuv*."

"Sarah..." Mommy gripped the iron railing and scanned the sky intensely. "This could be...this might be the beginning of something. The army might know that something is up. Maybe they're getting ready for some big reaction on the part of the Arab countries to Abu Nidal's death."

"Abu Jihad."

"Yes."

For the next half-hour, Mommy and I kept dashing out to the *mirpesset* to gaze solemnly up into the heavens. As another formation soared overhead, she noted that many people on porches in adjacent buildings were now, like us, pointing and staring. She looked down the four flights to the grassy expanse below, where mothers sat placidly on park benches watching their toddlers. Children bicycled. Over to the right was a small knot of giggling teenage girls. "Isn't that interesting," Mommy said quietly. "It's so ironic that we can see these people carrying on as if everything is normal, and they aren't aware of this drama happening right over their heads, and of what this might mean to their lives. This might mean...war."

"Shhh!" I pointed to Elisheva, who had snuggled up against me.

My mother turned to me. "Sarah...What do you think...of taking you and Yaacov and the children back with me? What do you think? Shouldn't we think about this?" Her fingertips flew instinctively to her mouth, as if to hush her thoughts. We stared at each other and then, together, up at the blue sky. "Mr. Israel is also looking," she said.

I craned my neck to see the next-door window, where our English neighbor was leaning out, perusing the sky as were we. He puffed blithely on a cigarette and nodded cordially. "Good morning. How are you?"

"What do you think of this?" I called out to him.

"What do I think of it?" He gave a little wave toward the sky. "You mean all that business?"

"Yes," answered Mommy. "You know, this could be a—"

"You think the bombs are going to start falling, do you?" He smiled agreeably.

"Yes," Mommy and I responded in unison.

"Pshaw!" He pouted and flicked his hand to dismiss our concern along with the ash, as if to say that we were overestimating the quality of entertainment this country provides. He took another puff. "Getting ready for Independence Day, that's all!"

"Independence Day?" we rang out together.

He nodded and blew a smoke ring.

Happy 40th birthday, Israel.

April 22, 1988

I went with Mommy to the airport, and let Rachel come along. We got there with twenty or so minutes to spare, but they wouldn't let us in the gate. "Too late," said a Swissair stewardess.

"What? How could it be too late?"

"I'm sorry, madam, but the gates are closed. For international flights you must arrive two hours ahead."

"But the plane is still here! Please! Please let me run to the gate! My husband is expecting me in Los Angeles and I just must get on that flight! Please!"

The security guards all shook their heads. Too late.

No harm done. A friendly clerk finally figured out a way to transfer her to another flight two hours later.

Goodbye, Mommy. Goodbye!

You saved us all. Thank you.

April 25, 1988

This morning there were all kinds of things I had to get done while Avivah slept, but I suddenly got it into my mind to move one of the upstairs bookcases down to the living room, where it would cover the peeling wallpaper. And by moving it out of there we'd also get more room on the upper landing, which I'm planning to transform into an official children's activity center.

I just couldn't wait to see this marvelous idea become reality. I emptied out and removed all the shelves, turned the bookcase on its side and pulled it to the stairs. Hmmm. A lot heavier than I thought. Should I leave it here and wait for Becky to come home from school, and we'd do it together? Ah, but I want to get this accomplished right now! Now...How should this be done, exactly? If the stairs proceeded down in a straight line, there would be no problem, but they hook sharply to the left and then around in the opposite direction.

I was determined. Down I let the bookcase slide. One corner smashed into the wall lamp. Pull it back up! Twist it around! Set it back up on its end! Now, slowly!

Bump!

Bump, bump!

Bump!

Each tremendous bump made me think the bookcase would wake up Avivah and then fall apart. It did neither. Onward! The bookcase was perched now upon the slender triangle of stair that pointed the stairway around towards the living room. I was holding on with all my might, envisioning how all I'd have to do in order to have a tremendous disaster would be to loosen my hold even the slightest degree, and this escapade would end in a terrible crash, the bookcase smashed, the wallpaper scraped, and me a fool...my ambitious little home improvement an embarrassing mess. "No", I thought to myself as the bookcase and I teetered on the edge between catastrophe and success. "I really don't want that to happen. I can do this if I just hold on! Now slowly!"

So...The bookcase looks even nicer in its new spot than I had anticipated. I'm very proud of myself for having accomplished such a great feat, and also excited about making the upper landing into a place where the children can crayon and paint and play with clay—everything that they've never had a real place to do before!

With intense pleasure I ran up and down the stairs getting *Duties of the Heart, The Ways of the Righteous, Rejoice O Youth.* Yes, that's me, Youth! O, I do rejoice! I thought of the midrash in which Har Sinai is held over the heads of the Jews. *How apt! Just like the bookcase!* If they had not accepted the Torah, the mountain would have been dropped upon them. What kind of a choice is that? I used to wonder. They were forced to make their decision, so how can they be given credit? But so much of life is engineered for us like that: we are indeed given free will to make our choices, yet are compelled by frightening alternatives to choose correctly.

April 28, 1988

There is no material thing in my house that I love more than the window boxes on the *mirpesset*, which now, after three years of impatient waiting on my part, overflow with pink geraniums, tangled vines, purple nasturtiums, strange orange blossoms that open in the morning and close up at evening, and assorted other flowers that, to my astonishment, have all succeeded in blooming and proliferating. Each time I catch sight of that whole garden out there, either from inside or from down below when I'm coming up the path, my heart overflows. It's a feast for the eyes. Those window boxes prove that we live in a real home. They are the incarnation of my childhood dreams, that one day I would possess my own corner in this world, one full of beauty.

Another thing I've always enjoyed is Daniel's enjoyment of

these same plants. It is he who has always informed me when this or that flower is blooming. It is he who has always taken care to water them when I forget.

A few days ago, I found Danny digging around in one of the boxes. I felt like yelping out loud as if my own skin were being scratched open, but I caught myself in time. "What are you doing, Danny?" I inquired, straining to suppress my real feelings.

"I'm cleaning out the dirt," he told me cheerfully, with confidence. "See?" He peered up at me to take in my happy appreciation. I looked and was aghast. On the floor, all along the wall of the *mirpesset*, black soil had fallen in clumps. The "dirt" to which he was referring, I supposed, was the brown, dead leaves shed by each plant, which had mixed in with the soil as they are supposed to. This self-fertilization had proceeded unhindered for three years. To my horror, I saw that the delicate upper roots of the plants had been exposed, some having been broken in the course of Daniel's "cleaning."

I knew how much I would regret it if I discouraged Daniel from his gardening by getting angry. I told myself firmly to take as much care with Daniel's roots as with those of my flowers, that the most important thing was that Danny not be made to feel bad about himself. He had acted with good-hearted enthusiasm and the best of intentions. I told him with forced calm that thanks to him, we wouldn't need to clean the dirt out like this ever again, and that he would have to go get some more dirt from outside, so that we could cover up the roots that were now exposed. He agreed, but forgot.

I was looking out from the *mirpesset* today to see how Dinah was faring with Avivah down on the grass, and I noticed once again the naked roots. *Oh! Why must the things I love be ruined! Can't I have anything in this house that doesn't get destroyed?* "Danny!" I snapped. He was on the couch reading.

"What?"

"Danny! These plants will die! Go downstairs and get dirt for them right now! Look what you did, Danny! All these years I've been waiting for these plants to grow, and now they'll all die in a

few days! Don't do anything to these plants without asking me, all
right? ALL RIGHT? Danny! Go downstairs right now!"

"My head hurts me."

"Well, I don't care! Go downstairs!"

"If you don't believe me, I don't care, then. My head hurts
me." He sat up and started to cry, rubbing his eyes. I remembered
that he had indeed come home with a headache, and hadn't
wanted to eat. You're losing control of yourself, I told myself. Put
on the brakes, fast! "O.K., Danny. All right. You can get the dirt
tomorrow."

Then I got an idea. Out in the little laundry room off the
kitchen, there were a few old flower pots filled with dirt, just
sitting around because the ferns they had contained had died. I
scurried in there, pulled out the pots from the corner and rushed
with them out to the *mirpesset*. Lo and behold, in a matter of
minutes, all the dirt was nicely emptied into the boxes and the
naked roots looked safe and sound, invisible once again. I felt my
heart settle back down peacefully, like a cat that had been badly
startled and had now been put at ease.

But as I stood there looking into one of the window boxes,
enjoying the work of my hands, all at once I noticed something
strange. Several tiny insects, weird little creatures with which I
was unfamiliar, appeared in some of that soil that I'd just added
on. As I stared I became aware that it was not just a few: that soil
was absolutely teeming with hundreds of them! What were they?
Parasites!

I madly began scraping all the new dirt out now. Oh! If I
neglected to find even a few of them, they'd probably proliferate
and kill all my plants! "Danny!" I yelled. He was still on the couch
reading. "Danny!" He looked up. I burst into the living room.
"Don't touch those plants ever again without asking me! What a
mess you made! Don't touch them!"

A silent stream of tears erupted down his face, his sweet face.
"I hate you!" he blurted out. "I don't want to be near you!"

Stop yourself, Sarah!

"Oh, Danny, I'm sorry!" I hated myself. "I'm just nervous. I'm sorry. It's because of you that these plants look as beautiful as they are!" *Oh, what have I done?* His silent tears continued to stream forth. "Danny, I'm sorry, forget it, please. I'm just nervous." He rubbed his eyes.

"My head hurts me."

Danny agreed to eat two bananas and I ran upstairs to write this in my journal, to get a hold of myself before lashing out again. Danny joined me in my room a little while ago, threw himself down on my bed and said: "You know why I wasn't able to get a book from the library today? Because the boy who works in the library is too busy getting ready for Lag BaOmer and he says he doesn't have time." I was so relieved that he seemed to have survived my assault with a fair degree of equanimity. But to what extent had I damaged his enthusiasm for the flowers? "Tomorrow when you feel better you can go get some dirt, all right, Danny?"

"All right," he said quietly.

Oh, to be a mother!

May 1, 1988

The day after my mother left, I came down again with the same general illness. I spent the whole morning feeling dizzy and strange, wondering if I was imagining it. When I finally took out the thermometer, I found I had a temperature of 102°. I got into bed. Yaacov came home early. Neighbors sent over food for the family. "You might have mononucleosis," Yaacov told me. "That would account for the temperature and the weakness and the lack of resistance."

My hopes jumped up like a happy doggy. Oh, if I had mono, then maybe I could go on a vacation! My fever seemed to soar. The rest of the day I lay in bed like a sack of potatoes. Maybe I could take another trip to America!

But this morning, no sooner had I opened my eyes than I could tell my inner weather had taken an irrevocable turn for the better. I don't know what it was, but I could sense right away, even lying there in bed, that my feet were back on the ground. My fever would not return. I was tired from having been up a lot through the night with Avivah, but I was no longer sick.

Later this morning, I went shopping in the neighborhood supermarket, one of the few times I'd done so since before Pesach. As I turned the corner of one of the aisles to search for something on the shelves, without thinking I rested my hands on somebody else's shopping cart. Feeling her eyes upon me, I turned to find myself facing the wife of one of my husband's fellow kollel members. They live in another part of town. "Oh! Pnina! How funny, is this your cart? What are you doing here?" I didn't give her time to answer. "Shopping, obviously!" I joked.

"Hi! Up and around? I heard you've been sick."

What did I feel guilty for? "Yes, I have been, but I feel better today."

"Oh, that's good."

"No, I wanted to be sick. I'm disappointed."

Only in her startled face did I realize what had slipped out. "Well," she said politely, "glad you feel better. I'll be seeing you!" And off she went, doggedly pretending not to notice me when we met again in front of the applesauce and tomato paste.

May 2, 1988

For the longest time, my friend Happy has been urging me to accompany her to Rabbi Berkowitz's Tuesday morning *shiur* at Eyaht, and I have always protested that I can't because of the baby. But when my cleaning lady came last Tuesday, as she does each week, it dawned on me that I could put Avivah to sleep and return in two hours. That's what I did, bolting from the house, when Avivah's eyes closed, like a horse whose gate has been lifted.

I walked in on his introduction to a series of lectures on the laws of Shabbat. "Why do we observe Shabbat?" he was saying. "It is not only in order to recognize that G-d created the world in six days, and on the seventh He rested. It is also to remember that the world is a perfect system. From candlelighting to havdalah, you do not add to creation. This is the time designated for man to remember that the world is perfect; it does not need anything from him. It doesn't need man in order to continue perfectly. One day a week, man stands back and the world still operates.

"It is forbidden to run on Shabbat. Yet there are exceptions to this. You're allowed to run if you're running to shul, you're allowed to run if somebody's waiting for you. You're allowed to run if it gives you pleasure. There are various other exceptions as well.

"So it is not on account of the exertion involved that running is forbidden. It is on account of the involvement in the physical that running implies. Shabbat is the time to step back, to not be so involved in unspiritual activities. If you're involved enough to be troubled on Shabbat, something is wrong."

Listening to Rabbi Berkowitz, I got an uncomfortable feeling. "Happy," I whispered when he had finished, "I'm so far away from what he was talking about. I work so hard on Shabbat, and I have such a feeling all Shabbat of having to do so much to keep everything going, and get so nervous about getting everything done right: serving the meals and making sure that the children eat, and keeping everything clean and in order. How in the world can I experience the fact that the world doesn't need me?"

"That's a very good question!" Happy encouraged me. "That's a very good question! Ask him!" I myself doubted that it was a very good question. I felt that it was merely an indication of my own spiritual lowness, my own personal failure as a Jew. But I asked him.

"Rabbi Berkowitz," I began, feeling silly. "On Shabbat I'm so worried about everything, particularly about the children—that they should be dressed in reasonably clean clothes and that they shouldn't eat junk food all day, and that they shouldn't drive me up a wall from boredom. There's so much work on Shabbat. What can I do to give me an awareness that the world is a perfect system without me? I mean, if I don't make sure they eat the cholent, who will?"

Rabbi Berkowitz smiled. I could tell from his smile that he has children. "You have to live," he said, "according to a paradox. You wouldn't be a good mother if you weren't worried about your children. That is part of the fulfillment of the role into which you have been placed by the Almighty. Yet deep down, you have to know that actually they don't need you. *HaShem* is taking care of them. A doctor once spoke to me about his own paradox. He was becoming a believer in G-d, and he began to wonder what in the world he was doing: he saw that he could take very good care of a patient, do all the right things and not make any mistakes, and the patient would develop double pneumonia after his operation and die. And then with someone else, he could make mistakes and the patient would be just fine. So he began to see that what he was doing was just a game, that the patient's recovery was really not in his hands. So, he has to live with a paradox. He has been placed into this role of doctor, and it is his responsibility to do his utmost to save the patient. If he does his utmost and the patient dies, he is not at fault. If, however, he thinks to himself, 'Oh, G-d will take care of this one. Why should I try so hard?' then he is indeed guilty, even if the patient recovers without his care. We are not allowed to push off the responsibilities of our roles in life. We're not allowed to stand aside and say, 'G-d will take care.' Yet at the same time, we must live with the consciousness that actually we're not needed. *HaShem* is doing it.

"Deep down you've got to know that *HaShem* is going to take care of your children. They don't need you. You have been put in this role in order to become a great person who can keep your family together."

Once again, I hark back to Aunt Sophie. I carry out the responsibilities of a wife and mother for my own sake, and for the sake of my private relationship with G-d.

May 3, 1988

Today was the day my cleaning lady comes. I left the house in the morning, confident that the mess from which I was taking my leave would not be there when I returned.

I opened the front door at quarter to one, ready to make lunch for the children, and—could it be? The disaster was still there in its every detail. It took me a few seconds to take it in—the crayons Avivah had been eating were still under the coffee table, the toys were scattered all about, the pajamas, that gunk on the kitchen floor (thanks Eli), the piled up sink.

Turned out Chanah had decided to leave the living room and kitchen for last today. She was still cleaning the bedrooms and the bathrooms.

I wandered around, disoriented and out of whack, picking up this and that, buzzing around like a confused fly trying to make order. How agitated and angry I felt! Not until the house was clean and lovely did my soul return to its proper nest.

Miriam Adahan always tries to get across the idea that one's worth as a person does not rise and fall according to the cleanliness of one's house. Yet there, to my mind, went mine, down with the dirt and up with the shine and the glow! G-d doesn't make mistakes; it could only have been by intention that women were implanted with this extreme identification with their houses, this extreme aversion to messiness. Perhaps we would never do the cleaning otherwise. But I must strive to dislike the disorder and dirt without disliking myself, and bear in mind that even less-than-super *balabustas* are also made in G-d's image.

Yaacov once told me that one of the rabbis at his yeshiva said that for a woman, keeping house can be a spiritual pleasure. I bridled at this. "Ha! That's because he's a man! Any time he wants some inspiration, tell him to feel free to come on over and do my housework." But the rabbi's words had an effect. From then on, I tried letting myself feel the full measure of my pleasure in getting the house orderly and clean. Until then, I'd always put a damper on the satisfaction, as if to feel so terrific about a white cabinet was stupid. Now, putting a different interpretation upon the experience, it doesn't hurt my pride to indulge in the sheer feminine joy of a nicely cleared off kitchen counter, towels folded in a neat pile, an unsmudged mirror. It is a spiritual happiness, if you permit it to be.

14

The Purpose of the Darkness

May 4, 1988

What is heaven?
A mother knows.
When the wash is hung
and the kitchen glows.

The children are fed
and all in bed,
each a heap
of innocent sleep.

The stars are necklaces strung out over the dark, vast deep.
Clothes flying on the line dry under the speechless moon.
She turns out all the lights but hers.

                Nothing stirs.

What's heaven?
When earth is completed.
She looks around and finds
nothing else needed.

                The children are all right,
                each one,

and now dreams
        unwind
            until the rising of the sun.

May 5, 1988

Today to my horror I saw that one of the plants on the *mirpesset*, a large tangle of delicate purple blossoms, had been inexplicably pushed over to the other side of the window box. Being shoved around like that could have broken many of the fragile stems. I immediately blamed Daniel. What in the world would have moved him to do something so destructive? A few minutes later on my way to the store, I caught sight of him on his new bicycle, the one my mother bought for him when she was here. What a dignified bearing he assumes upon his bike! Ever shy to let on in public that he has a mother, he glanced about to see if friends were looking, then flashed me a soft smile. "Danny!" I called. "Come here a second!" As he pedaled toward me, I reminded myself of something Miriam Adahan once told me: when she wants to say something to one of her children, first she asks herself if it's going to damage his self-esteem or build it.

He screeched to a stop. "What, Mommy?"

"Danny," I said quietly, restraining myself. "Did you move some of the flowers on the *mirpesset*?"

"What?"

I pointed up to our balcony. We could see from where we stood how the purple flowers were sticking out over the edge. "There, Danny. Did you move them?"

"Yes, I did! You want me to tell you why? Because some of the flowers couldn't even breathe and they were covered up by the other flowers!"

"Oh, all right, Danny," I said, "it's so good that you're taking care of them. But don't move them again, please. All right, Danny? Next time you see something wrong, tell me and we'll try to fix it together, all right?"

"All right," Danny nodded genially as he waved goodbye and sailed away, his dignity intact, as was my own, *baruch HaShem*.

May 6, 1988

Now that Eli can get out of his crib by himself, whatever rough approximation of a schedule we used to have in our household has been swept away. Gone are the days in which I popped him into his crib, reducing by half the general mayhem in one easy blow.

Nowadays, Eli wakes us up at five—not only Yaacov and me but his brother and sisters as well, and at night he doesn't go to sleep until eight or nine, only when his exhaustion is overwhelming. Naps in the afternoon have become hit-or-miss affairs. Instead of disappearing politely between one and three, as he once did, he now catches ten winks in odd places around the house—on the floor by the front door, under the kitchen table, wrapped in his blanket with half-closed eyes, thumb in mouth, wobbly head nodding.

I have sometimes been driven to distraction.

As of this week, however, I see us moving in the general direction of a solution: first of all, I moved Eli's crib next to Avivah's. Her companionship, especially if she's crying, seems to take the edge off his own misery at being confined to bed. Secondly, I resolved inwardly to outlast him no matter how long the battle takes, and to remain calm and loving throughout. What this means in practical terms is that each time I put him into his crib and he climbs out, I must immediately stop whatever I'm doing and go put him back inside. If he jumps out for the fiftieth time, I must with alacrity put him back in for the fifty-first. I cannot afford to let him win. He has to be the loser, but I have to kiss him and hug him and speak his name lovingly, and tell him confidently that no, Eli is going to bed now.

Today, when we were doing what felt like the ninetieth repeat performance, I reinforced my determination by telling myself: "If I can win this time, then it will make it easier next time. But if I give up and let him get out—even though that appears right now to be easier—then forget about ever teaching him to stay in his crib." Thoughts would come to me, such as: "Oh, maybe this isn't right," or "Maybe I should wait until he gets really tired, and then it will be easier," or "Maybe he's outgrown his nap." Wisely, I ignored these sentiments. It's feasible that Eli could manage without his nap, but I cannot.

Eli finally gave up. I looked on at the crib with satisfaction as he wrapped himself up with his blanket and thumb and slipped off to ignominious defeat. He would not go so far as to lie down, however: he fell asleep sitting up.

It's a new thing for me to trust myself and respect my needs enough to be able to bear a child's grief. Sometimes it's not wrong for a mother to take outright advantage of her superior physical size and strength, and play a test of one-upmanship. I can win without guilt.

How pleasant art thou, victory!

May 8, 1988

Our downstairs neighbor, Gila, asked me if I know any girls who would be interested in a baking class. "Yes!" I replied. "Rachel and Dinah would love it."

"Well, I was thinking more of teenagers, or brides."

"Oh, all right, but why don't you also do one for little girls?"

She thought it over. She was reluctant to take on Dinah, who is only seven, and tiny of stature, but I assured her that Dinah would do every bit as well as Rachel. The classes begin next week. Rachel and Dinah are so excited.

May 14, 1988

A new school for girls is going to be started by Rivka Rappaport, the granddaughter of Rav Moshe Feinstein. They won't have a class for Dinah's age group, but we plan on sending Elisheva and Rachel there next year. In reference to teaching, she said: "Well, it's like being a mother. The main thing is to smile when you tell them to do something. If you say it angrily, they'll probably do it anyway, because 'She's my mother and I have to,' but they'll be doing it resentfully."

May 15, 1988

I was doing the breakfast dishes when Eli, standing on a

kitchen chair, reached for the sugar jar. I snatched it away just in time. Then he pulled out the silverware drawer and grabbed the spatula and some spoons I'd just dried and put away. "No, Eli! No!" And I replaced them in the drawer. The next thing I knew, the broom was swinging around wildly in back of me. He was sweeping the floor. "No, Eli! No! Don't do that!" But not in time. The broom handle knocked over a pot on the stove. "Oh! Eli!" I moaned as I leaned down to wipe up the splattered cereal from the floor. Honestly! He makes it so hard for me to get my work done!

But as I rose from the floor to wash out the rag, a thought crossed my mind: I suffer more each time I groan and sigh and moan. Every complaint engenders more anger and increases the load of frustration that weighs me down.

Eli is my baby. I love him. I do love him with all my heart. It is a two-year-old baby's profession—in fact, his very identity—to be curious and get into all kinds of things and undo my work and prevent me from finishing as fast as I would otherwise. Shouldn't I expect all this of him, rather than feel disappointed and exasperated and sorry for myself each and every time I have to face this situation? Why should I increase my own suffering?

This behavior is part of him. Accept it. Expect it. I'd be making it easier on myself that way.

May 16, 1988

Dinah has been cranky lately, so I resolved this morning to take her out by herself today for a little outing. I thought we'd get ice-cream cones. But I wasn't able to get a babysitter, so I forgot about it.

In the late afternoon the house became quiet. Rachel was at home doing homework, Avivah was asleep, Dinah had gone to a friend, Danny and Elisheva were bicycling. I put Eli in his carriage and told Rachel to stay home with Avivah while I did some shopping. Downstairs, as I turned left out of the building, Dinah came running up. "Where are you going?" she called.

"To the fruit and vegetable store on Shmuel HaNavi. You want to come?"

"Yes!"

She fell into step beside me as I hurried along so that none of the other children would notice us. As we turned the corner, safely out of sight, I sent a word of thanks heavenward. Our time alone, after all.

First we went shopping, and Dinah picked out the oranges and peaches and grapes. Then I decided to go to the pharmacy, and I let her choose a new hairband. Then we walked home by a roundabout, unfamiliar route, crossing through a playground we'd never seen before. By the time we got back almost two hours had elapsed, and I was worried. Was Avivah awake, and crying? Was Rachel scared to be alone so long? Had Danny and Elisheva come back home?

As I rushed to maneuver the carriage into the elevator, I heard Elisheva's little voice from far away. "Mommy! Mommy! Wait!" As quickly as I could, I closed the door behind me. I had to check on what was going on upstairs, I couldn't be delayed. At home, my expectations were unfulfilled. Rachel greeted me with blithe indifference, Avivah was still asleep. I set about cleaning up. Ten minutes later, Rachel drifted into the kitchen. "Elisheva's crying downstairs," she told me. "She's lying down on the grass."

I wanted to get the towels folded. "Tell her to come up." Rachel ran back in a minute later. "Mommy! She's calling you! Go get her! She's crying SO LOUD!"

I went out to the *mirpesset* and looked over the side. There was Elisheva, sure enough, splayed out on the grass, hysterical. "Elisheva!" I called. "Come upstairs, darling."

Her sobbing, muffled reply wafted up the four flights. "No!"

"Elisheva, come upstairs, darling. Come."

"No! YOU!"

"Elisheva, come up, darling. It's hot outside."

"YOU COME!"

Shall I let her dictate to me like this? I asked myself. *Shouldn't she learn that I don't have to go to her, that she should come to me? Should she get into the habit of disturbing me from what I'm doing?* I went back to the kitchen and cut zucchini for Yaacov's dinner. Eli wandered about the living room with his big, deflated plastic ball.

Rachel burst into the kitchen. "Mommy! She's crying!" I was about to strengthen my resolve once again not to give in to this pressure, when a little voice within me said: *What could Elisheva be so upset about?*

I remembered...Wiping my hands, I hurried to go downstairs. *Give her in the next few minutes,* I told myself, *all she could wish for from her mother.*

She was stretched out on the grass, sobbing. I gave her my hand, she rose, we went inside to the shadowy, cool entrance of our building and sat down at the bottom of the stairs. It was apparent by the already satisfied set of her little tear-streaked face that half her pain had dissolved by my coming. She had wanted proof of my love. "Elisheva, what happened?"

"You didn't wait for me!" Her sobs exploded once again. "I called you! WHY didn't you wait? WHY?"

With all the gentleness of which I was capable: "Elisheva, sweetheart, I'm so sorry. I was in a big hurry to get back, and I was running." I encircled her in a soft embrace.

"I wanted to come upstairs with you!"

Gently: "I'm so sorry! I understand!" She looked long into my face, smiled and stuck her thumb in her mouth. "I'm going upstairs now," I said. "Do you want to come with me?" She nodded and we entered the elevator. "What shall we thank G-d for this time?" I inquired. My friend Margerie once told me that she had resolved to thank *HaShem* for something else each day upon awakening, right after *modeh ani.* I had decided to try doing it every time I stand there bored in the elevator.

She thought a moment, then took her thumb out of her mouth. "That I have a good mommy," she replied.

Back in the apartment, I looked around for Eli. Good, he's with Rachel on the *mirpesset.* Wow, six o'clock! I have to get dinner ready! Let's see, where is everybody? Rachel's all right. Danny's having fun on his bicycle. Elisheva's all right now. I'm so happy I went down. Dinah's all right. How wonderful we could go alone, after all. Amazing. Avivah's asleep. Eli's exhausted from his long outing in the hot sun—I have to get him fed fast, before Avivah wakes up.

Like a mother hen that counts her eggs and comes up with the right number, I felt good that all of them were safe...under my wing.

May 29, 1988

This Shabbat we had challahs baked by Rachel and Dinah. They are so proud.

I was remembering today a comment made to me some years ago by a visiting second cousin. She asked me pointedly if I hadn't already made an adequate contribution to the population of Israel. "There's more to life than diapers," she advised affably. At the time, I bristled for lack of a suitable retort. Now I've got one ready if she ever comes again: "Yes, how true. And there's more to children than diapers."

June 2, 1988

I heard today that an eighteen-year-old yeshiva student was shot by an Arab girl in the middle of town, in Sacher Park. He was walking home from a wedding with a friend, and had sat down on a bench with him to relate what had been in a *shiur* that his friend had missed.

When I heard the murdered boy's name, Schlesinger, and that his family lives in Bayit Vegan, a shiver ran up my neck. Could that be the Schlesinger family I know? Mrs. Schlesinger taught me *taharat hamishpachah* before I was married, and I used to look on at that family entranced. Such warmth. I found out later that it was indeed that family. I cannot stop wondering how the mother is taking it.

I was there ten years ago, so he must have been that little boy with curly reddish hair running around in pajamas, smiling at me shyly, curiously, as I waited for his mother.

June 4, 1988

When the children are raising their voices, I feel compelled to raise mine higher than theirs to get their attention. Invariably, they continue yelling at each other and pay me no heed. I just end up tense and depleted.

But sometimes I notice what's happening. *Loosen that tight knot within. Just because they're yelling doesn't mean you have to get all tied up in knots along with them. Untie, relax. Breathe.*

Then I can speak quietly.

June 7, 1988

Yesterday Eli and I had another in-and-out session. His wailing and weeping was too much for Elisheva to bear and she burst into tears. "Mommy! Stupid! Eli's crying so much! You can't hear him? Poor Eli!"

"He just has to go to sleep, Elisheva. And you should not call your mommy 'stupid.' "

"But Mommy! He's CRYING!" She went to his room, dragging her pink pillow, and curled up on the soft rug beside Eli's crib. He grew quiet. When I peeked in some minutes later, Eli sat there entangled in his blanket, sucking his thumb, appeased by the presence of his sister...who had herself fallen fast asleep.

June 10, 1988

Daniel no longer waters the plants each day, and my downstairs neighbor is relieved that muddy water no longer drips down onto her windows. I'm relieved, too, because he was flooding the flowers, but sad and remorseful. Am I nipping his enthusiasm for gardening in the bud?

June 13, 1988

Last night I went to a bridal shower organized by Aish Ha-

Torah. The proceeds are to be given to needy brides. A teacher from Eyaht said that it is written that "The wisdom of women is in weaving." "Does this insult you?" she asked us. "It doesn't insult me. What this means is that what a woman does with her child is not like a paint job, which can come off or be removed; it is woven into the very fabric of the person."

She related this story: After the war, a rabbi was searching in a Christian orphanage for Jewish children. The orphans were assembled in a large room, their chairs arranged in long rows. He began walking up and down the aisles muttering under his breath, *Modeh ani lifanechah...*and *Shema Yisrael HaShem Elokeinu...*and *Reishis chochmah yiras HaShem...*From every side he was besieged by children reaching out for him, grabbing onto his jacket, pulling at his hands. "You know my mommy!" they were crying. "You know where my mommy is!"

June 14, 1988

I'm so busy and distracted that I never toilet trained Eli. The potty just sat there in the bathroom and that's the best thing that could have happened. He takes pride and pleasure in his success at this new game. When he jumps up to look around at what he has produced, his exuberance has no bounds, and when he runs with the potty to the bathroom to dump it out...keep your distance!

June 19, 1988

Daniel has started, gradually, going to shul on Shabbat. Yaacov finally found out why he didn't want to go in the first place. It wasn't because he's rebellious or lazy. It wasn't because he is disinterested in praying. Quite the contrary. In the course of a long, private conversation, Daniel admitted that it's his embarrassment about davening in front of his peers that stops him from going. So Yaacov suggested they go to Ohr Somayach Yeshiva, where none of Daniel's friends go.

Yesterday, after spending many hours together with Yaacov in shul studying, Danny was so happy that when it came time to go to bed, he couldn't stop saying good night. "Good night, Mommy," he called from the stairs.

"Good night, Danny. Sweet dreams."

He came down for a glass of orange juice. "Good night," he said, and threw me a kiss.

"Good night, Danny."

"Good night!" he called as he left the kitchen.

A few minutes later Danny wandered downstairs with a shy smile and threw himself onto Yaacov, who was in the living room on the couch, reading. "Good night, Daddy!"

"Go to bed, Danny," I said.

He waved and went upstairs.

June 20, 1988

Yesterday afternoon I paid Dinah and Rachel a shekel each, as usual, for their babysitting hours. Some time later, they slipped furtively into Dinah's room and quietly closed the door. Of course, this meant they had gone and bought junk food. I burst into the room and yes, there they were, sharing a bag of what must have been ten chocolate candy bars. Evidently, they'd been saving up their shekels from the past few weeks. I exploded, spanked them both, and shouted at them that they know they're not allowed to have junk food during the week. They cried.

What a hot item candy is for me! Too hot! I was sad and regretful about the ridiculous way I handled it. Sure enough, in those instants before I became enraged, I remember thinking: "It's my fault! I should have had carrots and cucumbers and red peppers out on the table for snacks. I'm not feeding them right." No doubt about it, I felt that I'd failed...then came the fury.

How did the girls feel when I burst in upon them like that? It reminds me of that woman in our old apartment building, whom Elisheva and I watched that morning as she broke in on her little boy's play. Rachel and Dinah must have felt that they had done something horrible. As a mother I know it's not they who are guilty, it's me I'm really angry at, but they don't know that. One day, when they're adults, will they carry around in some corner of their hearts a shadow—however faint and forgotten—of yesterday afternoon's "sin"? How many such incidents—one? ten? a hundred?—are enough to make them feel they're bad people?

This morning before they went to school, I rounded up the two of them. "Rachel, Dinah, I have to tell you something." I anticipated resistance. I thought they'd protest that they were going to miss their bus. To my surprise, they listened intently. "Yesterday when I got so mad at you for eating the candy upstairs, what did you feel?"

No answer. They both looked deeply into my eyes. "Well, I want to tell you something very important. Getting that candy was not a terrible thing and you were not bad for doing it! It's just that I'm worried because it's so unhealthy. Please, just have it on Shabbat, and not so much at once. I was upset that you were eating all that chocolate, but you're not bad because of it! Do you understand?" I stroked Rachel's face gently and put my hand on Dinah's back.

They said nothing, but I could tell: they heard me.

June 21, 1988

The two babies are here on the porch in the plastic wading pool. They are so funny, it's like watching a comedy routine. They splash, they coo and exclaim, push each other down and giggle delightfully as they get up. Such a complex relationship they have, this one-year-old and this two-year-old!

It's work taking care of the two of them. I have to be constantly on guard when they're together, lest he sit on her or bite her or stick a pencil in her eye...the sky's the limit as to what he might do. However, there is the pleasure of moments like this one, the privilege of beholding their purity, innocence and beauty. The sweetness is so intense sometimes, I feel I'm going to burst.

The two of them like to dance together, but they only know one step: they turn around and around and around until they get dizzy and fall down. Any music will set them off, even the thirty-second musical interval before the morning news. This afternoon I was in the kitchen putting away some pots and pans, humming mindlessly to myself as I thought about what to have for dinner, when I became aware of the two babies behind me, spinning like dreidels to the meager music I was providing.

I'm subdued and humbled by the memory of not having wanted her. Little did I know what I was getting.

June 23, 1988

We had a farewell party for Yaacov this morning at 6 a.m. We served the cakes that Dinah and Rachel made in this week's baking class, and as he took his leave, I cried, which was just the final touch I would have wished for. "If you're crying because you'll miss me," he said, "that's nice. But you don't need to feel sorry for me. Army training's fun. I always wanted to go to summer camp, and the army's like summer camp except we don't get a canoe." He was to be gone for a month.

Two hours later, there was a knock on the door. It was Yaacov. "What in the world are you doing home?" I exclaimed incredulously.

He laughed, dumped his huge backpack on the table and plopped down on the couch. "Three guesses."

"Yaacov! Stop it! Why are you home? What happened?"

He kicked off his shoes and laughed again. "The guy in front of me in the line to get boots wore the same size as I do."

"So?"

"So he got the last pair."

"So?"

"So they looked for my size for a while, then they got fed up and told me to go home."

June 28, 1988

I hate being a mother today. I feel discouraged. So I'm reminding myself how two weeks ago, our Shabbat guests commented on how well behaved our children were, and that two days ago a babysitter said the same thing, and last night, when Yaacov and I had to go to a *shevah brachos* and I couldn't find a babysitter, the children took care of themselves.

My mood today will pass.

Last night, as my negative mood was just coming on, I lost patience with Dinah because she called me a stupid mommy. Suspecting that she was right, I snapped: "You should beg me for forgiveness, Dinah!"

Her eyes narrowed. Her English vocabulary had not gotten this far. "All right," she conceded. "I forgive you for my bigness."

It's ten o'clock at night. A friend of mine who has just re-married this week brought her four-year-old son here while she and her new husband go on a four-day vacation. Needless to say, the little boy is going through hard times, losing his mommy to an intruder, and once here, he cried. For me the nice thing is that my depression lifted with the effort I expended in empathizing with him and trying to make him feel loved. I figure that a separation like this, right on the heels of a remarriage, could really make him feel abandoned, but that we can make a difference. If he has fun here and feels loved, his dismay will be much diminished. Doing such an important mitzvah has broken through my depression.

To top it off, I have had the joy today of seeing Rachel, Dinah and Elisheva reach out to this little boy in his pain. Looking on as he cried pitifully for his mother, they were sensitive and generous, and behaved like mothers. In spite of all my mistakes, I have given the children a lot of love and understanding, and it looks like they're going to be loving, understanding people themselves. At one point Dinah whispered in my ear: "Right, every minute we're taking care of him we're getting a thousand mitzvahs?"

Not only did they put themselves to bed tonight, they also put him to bed.

June 30, 1988

I met someone in the store Friday morning who mentioned that she was horrified to have not yet finished cooking for Shabbat. "Gee," I said, rather crestfallen, "I haven't finished cooking either, but it's always like that Friday morning."

"Oh, I'm not the type to put things off," she said. "I hate rushing at the last minute. At our house, Friday is a vacation day. We go places. We have picnics. But today I don't know what happened."

I listened to this, getting sadder by the minute. "I *am* the type to put things off. Every week I procrastinate doing all the Shabbat preparations, and as Friday goes on I become more and more exhausted and nervous." *Oh dear!* I cried inwardly. *I'm not fair to my family! Why don't I change?*

She must have sensed how this was killing me, because she abruptly changed her tune. "You know, don't worry about it. Your children are probably already used to the way you are, and they work around it." She waved her hand dismissively, as if to shoo away my flood of self-doubts. "Don't you worry about it. It's all right."

Thank you, lady. That was nice.

July 2, 1988

I awoke this morning to the pleasant sound of Rachel's voice. She was babysitting for Eli while Yaacov and I slept. When I went downstairs, Eli was stuffing himself with cookies, and that all-too-familiar arrow of guilt shot through me. "What kind of a mother am I to let my child have cookies before breakfast!" I grabbed them out of his hand and said to Rachel, "Don't give him cookies until after he's eaten!" That was all, and I forgot about it.

Rachel was in a terrible mood all Shabbat, pinching Dinah, hitting Elisheva, fighting with Danny. My thoughts caved in on themselves. "Oh, no, she's going back to the way she was two years ago, before our trip." I peered into the future and beheld darkness. I asked her what was wrong but she wouldn't answer.

Finally, at bedtime, she responded: "This morning you yelled at me when I gave Eli the cookies, and you didn't yell at Dinah or Elisheva! So I was jealous. I was SO JEALOUS!"

After this, she sprang back to life again.

July 11, 1988

Yesterday I left the baby with Rachel and attended an all-morning seminar at Eyaht Yeshiva. When I returned, I found that Rachel had been invited to a friend's house, so Daniel had babysat instead. I never would have thought to ask him to do it for so many hours. It shows how a mother's limited image of a child prevents him from growing, for, given the opportunity, Daniel was happy to be entrusted with a big responsibility.

Some notes from Rebbetzin Weinberg's class:

—"There is a principle in psychology that a person's ordinary, daily self fears and retreats from the real self. The real self is the one whose powers are far greater than those exercised by the person normally. So the ordinary self locks up the real self in the unconscious, because it is frightened of its ability to fulfill its potential."

—"Stop thinking about everyone's approval/disapproval. Do what's right no matter what anyone says about it."

A woman asked about the approval/disapproval of her mother-in-law. Rebbetzin Weinberg said: "Do as much as you can without violating *halachah*. Pleasing one's mother-in-law is a value; there's no upper limit on it. I regret that as a young woman I used to be opposed to the candy that my mother-in-law would bring for the children. Now I recognize that even though I'm opposed to letting children have junk food, giving pleasure and respect to my mother-in-law is a more important value."

—"Don't be a religious robot. There are plenty of people around who do the right things...they wake up in the morning and wash their hands, and they pray, and they even say *baruch HaShem, baruch HaShem*. Yet they are a far way off from fulfilling what it means to be a religious Jew."

—"Someone I once knew was in the hospital with a terminal illness. A group of visitors were standing around talking about various things, until the woman they were visiting protested. 'What are you doing to me? Here I am not knowing whether I'm still going to be alive tomorrow, and you're talking about all this meaningless nonsense! Talk about things that matter.' Isn't her predicament our predicament? We don't know whether tomorrow will be our last day here in this world. Shouldn't we see to it that what we speak about are the important issues?"

—A woman asked: "Some people say you should let a child cry and not spoil him, and some people say you should never let him cry because he'll feel unloved. What do you think?"

" 'Never' is not a good word in any case, but in principle, it's definitely better not to let a child cry. However, you do have to go along with your own needs; otherwise you'll be aiming so high that you can't do anything but fail. Even if it's just because you want to sit down for a minute and have something to drink, that's a legitimate reason to let him cry for a little while. Sometimes, the firstborn child is never left to cry, the second child is sometimes left to cry, and by the time the third one comes around, it's 'Oh, let him work it out by himself.' In general, it's cruel to just let a child cry."

—"Shabbos, being a time of *kedushah*, gets a double whammy of the *yetzer hara*. It's so hard for a mother to balance all the different requirements of Shabbos. There are two things to do to make the Shabbos table as pleasant as possible. 1) Pray. 2) Plan. Pray, because with this many things to do, you'll need the Almighty's help. And plan. Have special toys that you take out only for Shabbos, and special books. You can have dinner quickly, and let the children get up from the table after the amount of time that's reasonable according to their age. Don't think a young child is disobedient just because he wants to leave the table. Some people go too much to one extreme, and insist on perfect behavior, and some are too relaxed. 'Oh, I'm so exhausted. Just let the children eat in the other room and not bother us.' The main thing is not to demand too much of a child. Go according to his age and his temperament."

—"It would be disastrous for a woman to define herself and her potential only in terms of her children. There must be many tracks running simultaneously. She has to dig inside herself: 'Who am I? What contribution can I make to the Jewish people?' When she arrives at the age of fifty, if she hasn't been developing the other parts of herself all along, it is going to be very, very hard."

—"Get rid of *I know*. Replace it with *I think*. Diminish direct confrontation. Get so much into this habit that even if someone comes late to an appointment, your response is: 'I could be mistaken, but you might be late.' "

The women laughed.

—"Every husband is dying for the respect of his wife, even if he doesn't respond to your compliments, even if he seems not to listen when you praise him. He needs the appreciation as much as your children do. It's his bread and butter."

Rabbi Aharon Feldman then gave a talk on *shalom bayis*. Some notes: "The drive to be a wife is the drive to be loved. The drive to be a mother is the drive to nurture. These drives can be expressed in different ways in different women's lives. A female neurosurgeon can be manifesting the same need to nurture as the woman who is diapering her baby.

"Most men do not have these two drives to the same degree as do women. In general a man has a drive for power, for honor, for domination. A man can be extremely threatened by what he interprets as competition from his wife. In his own home, he wants to have domination. You can feed his need to feel dominant. While it's his responsibility to feed your need for love, it's your responsibility to feed his need to be honored. Neither husband nor wife should consider the other's need a weakness. Then they start thinking, 'I shouldn't indulge her need for approval,' or 'I'm not going to pander to his ego problem.' Each one's duty is to feed the other.

"If his desires for domination or honor exceed the normal bounds of the male nature, in other words, if they bring pain to others, then it's advisable to get somebody else to talk to him about it. Most men will not accept *mussar* from their wives."

July 12, 1988

When I returned home from the second day of the Eyaht seminar, Dinah said she wanted to make bread. That was the last thing I felt like having her do. I was tired, there was work from the morning to catch up on, I didn't want to clean up after her. I told her no.

"Please, Mommy," she begged me. "I'll clean up everything."

I let her do it.

All the children had Dinah's delicious, warm, whole wheat bread for dinner, and she cleaned everything up. Most important was her solid good feeling about the success, and her expanded sense of her own capabilities.

July 17, 1988

From a tape by Avigdor Miller: "To deny the truth is the greatest form of suffering. The truth is the greatest happiness, and at the same time the greatest sadness.

"In this world, truth is not easily apparent, and this is not an accident. 'You, *HaShem*, made darkness and it became night.' *HaShem* made this world a place where it is not easy to see. The purpose of the darkness is to test mankind, whether they will exert themselves to find truth despite the darkness."

15
Mother's Helper

Out on the porch Elisheva is doing *sponga*. As usual, whenever one of the children volunteers to help in a way that might actually end up meaning more work for me, I wanted to say no. Then I caught myself and said all right. For the past fifteen minutes, she's been dragging the sopping-wet rag, which keeps falling off the stick, back and forth from one side of the *mirpesset* to the other.

A jet just roared overhead. Elisheva raised an arm and opened and closed her fist a few times...she was waving. She stood there with the stick in one hand, the other hand shielding her eyes from the bright sky, and waited a minute with innocent goodwill. Did she expect the people in the plane to look down onto our porch and see her friendly little gesture, and return the greeting?

How far from the adult's mind is the mind of a child! Another reality. A frontier untraveled by adults. One day she herself will have left it and won't be able to regain entrance.

Ten minutes later, the heat of the day has already evaporated every drop of water out there. It looks nice and clean and white. Elisheva's work really was useful. Now I don't have to clean the *mirpesset*.

October 10, 1988

Someone pressed the "record" button on the tape recorder while Handel's "Water Music" was playing. When I put it on tonight and realized that some of my favorite music had been lost, I was sad. Never mind, I instructed myself, these are your child rearing years: many relatively unimportant things will be lost in the trade-off for the gift, the children who are of eternal and incalculable value to you.

So while I cut up vegetables for dinner, the children clustered excitedly around the tape recorder. We listened to the sounds of pots and pans clattering, cabinet doors opening and closing, and of our stray voices that had been inadvertently recorded. A woman's voice came on. It was so warm, resonant and comforting, it could have belonged to the star of some children's radio program, yet it was mine! I couldn't believe it. I stopped what I was doing and came closer to listen. "Is that what I sound like?" I asked the kids. They nodded. Gee, I must have changed. I used to be embarrassed to hear myself on tape, but I admired the sound of this woman. Yes, unbelievably: not a girl's, but a woman's gentle, tolerant voice. "I don't want one like that!" Dinah was crying. I was answering kindly and educationally in mellow tones, on and on in response to Dinah's anguish and frustration. Unforced patience. A while later: "It's not *this* dish, it's the other dish." Dinah, still sounding sad, but calmer now.

Handel's harpsichord came back on, the children drifted off, then a half-minute later, live from our kitchen, there we were again somehow. (Eli! It must have been him playing with the buttons!) Cooking, I listened to the sounds of our life—the crying of a baby, fragmented conversations, my footsteps, the door slamming, even the telephone ringing. So that's the texture of it as heard from the outside. Then, all of a sudden, in sharp relief against the muffled background, this: "Come right now! It's not *fair* that I should make dinner and have to call you so many times! It's not *fair*! All of you! Danny!"

My voice again, but quite different now. If only I had known how transparent...why, anyone hearing it could have seen right through me: that voice was positively dripping with self-pity. A grown woman whining that she's the poor victim of her children, agonizing over her martyrdom, trying to sway them with guilt. Ugh.

October 13, 1988

It's 5:20 a.m. Just now I was groggily holding Eli up on the bathroom sink to wash off the remains of his nighttime diaper. His arms were draped sweetly around my neck as I scrubbed, and as he nuzzled his face against mine, all my agitation at being woken up melted away. He was like a little puppy. I watched him in the mirror then, as he pulled back his head to look pointedly at something near my ear.

Oh. Eli hadn't been nuzzling from love. He has wiped off his nose on my scarf.

Hmmm.

October 14, 1988

Every so often through the years it occurs to us what a good idea it would be to get someone to live-in and help me in the house in return for room and board. Several young women have called up in response to the most recent of our "Mother's Helper" signs, which Yaacov posted in various places around the city last week—Richie's Pizza, Neve Yerushalayim, the Israel Center. One of them, Amanda, a soft-spoken, dainty, twenty-four-year-old blonde from London, drank tea in my kitchen yesterday as she explained that the Hyatt Hotel couldn't hire her as a waitress because she didn't have a work permit. "Do you require a work permit, too?" she inquired.

"I didn't even know there was such a thing," I said.

"Well, I suppose you never needed one because you're Jewish, obviously."

"Oh." My little brain computer whizzed accordingly. A missionary? She didn't seem the type. "So what are you doing here in Israel?"

"Well, I plan to be married shortly."

"Oh."

"I was just at the Rabbinate today, actually, getting my conversion underway." Her large, gentle brown eyes widened and she smiled a proud little smile.

"Oh. You're converting because you want to get married to a Jew?"

"Yes." Again a little smile.

I busied myself around the kitchen, kids burst in and out, a dozen crises fizzed up and fizzled out. Then the kitchen emptied and it got quiet again. "Do you feel that you're converting out of conviction or mostly because of the marriage?"

She tipped her head to one side and shrugged ever so slightly. She felt something coming. "Well, I suppose you could say because of the marriage."

I told myself: Don't dare be shy. "You know, Amanda, people who convert are held in high esteem. They choose to be Jewish even though it's hard in many respects, as I'm sure you know. In most cases it is something that happens over many years. It's a whole development. They belong in this world here in Israel and are especially respected by religious people, because to choose the commitment for the sake of one's belief is an exalted level of observance. We're told in the Torah to love the stranger. We were strangers in Egypt, and we're supposed to realize how hard it is. A convert chooses to be tested: he doesn't get anything for free. He earns it. But if you're converting out of love for a person rather than for religious principles, then it's not fair to the Jewish people. It's not fair to your children, to put them into this society." She crossed her legs nervously and put down her teacup. "I don't want to hurt you," I went on. "I hope I'm not. I was really a stranger myself in my life. I felt like one. I grew up in a non-Jewish town, with Christians, so I know what it is to feel like an outsider. This is not a tolerant society when it comes to something like this. You'd just be paying lip service to the word 'Jew.' You might suffer, G-d forbid. Maybe your children would suffer. Are you aware of that?"

Amanda stared. "I've wondered."

"Now you're in love and what I'm telling you seems shallow, right? Like I'm being self-righteous and cruel and unfeeling and bigoted. Right?"

Amanda's face closed.

I pushed on. The fearless and forthright tell-it-like-it-is role is one to which I aspire but don't usually carry off gracefully. I hoped my pompous disregard for her feelings was called for. "Someone I know who converted happened to have a run-in with a group of Jewish women. She was bitter for quite a few years because she thought it was because she was a convert, then later on she realized why it actually happened. It was for other reasons. But anyway, it was a bad experience, and it was with religious Jews. So while it was going on, she told me that she no longer defined herself as a Jew. She said she didn't want any part of the Jewish community. So I asked her, why do you go around with that scarf on your head, then, and eat kosher, and do the holidays and all the mitzvos and everything else, if you don't consider yourself a Jew? And she said: 'Because the Torah is true, that's why. I consider myself an Irish Catholic who has discovered that this is where the truth lies.' Can you imagine that? For the sake of her belief, she continued living in a community by which she felt rejected."

Amanda cleared her throat. "Well, I'll certainly give some thought to what you say."

I wanted to stay in touch with her, so I asked if she'd like to give the job a try, starting at twelve thirty the next day, which obviously pleased her. I was so glad that she didn't seem to be mad at me, and wondered how I'd react if the roles were reversed. She even stuck around for another quarter-hour or so, cheerfully feeding Eli his rice pudding. He opened his mouth obediently, keeping an eye on her, enjoying warily the luxury of being fed. She appeared to have taken my remarks with goodwill.

No luck. Her Israeli boyfriend must have gotten wind of my

comments and feared losing her. "Are you kidding?" he probably said. "Don't go back to that crazy lady!" And she didn't.

October 16, 1988

This morning I got a call from a newly arrived Italian. "I am twenty-two years old. I am Sephardic," she told me on the phone. "I am religious, but I am not fanatic. I know to cook very well and to sew and to take care of kids. I love to clean. So if you wish we can meet together and speak about it."

As soon as Sonia walked in and I looked into her intelligent, bright eyes, her warm smile, her elegant bearing, I thought, "Yes, yes. She's good." For a few minutes I put up a fair show of interviewing her, then asked if she would like to start right now. "And you know, my niece has just moved out of her room to live in the dormitory of her college, so there's a possibility of living in, in return for a certain number of hours of work each day, if you're interested."

She lit up. "Yes, this would be perhaps a very good thing, because I want to stay religious here in Israel and the university is not conducive to this, and I have little money." It was decided.

Sonia sprang up at once and began to dart here and there, picking up toys, setting things in order, washing dishes, sweeping floors. "What can I do now?" she kept saying. I was delighted. This was just what I needed, someone who wouldn't wait around for me to give orders.

Around an hour later, Rachel and Dinah were in the kitchen talking something over when their conversation suddenly flared up with some disagreement. I don't recall what was said because I hardly paid any attention to it, but Sonia appeared at their side, her face stern and surprised. "Rachel," she said with hushed solemnity, "you do not need to raise your voice." Then she went back to what she'd been doing in the living room.

Rachel and Dinah looked over at me. Rachel's eyes were opened wide, Dinah's lips were parted in silence. They waited for some response from me. Well, I thought to myself, maybe this won't work out after all. A second passed. I changed my mind. No, maybe it will work out. A good influence on them.

Sonia returned to the kitchen a few moments later. "Rachel," she said, "I have never in all my life seen a child yell at her mother." My heart fluttered. "Never have I seen such a thing. A child yelling at her mother? And especially a mother like this—" she gestured to me. "So nice, and her hair covered, and modest, the long skirt! And she does so much work for you!" Sonia shook her head as if amazed.

Hmm, this was interesting, I mused, getting a nice warm glow from the praise. Rachel actually hadn't yelled at me, she'd been having a fight with Dinah. But I figured a little propaganda in my favor wouldn't hurt.

The afternoon went quite well, I thought, and I was excited at the idea of having help like this every afternoon. Why, I'd have her chop up the salad for dinner, scrub the potatoes, iron Yaacov's shirts, the children would eat on time...the whole household would get more organized.

At six o'clock I happily bid Sonia farewell until tomorrow. Her face became serious. "Sarah," she began in her precise and pretty Italian lilt, "I must tell you, though, that perhaps I cannot live here with you. Perhaps it would not disturb me to work here a few hours a day, then leave and go to my own place, but I cannot stand to see children yelling like this, and being disrespectful to their mother. I have never in my life seen such a thing. In our house, there was a high quality of life; nobody ever raised his voice. We used to fight among ourselves only for who would have the privilege of washing dishes for our mother. That is the way we lived. I never heard my parents raise their voices to us or to each other. In a religious family, the children say, 'Mommy, please,' and 'Mommy, thank you,' and 'You're welcome, Mommy,' and 'Excuse me...' And also, Sarah, I cannot live in a house that is not tidy." She smiled kindly and my insides shriveled. "When a house is nice and tidy, it gives peace of mind to everyone who lives there."

The moment froze. I see now in my mind's eye a photograph of Rachel, Dinah and Elisheva all staring at me. I hear Eli banging on something in the next room, and Avivah making soft conversation to herself. And there am I, my self shrinking into a tennis ball, a tight little ball sucking itself speedily backwards into the distance. To get away from this. I felt a little dizzy. This cannot be happening...What's happening? What's the big deal? The children—the children are watching me. Why be so stunned? Hey! It's all for the best, take it the right way, it's not serious, just one of life's little corrective shocks. Don't worry: either she's wrong or else this is the truth, and if this is the truth, the truth is always for the best. Things will ultimately be better because of this criticism, it will make me more aware...Then I veered in the other direction: *How dare she say this in front of the children!* Now they'll be ashamed of their home! And of me! And of themselves! She doesn't know what she's talking about. Ignore her! She comes from a repressive family. (But she seems so self-possessed, alive, confident...) For goodness sakes, doesn't she understand that when all the kids are here, of course the house gets messy? This is rush hour, dinnertime! Eli and Avivah are still awake and at work! Doesn't she figure that after they all go to bed each night, I clean up? She's just inexperienced. You think I'm some kind of slob, don't you, Sonia! That I don't care if the house is messy. If anything, I've got the opposite problem. I care about it too much. I've cultivated carefully that chief trademark of feminine virtue: compulsive housecleaning. True, if you're looking for something really disorderly, take a little peek in my closets. But I'd drag myself across the living room with a broom even if I were on my last legs, just on the off chance that a neighbor might drop in. My pride is alive and well! You don't understand—Eli, Avivah...they remove the contents of every drawer and redistribute it according to their own sights. A place for everything and everything in its place, that's their motto. Just wait till you have children (may you have ten in five years.) You must come from some kind of a spotless Sephardic household, you have a whole different standard. Don't impose it on me...*It's ridiculous that this girl should get to me like this! Brush it off!*

My knees felt wobbly. It was as if Sonia had unknowingly tripped the switch of a secret trapdoor, and I had plummeted through into the cellar. Above me, in three seconds flat, the invisible construction work on which I'd built my life had collapsed with a whisper. I panicked. She's right! Look around! Open your eyes! Look at that dirty floor! Look at the stove! The home I've made is a failure, Yaacov and I are so far off the track, our children are missing out on a genuinely peaceful home life. You can't pass on something you just don't have, and our characters are missing...missing...what was her word? Quality. It's a sham, we're not deeply rooted in the religious tradition. Our children haven't tasted real *shalom bayis.* Dear G-d, we're so far away from what she's talking about! We're not teaching our children correctly! And we can't! What she's talking about just isn't in us...and it's too late to put it there, it would be like adding baking powder after the cake's in the oven.

I wanted to say something, to retort. "Well, if the house were tidy, dear, then I wouldn't have advertised for a mother's helper in the first place. Tidiness is not my greatest priority. I have more important things to think about. My children may fight and raise their voices, but at least they feel free to express themselves to me. You were probably raised in a straitjacket, but you're too repressed to even realize it. Besides, all kids are noisy, at least the normal ones, and gee, I thought the house was looking pretty nice. You probably just have different taste than ours. I bet I'd hate your wallpaper. You don't understand Americans; we don't make it our business to produce perfectly behaved angels and a perfectly tidy house, and thank goodness we don't."

But nothing came out of my mouth, for I thought: I'm lacking some essential ingredient.

I had been standing there numbly for perhaps thirty seconds in silence, with who knows what expression on my face. Sonia was looking at me in alarm. "Oh, dear, Sarah!" she began slowly. "Please excuse me! I hope you understand! I hope I have not...Perhaps you did not understand me..."

I shook my head. "No, I understand you very well."

"No, I think you did not unders—"

"I understand you, Sonia. I understand fine."

"I hope I have not hurt you."

I was going to shake my head no, I was going to summon up some line of defense, I was going to tell her where she was mistaken...but instead I just chose the path of least resistance. The words fell from me like flat slips of cardboard. "You did hurt me." Then my eyes brimmed with tears and spilled over, big wet drops, down my face. The children watched, abashed and amazed at all this, as was I.

"Oh, dear!" Now Sonia was really alarmed. "Oh, dear, what have I done! Please forgive me—to make someone cry like this, I have never done this in my life!"

"You've never made anyone cry in your life?" I asked suspiciously, wiping my eyes on my sleeve.

"My mother, my sister, but never someone who is not close. I am a stranger to you. Forgive me! Please! Do you forgive me?" I nodded half-heartedly. "I cannot wait for Yom Kippur to get your forgiveness, Sarah. I ask you again to please forgive me."

"I forgive you."

"Truly?"

"Yes." *Because she's right,* I thought, from the pit where my soul at that moment lay, under the fallen debris. *My children have not been sufficiently educated to be respectful towards their parents and towards each other. I am unaware, I am too permissive. They don't have in me a good role model. This young woman's only sin is that she said the truth.*

Sonia wandered from the kitchen, ashamed. The children dispersed, except for Rachel. While the inaudible, invisible crash still echoed, I turned to the sink, picked up a dish, but had no strength to wash it.

Suddenly, two little hands were holding my face from behind. I turned around. It was Rachel. She stood on tiptoe and took my face between her tender, long-fingered hands. "Mommy!" She pressed her face to mine and kissed one cheek and then the other, one and the other, again and again. I felt like a rag doll. "Don't listen to her!" Rachel whispered fervently, glancing back into the living room to make sure she wasn't being heard. "I hate her! She doesn't know! The house is tidy enough! *She's* not right. I love you! *You're* good, not her! You're good!"

Ah, this was sweet...I could have turned into a puddle of chocolate right there on the kitchen floor, but alas, I was off somewhere under a pile of the years. Everything had fallen on top of me.

Sonia wanted to work for free now for a few hours, as atonement. "I am your prisoner, now, because of what I have done," she proclaimed cheerfully. But whatever little flame of indignance I harbored toward her had been snuffed out by other sentiments. Her sincerity sufficed to appease me; I didn't need her slavery. Toward my critic my anger died, but toward the culprits, my children...Tonight, after Mother's Helper took her subdued leave and Mommy put the babies into their cribs, a metamorphosis took place. The poor, boneless mother turned into a...a lion, a hurricane, a pestilence. "GET IN HERE!" I hollered at Rachel. She jumped. "WHO MADE THIS MESS! CLEAN IT UP!" And: "STOP FIGHT-ING, DANNY!" "WHAT'S WRONG WITH YOU!" "DINAH, DON'T TALK TO ME THAT WAY!" "ELISHEVA, FINISH YOUR DINNER!" "STOP FIGHTING! DANNY, GET TO BED! DON'T LEAVE THAT MESS IN THE LIVING ROOM! HOW COULD YOU DO THAT TO HIM! WHO DID THIS! CLEAN IT UP RIGHT NOW! GO TO BED! STOP FIGHTING!"

And what was I thinking?

It's my fault. I can't let them get away with this anymore. But it's too late to change things. They're showing everyone that they don't come from a good home. They need to be smacked! They don't deserve my patience, they're going to be punished.

October 17, 1988

The house was at sixes and sevens last night, as British Amanda might have said. I couldn't make dinner, couldn't put the kids to bed, couldn't clean up. When Yaacov came home, I told him that the au pair girl had said the children shouldn't speak to me disrespectfully, so it had made me a little nervous. He lifted his eyebrows. I could tell he was about to say she had no right to interfere. "No, she was really very nice about it," I said, wishing she had been stupid and cruel instead. Then I could have been self-righteous. "And she apologized."

Extricating myself from the house as if from an amusement park maze, I fled to an EMETT group. "Your dinner's on the stove, just warm it up," I called to Yaacov as I rushed out the door.

At the first opportunity, I brought up my "example." Smiles of recognition and understanding came over some of the women's faces. Shaking of heads, sympathetic sighs. But I kept worrying, paranoically: if I tell them that somebody said my children are badly behaved and my house is messy, then they'll think it's really so. They'll think I'm a failure.

"How many children does she have?" asked one woman.

"No, she doesn't have children yet," I replied, anticipating the laughter and "Oh!"s and "So!"s which this elicited. Yet reassurance, however comforting, didn't do the trick, and I looked to Miriam Adahan for some insight. She began taking me through the EMETT steps: What had been my insecure thoughts? Condemnations of myself and others? Romantic expectations and unfulfilled demands? Harmful impulses? Upsetting physical sensations? Upsetting emotions? As the structured analysis of my reactions continued, a meek, cautious thought appeared in my brain, like a friendly little spider waving one leg at me: *Maybe your feelings are not facts.*

Miriam said: "Can you say to yourself that you will it to be this way? That you will it to have happened?" I winced. "I have found that saying this, even though you don't feel it, is one of the best ways to reduce the fear and discover the meaning in painful events."

"Yes, I'm so glad she said what she did," I began tentatively. "I am so glad she said those things tonight." I repeated this several times before getting into the swing of it. "Yes, I am! I'm really just jumping for joy that she said it to me!" I burst into laughter, but it was quickly becoming the truth. Yes! I was glad, even thankful, to be shaken up, awakened. If she's wrong, then this will just strengthen my self-confidence. And if she's right, if I need to keep my house tidier, if I need to be stricter with the children about obedience and respectfulness, I should know it, the sooner the better.

One of the women commented that each mother relates to her children in her own way, according to her own nature and character. I nodded. Yes. That's something else I can learn from this. The personality and background G-d gave Sonia from Italy is not what He gave me: there is an inscrutable divine justice. I've been bequeathed a certain character, certain circumstances and challenges, which were not intended to be identical to those which were given her.

I can trust my fate.

I left the class invigorated and joyous.

October 18, 1988

The next morning, another young woman named Rebecca came over in response to the ad. An American, nineteen years old, from—of all places—Fairfield, Connecticut! Why, we were cooked virtually in the same pot! In the course of our conversation, I asked her what she thinks about children yelling.

"Oh, well. It happens." With one well-manicured hand she flicked her long, glossy, disobedient brown hair back from her forehead. "My brother and I used to fight all the time."

"And you're friends now?"

She shrugged. "Sure, we're fine now."

"But what if a child yells at his mother? What do you think of that?"

She pouted, casually arched an eyebrow. "Oh, well, I guess it's healthy. To get it out. Even adults have to get it out." How refreshingly American! Our culture's pop psychology. I wish I could swallow it, but if you gulp it down whole, it leaves you half-empty. It's only a fragment of the truth.

Rebecca and I were still talking over our coffee cups when the phone rang. "Is this Sarah Shapiro?" It was that exquisite Italian accent.

"Yes," I murmured. My mind grazed over all the events of the day before.

"Sarah, this is Sonia. I want first to ask you how you feel, if you are all right."

"Yes, Sonia, I'm fine." *She has no idea how much I went through last night because of her*, I thought. *She has no idea how much I've learned in just one day on account of her colossal insensitivity and arrogance. I have reaffirmed myself.*

"Well, I would like to say that if you wish, I would like to try being au pair at your house."

I glanced over at Rebecca, who was gazing around the kitchen. I felt like a woman with two suitors. "But...what about all the things you objected to—that it's not tidy enough, and the children. How—"

"Well, Sarah, I have not been able to sleep all this night, for my worry of what I did to you. And I just pray with all my heart that *HaShem* shall forgive me. They say that you should not judge a person until you are in his shoes, and I do not know—I do not have this experience of being a mother of six kids, so I pray that *HaShem* will one day give me this privilege, to have an untidy house very full of noisy children. For that is the blessing, if you can open your eyes to see."

October 26, 1988

So I have decided not to run away from this potential critic, and figure I'll end up the stronger for it. Sonia brought some of her stuff over, but didn't move in, finally, because the university offered her a dormitory room for only seventy shekels a month— too good a deal to pass up. And if that was not her only reason for declining our gracious hospitality, I didn't probe. It's all right if she doesn't like the noise and the disorder. Even if she'd like to be tolerant, this is a matter of personality and background, and she probably never would have been comfortable here.

So at five shekels an hour she has been coming in the afternoons to help me from four to seven, and I have enjoyed her conversation as well as her efficiency. I have a problem, however. I see the children now through what I imagine are her eyes. I can't shake this idea that my children are bad, and that I have to crack down on them. The more I perceive them in a negative light, the more they resist me and fight with one another, which makes me ashamed and more angry. It's a vicious circle and I even see it happening before my eyes, how my anger makes them angry, how my low expectations make them disobedient, how my intolerance makes them behave intolerably...but I can't get a hold of it. It's a whole process with a life of its own. I'm out of control. I'm so mad at them, these emblems of my failure. I feel helpless to change their behavior, the behavior that advertises my weakness, so I've been seizing upon one punishment after another, and every once in a while I get a wisp of anger at Sonia. *It's all her fault! That Sonia really set me off!* But I can't get away with that, because this entire syndrome is nothing if not familiar. This was once the whole story of my motherhood, and now I am seeing an awful rerun. Not only seeing it. I'm up there on the screen. I've got the villain's role.

I'm really so scared that I won't be able to get out of this.

How very frightening and awesome, that the well-being of my children depends upon my pride, my fragile and ignorant pride.

Danny is getting the brunt of it. Each time he gets out of line, I jump on him. STOP IT! I yell. STOP IT! What am I thinking? I'm thinking, he's acting terribly, I can't allow it, he's doing it on purpose...Danny is getting nervous and troublesome right before my eyes. Ironically enough, right when I'm in the act of spanking him or yelling at him to stop whatever it is he's doing, at that moment, when I'm hating myself, is precisely when I feel most self-righteous. I DON'T DESERVE SUCH AGGRAVATION! HE SHOULD BE TAUGHT!

On top of this, I can hardly bring myself to keep things in order. My self-image these days is that of an incompetent house-keeper, and I behave accordingly.

Tonight was Dinah's birthday party. She is eight years old. I bought a colorful Carvel ice-cream cake in the shape of a bear, and she and Rachel set the table elaborately to surprise Yaacov when he arrived home.

As the party got under way, I was proud in front of Sonia. The kids were expectant and jubilant, Yaacov and I on our best behavior. See, Sonia! I was thinking. See what a happy, wonderful family we really are! Daniel turned off all the lights in the kitchen. "Pray for whatever you want, Dinah," said Yaacov, as she leaned forward in shadow, hands spread before her in the flickering light. She made her wish and blew out the candles. Danny fumbled for the light switch. In those pitch-dark seconds when all of us disappeared and automatically strained to see each other through the empty void, I sensed keenly our wealth. We are together, a family, we are alive.

"I want to cut the cake myself!" declared Dinah when the lights came back on, along with our voices. "No!" implored Danny, desperate. "I want Mommy to do it!". "I want to do it!" A mighty chorus now: "I want the pink frosting! I want the blue frosting! I want that part there! No, that's my piece! Mommy! I'm getting the whole head! No, you're not! I want the stomach! NO! NO! She doesn't know how! Tell her, Daddy. She'll give herself the big piece! Don't let her! It's not fair! It's not fair!"

I stole a glance at Sonia, but she seemed to be taking it well. She's getting the hang of it, I thought hopefully and smiled at her conspiratorially, as if to say, Right? Now you understand that this is all just normal.

But after the party dwindled down and Dinah was carefully secreting away the single leftover slice into the freezer, Sonia approached her quietly, with her solemn face: "Dinah, I must tell you that I have never in my life been at a birthday party where the children fought over the birthday cake."

Dinah lifted her chin sadly and gave an almost imperceptible shrug.

October 27, 1988

When I got back from Geulah this afternoon, Sonia gave me a telephone message from a Sheina Deutsch, whose name I didn't recognize. Sheina Deutsch was looking for a Mrs. Sarah Shapiro who used to be a friend of her mother's. Sonia told me she had said, "The woman I am thinking of is tall and thin and beautiful."

I brushed this off with a modest guffaw to conceal my amazement. Later, when I dashed out to Shmuel HaNavi to pick up fruits and vegetables, in each store window I sized up my reflection. Tall, thin and beautiful. Could it be? Could people really see me like that? I pulled in my stomach. Maybe I really am and don't realize it. A warm wave of self-confidence filled me with goodwill toward mankind.

Sheina Deutsch called back at seven. In a European accent, she asked me if I used to live in Tsfat.

"No, I didn't."

"You did not live in Tsfat in the late seventies? '78 or '79?"

"No, I didn't."

"So you do not know my mother, Henya Deutsch?"

"No, I don't think so."

"Ah, so, excuse me, I am very sorry that I bothered you, it is a mistake. Shalom, and excuse me."

I hung up and went to take a load out of the washing machine. Yes, Sheina dear, whoever you are, of course I excuse you. It was no bother. If you only knew how your description of Mrs. Shapiro, bless her heart, whoever she is, impressed itself upon me! Why, here it is five hours later and I still have to remind myself not to feel cheerful because of that misaddressed compliment!

Tall, thin and beautiful...For how many years has that image haunted me as the utmost achievement of the feminine will! Though many yardsticks measured one's value as a person in suburban Connecticut society (friendliness, creativity, kindness, intelligence, honesty) two things were taken most into consideration when determining a female's worth: her academic performance and her measurements. Any fool can be "nice," but not everyone can get nineties in French and twenty-three around the waist. For lack of any other viable, unambiguous philosophy of self, her stature as a human being was ascertained by her grades, while the surest sign of self-mastery was a body over which she, the owner, visibly retained firm control.

I thank G-d each morning in *modeh ani* for returning my soul. I wish I could identify as consistently with that *neshamah* as I do with my physical self. Would that I mourned and rejoiced as sincerely for the perfection of my soul!

October 29, 1988

I was groping for something today, something to help me calm down, and I found it when I recalled one of Miriam Levi's remarks from the workshop: "It is your responsibility to teach your child to be a *mensch*, but you have to do it in a kind way." A statement so foreign right now as to seem from another world. Oh...Kindness. I forgot.

These words served as an anchor in the chaotic sea. I threw out a line to that anchor and I am being pulled ever so slightly in the right direction again. This afternoon, I can imagine that even if I have failed with them, even if things are hopeless, even if hypothetically my children are, G-d forbid, the worst in the world, along with their mother, I am still obligated to be kind. It's well within my capacity.

This evening Danny was drumming on the kitchen counter and singing at the top of his lungs. I noticed myself feeling that his happy exuberance was sort of nice, and recalled that yesterday the same behavior made me angry.

October 31, 1988

Sonia told me today that my children are the most badly behaved children she has ever seen. This time I told her that such a remark is uncalled-for, that she has no idea how badly it affects a mother to be told something like that. I don't want Sonia in my house anymore; to have her here every day would be ridiculously masochistic. But still, I find that I don't wish to part with her entirely. Something tells me that if I run away from her, I'll never figure this out. We decided mutually that perhaps once a week is better for both of us, and rather than deal with the children, she'll just concentrate on cleaning.

But within myself, the whole thing started again. Are my children really that bad? What have I done? My soul tottered, as if my legs had been cut off at the knees.

I'm in such a depression this evening. I look around me at my failure, like walls that have collapsed around me, and I pick my way through my self-made rubble. How can I be so weak, to let that young woman shoot me down like this, and why do I believe her? Why am I so shattered? Who is she, anyway? Where's my pride?

But the fact is, my pride is very much in evidence.

I hurried at ten this morning to an appointment at Dinah's school. Her teacher is very miffed that Dinah's handwriting doesn't stay along the lines. "Look at this. Look at this." She flipped through a pile of papers on her desk, pulling out eight or nine sheets. "Look at the way the other children wrote on the test we took yesterday." Then she showed me Dinah's, a wavering, tiny scrawl. But Dinah's handwriting isn't always like that, I wanted to say. Can't you see she was scared of the test? Besides, ever since first grade she hasn't had a lot of confidence about the way she writes, because...

"Do you study with Dinah at home?" the teacher asks me.

"No, the Hebrew is very difficult for me."

The teacher looks at me askance, telling me with her cool eyes that this situation will have to change fast. I want to say to this woman: "Dinah's handwriting at the age of eight is not as important to me as her general self-confidence or lack thereof. It's all right with me if her handwriting is unusual. Don't make such a big deal about this and her handwriting will sort itself out." Naturally, I mumble awkwardly and can't get it out. She stares me down, awaiting something intelligible to cross my lips, to no avail. When I walk out of the school into the cloudy daylight, I feel strange, as if I'm stumbling. Does Dinah need a psychologist? It's my fault.

When I get back home I'm unhinged. I urgently need something...a cup of tea with honey? A vitamin pill? Maybe I should open the windows and get some air...Some music, some nice, calm classical music to ground me. Music. I go to the kitchen and switch on the radio. Arabic music...A man talking in fast Hebrew...92. I want 92 on the dial...Wait, what's that? A familiar sound from many years ago.

> If the sky above you
> turns dark and full of clouds,
> and that ole north wind begins to blow...

Oh yes. Candis and I used to sing it to each other all the time. How I wish I could be with Candis now!

> Close your eyes and think of me,
> and soon I will be there,
> to brighten up
> even your darkest night.

I listen to that melody, amazed. Whoever wrote that song must have been through some kind of really bad time, as I am now. Could it be? That I'm not the only one?

> You just call out my name,
> And you know, wherever I am,
> I'll come runnin',
> to see you again.
> Winter, spring, summer or fall,
> All you gotta do is just call,
> An I'll be there, yes I will.
> You've got a friend.
> You've got a friend.

I twiddle with the dial carefully now. There, that must be 92. An exquisite, orderly harpsichord. Just right. No, a little too fast, not quite peaceful enough, but I rest my elbows on the counter and lean forward into the music to drink it in.

All those rich harmonies, like a radiantly colorful prism.

Yes.

Of course.

People experience failure and survive, in every corner of the globe, every hour of the day. But the hour passes, life itself interferes, and it feels as if maybe it was all just a nightmare. The horrific spector subsides...things don't seem so bad anymore. Yes, it happens all the time, so then why do I feel unique? Who can I talk to about this? I can't call Yaacov until three o'clock when he has his break, Miriam Levi's in America, Miriam Adahan's telephone answering machine is on, Mommy and Daddy are available but at ten shekels a minute...

Beyla! I dial her number. Busy.

Angie? Her daughter says she'll be back at eight o'clock tonight.

Esther...no answer.

Beyla again. Still busy. Beyla, how could you!

I scan my list of close friends but fear there must be something very wrong with my life. I'm missing a friend like the one in the song. Pigeon's in Boston, Candis is in Oakland, Diane's in Brooklyn, Rose just got married, she doesn't have children yet, Menuchah will give me examples of all the wonderful people she knows whose children are absolutely wild and I won't believe her. Yaacov is obviously too close to the situation. Everyone else is too far: maybe they'll believe it, maybe they'll think I really have failed. They don't see Dinah when she's kissing me tenderly good night, they don't see Rachel taking care of Elisheva with such depth of understanding, they don't see Danny thinking his subtle questions or playing with the babies, Elisheva giving me *mussar*, or Eli giving his bottle to Avivah. They don't see the children dancing with joyous abandon in the kitchen, a circle around the two babies.

But these charming details, though accurate in themselves, sound so phony somehow. Must I whitewash the truth in order to accept it? Apologizing for the negatives by glorifying the positives is missing the point.

The point is that each one of my children is engaged in his own struggle. And that's what bystanders can't see. A child's behavior must be viewed within the context of his age, his nature, his efforts, his entire development. But what friend understands all that? Whom can I talk to? People are biased, quick to judge. Their phones are busy, they go out of town, they're thinking about other things, they'll criticize you when you want support and soothe you when you need the truth instead.

Then it occurs to me. There is no such human friend—ever-accessible, ever-patient and understanding, but the description does fit G-d to a T. If I had a say in the matter, I wouldn't mind having a friend like the one in the song, a human being you see and hear, someone who can meet you in Geulah at 10 a.m. for a heartfelt tête-à-tête over café au lait, someone who will jump into a taxi whenever you call. Who will *want* to come, no matter what. But perhaps it's time to put aside the dream. If I were to believe in *HaShem*'s existence as completely as I do in my own, or in that of the announcer on the radio or the woman who cleans my house on Tuesdays, I would take advantage of the fact that, dear G-d, You're always available, always on line, never on vacation, ever-prepared, even happily, to accept a collect call. From You I can beg for help without forgoing my pride, and You're so brilliant, You understand the whole story far better than I do, but are eager to hear my version. I can trust Your admonishment to be for my benefit and Your comfort to be meaningful, not condescending. And You always have time for my endless requests—if I can just bring myself to ask.

November 6, 1988

I'm on my way home from a parent-teacher meeting at Rachel and Elisheva's school. Rachel is sitting here on the bus next to me. I wanted a chance to be alone with her, so I accepted her offer to come with me tonight to show me how to get there.

I'm on a buoyant cloud of joy.

Halfway through my conference with Nina, Elisheva's teacher, she said: "If you don't mind, I want to ask you—perhaps it could be of help to me with my own children—what do you do with your children?"

I braced myself. "What do you mean?"

"Both of them are such fine children. Just so fine."

"Thank you." I was waiting tensely.

"I have never seen a happier child than Elisheva. I'd like to know what you do."

My mind reeled. I looked her in the eye. Was she serious? Yes. Nina was serious, inquisitive. "What I do?"

"Yes. Elisheva tells me that in your house they have to sit down for five minutes if they hit each other. Is that so?"

"Yes." *But that's not the whole story. What can I say?* "Nina, thank you so much. You have no idea how much this means to me."

She seemed surprised by my surprise. "You mean you don't see that about them?" I was speechless. "It's in your *zechus*. You're the one who did it."

I could float away on my joy. What miraculous timing. It's as if *HaShem* made a concession to my pride at this point, because otherwise I could not, or would not, go on. "You want a bouquet of roses now, don't you, My daughter? All right, here! Catch!" As my friend Angie always says, G-d has such a good sense of humor.

November 7, 1988

Sonia came today. I told her that though I forgave her the first time she hurt me, I was having a hard time forgiving her for the second. "It was unnecessary for you to say that my children are the worst behaved kids you've ever seen, Sonia. I already knew how you felt. Why did you have to repeat it?" I was bursting at the seams to tell her what Elisheva's teacher had said, but didn't. A form of abstention.

She leaned back against my refrigerator and looked me straight in the eye. I expected her to apologize now the way she had the first time. Oh, how tranquilizing that would be. "But Sarah," she asserted calmly, "it is true."

"What makes you think so?" I wanted to hear all of it.

"I have told you already, have I not? That I have never seen children fighting over the cake at a birthday party before. This to me is something—" She threw up her hands, as if to say that this was something beyond her comprehension. "I see now that when, G-d willing, I have children, this will be one of my biggest priorities: to teach them not to raise their voices, and to share. What good is it to recite a blessing over a lovely piece of beautiful birthday cake if it has been acquired through fighting?"

"But Sonia, I agree with you that learning to share and not raising the voice are priorities. But you have to keep it in perspective. We can teach this to children without being so shocked when they don't live up to our ideals. Generosity is a long-term goal, and so is controlling one's anger. It takes a lifetime to learn these things."

She squinted skeptically. "A lifetime?"

I faltered. Perhaps she already had these things under her belt, and once again I was just bumping up against my own inadequacy. "Well, for me it's a lifetime job. Yes."

"You know, Sarah, the only time in my childhood that I fought with one of my siblings over a physical object was when I was three years old, and my sister and I fought over a doll. So my father told us, 'All right, girls, if you wish to fight over the doll, you may both have her. I shall cut her into two pieces.' This taught us, and we never fought again."

Now it was my turn to be skeptical, but I allowed for the possibility that what she was saying was factual. Either Sonia had been born into an angelic family so far above my own level that I need not compete, or she just didn't remember her childhood accurately. In any case, after these weeks of torturing both myself and my children, a little ray of light peeked through. *Could it be? My whole being heaved a sigh of relief. Fighting over the cake? Something like that really bothered her that much? How wonderful! How wonderful! For that's one thing for sure that's normal. Maybe my children are all right! Maybe they're just normal!*

"That's a good line your father used," I grinned. "I'll try it sometime. I have to pick Eli up from *gan* now. You want to come?" Sonia gathered up her things and we walked out into the sunny, cool autumn day. Leaves blew around our feet as we passed under the trees. "You know, Sonia," I said, "my mother taught me to share. Thank G-d, I really did get the message and so now, as an adult, I do feel obligated to share with others, and I'm grateful for having been well educated. But the thing I didn't learn in that society is that it's a normal human reaction to *not* want to share, even though we're obligated to do so. I disliked myself as a little girl whenever I saw my selfishness. I thought it was horrible. I grew to be ashamed of my own natural self-interest and tried to hide it. That's what I want to avoid with my own children. I want them to know that we're all in the same boat. *HaShem* gives us the *yetzer hara*. It's *meant to be* that each one of us should have to struggle in order to transcend the selfishness."

We walked along. "Yes. This I can understand," said Sonia. "*Be'ezrat HaShem*, with my own children, yes, perhaps I will be able to teach them to share and yet that they are not horrible for not wanting to. It is difficult for everyone."

November 8, 1988

Dinah's backpack broke this morning, and Yaacov fixed it when he came home from davening. Dinah then asked me to write a note for her teacher explaining why she was late. As I sat there trying to figure out how to write "her father had to fix it," in Hebrew, Dinah became distraught. "OOOOHHH! You don't know how to write it! Because of you I'll be more *late!*"

"All right, Dinah, now this is a problem, and we're going to find a solution."

"What's SOLUTION?" she wailed.

"That means that we have a little problem and we're going to find a way of fixing the problem. We'll find the answer." I went back to my note. Hmmm. If *letakain* is to fix, then, uh, let's see...third person singular, masculine, must be...

Dinah threw her head back on the couch, exasperated. "I HAVE TO GO TO SCHOOL!" I went downstairs to my Danish neighbors to ask for help.

"Here it is, Dinah," I said brightly upon my return. "Mr. Yaacovi wrote it out for me, and I'll copy it down."

Dinah looked over my shoulder as I worked. Out of the corner of my eye I saw her mouthing the words silently. Then she exploded. "HE DIDN'T DO IT RIGHT! I DON'T WANT IT! HE DOESN'T KNOW HOW TO DO IT!" She ran to the couch and dove into the cushions, sobbing. "STUPID," she yelled, "YOU DON'T KNOW! IT'S YOUR FAULT!"

At this point I lay down the pencil and rose from my chair, hoping it was not apparent that I was hurt. "All right, Dinah," I announced softly. "I'm sorry that I can't help you anymore."

An hour later, Dinah sidled up to me in the kitchen, where I was putting away breakfast dishes. "I'm sorry, Mommy."

I smiled, and hesitated: should I kiss her? Would that be leaning over too far? Shouldn't give in too easily? No...of course not, kiss her.

She returned my kiss, passionately. "Mommy, I don't like the way he wrote that note," she said, coming suddenly to the verge of tears. "All you Americans don't know how to write."

"All right, Dinah, I understand."

It was much too late for Dinah to go to school now, but I had no regrets: she'd seen that as long as she's not being rude, she can tell me what bothers her and I will listen.

Sonia did make me more aware. Rudeness to a parent should not be overlooked.

November 9, 1988

I called Miriam Levi this morning to solicit her opinions about my experience with Sonia. After relating the whole story, including what she said about my housework, and the contrary feedback I got from Elisheva's teacher, the question I really pined to ask was: *Miriam Levi, are my children all right or not?*

But I couldn't just shamelessly lay my fate at her feet like that! So I said: "I think it's much better for children to be noisy and rambunctious than turned in on themselves. Don't you?"

"Well, I wouldn't go along with that, no."

"But they say that a lot of times children who are very passive and overly obedient turn out to have a lot of problems."

"I don't think it's wise to generalize like that. A passive, obedient child can be just fine, while another one who acts like that might indeed be having some problems. You'd really have to find out what's going on with him. There are so many factors to take into consideration. The behavior itself in such a case is neither positive nor negative. Take noisiness. Now, noisiness in itself is neither good nor bad, unless there's someone whom it bothers. Say there's a grandfather in the house who's sensitive to it—well, then the children have to learn to accommodate themselves to the reality of the situation, to be considerate, to not cause him discomfort. I think that at this stage in my life, if I had young children around, I'd have to tell them: 'Children,'" Miriam's voice contracted to a whisper, "'children, please. A little quieter.' But when I was younger it didn't bother me very much, and in fact, I remember one babysitter telling me she preferred to sit for my boys because they were enthusiastic about everything. Somebody else might have perceived them simply as noisy. See, my boys were enthusiastic, as she put it, because that's the way I was. Oh, taking them to the Bronx Zoo and what have you. It was a lot of fun. That happened to be my priority.

"I suspect, Sarah, that though noisiness may bother you at times, it's not one of your main concerns, so you let it go. It's not one of your priorities.

"And the same goes for the housework. I wish I could say to mothers of young children: 'Just make a decision to forget the house until they're in bed. While you're with them, just be with them and enjoy it.' But of course when I once suggested this to a group of mothers, they sent up a great hue and cry that it was easier said than done, that I didn't understand, they're too exhausted to do the work at night, by bedtime they'd be in garbage up to their ears if they didn't keep after it, it would drive them crazy, and so on. And perhaps they're right." Miriam half-sighed, half-laughed.

"So a child's development is what emerges out of the interaction between him and his parents," I said. "A mother can seek other people's advice, but she has to realize that they have no way of knowing all the variables as well as she does, if she puts her mind to it. The relationship between each and every mother and child is unique, unlike that between any other mother and child."

"Yes, I'd say so."

I sensed myself at that precise moment taking a stride forward. I had heard this principle before, but had never really arrived there. *I can look into myself for the answers. I can listen to other people's advice or criticism, but in the final analysis, the correct way for me to apply Torah principles must be according to the grain of my own personality.* "I guess I have to grow-up," I said, "and be my own judge."

"Yes, yes," said Miriam. "That's true for all of us."

November 10, 1988

I try to bear in mind that Sonia didn't *make* me have the response I did to her criticisms. She merely elicited it. Sonia was the necessary condition to my facing the full measure of my underlying, ever-available sense of failure, and the anger that comes with the territory. A burnt cake, a child's tears, a friend who doesn't return a call—all can elicit the same sense of guilt and defeat.

Nonetheless, even if Sonia is only the external stimulus for what's really an internal conflict, I don't need to invite such painful self-revelation on a daily basis. As much as I must learn to live with my own and others' human fallibility, to be on speaking terms with it as I would with an insensitive neighbor who insists on coming in without knocking, at least I can shut the door. So I sent Sonia a note, saying that I couldn't afford to have her even one day a week anymore. It was not a lie: I could not afford her, I decided, neither emotionally nor financially. I could hardly pay the grocery bill last week, much less recover from her off-and-on approval and disapproval. And though my natural inclination was to keep her around, hoping to impress her (as if the only way to restore my own equilibrium would be if Sonia saw how tidy and obedient my children were), this time I chose to let go of my critic.

I was thus taken aback to answer a knock at the door and find Sonia there this morning. "Oh, didn't you get my note?"

"No. What note?"

"I sent a note to the university with Ayelet, telling you that I couldn't really afford to have—"

"It's all right, Sarah. What I would like to tell you is that I am willing to work for less money, but to work here, rather than continue at the home where I have been this past week. Because this has been a—" She held up her hand as if to say: stop. "This week has been a bad time."

I made coffee and we sat down at the kitchen table. "I have been working at a home," Sonia said, "in which the children—there are three—are always respectful to their parents, and they do not fight with each other, and the house is extremely tidy. But they are sad, these kids. They are frightened of the mother. And though it is hard for me to see your kids say 'no' to you, and fight with each other, I would rather be around you and them, for you are respectful to me and your children are always respectful and kind to me, than to be in a home where such a price is paid for tidiness and obedience. I am grateful to have had this opportunity to see two different families, and I have thought a lot about it this week, for I see now that what the Jewish people need is families with a lot of kids, to give us back the many children Hitler killed. And if that is the sacrifice one agrees to make in return for bringing down more souls—a house that is not always as perfectly tidy as the house in which I have been working, then so be it. Everybody likes an orderly house, so G-d must recognize this sacrifice. I had to ask myself this week which I would prefer for my own family, if I will have this opportunity to choose. And I decided that I would want my children to be like yours because you can see in them their flames. Your children fight with each other but they also kiss, but in this other house they neither fight nor kiss."

Thank goodness for small favors! In this city she could have so easily come across a very tidy house where the children were happy, loving and obedient, too!

She might see things in a different light soon enough, but for now I crowed. "Thank you, Sonia, thank you!" I felt like raising an arm in a triumphal salute. And when I ran later under the trees to pick Eli up from *gan*, it was the image of swimming that came to mind. My critic, now on my side, had called to me: "Jump in! Swim freely in the way you know! You'll make mistakes but all of you will stay afloat."

16
The Smile

Today I prepared a super-duper vegetable soup for Yaacov, along with an interesting bean sprout and pepper salad and a rice dish with turnips and carrots. "I can't tell you what it means to me to have a lunch like that," he said as he got up after the meal. "It's not just a physical need but a spiritual one."

A deep sense of satisfaction spread through me. "And it's a spiritual need for me to do it," I replied.

It was only as I said it that I realized it was true. I have a *spiritual* need for the simple, physical, earthly chores—the shopping and the chopping, the slicing and the simmering, the bringing to a boil and the blending of tastes, the setting of the table and the serving—all that's involved in taking care of him and the children, in giving...in feeling needed.

I wish I could have come to that realization years ago, but I have to trust that there's a time for everything, and growing takes time.

November 14, 1988

This morning I dreamed that I was seized with fury at Rachel over something. I was about to explode but I stopped myself.

While the children were having breakfast, I remembered the incident vaguely and tried to figure out when it had happened. Then I realized it had been a dream. The process of restraining my anger has entered deeply enough into my consciousness to be reexperienced in dreams.

Getting angry is like climbing up a rope. Fast! Faster! Grab hold and pull yourself up higher! Higher!

Letting go of the anger is like letting go of the rope. You're afraid you'll fall. It feels as if you'd be giving up all your strength.

But you don't fall, and you don't give up your strength. Precisely the opposite.

November 15, 1988

I see myself as having found a safe harbor in life, if there is such a thing as safety, and within those boundaries a place to grow and develop and experience the beauties and pains and rough seas that abound in this world. But a few nights ago when Avivah awoke me around two o'clock in the morning to nurse, I couldn't go back to sleep. I lay there looking into the dark and getting scared. Some authenticity lacking in my life, some unreality...not really treading on solid ground. It reminded me of that song from the sixties that I used to hum along to merrily as I bopped my way home from high school in the Volkswagen each afternoon: "I'm not really making it. I'm really just faking it."

I peered through the dark at Yaacov, who was sleeping soundly. I wondered if he, too, sometimes feels like this in the middle of the night. Does everyone get it? Probably. Nobody's immune. There's no guarantee that you're living up to your ideals, no guarantee, deep within, that you're living authentically, leading a real life. Hello again, Coca-Cola. The real thing in the back of your mind.

Hours passed. My life seemed a lie.

At last a glimmer of light glowed in the window, and with dawn's pale arrival the fear vanished I know not where. With a little shadow of gratitude for life's myriad practical demands and details, I got up eagerly, boiled up some water, and went on about my business as usual.

November 16, 1988

Dinah doesn't eat breakfast in the morning. She takes a few sips of orange juice, perhaps, and goes on her way. I let her get away with this, as I don't the other children, simply because she is so determined once she decides something.

Yesterday morning the weather was terrible: hail, terrific winds, driving rain. I insisted that each child have toast and eggs before going out into that freezing storm. "Dinah," I proclaimed firmly, "today you're having breakfast."

"Oh no, I'm not."

"Yes, Dinah. I'm giving you toast and eggs and orange juice. On a day like this you can't leave without eating anything!" Dinah was quiet. I thought I had won and I turned to the stove, then heard her exclaim:

"You can't force me to eat!"

How these words reverberated, oh...those are the brave words I would have liked to say to my own mother. Should I press on? Is the loss worth the gain? I looked out at the trees blowing wildly, clouds rushing...flocks of birds appearing and vanishing fast as thoughts. *Should I force her?*

"All right, Dinah. Bye-bye."

Dinah, who had started putting on her backpack with the defiant air of one who's expecting a fight, paused slightly and looked over at me out of the corner of her eye. She had won so easily? I casually carried on about my business.

She needn't have suppressed the little smile that came over her lips; I know how lovely a gift it is to get an unexpected victory. She rose, opened the door, and leaned back inside to blow me a kiss.

November 17, 1988

I asked Elisheva today if she likes going to school with Rachel on the bus each day. She nodded and took her thumb out of her mouth to speak. "Rachel is *so good* to me."

November 20, 1988

A friend of ours was telling Yaacov and me last night what it was like when she was in the army as a teenager. She had been ridiculed for her English accent. "You get these people who think very little of themselves," she said, "and you put them in a position of power."

Sounds like a perfect description of parenthood.

November 21, 1988

In an EMETT class tonight, Miriam Adahan said that she lets her ten-year-old son stay up late just so that they'll have private time together. She said she knows that as he gets older such intimate moments will become rarer, and she figures she has around one year more in which to establish this emotional bond. They talk about all kinds of things—what happened during that day to each of them. Miriam said that it's good for him to listen to her feelings as well.

She quoted a friend of hers who says, in contrast to the popular "I'm O.K., you're O.K." psychology:

"I'm not O.K., you're not O.K., and that's O.K."

November 22, 1988

I learned in Rabbi Berkowitz's shiur in Eyaht this morning that in the time of the Temple, a rabbi on the Sanhedrin was required to have either young children or grandchildren, so that he would learn to judge with compassion and grasp how people's minds work. He had to know that people frequently do hurtful things not out of malice but out of some misinterpretation of reality. They're in their own world; they're acting out of some convoluted personal fantasy. And it is parenthood that best teaches us this fact. A parent learns by experience that the harm a child inflicts on others is most often a manifestation of his own fallible, distorted version of events. To judge with a high degree of compassion as well as accuracy, a rabbi on the Sanhedrin had to understand that adults are overgrown children. Most of us inhabit our own little dream worlds; we haven't learned to face reality. How many of us are more concerned with what other people think we're doing than with what we're really doing? We treat our lives as if they were childish games. When a person gets old and senile, he returns wholly to the dream, in which he has reached all his dream goals.

In the Gemara it says that destroying a child's toy is equivalent to taking away an adult's livelihood. If you empty out a child's bathtub full of toy boats, you have sunk a major fleet with two thousand people. Before you go and pull out the plug, know exactly what you're doing. Just as one has to enter into the world of a child in order to correctly interpret his behavior, said Rabbi Berkowitz, you have to enter into an adult's world as well, in order to discern what he's really up to.

The *yetzer hara*, said Rabbi Berkowitz, may be described simply with these words: being an infant.

November 23, 1988

Danny has been unhappy and nervous lately, ever since I started getting angry some weeks ago. It's always been easier for me to figure out what to do when one of the girls is unhappy; I can sense what they're feeling more instinctively than with Daniel. But what has dawned on me now is that in spite of his boyish, rambunctious manner, he needs precisely the same tenderness and closeness that Rachel, Dinah and Elisheva do. I just need to alter the style a bit, so as not to offend his male dignity.

It has been a long time since I really focused on him. G-d willing, I'm going to spend time alone with him each night and talk, and I'm going to go out with him alone to choose birthday presents next week. I have to figure out some way that he can play his drum without bothering the rest of us, or the neighbors. He loves music so much, and I'm always telling him to keep it down, the babies are sleeping, Daddy's studying, the girls are doing their homework...

November 24, 1988

Chava, Dinah's English teacher here in the neighborhood, sent home a note after the class last week. I read it out loud: "Dinah did a terrific job today." Dinah showed little reaction at the time, but ever since, she's been trying to read all of our English books, asking me the words she can't decipher.

I met Chava in the supermarket today, and told her how much that praise had meant. "If only the teachers in school understood that what children need more than anything else is encouragement."

"Oh, yes, I know what you mean," she said. "We once asked one of our son's teachers to give him more encouragement, and he said he just didn't have time for more individual attention. And I realized how often all of us say that. If a child says, 'Mommy, can you do this?' it's: 'I don't have time, I don't have time.' But it's not so. We do have time. Who gives us time in the first place?"

As I maneuvered the twin carriage through the entranceway of our building, Eli jumped out of his seat and ran back outside. He often does that, I'm used to it, but this time I didn't sweep him up into my arms and put him into the elevator. I said to myself, *You have time. It's a matter of making time. Let him explore a little bit.* "Avivah, you want to go play with Eli?" She let this invitation sink in. Carefully, deliberately, she wiggled backwards down out of the carriage. I followed her.

Eli was standing in a puddle. I cringed. "Come, LaLa!" he told her. "Come!"

She shrugged. She didn't want to stand in the puddle. "No, no," she murmured, shaking her head, which was to say, "Don't you see that Mommy's here?" Eli looked at me and grinned from ear to ear, for the most fantastic thing in the whole wide world, the most exquisite, exciting and forbidden thing that could ever be, was to be right then in Eli's shoes, right on that spot where Eli stood, stamping his feet, drenching his pants, splashing the dirty water all around.

Enough joy. I grabbed him.

November 27, 1988

The fighting around here has really gotten out of hand lately. It is apparent that five minutes in a chair is no longer appropriate for them at this age; they can develop more self-control. Last week I told the kids that from now on they can expect to sit down a half-hour for hurting each other.

They took in this news soberly. "A half-hour?" said Dinah.

Good. I saw that this was giving all of them pause. "Yes. A half-hour. That's how important it is to stop ourselves from hurting anyone."

"And what if we say something bad?" she asked. "Will that also be a half-hour?"

Hmmm. I didn't know what to say. I wasn't equal to the task of getting them to sit down that long every time they said something bad. Was that laziness on my part? What was the right answer? If I penalized them for inflicting physical pain but ignored verbal abuse, wouldn't they get the idea that hurting people's feelings isn't that important?

I let it go, hoping that Dinah wouldn't come to any wrong conclusions because of my silence.

Today I got an answer. For causing physical pain, it's appropriate to restrict the body. For verbal attacks, a different penalty has to be found, something to do with the mouth...Ah hah! A restriction on junk food! When I found myself in the kitchen with all of them this evening, I brought it up. "I figured out why it is that for hitting, it's right to have to sit down in a chair, but for bad words, not. You know why?"

"I know!" Elisheva exclaimed. "Because even if we're sitting down, we can still be saying bad words, but we can't *hit* anyone if we're sitting down!" She smiled brightly.

"Very good, Elisheva. Right! Can anyone think of a good punishment for words that hurt?"

"We can put Scotch tape over our mouths," suggested Dinah.

"That's interesting. You want to do that, then?"

Dinah changed her mind. "No, because then when the Scotch tape isn't on our mouths anymore, then we'll feel like we can say the bad words again."

"Well, what we're going to do is this. I'm going to mark down on a paper every time I hear one of you saying something that hurts someone's feelings. Anyone who gets ten marks won't get ice cream on Shabbat. And anyone who hasn't gotten any marks at all will get an extra ice cream on Shabbat."

This was a powerful inducement. This Shabbat, no one went without ice cream. Rachel had an extra one.

November 28, 1988

Eli grabbed Avivah's blanket from her a few minutes ago, and with shrieks of excitement scurried up onto the couch. "Icky LaLa! Icky LaLa!" he taunted, waving the blanket around like a flag and pouncing up and down with sheer glee.

Avivah was devastated.

He's being mean! I thought. He's always had such a big heart, and now he's starting to be mean! *No, no, dear, I corrected myself, this is normal behavior for a two-and-a-half-year-old.*

I furrowed my brow, shook my head solemnly and intoned in a grave, low voice: "Eli. LaLa is crying. Look at her. She's crying." Eli, instantly drained of all joy, froze, lowered his head and pouted fiercely. His face reddened. "Eli *motek!*"

"Yes, darling, Eli *is motek.* You want to give LaLa her blanket? She's crying."

Eli clutched the blanket and drew himself tightly unto himself. I recognized that look: of the dam about to break, of the tears about to burst. The mighty storm. I repeated myself sternly yet kindly. "Please, Eli. Please give LaLa the blanket." But it wasn't working. Years ago I would have simply snatched it away and restored justice myself, for Avivah was pining. She loves her blanket deeply. She looked up at me now and pleaded with her eyes: Mommy, aren't you going to help me?

The guilt wasn't working, nor the gravity of my tone. I changed my tune. "Don't worry, LaLa," I exclaimed happily. "*Eli* will help you." He eyed me suspiciously. "Don't worry, LaLa, Eli will give you the blanket. Eli *motek* will help you." His pout deepened as he tried to figure this out. What was Mommy up to? Teasing that baby is such fun, but Mommy's so confident I'm going to stop!

That positive image of Eli Big Helper was too alluring. Against his better judgment, he edged off the couch. "Good, Eli! Good, Eli! Look at that, Avivah, Eli's giving you the blanket!" He held it away from her at arm's length, and she whimpered. Then, sweetly, he cooed to her condescendingly like an indulgent daddy: "*Hineh, LaLa, hineh anket,*" and with magnificent magnanimity he threw it on top of her.

Eli pranced off, very pleased with himself. Avivah smiled.

November 29, 1988

Avivah is beginning to say the word "no." She says it to me, she says it to Eli, she says it to Elisheva and Danny and Dinah. "No." Through those tender little lips she sighs the word as if it has two musical syllables, and delivers it unto us as airily as a sparrow feather or a rose petal on a breeze, but she means it.

I have often thought I should write about Avivah, but the only suitable form of expression would have been a sonnet as delicate as crystal, and the words would probably be rhapsodic and corny. So it's better left unsaid. She's been so easy, so gentle, a heaven-sent pleasure, a sweet treasure, a precious light, a special gift of sunshine to each one of us, even Eli. He will not go to sleep without her, wakes her up at five for conversation, plays doggie with her all over the house.

The "no" is a sign that her self within is budding. Her wishes will start conflicting with mine and soon I'll have things to write about.

November 30, 1988

I was just looking out the window at Eli, who is with a babysitter. I won't hire her ever again. She's sitting there with her friends talking, ignoring him almost completely! Eli is carrying on adequately, albeit a bit bored, but at four and a half shekels an hour I think I deserve a babysitter who plays with him. A simmering anger stirs within me. Every few minutes I have to rein myself in as I would a horse that's chomping at the bit. "Calm down there, girl. Whoa! Ain't nuttin' to get so worked up about. She ain't doin' nuttin' any other babysitter wouldn't do."

Eli, meanwhile, stumbles around the sandbox, wending his way cautiously among the big four- and five-year-olds. As my eyes follow him around on his little trails, I take note that only he, my little boy, is enclosed in a bubble of light. He carries a halo around his whole little self; it makes it easy for me to spot him if I go into the kitchen and come back. My eyes alight at once upon that portable radiance.

Could it be that some other mother, glancing out her window to check up on her Avi or her Shmuli, might scan the sandbox and easily find him among all those nondescript others, because, of course, her baby is the one who glows?

December 1, 1988

My cousin Shoshana took me to Hadassah Hospital to help with a baby there who has been abandoned by his mother. There seems to be something wrong with the shape of his head; it frightened me to look at him. The skull was too small. They are looking for volunteers to come to the hospital to hold him and rock him, because the nurses just don't have time.

On the way out to the car after our visit, Shoshana's husband Avraham told me about a news article he read concerning the Armenian earthquake. A woman and her daughter were trapped for several days, and the little girl, age seven, survived because the mother cut her own fingers and fed her daughter blood from the wounds. I thought: Yes! That's what it is to be a mother!

Then I thought: To be a mother is also to abandon your child because he's not well.

December 3, 1988

The earthquake in Armenia. I can't get it off my mind. What must it be like for people there now? Maybe there's a woman, and she's trapped under a building, and she doesn't know where her husband and children are, or what has happened to them. What a horror! Please, G-d, spare me that in my lifetime.

There has been a lot of news lately about Libya's chemical weapons factory. I try not to think about it, but my mind wanders. What if...

I read an article a few months ago about the *mikveh* lady of Moscow, in charge of what I think they said was Russia's only public *mikveh*. She reminisced about the Holocaust, and how for a long time she had gone virtually insane: "They killed my children," she said, "and I lost my mind." I think about that sometimes. I think about poison gas, and what would be if...and then I try to turn away my mind.

Miriam Levi is a cousin of Mrs. Schlesinger, whose son was murdered last year by an Arab girl. Miriam told me that Mrs. Schlesinger said: "I'm grateful for the privilege to have had him on loan for eighteen years."

"And this is not just words," Miriam told me. "This is who she is. This is the kind of attitude toward life that she has internalized."

Tonight as I was carrying Eli upstairs to bed, he lay his head on my shoulder and stuck his thumb in his mouth. With his enormous blanket trailing heavily and getting entangled in my feet, I hugged him close to me. *He's on loan*, I thought. *Train yourself to relate to your children with the awareness that they are not your possessions. You have them on trust.*

December 4, 1988

Last night a little hand patted me on the forehead in my sleep. Elisheva. "Mommy, I had a scary dream." I picked up the warm blankets for her to crawl into bed with me, and I knew just how happy she was to be safe with Mommy. That's how it was for me as a child in the middle of the night, feeling my way along the dark hall to my parents' bedroom, opening the door. "Mommy," I'd say into the dark.

"Yes." She'd sit up suddenly in bed. "Come in, Sarah."

I'd scurry over and cuddle up under her warm blankets—there was no other place in the world as good as that—and she'd wrap her strong, warm arm around me. After a minute or so it would get hard for me to breathe.

"Is my arm too heavy?" she'd ask in a low voice.

"No," I'd whisper back, and I'd take careful, shallow breaths so she wouldn't take it off.

December 5, 1988

I hired a babysitter this afternoon so that Daniel and I could go out alone to choose his birthday presents. Rachel couldn't accept the idea that I was doing it first with him, and that her turn would come next week. "Why Danny first?" she kept imploring, but I was adamant. I was sure that the best thing would be to give each one private time. To my surprise, it was he who said it was all right if she came, too.

Daniel wanted to go to the Mashbir department store, which is one of the most expensive places in Jerusalem. I said no, knowing how much you can spend on a pencil there, but it became apparent that he had some image in his mind about the Mashbir, that the best presents possible would be found there. So I said all right.

First they had ice-cream cones, then we went to the department store. I resolved not to hurry, not to press: they would lead the way. They browsed and carefully investigated. Rachel took special interest in the stuffed animals, and understood readily that forty shekels for a small rabbit was out of the question. "It's all right," she said. "I don't need it." Danny looked over every board game, but found none he liked under seventy shekels. Finally, after an hour and a half, they decided on two decks of cards. What an educational experience this was for me: once I realized that the glamor of browsing in the Mashbir was in itself part of the birthday present, I took it easy and they themselves found something reasonably priced. It amazed me: there we were at the Mashbir, and they came away—totally satisfied—with two decks of cards! What had really produced that sense of satisfaction was the completely happy, relaxed attention they were getting.

Afterwards, we browsed in some other stores and got various odds and ends: silver balloons, tiny figurines, things of that sort. Then Danny asked if they could have pizza. This was the day of Yes, so that's what we did. When he finished it, he asked if he could have another. Yes again.

On the way home, Danny reached out for my hand and stood on tiptoes to whisper something in my ear. "You let us do whatever we wanted. Thank you!"

He hadn't been able to get any of the big presents he had envisioned, but Daniel came away from the experience feeling he'd gotten the world.

Upon our arrival back home, Dinah and Elisheva burst into tears when they saw Daniel and Rachel's loot, even though I had taken care to get them something, also. But this didn't catch me by surprise; I'm used to it. *Isn't this a perfect example of human nature,* I thought to myself. *The other guy gets, therefore I'm deprived.* From the sidelines, I looked on with pleasure at my reaction to their complaints. *Gee, here they are making such a commotion and you feel sorry for them but it doesn't faze you. How wonderful!* I listened to their agony empathetically. It passed, and a few hours later both of them came to thank me for their presents and say they were sorry.

December 7, 1988

It's so important to have time alone with each one of the children. It makes such an incredible difference. That afternoon with the twins, even though it was a threesome, was so valuable, and achieved so much: just that relaxed time together. It's a necessity, it's worth a million dollars. I'm going to hire a babysitter once a week, G-d willing, and take turns alone with Daniel, Rachel, Dinah and Elisheva.

December 8, 1988

Daniel has been so happy these past few days.

Candis once told me, years ago, that if a sailboat sets out from the Pacific coast, a difference in just one degree determines whether it will end up in Australia or Japan.

That's the way it is with a child. A minor adjustment, a modest effort, makes all the difference.

December 11, 1988

In the mail today Daniel got two presents from my mother for his birthday: a harmonica and a cymbal to go with his drum. He kept calling out, "I'm so happy! I'm so happy!" and dancing around the living room blowing on his harmonica. I let him play the drums as loudly as he wanted for two whole hours. He made a recording of himself and played it back for me, listening to his own music with such satisfaction.

Rachel's presents are on the way.

December 13, 1988

Daniel and Dinah often ask me to help them with their arithmetic homework. It's a pleasure for me to do so, but when they're tired and frustrated they just want the answers and no education, please. "My head is breaking already from all these numbers!" Dinah cries.

The other day, Danny was in one of those moods. He'd had his fill of homework and just wanted me to do it for him. "No, I can't just tell you the answer, Danny. Your teacher wouldn't want me to." This sent him into a tailspin, and he worked out the example in agony.

Ten minutes later he reappeared. "Mommy, can you help me?"

This time I took care to say yes rather than no. "Yes, Danny, I'll help you. Sit here in the kitchen and we'll do it while I cook." He took a seat, I went on cooking, he concentrated on the problem and finished it off.

"I did it!" he exclaimed.

December 14, 1988

A household repairman came today. He fixed the leaky sink, the closet door that has never closed properly, replaced the broken bathroom window and the dead doorbell. It is a revelation. I had gotten accustomed to these small handicaps and resigned myself to the inconvenience. Now, I see I didn't have to live with them. I could have had them fixed long ago.

It's possible to fix things, and gee, it's so nice. It's as much of a surprise as finding out you don't have to live forever with a bad habit.

December 15, 1988

I was remembering today the feeling you get when you're walking along a beach and a wave powerfully draws the wet sand from under your feet. You stand there tottering a second on the teeny, fragile platform which remains, then it collapses. There is a pause, like a grand intake of breath... then the wave sweeps back in a cool rush around your feet. The water fans out and the ground beneath you is solidly restored. You're on a warm, damp, firm, luxuriously smooth expanse.

Then a tremendous surge sucks the ground out from under you again, and in the sound of the waves, something's whispering in your ear: It's bigger than you are, it's bigger than you are, this wave belongs passionately to the distance and the unknown.

In those moments—perhaps each day has its unnoticed share of them—when one thing or another brings me to fear I'm not on solid ground, that is what it's like: the land slips and I'm scared and unsteady. Then the ground is reinstalled and I'm set back on my feet again, held up by a great unseen hand.

Many women become who they are capable of becoming without motherhood. No doubt about it. If it were impossible to fulfill one's potential without being a parent, G-d wouldn't deny the experience to anyone. But how lucky I am to have this challenge all set up for me, prefabricated. It's designed to bring out all the worst in me, and therein, potentially, all the best.

December 19, 1988

Mazal tov and *siman tov*! The moment I've been anticipating all these years! I just found my first gray hair!

Actually it's white, not gray. No compromises, please.

I didn't pluck it out.

December 20, 1988

In an old notebook I found some notes from a class by Chaya Rochel Blatt. "The only time a person sins is when he believes no one is looking. Be as afraid of *HaKadosh Baruch Hu* as you are of people." Then there's a note: "Yelling at children—a stranger present." I remember what that was: A friend of hers was busy giving the children dinner one evening when one of their friends came to the house to speak to her husband. "My husband's not in right now," the woman said, "but he'll be here any minute. If you'd like, you can wait for him in the dining room." She showed him in, gave him a cup of tea, closed the door, then went back to the kitchen. She was so busy that she forgot all about her guest and started yelling at the kids as usual. All of a sudden, after a half-hour, she remembered with a start that their friend was right there listening to her. Her embarrassment was overwhelming.

"We live with a pack of lies," said Chaya Rochel Blatt. "In front of people we are ashamed, but don't feel embarrassment before *HaKadosh Baruch Hu*. We don't really believe He sees us."

December 24, 1988

Daniel, Rachel, Dinah and Elisheva were having a fight in the kitchen over something, I think it was candy—who had gotten more or less. Their screeching, their weeping, their wailing and their recriminations, the shrieks of pain beneath the blows—oh, dear. I was on the couch nursing, feeling very tired, but I would have gone in to stop them had the intensity of their fighting not evoked such fear in my heart. *What kind of children are they? I've failed as their role model.* Numbed by the challenge, I just stayed put.

Some moments passed as the incredibly bitter fighting continued. Then I heard what sounded like laughter. Yes, that did sound like laughter. I rose and took a few steps towards the kitchen, keeping enough distance so as not to attract attention. With a face wet with crying and sobered by the adult-like depth of her suffering, Dinah, sitting on the counter, was laughing even as tears still ran down her face. Rachel was doubled over. Daniel and Elisheva were out of my line of vision, yet I thought I heard them, too. I peeked. Yes! Dissolved in laughter.

December 25, 1988

The system whereby I record each insult or bad word that any of the children says, rewarding those who get no marks with extra junk food on Shabbat and penalizing those who get ten, is successful. During this, the second week, no one has more than three marks, and two of them have none.

The half-hour in a chair has also been remarkably effective in instilling self-control. I see them sometimes on the verge of hitting, yet holding themselves back. I can't recall at this moment having seen any of them hurt each other this week.

December 28, 1988

I have just returned from Hadassah Har HaTzofim Hospital, where Beyla Potash has given birth to her eleventh child, *beli ayin hara.* Her oldest child must be around eighteen by now. On my way there in the taxi, I was surprised to see how close it is to our house. The meter read just three shekels as we pulled into the entrance. Gosh, I thought, if I had to give birth it would be so convenient, such a short, cheap ride to the hospital...what a pity not to take advantage of it. Dear G-d—

I squashed that prayer just as fast as I could. Are you crazy? Here you are with your own world again, a little bit. There's a semblance of sanity and order, the older children babysit for the younger ones, Yaacov and you can go out at night and the children send you off with their best wishes. *Don't play with fire!* Just when some of the problems of the past few years have ironed themselves out: Rachel's happy and wonderful. Daniel goes to shul with Yaacov on Shabbat. Dinah gets herself to school on time every day, her homework meticulously prepared; that fierce need for autonomy is channeling itself into constructive independence and her handwriting stays along the lines. They put themselves to bed, pretty much, and Danny helps me get the babies to bed. Elisheva hasn't been having tantrums for a long time, *baruch HaShem*, and doesn't seem to be jealous of Eli anymore. Eli's getting to the stage where he understands the word "no," Avivah is no longer the fragile newborn...And as these problems get ironed out, other wrinkles are bound to take their place.

Beyla and I sat down together for coffee and pecan pie in the cafeteria. She was worried because her baby's running a fever and has lost weight. "Don't worry about him losing weight, Beyla," I told her, pontificating on one of the few subjects about which I can act like an authority. "That's the way it's supposed to be after birth. I can't figure out why nurses don't comprehend that! When your milk comes in after a few days, then, you'll see, if you just keep nursing, the baby will gain back the weight right away. There's a natural system after birth. There's some reason that babies lose weight for a few days; they're supposed to. They start gaining it back when the milk comes in around the fourth day. It's designed perfectly. G-d doesn't make mistakes."

"You know, I was so scared this pregnancy," said Beyla. "G-d has been so good to me, I get so much joy from the kids. My eldest daughter just won a writing prize, did I tell you? Yeah, really. A big contest. When she told me about it, it was great, then I said, 'O.K., do the dishes.'" Beyla laughed. "I've been getting such *nachas* that I thought it must be my turn for—you know. Dum dee dum dum. But the baby was normal. I couldn't believe it. You know, I have this relative who's always said these slightly cutting remarks about my having one baby after another. He came to visit us at Maalei Amos and he was looking around at all the kids, and at the end of the day he said, 'Beyla, you're not a millionaire. You're a billionaire.' Good coffee, isn't it?" I nodded. Anything in a restaurant is good. "Oh, I wanted to tell you. This morning a whole group of Meah Shearim women were here visiting somebody. They were around our age—"

"Twenties, you mean?"

"Yeah, right." We guffawed. "Anyway, so they were looking for one of the mothers here and the nurse couldn't find her, so they all were waiting by the nursery. I was looking at all of them, and I felt proud. They have dignity." I knew what she meant—these women aren't frivolous, they don't go around trying to be sexy and cute. "So all these women—each one of them must have at least ten children of her own—they were standing there at the nursery window oohing and aahing over the newborns as if they'd never seen any before. You know, 'Oh, look at that little mouth!' and 'Oh, look at that one over there!' They aren't afraid to show what they feel is important in life. They're not influenced by all the garbage. They just know that a new *neshamah* has joined us down here, and they really know how to welcome it into the world."

In the taxi back home, I kept glancing at my watch. I had to get back in time to pick up Avivah at the babysitter's, and get Eli from *gan*, and get lunch ready. Dear G-d.

Dear G-d.

Uh, do you think—

No. Forget it. The children...it wouldn't be good for them. Too hectic. Too crazy. The migraines, and the eye problems...but then again, surprisingly enough, I never did get those problems when I was pregnant with Avivah.

No. It wouldn't be fair to the others. They need space. They need some peace in the house, and enough individual attention. Especially Danny.

Ah, but if I had been "fair" to Daniel and Rachel, I would have stopped at two. And deprived them of the brother and sisters who are as much a part of them as my sisters are of me. I can't bear to imagine life without my sisters, and I can't imagine Danny without his sisters to fight with, to play with, to grow with. I can't bear to imagine him without Eli and Avivah.

Dear G-d. Could You—

?

Yes.

May I—

January 3, 1989

Notes from today's class by Rabbi Berkowitz: Prayer is not a ritual. It is the emotional attachment between G-d and His creations. There is a conversation between each person and *HaShem*. A person speaks with his prayer and G-d answers through all the events of the person's life. We're saying, "G-d, smile at me." We seek the message that G-d is smiling at us, whether or not we realize that this is what we're after. What's really bothering us when we're depressed is that we feel G-d is not with us.

Everything that occurs in our lives is a message, and the job is to decipher what He's saying. But you can't decide that what you're doing is right or wrong according to the messages; for example, if you're on your way to do something that your conscience tells you is wrong, and the way just opens up for you, you're getting a green light and everything is moving along easily, you can't conclude from this that *HaShem* is on your side and rooting for you. If you're on the way to do a mitzvah and it starts to rain cats and dogs, you can't say, "Ah, *HaShem* is giving me a message that I shouldn't go!" That's what superstition is. The only way to find out if what you're doing is right or wrong is to find out if it's right or wrong. He could be making things harder for you in order to hint that you should stop, or it could be that what you're doing is right and He's just increasing the challenge.

As a matter of fact, if you run into trouble, chances are you're doing the right thing. You were created to repair your character, so you'll run into situations that bring out just those defects. You'll be exposed to the people who are just right to bring out those problems. *HaShem* is bringing out the best in you. In difficulties, your hidden potential comes to life. How many people were made by their troubles? And we survive. Look back on all the times that you've been in a situation that looks impossible, but you came out of it somehow and you're here today. It's not that Jews believe we're supposed to suffer; if we can grow without the suffering, all the better. But so often when G-d gives us bounty, we rebel. On Rosh Hashanah we pray for a good, sweet year. Good: good means meaningful. Sweet: we hope that we can have a meaningful year without it having to be a bitter one. We hope to be able to grow in the midst of sweetness. But human nature is such that when G-d is giving you trouble, when He's giving you a good spanking, that's when you don't have to ask where He is. You know precisely where He is. When we have trouble, we feel close to G-d.

Why did He create us in the first place? Because He wants to give to us. But we have to earn it. No spoon feeding! If we're spoon-fed we don't develop. He created the *yetzer hara* so that we can earn our life. When He gives you a challenge, what He's really doing is pushing you along in your growth process. G-d is saying: "Grow. Become a better person. Take. Take more." Like the Yiddishe mama. Eat more, my darling. Help yourself to more.

G-d has a craving to give. "Please, earn more," He's saying. "I want to give more. Earn more."

And our message in return is, "G-d, come closer. Give more."

January 5, 1989

Tonight Daniel said to me: "You're a good mommy. Not just now. All the time."

That's the praise I need most. If I look back over the afternoon and evening, yes, we had a good time, all of us. Whatever bothered me, I reacted calmly. Whenever I wanted to get somebody's attention, I automatically lowered my voice. When I asked Danny several times if he wanted vegetables with his rice and he didn't answer, that taut bubble of anger swelled up inside me. What was I thinking? That he was being disrespectful, that he was ignoring me on purpose, to "get" me. I repeated myself, almost in a whisper. "Do you want vegetables with your rice?"

"What?"

"I said, do you want vegetables with your rice?"

"Oh." He narrowed his eyes and thought this over. I could see that this was the first time he'd heard me. "No."

"How do you say that?"

"No, thank you."

I knew I was being a good mother tonight—a solid sense of it. I don't think anyone could have come along and knocked me off my feet so easily. To that ever-present question, "How am I doing as a mother?" a degree of certainty is possible. Your conscience will tell you if you're harming them or helping them.

It is normal (yes, Sonia, it is) for children to yell, squabble, fight, complain, be fearful, balk at orders, refuse to cooperate, not want to share...It is normal that they should manifest infinite varieties of human negativity. Generally speaking, it shouldn't be overlooked. But a mother creates extraordinary difficulties by not recognizing that the normal difficulties are normal. Isn't it intriguing how we expect children to be *tzadikkim*! They should share their belongings happily, be cheerful and obedient, and should not complain about their lot in life. We find it hard to face the fact that we ourselves are not on this level. If we were able to accept the reality of our own human weaknesses, then we would be able to deal with those same faults in our children with more equanimity.

It's not a mother's fault that life is rocky. For the ups and downs and ins and outs of the human condition, she is not to blame. At the same time, however, it is indeed the mother's thoughts, feelings and perceptions that create reality in the home, for it's her interpretation of normal events that determines the direction those events take. If she recognizes that most of the children's behavior is a normal manifestation of their growth, then the succeeding stages of their development will be sloughed off as time goes by, like the snake's many skins.

So what happens if I'm in the midst of things, if I'm bored or unhappy? What if at a given moment, I'm so exhausted or nervous that I don't remember to get a hold of my thoughts? Eli's throwing a ball against the sliding glass door, Avivah's crying to nurse, Dinah and Danny are having a loud fight over a card game, Elisheva asks me to read her a story, or bursts in the door with a scraped knee, and Rachel asks me for clean socks...Shall I regret, G-d forbid, that I have all these children, feel guilty I can't devote myself as much as I'd like to each one's needs?

No. I can concentrate on keeping my voice as low as possible, and ask for strength from the One Who understands everything, Who in spite of His awesome greatness, is waiting for a word from me.

Now I can thank you, Sonia, for criticizing me honestly (though you shouldn't have done so in front of the children). You were just the right person to propel me through a rerun of my personal history as a mother, and bring me face to face with my own inner critic—the one who's far less concerned about my feelings than you were.

You made me reassess.

You were in every sense a true mother's helper.

March 2, 1989

Yesterday was the Bais Yaacov seminary's annual fair to raise money for poor brides. I let Rachel go with Hanny Israel, and Daniel with his friend Ephraim, while with some trepidation I let Dinah and Elisheva go together by themselves. They're old enough now, I told myself. They'll be all right. Daniel was to go afterwards to his friend's house, and the girls were all due home around four or five.

At six o'clock, the telephone rang. "Mommy," came Rachel's earnest, tender murmur, "is Dinah home?"

"No! What do you mean, is Dinah home? Isn't she with you?"

"No. All right. Bye."

"Rachel! Wait! Where's Dinah? Where's Elisheva?"

"I don't know! I've been looking for them for an hour already. They were supposed to meet us at the bus stop at four thirty."

"SO WHERE ARE THEY?"

"I don't know. I'm going to look again."

"RACHEL! CALL ME BACK IN A LITTLE WHILE!"

I knocked on the Israels' door. I tried to smile and told him the problem. "All right now, don't worry," he said calmly. "They're certainly all right. The next time Rachel calls, if they haven't turned up I'll go there in my car. Angela will be back with it any minute."

The next half-hour was a jumble of phone calls. "Tell the teachers there to call them over the loudspeakers," Mr. Israel told Hanny. He paused. "They did? Tell them to do it again. They did? How many times?"

I stuck my head towards the receiver. "HOW MANY TIMES?"

Mr. Israel lowered his chin and looked at me over his glasses. "Four times."

"FOUR TIMES! OH! OH!" *Act more British, Sarah,* I told myself. *Control yourself.*

"Now don't worry," he went on. "It's probably just such a *balagan* there that they couldn't hear the calls."

"Right, but now that it's the *intifada*, you never know. Maybe a terrorist...I'll call my husband!" I dashed to the telephone.

"No, no. A pity to disturb his learning. Don't worry. If you'd like I'll stay with the babies and you can go there in a taxi to look for them yourself."

Ah, waiting for that taxi. The wringing of the hands and the self-recriminations and the horrendous possibilities. *Maybe—maybe they'll walk up the path right now, giggling and swinging their arms. But no! No! What about those children out there playing on the new slide...No! Not them! No! Oh, why did I let them go? Maybe they...Maybe someone...Oh! Oh, if anything happened! Dinah! Elisheva! If only you're all right!* I ran to the *mirpesset* to look out, gripping the iron railing as I stared into the twilight. I recalled how annoyed I'd been last night at Dinah when she had refused the dinner I made. And my darling, my darling Elisheva, my mild child. Oh, if only they'd walk in now! I hurried into the living room, paced back and forth, peered intensely through the peephole in the door. Silly! What good will that do? *Dinah...Elisheva...Dinah...Elisheva...*

Well, as my taxi was turning into the school, a message came over the car radio that my children had arrived home and had been playing downstairs the whole while. Mr. Israel must have called the taxi office and asked them to notify the driver. I picked up Rachel and Hanny and set off for home, as happy as a cloud, as buoyant, as grateful as a prayer. My children. My children. Daniel. Rachel. Dinah. Elisheva. Eli. Avivah. My children. I have all my children. What more can I ask for?

March 3, 1989

I put a hundred shekels in my purse yesterday. I was on my way to town to meet Robin for coffee and I hoped to buy a pair of shoes, but as it turned out, I didn't have time so I came right home. This morning, when I looked into my purse, the money was gone.

"My money!" I grunted. "Where's all my money?" Rachel looked on as I dumped out papers and paper clips, lipsticks, telephone bills, broken pencils. Once, twice. Again. I rummaged through my mind desperately for clues. Danny's friend Ephraim? Could he have taken it? When I wasn't looking? Did I leave my purse unguarded in the kitchen?

Before Rachel left the house for school, she stretched out her arms and wrapped me in her dear and delicate embrace. "Don't worry, Mommy. *Gam zu letova.*" I melted. Yes. A *kapparah*, I thought as she held me, remembering what it was like yesterday when I thought I'd lost Dinah and Elisheva. *A blessing to lose a million shekels every day rather than any one of them.* Today, when it finally dawned upon me that I had paid for Eli's *gan* yesterday afternoon, and that I hadn't lost the money after all, I recalled her words: "It's all for the best, Mommy! It's all for the best!"

March 6, 1989

I went to a lecture by Rebbetzin Esther Greenberg. From my notes: "Get up each morning before your children. Fix yourself up. Don't walk around in your nightgown and robe all morning. Get dressed nicely. Say the blessings. Have something healthy to eat."

She told a story about a certain friend of hers. This woman noticed that one of her sons hadn't gone to *minchah* but was hanging around outside with some other boys. "Most parents would be angry and indignant at such a thing," said Rebbetzin Greenberg. "But when her son came upstairs, she said to him gently, not concealing her sadness: 'We have lost something very precious today.' He asked her what. 'Your *minchah.*' He started to cry."

She said: "Most mothers are stingy with their words of love. Give encouragement to your children. You can't give them enough of it. It makes them grow. Your words give them life. Every child is desperate for words of warmth and encouragement.

"Your first priority is you. There is a story about a penniless family. The mother found an egg outside one day and hurried home with the thought of dividing it among her ten children, but she realized that obviously none of them would get any benefit that way. When she arrived home, she went into a room, closed the door and ate the egg by herself. The children knocked at the door and cried, 'Mommy, what are you doing?' She called to them, 'I'm making a mother for you.'

"Do the best you can with each day.

"Start training yourself to see the *chessed* in everything. There's a saying: Why doesn't a man have what he wants? If he wanted what he has he would have what he wants.

"When you awake in the morning, look at the world as if you have never seen it before."

March 12, 1989

Sometime before five thirty yesterday, Eli woke up Avivah,

helped her squeeze through the broken slats of her crib, and together they woke up the rest of us. At quarter to seven, there was Yaacov doing his Shabbos morning stint at the kitchen sink, silent and intent. I had just stretched out on the couch with a new book, Daniel was reading on the other couch. Elisheva was up-stairs with the two babies. I had asked her to take care of both of them, something I've been trying to do more and more lately, not only to cultivate another babysitter in the family but as one aspect of the slow shifting of her self-image from jealous competitor to competent and kind big sister.

The book I had just begun was one Yaacov and I first heard about in a lecture given by Rabbi Avraham Twersky at the Israel Center last winter. Rabbi Twersky, author of *Let Us Make Man— Self-Esteem Through Jewishness*, is a professor of psychiatry at the University of Pittsburgh School of Medicine. Resplendent in *streimel* and *kapote* (it was *motzo'ei* Shabbos), he told the audience how he had sent a copy of Patricia Berne's Building Self-Esteem in Children to each of his sons and daughters, now that they them-selves were parents. "I hoped it would help them avoid some of the mistakes I made as a father," he said. "I wish I had had it when they were growing up."

My interest was piqued, naturally, and for the next few months I'd check the Jerusalem bookstores whenever I went downtown, but to no avail. Finally, I asked Pigeon if she could look for it in Cambridge. She came through for me, as always. We received it in the mail on Thursday. I was now on page 1:

> When I agree to be available to a child, I try to remember to present myself in such a way that the child knows I choose to be available specifically to him or her for this period of time...This may mean hanging up the telephone, putting down my pen or closing the book I'm reading...
>
> I find [that] it's just as important [to] me to be listened to by the people I approach...
>
> Children appreciate not only your availability, but also your full attention...Once I stop being busy and become

totally present to a child, whether it's for five minutes or five hours, I'm giving them prime quality time. And that helps build self-esteem because my total attention to them clearly affirms their value to me...

Children's self-esteem grows when they know you care enough to be with them.

These words touched me in their elegant simplicity. She was telling me that each interaction between parent and child *is* important, that it *does* have a lasting effect, whether for good or bad, because every encounter becomes part of the child's self.

I looked over at Daniel on the other couch. *There is no creative endeavor that could possibly be of more real value than relating well to my own children. There is nothing I could ever find to do in this life that would have a more lasting impact upon the world than giving respectful attention to the child who's right there before me.*

A deep, soft tranquility came over me. I turned to Daniel. "Daniel?" I said.

He didn't respond.

"Daniel, is that a good book?"

He looked up.

"Is that a good book?"

He nodded.

"It's about the Holocaust, right?"

He nodded and stared at me absently; his mind was elsewhere.

March 16, 1989

Every night I hate taking out the garbage.
I hate it. Handling the pail
carefully,
I hold it away from me (which makes it heavier)
and avert my face,
and my whole body holds its breath.
                              I hate
being splattered by some evil wet schlop

as I make my way out the elevator
and along the sidewalk by the parked cars.

                    Then
each night the night
sky's a surprise.
How unbelievable the endless blackness!
Thousands of stars!
Thousands of them!

With my free hand I swing open the noisy metal door and pause
as it bangs back and forth,
peering into the dark smelly hut of the garbage bins
where invisible cats

wait
to pounce upon their sustenance.   Are they in there?

                    They jump out and scare me.

Oh, dear G-d, I'm
alone in this life,
though my children are around me and my husband's near.

                    I am
so small

and life is
so big,
and hidden, and dark,
and beautiful beyond words.

Afterword

November 19, 1989

My publisher has asked for an afterword, yet now that I'm out
of the habit of writing my thoughts, it has taken me an inordinate
amount of time to find anything to say. The only thing that occurs
to me is that I miss recording daily events in the diary. Doing so
helped me to recognize the importance of the commonplace and
mundane details of everyday life. I miss the extra awareness it
gave me of my own behavior, and the increased appreciation for
the idiosyncrasies of my children's unfolding personalities; it was
like watching flowers open before my eyes. Nowadays, it is the
swift flight of the days that makes the most conscious impression:
these last eight months stand behind me only as a mute and
mysterious block of time in the abstract. Even yesterday is dim.
What stories have occurred that I don't recall, or didn't even notice
as they happened?

I kept this journal for my own benefit, but if there is anyone
anywhere who is encouraged by reading it to believe that it is
possible to improve one's behavior and change long-ingrained
habits, it would be for me a source of unexpected satisfaction. If
someone were encouraged in a low moment to believe that all of
us go through such tunnels and come out the other side, that

there is forgiveness for mistakes and that mistakes can be repaired...If anyone were encouraged to believe that an ultimate purpose is always there—amidst the diapers and the dishes and the dirty floors—then I would be amazed and thrilled that my experience could be of help to someone else. For if there is anything that I am sure of now, it's that there is indeed meaning for each of us in everything about our lives that appears insignificant and cumbersome. More and more as time goes on, it seems that to be a mother is to be engaged in the most important work one could wish for in this world, that having children is a gift to be relished.

So even if we don't write down the stories of our motherhood, we can be sure that each and every detail, enclosed in all of its meanings, is indeed being completely and permanently inscribed upon our children's souls. May the living histories we create be ones that can bring us joy forever.